Hurricane

Also by Leo McKinstry

Fit to Govern?

Turning the Tide

Boycs: The True Story

Jack and Bobby: A Story of Brothers in Conflict

Rosebery: Statesman in Turmoil

Sir Alf: A Major Reappraisal of the Life and Times of
England's Greatest Football Manager

Spitfire: Portrait of a Legend

Lancaster: The Second World War's Greatest Bomber

Hurricane

Victor of the Battle of Britain

LEO McKINSTRY

JOHN MURRAY

First published in Great Britain in 2010 by John Murray (Publishers)
An Hachette UK Company

1

© Leo McKinstry 2010

A CIP catalogue record for this title is available from the British Library

HB ISBN 978-1-84854-339-3
TPB ISBN 978-1-84854-340-9

Typeset in Monotype Bembo by Servis Filmsetting Ltd, Stockport, Cheshire

Printed and bound by Clays Ltd, St Ives plc

John Murray policy is to use papers that are natural, renewable and
recyclable products and made from wood grown in sustainable forests.
The logging and manufacturing processes are expected to conform to the
environmental regulations of the country of origin.

John Murray (Publishers)
338 Euston Road
London NW1 3BH

www.johnmurray.co.uk

This book is dedicated to Nancy Luttner and the memory of her brother Bill, who died in the cause of freedom.

Contents

Illustrations

23. A damaged Hurricane lifted on to a Queen Mary trailer in the western desert
24. A pilot showing the manoeuvrability of the Hurricane
25. Hurricanes of 1 Squadron, South African Air Force
26. The 'Tankbuster' demonstrating its firepower
27. A Hurricane Mark IIC under construction
28. Wooden fuselages lined up at the Hawker factory in Langley, Slough
29. The instrument panel inside the cockpit of a Hurricane
30. Fitters and armourers of the Women's Auxiliary Air Force servicing a Hurricane
31. A pilot of 121 Squadron tests the engines and guns of his Hurricane
32. A crated Hurricane is unloaded at the Vaenga airfield, north Russia
33. Hurricanes of the Soviet Air Force go on the attack
34. A British anti-aircraft gun crew in Bengal wave to a Hurricane
35. A Hurricane Mark IIC attacking a bridge near a Burmese settlement
36. An ox cart passes a Hurricane Mark IIC of 34 Squadron at Palel, Burma
37. The Mark IV: the last Hurricane type to go into service
38. The very last Hurricane to be built by Hawker

Picture Acknowledgements: Aviation-Images.com: 6 centre, 7 below, 12 above. Cody Images: 12 below. Corbis Images: 14 below (photo Yevgeny Khaldei). Getty Images: 3 above, 5 below, 6 below, 11 above, 13 below. Imperial War Museum London: 2 above (HU3664), 3 below (C465), 4 above (C188), 4 below (C1518), 5 above (CH1503), 6 above (H4219), 7 above (CM3513), 8 above (CH1934), 8 below left (ME/RAF1260), 8 below right (CH8459), 9 above (CH2250), 9 below (A11159), 10 centre (CM3021), 10 below (CM2240), 11 centre (CM2184), 11 below (CNA863), 13 centre (CH10090), 14 above (CR132), 15 above (896), 15 centre (CF175), 15 below (CF196), 16 below (CH13671). Private collections: 2 below right, 13 above. Royal Air Force Museum: 1 (PC98/173/5925/9), 2 below left (PC98/173/5684/5), 10 above (X003-2674/543), 16 above (PC98/173/5974/15).

Introduction

'She was a dream to fly'

O N A GROUND-FLOOR corridor at the RAF Club in Piccadilly, London, just off the main lobby, there is a row of three bronze busts, each of them representing a great figure in British aviation design. One is of Reginald Mitchell, the creator of the Vickers Supermarine Spitfire, the most famous fighter of the Second World War. Another is of Roy Chadwick, the genius behind the Avro Lancaster bomber, that mighty aerial destroyer which smashed the capacity of the Nazi war machine. The third bust is of Sir Sydney Camm, the Chief Designer of the Hawker Aircraft company for more than forty years. Though Sir Sydney was the only one of the trio to have been knighted, his principal wartime achievement, the Hawker Hurricane, did not win him anything like the same renown as the Spitfire or the Lancaster did for their designers. The former became the public symbol of national defiance in the Battle of Britain from July to October 1940. The latter gained lasting public affection for its heroic determination to take the war to the heart of the Third Reich. But similar recognition was never attained by the Hurricane, either during the war or in the decades since. Its record was ignored, its triumphs belittled. A graphic indicator of this indifference could be seen in the mass fly-past over London in September 1945, held to celebrate the fifth anniversary of the Battle of Britain, when not a single Hawker Hurricane was included in the RAF formation.[1] This was a glaring omission, not only because the Hurricane had been successfully fighting in the Far East right up to the end of the war, but even more so because of the central role that the fighter had played in the defeat of the German Luftwaffe in 1940.

Indeed it is no exaggeration to say that without the Hawker Hurricane, the RAF would have probably lost the Battle of Britain.

Sydney Camm's plane was the key weapon of Fighter Command during the crucial months that decided the fate of Britain and the whole of western Europe. If the Hurricane had not been available, the RAF would have been too limited to mount an effective defence against the Germans, especially because there were insufficient quantities of Spitfires emerging from the aircraft factories and into service with the front-line squadrons. Hurricane pilots and ground crews made up the majority of Fighter Command's front-line strength in the heroic national battle for survival. When Winston Churchill made his famous tribute to the men of the RAF in August 1940, telling the House of Commons that 'Never in the field of human conflict was so much owed by so many to so few,'[2] it was the Hurricane squadrons that deserved the lion's share of the Prime Minister's accolade. According to Air Ministry figures, Hurricanes made up around 63 per cent of Fighter Command's forces during the Battle of Britain and were responsible for 61 per cent of all Luftwaffe losses. As the historian Stephen Bungay wrote, 'Camm's Hurricane was cheap to make, easy to repair and robust, and gave Fighter Command the numbers it needed in the air in 1940. Without it, the thin blue line of defenders would have been too thin to hold.'[3] One Fighter Command ground crewman, Arthur Hudson, commented in a post-war interview: 'All the glory went to the Spitfire but the real damage was done by the Hurricanes. It was a fantastic aircraft.'[4]

Victory in 1940 rightfully belonged as much to the Hurricane as to the Spitfire. But it is the Spitfire whose name became synonymous with victory in the air despite its lesser numbers. This was partly a result of wartime propaganda, as the government exploited the image of Mitchell's fighter to boost morale. Tellingly, the official campaign in 1940 to raise money for aircraft production was called 'the Spitfire Fund'. A phenomenally successful initiative organized by the dynamic, unorthodox minister Lord Beaverbrook, it brought in more than £13 million, but in the process it cemented in the public's imagination the idea that the Spitfire was more important than the Hurricane to the war effort. When a group of citizens in Hampstead, north London, tried to set up a 'Hurricane Fund', they encountered widespread local indifference and even ignorance about the plane. As the social research group Mass Observation recorded, 'the reasons for the lack of interest were thought to be the limited sense of community in the area, the confused campaign which meant that people weren't sure whether the aim was to collect for a bomber or a fighter, and the competition with "Spitfire Fund"'.[5] Newsreels, press articles and films such as *The First of the Few*, the 1942 biopic in which Leslie Howard played the part of Reginald Mitchell, added further lustre to the Spitfire's image. Nor can it be denied that the Spitfire, with its elliptical wing and natural elegance, had greater aesthetic appeal than the more rugged Hurricane. Moreover, the Spitfire was undoubtedly the superior fighter in the long term, capable of greater speeds and manoeuvrability. It also had a much greater capacity for development because of its more advanced design. By late 1940 the Hurricane's airframe had reached its technological limit. The only significant future changes to the type involved different armaments, introducing greater firepower and the ability to carry bombs. Though the Hurricane continued to fight against Japan until the cessation of hostilities in August 1945, the last of the 14,533 planes came off the Hawker production line at Langley in Slough in July 1944. By contrast, the Spitfire became a much faster, heavier and more powerful aircraft through a never-ending process of evolution right up to 1948, covering no fewer than nineteen different types and thirty-seven variants.

Later in life Sir Sydney expressed regret that the urgency of putting the Hurricane into production in the late 1930s had inhibited its potential for development, not least because its fuselage and wings partly relied on the wood and fabric construction that had prevailed in the biplanes. 'If we'd had more time it would have been the greatest aircraft of all time,' he said. 'As a matter of fact, I felt that the Hurricane was somewhat outdated back in 1937. Yet if we had not gone ahead we should have had nothing when we went to war with Germany.'[6]

So strong was the bias that a form of Spitfire snobbery arose during the Battle of Britain, whereby victories by Hurricanes were sometimes credited to the more glamorous Supermarine fighters. In his vivid memoirs the former Hurricane pilot Tom Neil of 249 Squadron recalled going to a cinema in Leeds to see a newsreel report of an encounter in which one of his sections had shot down a Junkers (Ju)

88 bomber over Flamborough Head on the Yorkshire coast. 'The British Movietone News commentator credited the Spit with shooting down the German aircraft, producing whoops of disbelief and annoyance from our seats in the stalls. Such, we decided, was the folklore surrounding the Spitfire. People believed only what they wanted to believe!'[7] The same snobbery extended to the German enemy, some of whose pilots seemed to regard the idea of having been shot down by a Hurricane as an insult to their honour, as Eric Seabourne, a pilot with 238 Squadron, discovered. In a fierce dogfight over Portland in Dorset, Seabourne's Hurricane had come under attack from three Messerschmitt (Me) 109s. Having been badly burnt as the fire raged in his cockpit, he managed to bail out, coming down in the English Channel where he was picked up by a rescue launch. He was then taken to the Haslar naval hospital in Portsmouth, Hampshire. 'I was dumped in a bed next but one to a German pilot who had been shot down. He was an English speaker and he was creating because he had been shot down by a Hurricane, which he thought was much below his dignity. If it had been a Spitfire, it would have been OK, but not a Hurricane.'[8] Typical of this contempt was the view of Adolf Galland, one of the leading German fighter pilots, who once said witheringly, 'the Hurricane was hopeless – a nice plane to shoot down'.[9] But such an arrogant, complacent outlook severely underestimated the capabilities of the Hawker fighter. Nor would Galland's opinion have been endorsed by the thousands of Germans felled by the Hurricane in France and England in 1940, or by Field Marshal Erwin Rommel's troops who came under ferocious low-level attacks by Hurricanes in the North African desert in 1942.

Far from feeling inferior to the Spitfire airmen in 1940, most of the Hurricane pilots were full of admiration for their aircraft, cherishing its resilience, stability, ease of flying and sense of menace. That spirit was captured by Wing Commander Peter Townsend of 43 Squadron, who flew with heroic distinction in the Battle of Britain. On the eve of war in 1939, he later wrote,

> we were at one with ourselves and our machines. It was the Hurricane, really, which gave us such immense confidence, with its mighty

engine, its powerful battery of eight guns and its feel of swift, robust strength and the ability to outdo our enemies. Months would go by before the real test of combat but we believed in the Hurricane. Performance figures – those of the Me 109 and the Spitfire were in many respects superior – did not in the least dismay us. The Hurricane was our faithful charger and we felt supremely sure of it and ourselves.[10]

Those sentiments were echoed by Eustace Holden, serving with 56 Squadron at the beginning of the war: 'The Hurricane was a marvellous fighting platform. We were quite content with it. I had no apprehensions about its ability to take on the Luftwaffe.'[11] To Graham Leggett, who had worked as an apprentice at Hawker before joining the RAF, his very first experience of the Hurricane was a delight:

> I tightened the straps, did my cockpit check again and then opened the throttle. In no time at all, she picked up flying speed and the tail came up. The grass was very bumpy and she was bumping quite a bit. Then all of a sudden she bumped up in the air and was flying. After that, she just climbed up. It was like I had been flying her all my life. It was just too easy. She flew herself, she really did. I could just amble around the sky. I would ease the stick one way and she would respond immediately. I would move it the other way and again she would respond. She was a dream to fly, she really was.[12]

Many Hurricane pilots who also had experience on the Spitfire said that they actually preferred the Hawker plane because of its robustness and its stability as a platform for the eight Browning guns. 'The Hurricane was part of me. By the time I finished the war I reckoned I could do anything in the Hurricane. It really was a very operational plane,' remembered Ben Bowring, who served in the Battle of Britain and the Desert War in Africa. 'I flew quite a lot of Spitfires but as a general purpose aircraft the Hurricane would beat the pants off the Spit. That was because the Hurricane was the plane that won the Battle of Britain. It could take a tremendous amount of bullets since it was made of wood and fabric. It would keep flying almost after it was destroyed. If you put a Spitfire and a Hurricane in a dogfight together – not a question of speed or climb – the Hurricane would do better than the Spitfire.'[13] A story told by the legendary

Hurricane pilot Roland Beamont provided a graphic illustration of the feeling in his squadron, No. 87, during the Battle of Britain:

> One hears so much about the superiority of the Spitfire over the Hurricane. It is all rubbish. The Hurricane was more rugged, rather more pugnacious-looking and equally pleasant to fly. In fact in many ways it was nicer to fly because it was rather more stable. The Hurricane was also a better gun platform. You could aim the guns more accurately than you could with the Spitfire because it was better directionally. In August 1940, after we had been through the Battle of France and were well stuck into the Battle of Britain, we heard that we were about to be re-equipped with the new Spitfire Mark II. This should have made any fighter pilot full of enthusiasm but in fact, without much reflection, we all went to our Commanding Officer and said, 'Look, if this is true, please stop it. The right time to equip this squadron with Spitfires is after we have got this battle finished. At the moment we are doing all right with our Hurricanes. For God's sake, let's stay with them.'[14]

Even when outnumbered in the fateful conflicts of 1940 over France and England, the Hurricane provided the RAF with a lethal bite, shattering any belief that it was outmoded or too slow. In the hands of a courageous pilot, it represented a deadly foe to the Luftwaffe, as a host of combat accounts reveal. On 14 May 1940, in the opening days of the Battle of France, Donald Stones of 32 Squadron was on patrol with his section in northern France when he suddenly saw three Ju 88 bombers below him. Instantly he yelled 'Bandits! Bandits' over the radio/telephone, before diving on one of them. 'I felt the joy of firing my guns in hot blood and at a range of about 150 yards I saw my rounds flashing into the 88's port engine and his rear gunner firing tracer at me. The 88 started to turn to port and slowed down so suddenly that I overshot him.' Stones then told one of his fellow pilots to finish off the stricken bomber, while he went after the leader of the German formation. 'I pulled out the emergency boost plug for the first time ever, which gave the Hurricane its maximum speed of just over 300 mph.' Gradually he caught up with the leader of the Ju 88s, and the dark image of a German plane began to fill his reflector gunsight. 'Adrenalin was now pumping into my bloodstream and I tried to remember to give only

short bursts and make them tell. First his port engine and then switch
to the starboard, silencing his rear gunner. His port engine was smoking and I thought I could see his airscrew windmilling. Again I overshot and did a hard steep turn down above him and saw he was in a
spin. I straightened out and saw him go into the west bank of a river.
I felt nothing for him, only the satisfaction of victory.'[15]

A few months later, in the summer of 1940, the fight for national
survival in the skies over southern England showed the Hurricane at
its valiant best. For all the bombast of the Luftwaffe, the effectiveness
of Fighter Command impressed foreign observers. Alexander
Severesky, the celebrated American aviation pioneer and designer,
wrote in *Picture Post* in August 1940 of the 'poor performance' of the
German aircraft against the Hurricane and Spitfire. 'Unless Germany
can find some new model capable of meeting British pursuit planes
on equal terms, the English first line of defence cannot be
pierced.'[16]

In one astonishing action on the morning of 7 September, so
typical of the RAF's heroics, Tom Neil of 249 Squadron was sent on
patrol over Maidstone in Kent, the third time he had been scrambled
since dawn. Flying at 18,000 feet, he saw a large formation of German
bombers, escorted from above by a 'veritable cloud' of Me 109s and
twin-engined 110 fighters. There were just 12 Hurricanes from 249
Squadron pitched against over 100 Luftwaffe aircraft. Despite the
daunting odds, the cry of 'Tally ho!' went up across the radio/tele-
phone. As he headed in for the attack, Neil had a clear sight of his
quarry, a large group of Heinkel bombers 'huddled together as
though for warmth'. He switched his gun button to 'fire', all the time
watching the nearest Heinkels growing in his gunsight. As he surged
forward, he opened fire. 'The Hurricane's eight Brownings did not
chatter, the noise was of a thick, coarse fabric being ripped, a concentrated tearing noise which shook the aircraft with a vibration that was
indescribably pleasant. Ahead, smoking tentacles reached out in
clutching traces and felt about the leading vic of Heinkels with blind,
exploring fingers. The briefest ripple of twinkling lights. Like a
child's sparkler. I was hitting them! I couldn't miss!' Moments later
he realized he was at risk of collision with the Heinkel formation, so
he thrust the steering column forward and went into a sudden dive.

'My aircraft fell away like a stone, the slipstream rising to a scream, the distant earth plumb in my windscreen and dust whirling around my face.' Pulling out of the dive, he started to climb again, searching the sky for the bombers. He could not see them. But then, just to his right he saw an Me 109, flying in the opposite direction. 'I instinctively turned towards it and pulling hard, fired. The Hun ignored me, curving away in a slight dive. Emboldened and wildly excited, I shot after him, urging my aircraft on. Faster! Faster! Had he seen me? Surely he must have! Everything straining and shaking but catching up. I fired again. And again. A few bright strikes. A brief puff of dark smoke. A thin plume of white, then a slightly thicker trail of darkening grey.' Then 'like an animal, mortally wounded', the aircraft fell away, disintegrating as it plunged earthwards.

By now, having dived down to 10,000 feet, Neil had lost the rest of his squadron. But heading northwards, he came across another formation of Hurricanes and attached himself to the rear of it. Within minutes he was at the centre of a renewed combat, as the Hurricanes came across another armada of Luftwaffe aircraft, this one made up of light bombers, Dornier 17s, escorted by Me 109s. Instantly, the Hurricane leader dived, with Neil following him. 'It was a madly exciting twenty seconds, a cavalry charge of the wildest kind with all weapons bared. I found myself going down in a thirty degree dive towards the starboard front quarter of the bomber formation. One of a solid wedge of Hurricanes. Firing!' He kept hurtling towards the Dorniers, then suddenly he was past them. It was 'a chaos of wings, engines, fuselages and black crosses. A series of violent bumps after which, in an instant, they were gone and I was somewhere below, diving like a gannet, the wind screaming around my head and my controls tight and vibrating.'[17] Neil had expended all the ammunition in his eight Browning guns, so there was nothing to do but head back to base at North Weald in Essex, struggling to catch his breath as he returned homewards. His successful attack on the Me 109 was the first of eleven victories that he achieved in the Battle of Britain.

Even later in the war, when the Me 109, like the Spitfire, was undergoing continuous improvements and the Hurricane was sliding towards obsolescence as a fighter, it could still sometimes hold its own. Geoffrey Morley-Mower, who served in the Desert War as a reconnaissance pilot, left this account of a nerve-shredding confrontation with an Me 109 near the North African coast in November 1941. Having destroyed a parked Stuka bomber on the ground with a strafing attack, Morley-Mower was flying alongside another Hurricane towards a second Axis airfield. Then in the distance he glimpsed three Me 109s in line astern formation, 2,000 feet above him:

> I dived, automatically opening the throttle and selecting maximum revs, weaving slightly to keep the Messerschmitts in view, hoping they hadn't seen us. No such luck. The leader peeled off and headed towards me like a hawk after a hare. By this time, I'd reached ground level and pulled into a steep defensive turn. The situation had some advantages. The Hurricane had a lower wing loading than the Messerschmitt, and this meant it could fly in a tighter circle without stalling the wings and crashing to the ground. In order to shoot me down an attacker would have to fly inside my track to aim a deflection shot that would hit me. If I flew well, that was technically impossible. Also the Messerschmitt pilot would be worried about hitting the ground while concentrating on his gun sight.

Morley-Mower kept tightening up his turn at the lowest possible height, the Hurricane's airframe juddering slightly in the manoeuvre. Suddenly there was a flash of cannon fire, 'the shells kicking up dust outside my path and behind my tail'. But the German attack failed. The Me 109 flew off, only to be replaced by a second one. 'He came in slower and closer to the ground, holding his fire. This is what I feared most, that one of them might get inside me momentarily and blast my tail off.' With Morley-Mower continuing to turn frantically, the second Me 109 kept drawing closer. 'I was madly tempted to do something, to straighten out and turn the other way, anything to break the pattern. No! No! No! Lead us not into temptation. As soon as I levelled out he'd get me. I'd be a perfect sitter, big in his sights with no deflection for a second or two as I changed direction and his cannons would rake my fuel tanks and fry me.' Morley-Mower then had a flash of inspiration. If he put down 20 degrees of flap, he would reduce the stalling speed and therefore be able to tighten his turn further. Just as his left hand reached for the flap lever, the stalking Me 109 pilot opened fire. 'A real fireworks display this time, the shells

striking the earth behind me and bouncing over a wide area.' Then
something extraordinary happened. 'I took my eye off his aircraft,
and when I looked back, he'd disappeared. One moment he was
there, trying to shoot me down, the next instant he was gone. As I
continued on my circular path I saw a line of explosions and sheets of
flame.' What had happened was that the Messerschmitt had gone into
a high-speed stall, plummeting into the ground from about 100 feet
in 'a wild skid of dust, flame and assorted aircraft parts. Body parts
too, I imagined, poor bugger!' Drenched in sweat, Morley-Mower
climbed into cloud and set course for base.[18]

Armed with cannon, rockets or bombs, the Hurricane remained a
formidable air weapon in the last four years of the war, seeing action
in theatres as diverse as northern Europe, the Russian front and the
Burmese jungle. By day it could fly on convoy protection duties in
the Arctic; by night it could go on intruder sorties over occupied
France. But this versatility points to a fascinating paradox in the
Hurricane story. For the plane managed to be simultaneously both
modern and dated, revolutionary and conventional. It ushered in a
new era but carried an echo of the old. When it first entered RAF
service in 1937 it was the fastest, most heavily armed fighter in the
world, the first military plane to attain over 300 mph, yet its construction was a throwback to the era of fabric-covered biplanes. At
the end of the Second World War it was used to drop napalm, that
chemical weapon whose very name is redolent of sinister technological advance, yet the aircraft's fuselage was built using the methods
that Hawker had first devised in the 1920s. Paradoxically, too, the
plane's apparent weaknesses were also its strengths. Its wings were
much thicker than those on the Spitfire and the Me 109, limiting its
speed, but the thickness also brought tremendous stability in combat.
As Douglas Bader, the RAF's legless pilot who led 242 Squadron
during the Battle of Britain, put it: 'The aeroplane remained rock
steady when you fired. Unlike the Spitfire with its lovely elliptical
wing which sloped upwards towards the tip. The Spitfire was less
steady when the guns were firing because, I have always thought,
they were spread further along the wing and the recoil effect was
noticeable.'[19] Similarly, the fabric-covered wings and fuselage may
have seemed hopelessly outmoded in the new age of the all-metal

monoplane fighter, but the simple building techniques also meant that Hawker Aircraft could quickly produce the numbers when they were most needed. In the words of Dr John Fozard, who worked with Sydney Camm at Hawker and succeeded him as chief designer, the Hurricane's construction was 'right for its time and for the organisational skills and methods of its workforce on the shop floor. By 1937/8 a real fear of being outstripped by the Third Reich's production capability further dampened any ardour to change Hawker's production style. We can be thankful that common sense prevailed, for if the Hurricane had encountered half the production problems of the early Spitfire we would have lost the Battle of Britain because of insufficient fighters.'[20]

The Hurricane saga closely mirrors the narrative of Britain's war. There is the complacency and confusion of the early 1930s, when neither the politicians nor the country were facing up to the reality of the new threat from Nazi Germany, a mood symbolized by the Air Ministry's initial indifference to Camm's monoplane design. Indeed, the Hurricane was not a government project at all in its first years, and only received full official backing once the prototype had flown in 1935. This negative attitude was exacerbated by the Air Staff's dogmatic preference for the bomber over the fighter, reflecting the belief that the way to deter the enemy was through the threat of a strategic air offensive rather than through strengthened defences. A dramatic change in outlook occurred from 1936, just as the first contract for the Hurricane was awarded. Finally alive to the dangers of German militarism, the government put fighter production at the centre of its war preparations, pouring unprecedented sums into aircraft expansion programmes, pushing for increased output and encouraging firms to build new factories. The vast new Hawker factory at Langley in Slough was typical of this drive. Dispatched to France in support of the British Expeditionary Force in 1939 and dominant in the RAF's home squadrons, the Hurricane was at the forefront of the 'Phoney War', the name given to that strange, tense period between September 1939 and April 1940 when the Allies waited for Adolf Hitler to make his move. 'There was a lot of sitting around, rather tedious,' recalled Hurricane pilot Charlton Haw.[21]

The storm broke when Hitler invaded Norway on 9 April 1940,

with the Hurricanes fighting a desperate, unavailing action around the northern port of Narvik against the German onslaught. The effort was characterized by some of the bravest, most skilful RAF flying seen during the war. Soon afterwards there followed the devastating Blitzkrieg against the Low Countries and France. Once more the Hurricanes, based in north-eastern French airfields, were right in the front line, trying to deny the Germans air superiority or escorting bombers against the German ground forces. The Hurricane also played its full part in the Allied evacuation from Dunkirk in France between 24 May and 4 June 1940, though this was not always acknowledged by the retreating British troops who complained 'Where was the RAF?'

The Battle of Britain was the 'Finest Hour' for the Hurricane as well as for the nation. 'It was the aircraft for the right season. It came at a time when it literally saved the country. It was there, it was needed and it performed magnificently,' said Eric 'Winkle' Brown, the great test pilot who flew more different types of British plane than any other man.[22] But there was no sense in which the victor could bask in triumph. The months that followed were difficult for the Hurricane, as they were for the urban population facing the horrors of the Blitz. One of the Hurricane's primary duties in the winter of 1940–1 was to mount night patrols against the German bombing campaign. But, lacking airborne radar, the plane was ill-suited to this role and struggled in the darkness to achieve any successes. 'The idea of the Hurricane fighting at night in 1940 was an absolute waste of time. To see anything at night, approaching speeds of six miles a minute, just doesn't work,' said Dennis David, a pilot with 87 Squadron, who believed that the decision to put the planes up into the night skies was driven entirely by 'political pressure'.[23] Just as in the wider tale of Britain's war, 1941 was a year of gloom for the Hurricanes. They were involved in the fall of Greece and Crete in April and May respectively, as well as the failure to throw back the Axis forces in North Africa. Fighter sweeps over France led to crippling losses for little gain. Inevitably, when Russia came under attack from the Wehrmacht, it was the Hurricane that represented Britain's first military contribution to the Soviet Union's response. Two fighter squadrons were transported to Murmansk in September 1941, though their impact was limited, not least by the lack of Soviet co-operation over maintenance.

Yet the mood of failure was partly alleviated by the courage that the airmen showed against daunting odds. The doomed Allied campaign in the Balkans in 1940 and 1941 featured the phenomenal exploits of the South African pilot Marmaduke 'Pat' Pattle, the commanding officer of 33 Squadron. Killed during a dogfight over Greece in April 1941, Pattle is little remembered today. But he could lay claim to be regarded as the greatest RAF fighter pilot of the war, having been credited unofficially with around fifty victories, thirty-five of them in the Hurricane. A further example of remarkable heroism was found in the work of the Hurricane pilots on merchant ships in the Atlantic and Arctic convoys. Because these vessels were not proper aircraft carriers with landing decks, the planes had to be launched by rocket-propelled catapults when enemy aircraft were spotted approaching the convoy. Not only was the unorthodox take-off dangerous, but more disturbingly, each pilot had little alternative but to bail out into the icy sea when he had used up his petrol, since he had no hope of landing his plane back on a merchant ship. Even the installation of extra fuel tanks did not greatly increase the chances of a Hurricane reaching friendly territory. Yet the RAF was never short of volunteer airmen for these hazardous duties.

Again, just as with the overall British war effort, the early months of 1942 marked the nadir of the Hurricane's fortunes, as its squadrons were overwhelmed almost everywhere they fought – in Java, Singapore, Malta and Tobruk. Hurricanes took part in one of the most embarrassing episodes of the war, the notorious failed attempt to halt the 'Channel Dash' of February 1942 by three German battleships, which slipped out of the port of Brest on the north-western tip of France and then, in broad daylight, sailed up the English Channel to the safety of the Reich's home waters. But then, in line with the British nation, the Hurricane underwent an inspiring military revival. Though no longer effective strictly as an interceptor, it found a new role as a high-speed, low-level bomber and ground-attack fighter, using a wide variety of weaponry. In Field Marshal Bernard Montgomery's defeat of Rommel in North Africa in late 1942, the Hurricane proved invaluable as a tankbuster, its 40-mm cannons hitting with a lethal punch. It was also useful in weakening the German defences in occupied western Europe during 1943, especially with its 60-pound high-explosive rocket projectiles.

Just as ruthlessly efficient were the Hurricanes fighting the Japanese during the last two years of the war in Burma, where they elevated army co-operation to a new level. At the vital siege of Imphal in early 1944, where victory for General William Slim's forces marked the turning point in the war in the Far East, the Hurricanes dropped more than one million pounds of bombs on the Japanese. Flight Lieutenant E. D. C. Lewis, serving in Burma, wrote this commentary in 1945 about the widespread admiration for the Hurricane: 'The army displayed an enthusiasm for the Hurribombers as of no other combat in the India-Burma theatre. From the dispatches of commanding generals to the private mail of the men fighting in the jungle have come messages of praise for the Hurribomber attacks pressed home at the appropriate moment. It is the proud boast of the pilots that they have never failed to give prompt aid when called upon by their comrades fighting on the ground. Today the army has come to look upon the Hurribombers as an extremely adaptable artillery arm hitting the enemy at long range or within a few yards of the British front line, whichever hurt him most.'[24] Though American planes began to replace the Hawker fighter from late 1944, there were still three RAF Hurricane squadrons in Far Eastern service at the time of VJ Day on 15 August 1945.

As well as gripping, sometimes shocking combat incidents, the Hurricane story is also packed with vibrant characters and explosive controversies. No personality in the tale was more colourful than the designer himself, Sydney Camm, who was a strange mixture of loud irascibility and anxious shyness, his ferocious temper often serving as a mask for his insecurities. Among his several eccentricities was his dislike of using wind tunnels for testing his designs. 'There was never any doubt about who was the boss,' recalled Dr Percy Walker, who joined Hawker in 1933. 'His personality pervaded the whole atmosphere . . . He could spout aphorisms and epigrams with the rapidity of a machine gun, and with penetrating force. One of his favourite sayings was "aircraft design is an art, not a science". This may not have been original but it never can have been said with greater conviction.'[25] Former Hawker designer Harold Tuffen, who described Camm as 'an enigma', said that 'in the old days we all firmly believed his fury always grew with the moon phases'.[26] Another of Camm's former employees, Ralph Hooper, called him 'a man of moods; when in good heart he was excellent company and full of humour. When depressed, it became the duty of his staff to cheer him up. A martinet, an enigma, yet under him success bred success.'[27] For all Camm's foibles, his vision, talent and longevity were astonishing. Having designed biplanes in the First World War, he finished his career in 1965 as the driving force behind the Hawker Harrier, the world's first operational jet fighter with a vertical take-off-and-landing capability.

Other key figures in the Hurricane story include the Fighter Command chief Sir Hugh Dowding, who possessed an unsociable manner but a unique grasp of organization and strategy. His sacking at the end of the Battle of Britain remains to this day one of the most contentious episodes of the air war. Dowding's closest ally in 1940 was the tough New Zealander Sir Keith Park, commander of 11 Fighter Group that covered the south-east of England. Regarded with suspicion by the Air Staff, he was adored by his men, with whom he had regular contact during the Battle of Britain by flying to his airfields in his own personalized Hurricane. Almost as much as Dowding, he was the architect of the Luftwaffe's defeat. During the later part of the war, Park showed the same successful leadership as a commander both in Malta and Burma. Many of the Hurricane pilots, such as Douglas Bader and Bob Stanford Tuck of 257 Squadron, were compelling personalities, as was the night-fighter hero of 151 Squadron, Richard Stevens, who combined superb shooting with a seething hatred of the Germans after his wife and children had been killed in the Blitz. 'My God he was a bloody killer. His hatred was unbelievable,' said his fellow 151 Squadron pilot John Ellacombe.[28] On one occasion Stevens instructed his ground crew not to remove the blood from the wings of his Hurricane after he had blown up a German bomber at point-blank range. Politicians also feature strongly in this tale, particularly the Earl Swinton, the dynamic Secretary of State for Air during the push for expansion in the mid 1930s, and of course Winston Churchill, who took an intimate interest in all the

Hurricane's operations, regularly expressing his exasperation at the failure of the RAF to use its resources more effectively.

Through the wealth of original research, this book sheds much new light on the history of the Hurricane. Air Ministry papers at the National Archives in Kew, London, for instance, show that the early production of the Hurricane was much more troubled than has previously been claimed. At one stage, the Ministry, in its frustration with the slowness of deliveries, even considered taking the Hurricane project away from Hawker and handing it over to the Bristol company. Unpublished correspondence between Sydney Camm and the government is published for the first time, including letters showing Whitehall's disdain for the early monoplane fighter. Archival documents provide new insights on the technical development of the plane, such as the introduction of stressed-skin metal wings, the use of 100-octane petrol, the installation of more advanced airscrews and the creation of the Hurribomber. Also revealed are some of the bizarre experiments with the Hurricane, such as a plan to fly it on the back of a Liberator bomber to increase its range, or the proposal to tow it like a glider from a cable linked to a Wellington bomber. The previously uncovered episode of using the deadly incendiary napalm in Burma is told through both Whitehall records and interviews. It is a little-known fact that twenty years before the notorious chemical weapon was used by US forces in the Vietnam War, the Hurricane was dropping napalm on the jungles of the Far East. The strategic thinking behind many of the Hurricane's key operations, such as the siege of Malta (June 1940–December 1942) or the North African campaign (June 1940–May 1943), is further highlighted through an examination of the papers of Winston Churchill and the Chief of the Air Staff, Sir Charles Portal. On another level, the experience of fighting in the Hurricane is recounted through a large array of interviews with pilots, many of whose commentaries were taken from audio records in the Imperial War Museum sound archive, London. Interviews have also been conducted with several Hawker employees, who depict the wartime mood and conditions in the Hurricane factories.

But at the core of this enriching narrative lies the great fighter itself. In many ways, the Hurricane was a quintessentially British plane, evocative of the nation's wartime character: reliable, tough, determined rather than elegant, perhaps lacking in refinement but undoubtedly solid. It was a true bulldog of a plane, the instrument of salvation when the country was fighting for its very existence in 1940. As the Hawker engineer Beryl Platt put it to a post-war interviewer, 'without those Hurricanes, you and I would not be sitting where we are today'.[29]

I

'I'm only interested in designing fighters'

THE HAWKER HURRICANE was a fighter that initially the British government neither ordered nor even wanted. On 6 January 1934 Sydney Camm, the Chief Designer of Hawker Aircraft Limited, submitted to the Air Ministry a proposal for 'a High Speed Single Seater Monoplane', which he stated would be capable of flying over 264 mph at 15,000 feet, a significant advance on the current biplanes in RAF service. It was a plan on which Camm had been working for more than a year, and he assured the Ministry that the design offered potential for further development.[1]

But Whitehall was not interested. 'I am directed to inform you that your proposals for a High Speed Monoplane have been carefully considered and it is regretted that, at the present time, the Department is unable to give active encouragement to the scheme proposed,' came the reply from the Director of Contracts on 9 March.[2] This negative attitude was partly a reflection of the faith that the government had in other fighter projects, especially the new plane being designed by Reginald Mitchell at Supermarine to Air Ministry specification F7/30, which had been issued in 1931 to spur the creation of a new generation of high-speed military aircraft. 'It is clear,' wrote Major John Buchanan, the Ministry's Deputy Director of Technical Development, to his colleagues, that 'ultra high speed development must be associated with a monoplane and the Supermarine F7/30, if successful, may offer an opportunity to proceed with the work'. As a result, he continued, 'the Department does not propose to take any action in this matter'.[3]

Another cause of the initially unfavourable response was the wider conflict over the right air strategy to adopt. The Air Ministry of the early 1930s was a cauldron of competing pressures, as arguments raged over the modernization of the force. At the time, the RAF's fighter squadrons were largely equipped with biplanes, either Bristol Bulldogs or Hawker Furies, the latter of which had been designed by Camm himself in the late 1920s. Far-sighted strategists recognized that the biplane was reaching the end of its effective life. Slow, vulnerable and inadequately armed, it had become a liability in the air, as had been proved time and again in recent RAF training exercises when the biplane fighters were often outpaced by the bombers they were meant to be attacking in mock combat. Yet there lingered within some quarters of the air force a prejudice against the monoplane, based on the belief that it was more difficult to handle and less manoeuvrable. For many pilots, the key to success in combat was not speed but manoeuvrability, while they also liked the extra lift that the pair of wings on a biplane provided at take-off. The antipathy to the monoplane had deep roots. In 1912 two monoplanes had broken up in mid-air, and the Secretary for War, Colonel J. E. B. Seely, had immediately imposed a ban on their use in the Royal Flying Corps. The formal ban only lasted five months, but the hostility remained. When the Westland company designed a fast monoplane fighter called the Wizard in 1927, the Air Ministry refused to change its policy and none of the type were ordered.

Leaps in technological change led to a transformation in outlook at the Ministry. In the Schneider Trophy, the international seaplane racing competition first held in 1913, Supermarine's high-powered machines, including one capable of flying at over 400 mph, had not only brought Britain a succession of thrilling victories in the years up to 1931 but had also, in the words of one Air Ministry document, 'definitely proved the supremacy of the monoplane for pure performance'.[4] It was in 1933 that the first of the modern, all-metal monoplane airliners, the Boeing 247 and the Douglas DC-3, flew in America, again confirming the impending obsolescence of the biplane, though some of the old guard still remained to be convinced.

There were other obstacles to the development of the monoplane. One was the official impulse to spread contracts around the aircraft industry, both to provide employment and to encourage competition between the major firms in the industry. But this well-intentioned paternalism could act as a brake on rationalized efficiency, as well as promote a bewildering array of different aircraft types. Indeed, one of the reasons for the initial rejection of Camm's scheme was that the Air Ministry was already grappling with other fighter projects from Vickers, Westland, Bristol, Gloster, in addition to the Supermarine F7/30. Only a few months earlier, the Chief of the Air Staff Sir Edward Ellington, who had taken up his post in 1933, complained that the number of different fighter types under consideration was 'quite beyond the capacity of the department to deal with'.[5] Nor was there universal support throughout the RAF for the development of new fighter types.

The idea of deterrence through the threat of strategic bombing still held tremendous sway, testimony to the influence of Lord Trenchard, the RAF's founding father during the First World War. The very existence of the RAF as an independent service was predicated on the belief that it would be able to deliver 'the knock-out blow' against any continental enemy. The best form of defence, in Trenchard's view, was attack, and this required the creation of a powerful heavy-bomber force rather than wasting money on fighters. 'The aeroplane is not a defence against the aeroplane,' he once said, adding later that 'fighter defence must be kept to the smallest possible number'.[6] The 'Trenchard doctrine', as it was called, was theoretical nonsense. It took no account of the reality that, right up until 1941, the RAF had no heavy bombers in existence that could inflict serious damage on the enemy. Moreover, if Trenchardism had been carried through to its logical conclusion, Britain would have been defeated within less than a year of the outbreak of the Second World War. But for all its folly, the doctrine meant that the Air Staff had long sought to put far more emphasis on bombers than fighters.

Politicians, too, failed to provide any clear leadership in the early 1930s. The coalition government of 1931–5, led by the woolly minded, semi-pacifist Labour Prime Minister Ramsay MacDonald, oscillated between utopian dreams of worldwide military disarmament and an awareness that the air force should be strengthened to meet the challenge of the European dictators. Yet the political establishment also had a deep, corrosive sense of fatalism about Britain's inability to stand up to the looming military threat. It was an outlook epitomized by the notorious statement of the Conservative Leader Stanley Baldwin during a Parliamentary debate in November 1932: 'I think it is well for the man in the street to realize that there is no power on earth that can protect him from being bombed, whatever people may tell him. The bomber will always get through.'[7]

All these factors conspired to make fighter development a difficult task in the early 1930s. But Sydney Camm was not a man to give up easily. His near-tyrannical approach to management was matched by his bullish determination. Lack of support from the Air Ministry meant little to him. He continued to pursue his high-speed monoplane project as a private venture, certain that he could compel the government into ultimately awarding a contract for the plane. He had the record to prove that it could be done. Tall, balding and hook-nosed in appearance, with a stooping gait and a desperately short fuse, Camm had become one of the best-known designers in the aircraft industry by the early 1930s. Since joining H. G. Hawker Engineering in 1923, he had been responsible for a string of highly successful designs, most notably the Fury biplane fighter and the Hart light bomber. Both of these planes, distinguished by their attractive lines and superb handling qualities, went through numerous variants and sold all over the world. In fact, it was the swiftness of the Hart light bomber that helped to wake up the Air Ministry to the inadequacy of the RAF's fighter force.

Aviation had been the passion of Sydney Camm's life from his earliest years. 'I am one of those lucky individuals who've been able to convert a boyhood hobby into a profession,'[8] he told the BBC in April 1942, a reference to his youthful enthusiasm for model making. Like many driven men, his ambition was fired by a tough upbringing. He had been born on Alma Road in Windsor, Berkshire, on 5 August 1893, the eldest of the twelve children of Frederick Camm, an artisan carpenter, and his wife Mary Smith. The Victorian ethos of self-improvement prevailed in the Camm household, the father teaching his sons woodwork and construction skills. This informal tuition left a beneficial legacy, not just for Sydney but also his younger brother Frederick, who went on to become the long-serving editor of the magazine *Popular Mechanics*. Sydney proved a bright child academically as well as practically. He was admitted in 1901 to the Royal

Free School in Windsor, and in 1906 was granted a Foundation Scholarship, which meant that he received free school clothes and financial support, an indicator both of his own ability and his family's impoverished circumstances.

At the age of fifteen Sydney left school to become an apprentice carpenter, but by now his interest in aeroplanes had been fired and he started to spend much of his spare time making models or watching flying displays. One of the feats that particularly struck him was a landing at Windsor Castle by the engineer and daring aviator Tom Sopwith, with whom he later enjoyed a long association at Hawker. In 1912, less than a decade after the Wright brothers had made their inaugural flight at Kitty Hawk, North Carolina, Sydney helped to set up the Windsor Model Aeroplane Club. His strength of character and inherent talent for design were already obvious. As the dynamic secretary of the club, he led the construction of impressive gliders and other models, some of which were exhibited at Olympia, London, in 1913.

A sense of Sydney's restless energy at this time can be gleaned from the pages of *Flight* magazine, to which he sent regular reports of the activities of the Windsor club. In April 1912 *Flight* reported on the formation of the club: 'It is hoped that some good work will be accomplished during the summer as the club has unequalled facilities for experiments with rising-from-the-ground and hydro-aeroplane models. Despite the gale last Saturday week, some good flying was done by S. Camm.'[9] At the age of just nineteen Sydney had made it onto the pages of the national press. In February 1913 *Flight* further reported on his accomplishment in building a glider with a 30-foot wingspan, as well as the club's contribution to the Olympia model show, where its exhibits had been shown to 'very tasteful and pleasing effect'.[10] In April the magazine recorded that 'Mr S. Camm has been flying a five-foot racing monoplane. A hollow spar forms the basis of some of the construction, the type being tail behind. The model has accomplished some fine duration flights, flying very high.'[11]

Given this background, it seemed inevitable that Camm should embark on a career in aircraft industry. Just before the outbreak of the First World War, he took up a post at the Martin and Handasyde

Company based at the Brooklands racing circuit in Weybridge, Surrey, later to be one of the key sites in Hurricane production and also one of the early homes of British motor sport. At first he was a shop-floor carpenter, but his obvious ability quickly impressed the management and he was promoted to the drawing office. He said later: 'This period gave me a great deal of practical experience, and during this time I was also very fortunate in being able to inspect almost weekly the captured enemy aircraft which were shown at the Agricultural Hall, Islington.'[12] Throughout the First World War he worked largely on biplane fighters, but the end of the conflict brought difficult times for the Martin and Handasyde Company, as it did for many other aircraft firms, and in 1921 it went into liquidation following a slump in orders. For a couple of years Camm worked for George Handasyde, who had set up his own independent firm from the commercial wreckage of the earlier failure. The new venture enjoyed some public acclaim when one of its planes finished second in the hugely popular *Daily Mail* national glider trials of 1922. However, the success did not last. The following year the Handasyde firm, like its predecessor, went out of business.

But with his burgeoning experience Camm soon found another job. In November 1923 he was appointed senior draughtsman at the H. G. Hawker engineering company, based at Canbury Park Road in Kingston, London. The name of his new employer was something of a misnomer, for the enterprise was really run by Tom Sopwith, Camm's hero of the pre-war days. The son of a successful mining executive, Sopwith had been fascinated with cars and aeroplanes since his youth. But his boyish spirit of technological adventure was mitigated by an appalling incident that had occurred when he was just ten years old. During a family holiday off Oban in Scotland in 1898, he was on a boating expedition with his father. As they sailed across the water, a shotgun lay across the boy's knees. Suddenly, in a moment of horror, the gun went off, killing his father. It was an incident that haunted Sopwith for the rest of his life. Ironically, however, the substantial inheritance from this tragedy meant that he did not have to consider work, so instead he devoted himself to his pastimes of motor racing and flying. Then in 1912, just as Camm was forming the Windsor Model Aeroplane Club, Sopwith was operating on a grander scale, establishing the Sopwith Aviation Company. Almost immediately, his firm gained a strong reputation in the aviation world. Having won the prestigious Schneider Trophy for sea racing at Monaco in 1914 with a Sopwith Tabloid, the company then became one of the dominant aircraft manufacturers of the First World War, building no fewer than 18,000 aircraft of 32 different types, the most famous of which was the Sopwith Camel biplane, credited with 1,294 victories in combat.

Again, just like the Martin and Handasyde Company, Sopwith Aviation suffered badly from the loss of orders after the 1918 armistice. Attempts to stay in profit through the manufacture of motorcycles failed. Furthermore, Tom Sopwith feared that, in the new climate of austerity, he might be landed with a large retrospective tax bill for the company's wartime earnings. So he put Sopwith Aviation into voluntary liquidation while the firm was still solvent and could pay its creditors. Just two months later he returned to aircraft manufacturing by using £20,000 of capital to set up a new enterprise, H. G. Hawker Engineering Limited. The company's title, which he hoped would help him avoid further tax liabilities or financial ramifications from his past, came from his associate and close friend Harry Hawker, a heroic Australian aviation pioneer who had joined Sopwith Aviation as chief test pilot in 1912.

One of the most dashing airmen in the early years of flying, Hawker was renowned both for his risk-taking and his apparent good luck. His survival from a series of accidents, including one when he fell from an aircraft at more than 1,000 feet over Brooklands, led to his nickname among the sporting public: 'the Man Who Won't Be Killed'. During his association with Sopwith, Hawker established several records for altitude and endurance flying, though his two attempts to cross the Atlantic in 1919 both ended with him coming down in the ocean and having to be rescued by passing ships. Sadly, contrary to his reputation, Hawker's luck ran out on 12 July 1921 when he crashed at the Hendon aerodrome in London while practising for an airshow. Hawker was thrown about a hundred yards from the aircraft as it ploughed into the earth, and, despite immediate medical attention, he never regained consciousness. Commenting on his death, *Flight* magazine wrote: 'The name of Hawker deserves to live in the history of aviation, not for the performances associated with his name, but for his contributions to the increase in aeronautical knowledge.'[13]

The name did live on, but now the Hawker company was largely in the hands of Tom Sopwith. The recruitment of Sydney Camm in 1923 turned out to be an inspired move. Camm might have lacked academic qualifications, but his understanding of aircraft was instinctive. His very first design for Hawker, the ultralight two-seater Cygnet built in 1924, proved highly successful and helped him win elevation to the position of Chief Designer in 1925. Over the next forty years in this role Camm was to create 52 different types of aircraft, leading to the manufacture of 26,000 planes. It was a remarkable record for an entirely self-taught man. But the struggles of his early life turned Camm's personality into a difficult mixture of brutal intolerance and occasional self-doubt. 'He was very irritable and if people did not do things as he felt they ought to be done, they knew. He would lose his temper. He was a hard taskmaster,' said Beryl Platt, one of the few female senior engineers working in the aero-industry during the Second World War.[14] Dr John Fozard, who succeeded Camm as the Chief Designer at Hawker, wrote that he would 'brook no irreverence or argument from his men. His ability to give an instant and bowel-turning dressing-down to an errant draughtsman became well developed.'[15] At one stage in the late 1920s the staff in the Design Office grew so exasperated at his authoritarian manner that they signed a letter of complaint to Sopwith, though the subsequent years saw little change in Camm's behaviour. 'I can't imagine why his men put up with him. He was a genius, but quite often impossible,' said Sopwith himself.[16]

Yet men endured Camm because they admired him. They recognized that behind the brusqueness was a unique designer of unrivalled vision and practicality who had turned his team into one of the finest in the British aircraft industry. They joined him in his constant striving for perfection and determination to overcome every obstacle, whether it be a design fault or an exercise in bureaucratic foolishness. Besides, many understood that Camm's irascibility was sometimes part of an act, almost like a pantomime. Robin Balmer, who worked in the Projects Office at Hawker, had this memory:

He certainly kept people on their toes. He was wonderful at motivat-
ing people, more by fear than anything else. When he came in, you
made sure you appeared to be working hard. I can remember one day
walking down the back of the Drawing Office to see someone and the
old man was coming the other way, whistling, happy as a sandboy.
'Morning, Balmer.' 'Morning, sir.' I got to the other end, talked to
the other bloke. 'The old man's in a good mood this morning,' I said.
'Good mood my foot, he's just given me the biggest rollicking of my
life.' So Camm had done his day's stirring up and was feeling pleased
with himself.[17]

Another Hawker employee, Ray Braybrook, felt that some of
Camm's waspishness was a psychological ploy to create a special kin-
ship among his closest associates. 'Out in the vastness of the Drawing
Office he was willing to ham it up as the eccentric genius, but within
the confines of the Project Office he fostered – perhaps equally
shrewdly – a sense of close brotherhood of designers. Prime Ministers
were mere temporary nuisances and Chiefs of Staff were to be pitied
for their boring clerical jobs, but if you designed fighters for Sir
Sydney Camm, you were a prince among men.'[18]

Camm's pungent humour also helped to alleviate the effect of his
sharp tongue. The workforce at Kingston relished his stream of
maxims and insults, especially if they were not the target. 'I'm never
wrong except when persuaded against my better judgement,' was
one such adage. 'It looks like mother done it – all pots and pans,'
was another phrase he used when dissatisfied by a scheme for a component or an aeroplane. If the Hawker company came under criticism from the government or the press, he would tell his staff, with
an ill-disguised twinkle in his eye: 'I hope you're all working with a
proper sense of guilt and shame.' Some of his adages revealed his
personal philosophy toward aircraft design. 'I'm only interested in
designing fighters. There's no finesse in anything else,' he occasionally said. 'You've got to have an eye for a line' showed his belief that
a good aircraft should look attractive. His comment that 'every
modification begets a modification' highlighted his fear that med-
dling by the Air Ministry could over-complicate a design.[19]

Away from his desk at Kingston, Camm was a relaxed, genial
family man with a wide range of interests, nothing like the martinet

of the Hawker works. In 1915 he had married Hilda Starnes, the sister of one of his friends from the Windsor club, and they had one child, a daughter called Phyllis. The family house of Carradale in Thames Ditton was a place of warmth, as Phyllis later recalled: 'To the world at large, in his lifetime, he was a reticent figure, austere and reserved – a perfectionist in his profession. In private he had a well-developed sense of humour and derived great enjoyment from reading Damon Runyon and Evelyn Waugh novels.' He had, she continued, 'conventional tastes in music, enjoyed operatic overtures and orchestral pieces, was unimpressed by solo singers and considered violins should only be heard when grouped 1,000 strong.' She recounted how her father adored golf, which he played with a creditable handicap of eight, and driving performance cars, especially his E-type Jaguar. There were also more simple pleasures. 'At home, he would spend winter evenings being equally perfectionist, painting kitchen chairs, balancing his beloved golf clubs or repairing the family's shoes with stick-on soles and heels.'

The affectionate private man was also recalled by his granddaughter, Elizabeth Dickson, who said that when her own parents divorced he 'was like a second father to me'. Camm would drive over to Elizabeth's home to read her a bedtime story, and he would have her to stay at weekends. 'We would go out together to choose a new book, which I read in the orchard at Carradale, looking out from my perch in the apple tree to see Grandpa mowing the lawn or trying to catch me unawares with his camera.'[20]

As a designer, Camm was a mixture of the conservative and the radical, contradictory qualities that shone through the Hurricane itself. It was in the mid 1920s that he had first considered the idea of a monoplane, sketching out a plan for a small, single-seater fighter, powered by a Bristol Jupiter air-cooled radial engine. But because of the rigid Air Ministry policy in favour of the biplane at that time, Camm never tried to take the idea beyond the drawing board. From then on his concentration was focused on the Hart light bomber and Fury fighter, with all their myriad variants.

The cautious side of Camm was more strongly in evidence when the Hawker company decided to submit a tender in 1931 in response to the Air Ministry's specification F7/30, which called for a new day and night fighter to replace the ageing Bristol Bulldog biplane. The essential requirements were that the new plane should have a minimum speed of 195 mph at 15,000 feet, be of all-metal construction and carry four 0.303-inch guns. The Air Ministry felt that these demanding conditions would give Britain a world-beating fighter force. Though no wing configuration was stipulated, the Ministry's aim was to encourage a move toward the monoplane, as shown by a note on the specification by the Chief of the Air Staff Sir John Salmond in July 1931. 'There remains one point to which I attach importance: that is encouraging novel types so as to get away from the tractor biplane . . . If we are to get serious attempts at novel types to meet this specification, we shall have to provide the incentive.'[21] But Camm showed little willingness to embrace this spirit of innovation. Instead, the tender he prepared for F7/30 was a highly conventional development of the Fury biplane, known as the Hawker PV3. The only two major changes from the Fury biplane were, first, the introduction of a spatted metal undercarriage, with rounded metal covers over the wheels to improved the airflow, and, second, the replacement of the Rolls-Royce Kestrel engine by the experimental new Rolls-Royce Goshawk power-plant, which was meant to deliver greater power without excessive weight. The Goshawk used an evaporative cooling system in which steam was taken from the engine and then piped into a series of condensers that ran along both the upper and lower wings. The system eliminated the need for a radiator, but the complex network of condensers proved unreliable. Nevertheless, because of the Goshawk's early potential, most of the firms bidding in the race to secure the F7/30 contract, including Supermarine, opted for the new engine.

Camm's entry, the PV3, was never in contention. At a conference in May 1932 to review the Air Ministry's various tenders, his design was rejected for being 'too orthodox' and 'rather pedestrian'.[22] The 'most attractive design', decided the Air Ministry, was the Supermarine Type 224 'modelled on racing aircraft practice with a speed 25 mph faster than any other types'.[23] This was the Supermarine plane that would ultimately evolve into the Spitfire, though it was a fraught journey, involving a host of changes in specification and design, including the abandonment of the difficult Goshawk engine and the introduction of the unique elliptical wing. Indeed, the process was so drawn out that, in the meantime, the F7/30 contract was awarded to the Gloster company for its biplane design, the Gladiator. It is another illustration of the confusion in air strategy that a specification meant to herald an exciting new age in fighter technology should end up prolonging the reign of the biplane. In the end, 750 Gloster Gladiators were built. Though the aircraft was already obsolescent by 1939, it performed valiantly in several theatres of war up to 1942, most famously in the defence of Malta.

But Camm was too perceptive not to recognize that the biplane was finished. After the rejection of the PV3, the Hawker team began work on a low-wing, cantilever monoplane alterative. It was a step that Camm took with trepidation, as he later admitted. 'We embarked on this design with some fear as there was a natural reluctance to leave the biplane on which we had so much experience.'[24] But many of his staff were only too excited to be stepping into the future. Stuart Davies, who joined Hawker in 1931 as a project designer, said this of his office's activities in mid 1933: 'Such energies as we had to spare after coping with foreign enquiries were devoted to various abortive attempts to improve the Fury performance until finally, in the late summer of 1933, we were let loose on a monoplane version of the F7/30.'[25]

With the first drawings underway, Camm travelled in August 1933 from Kingston to the offices of the Air Ministry at the Aldwych in London. There, on a stiflingly hot day, he had a meeting with the Ministry's Director of Development, Air Commodore H. M. Cave-Brown-Cave, and the Deputy Director, Major John Buchanan. According to the project diary that Camm kept at Kingston, they discussed 'the possibility of building the Fury monoplane, a single-seater fighter armed with two machine guns in the fuselage and two in the wings'.[26] Air Commodore Cave-Brown-Cave is reported to have warned him that the political climate was not favourable to a further expansion of fighter types, on the grounds both of cost and the coalition government's continuing attachment to the idea of worldwide military retrenchment, a policy that reached its peak of influence during the League of Nations disarmament talks at Geneva between 1932 and 1934. 'All that I can promise is that I will put up the plans,' he said.[27] So Camm continued work on them. By 5 December 1933 the drawings of the plane, now alternately entitled the 'Hawker monoplane' or 'Fury monoplane', had been completed. That month, Camm had a lengthy meeting with Captain Roger Liptrot, another Air Ministry official, to discuss the details of this private venture.

By early January 1934 Camm was ready to submit the full plans for his new high-speed aircraft. True to form, the Hawker Monoplane was an amalgam of old and new. Despite its single-wing layout and fully enclosed cockpit, it featured a fixed undercarriage with spats. Furthermore, the construction of the fuselage relied on the traditional Warren girder technique that Hawker had utilized so successfully on its biplanes since the 1920s. The basic primary structure used four steel longerons connected in a zig-zag pattern by round steel or duralumin tubes. Each end of every tube was fabricated into a square section, which was then either riveted or bolted to the connecting plate on the longerons. The entire girder assembly was braced by wires with tensioning turnbuckles. Wooden frames were then attached to the metal structure, on top of which was laid a covering of fabric. The wings used much the same Warren girder method, in which the two main spars were held together by a web of metal tubes and then the whole structure was covered in fabric. Even though not exactly advanced, the plane was sturdy, light, straightforward to manufacture and simple to repair. More problematically, the design retained the Rolls-Royce Goshawk engine, despite all the severe drawbacks that it had increasingly displayed when installed in other aircraft.

Camm's proposal was circulated round the corridors of the Air Ministry in January and February 1934, but failed to win over the officials who were trying to cope with so many other projects in this time of flux. One of those who was not especially impressed was Sir Hugh Dowding, then the Air Staff's head of supply and research, a vital position with responsibility for the modernization of the RAF. He felt that Camm had been held back by the ethos of continuity with the Fury fighter, explaining that he 'could see Hawkers' point of view in wishing to stick with military utility', but feared that this 'rather handicaps' the Air Staff in pushing for greater speeds.[28] Yet the initial rejection, delivered by letter in March, worked in Camm's favour as it gave him the opportunity to improve the design greatly. One key change he made was to introduce a fully retractable under-carriage, operated by hydraulics, in place of the fixed, spatted wheels. Though this was an obvious step to reduce the amount of drag, it created a delicate engineering problem. The only possible place for the wheels when retracted inwards was flat against the fuselage floor, immediately behind the front spar in the wings. To provide enough room for the wheel tyres, the wing root had to be slightly thickened. With typical enterprise this obstacle was overcome, and indeed the resulting strength and efficiency of the wide undercarriage was to be one of the Hurricane's greatest virtues.

During the early summer of 1934 Camm also refined the Warren girder torsion bracing and revised the fabric attachments. A further key alteration was inspired by a visit he received from one of his clos-est friends in the aircraft industry, Group Captain A. C. Maund, Commanding Officer of the Aircraft and Armament Experimental Establishment at Martlesham Heath in Suffolk. Having examined the design, Maund bravely told Camm that he thought the wing tips were rather blunt. The Design Office expected one of Camm's instant explosions. Instead, he meekly said after a pause, 'I think you may be right,' and then proceeded to sketch out a new wing tip with a smaller radius.[29]

The most important change, however, was the introduction of a new engine. By the summer of 1934 it was obvious that the Goshawk was doomed to failure, as reported to the Air Ministry by Captain Roger Liptrot, who was being kept informed by Hawker of the progress of the monoplane. To test the Goshawk, the engine had been installed on a Fury biplane but it was proving a disaster. 'Hawkers are still experiencing great difficulty with the steam cooling system due to losing water. They are having a further discussion with Messrs Rolls-Royce and hope to devise a satisfactory modification. They are not very hopeful at the moment that they can get a system without a lot of further experimentation,' wrote Liptrot in July.[30]

But help was now at hand. At the very moment in 1932 when Camm had first been considering his private-venture monoplane as a successor to the Fury biplane, Ernest Hives, Chief Engineer of

Rolls-Royce, had embarked on a major private-venture project to create a successor to the famous Kestrel engine. The similarities between the upbringings of Camm and Hives were striking. Hives, born in 1886, also came from a humble working-class Berkshire family and, like Camm, was one of twelve children. His father was a factory clerk in Reading and Ernest's first job was working as a garage mechanic. His natural technical gifts meant that he was soon taken on by Rolls-Royce in Derby, where he was to remain for the rest of a long career.

After the First World War, having taken charge of all the company's experimental work, Hives confirmed Rolls-Royce's reputation for excellence with the Kestrel engine, from which evolved the R engine that powered Supermarine's Schneider Trophy winners in 1929 and 1931. Alarmed by the inadequacy of the Goshawk engine, Hives then poured his considerable energies into a further development of the Kestrel, the new engine taking the title of the PV12. With a 27-litre capacity, the PV12 offered much greater power in return for only a small increase in weight. First run in October 1933, it could potentially generate 1,000 horsepower, compared to just 700 hp offered by the Goshawk. Moreover, the PV12's coolant was the chemical ethylene glycol, which was first manufactured in commercial quantities in the USA in the late 1920s and was far more efficient than the Goshawk's awkward sprawl of steam-cooling pipes. Soon after its first successful run in October 1933, the PV12 was renamed the Merlin, taking its place in the Rolls-Royce birds of prey series, though after the power-plant achieved its international fame in the Battle of Britain, many people mistakenly but understandably believed that the title was a reference to the engine's magical qualities.

Not long after the Merlin's first bench runs, Hives made its performance figures available to Camm. Immediately, the Hawker designer saw the solution to his problems and set about redesigning his monoplane to accommodate the new power-plant. The small additional engine weight forward of the centre of gravity meant that the radiator had to be moved around eighteen inches further back than had been usual on the Hart light bomber and the Fury fighter. Nor did the new position and weight of the radiator allow it to be made retractable, as had been done on many variants of the Hart light bomber. Therefore, shutters had to be installed to regulate the cooling airflow, a particular necessity, as it turned out, during the Battle of Britain when planes often had to wait on the ground in a state of readiness with their engines running. But these were trifling difficulties compared to the significant benefits that the Merlin brought. Even the small increase in drag was more than outweighed by the component of thrust provided by the duct that enclosed the radiator.

By August 1934 a one-tenth scale model of the new monoplane had been built. Hawker did not possess its own wind tunnel, due to Camm's strange aversion to such equipment because of his scepticism about the applicability of the results. 'When you've designed aeroplanes as long as I have you can see the airflow,' was one of his aphorisms.[31] So for tests the company had to use the compressed-air tunnel at the National Physics Laboratory in Teddington, Middlesex. Camm was happy to learn, however, that the NPL tests on his model confirmed its aerodynamic qualities. Crucially, the wind-tunnel analysis further stated that little gain in speed would be made by reducing the thickness of the wing, news that came as a relief to Hawker staff as it meant that the arrangement for the retractable undercarriage would not have to be altered.

Camm was now ready to approach the Air Ministry again, six months after his first rebuff. On 4 September he sent Major J. S. Buchanan, the Deputy Director, Hawker's revised scheme for an 'Interceptor Monoplane'. In his covering letter Camm reminded the Ministry of the earlier submission in January. 'You may remember that our proposals were considered and we were informed it was regretted that the Department was unable to give active encouragement to the proposal.' But as he explained, the scheme had been greatly improved since then, which meant that 'a speed approaching 300 mph appears possible. We feel that this design is of some importance, and we respectfully re-submit it for your approval.' The enclosed written proposal revealed that the fighter would have an all-up weight of approximately 4,850 pounds, with the Merlin engine providing 810 horsepower at 15,000 feet. The new plane would be substantial in size, having a wingspan of 40 feet and a length of 31 feet. The wings, Camm's document explained, were constructed of two spars held together by Warren girder bracing 'to provide torsional strength'. Meanwhile, 'the fuselage and tail unit in general follow the standard Hawker methods, modified where necessary to suit the special conditions caused by fitting the monoplane wing'. The fuel system consisted of two 40-gallon tanks in either wing and a 27-gallon gravity tank close behind the engine, giving a theoretical total capacity of 107 gallons. The armament comprised two Vickers guns mounted on the fuselage.[32]

In contrast to the spring of 1934, this time the response from the Air Ministry was much more favourable. Less than a week after Camm had sent his proposal, Buchanan told his colleagues on 10 September: 'In view of the importance of high speed development, I recommend ordering this aeroplane. I am informed by Mr Camm of Hawkers and Mr Hives of Rolls-Royce that they expect to have this aeroplane flying in June 1935.'[33] Buchanan's boss, Air Commodore Cave-Brown-Cave agreed, just three days later. 'If Hawkers quote a reasonable price I recommend that we should order one of these aeroplanes against the money in the estimates for High Speed development.'[34] A single prototype of the 'Interceptor Monoplane' was ordered, the price of £8,000 having been agreed with Hawker to cover the cost. The Hawker Hurricane had been born.

The different reaction to Camm's fighter on this second occasion was prompted by a number of factors. One was the obvious great improvement in the design, with an estimated maximum speed of 298 mph, far above the original speed of over 264 mph offered back in March. The better Merlin engine, retractable undercarriage and strengthened wings all offered a 'much higher performance', to quote Cave-Brown-Cave.[35] In addition, the designer Reginald Mitchell was still struggling with his more advanced Supermarine fighter, which meant that the Air Ministry had to consider other monoplane alternatives. 'Supermarine are not getting the performance they hoped for from their F7/30,' Cave-Brown-Cave reported to his colleagues in July.

The political climate had also changed since earlier in the year. The world disarmament talks in Geneva had finally collapsed, having been rendered meaningless by Hitler's decision to leave the League of Nations and embark on a programme of aggressive remilitarization.

In response to the incipient German threat, the Chancellor of the Exchequer Neville Chamberlain, the most hard-headed member of the government, provided increased funds for air defence at home, offset by reductions in forces overseas. A cool realist, reared in the tough world of Midlands commerce and municipal politics, Chamberlain had no time for Trenchardian doctrinaires, naval supremacists or imperial dreamers. He believed that fighters must be the first priority for military spending. It was in part thanks to him that Britain was so well prepared for the Luftwaffe in 1940. As a result of his pressure, the Cabinet agreed in July 1934 to impose on the RAF a far-reaching expansion scheme, which provided for an increase in the Metropolitan force from 52 to 84 squadrons. This was the first of no fewer than thirteen different air-expansion schemes introduced by the government during the 1930s, each successive one betraying a mounting concern about the RAF's size and equipment as the menace of Germany grew. Crucially, Chamberlain's emphasis on fighters was shared by Sir Hugh Dowding, who as Air Member for Supply and Research had been one of the instigators of the drive for new monoplanes, though other figures, such as the inarticulate, uncharismatic Chief of the Air Staff Sir Edward Ellington, still clung to their enthusiasm for bombers.

Yet perhaps the most significant influence in favour of Camm's revised design was the new thinking within the Air Staff about the armament for fighters. There was a growing awareness that, in a world of high-speed aircraft, the traditional firepower of a couple of machine guns would be hopelessly inadequate. Even the most skilful pilot would not have time to get in a destructive enough burst on the enemy. More guns, with greater lethality, were needed. The official who was most deeply contemplating this question was Squadron Leader Ralph Sorley, a senior official in the Air Ministry's Operational Requirements Directorate. Having enjoyed successful spells in the Royal Naval Air Service during the First World War and in the Middle East during the 1920s, Sorley had embarked on his new role in January 1933. Soon he was immersed in the issue of fighter weaponry, as he later recorded in May 1945: 'My whole waking hours were devoted to one problem: what fighter could be evolved which would stand the highest chance of defeating the fast bomber.'[36] Sorley shared the growing consensus in favour of the monoplane, but the type and number of guns presented a more complex difficulty. After much 'burning of the midnight oil' during his research, Sorley decided the choice came down to two possibilities: the .303 Browning developed by the American Colt Automatic Weapon Corporation, or the new 20-mm Hispano gun, which had attracted the interest of the French air force. He later admitted that the contemplation of the decision was 'something of a nightmare during 1933–4', since he sensed that 'it was a choice on which the whole concept of the fighter would depend'.[37]

Amid 'great secrecy', Sorley travelled to the Hispano-Suiza factory 'in the bowels of a fort near Paris' to watch the 20-mm gun in action, but he was not especially impressed, for the gun was experiencing serious teething problems at the time. More effective, it seemed, was the Browning, which possessed a higher rate of fire than the Hispano. Sorley arranged for the tests of the .303 Browning to be conducted at the RAF's range at Shoeburyness, Essex, using eight Brownings harmonized to fire from 400 yards at the same target, an old disused aeroplane. 'Bursts of two seconds with solid and explosive ammunition were fired. To my joy the effect was all I imagined. The structure was cut through in so many vulnerable places that one could safely count on two seconds being the lethal dose.'[38] Sorley believed he had his solution: a multi-gun fighter with eight .303 Brownings mounted in the wings and firing 1,200 rounds per minute.

Sorley now put forward his case for the eight-gun, high-speed fighter to his senior colleagues on the Air Staff, pointing out that the big gain in firepower hardly disadvantaged the plane in other areas. In early July 1934 he wrote to Sir Edgar Ludlow-Hewitt, Deputy Chief of the Air Staff, that the difference in performance for the eight-gun installation compared to six guns was 'remarkably small', amounting to just 'half a minute more on the climb' and a 'one mile an hour drop in speed'. He was also dismissive of the traditional emphasis on manoeuvrability, long the biplane's greatest assest: 'As I see it, the principle of a short, decisive attack, does not introduce complicated and rapid manoeuvres.'[39] Dowding, with his usual perspicacity, became a convert to the idea, as did Hewitt, though others were more doubtful.

In a letter to Ludlow-Hewitt in early August the Commander of the Air Defence of Great Britain, Robert Brooke-Popham, said that he thought 'eight guns is going a bit too far. I should have been content with four. I should have thought that with eight guns you are bound to get a lot of head resistance and generally speaking I would prefer four guns with the same total amount of ammunition. You will, I think, find that the opinion of most people in the Fighting Area is that the guns must still be placed in the cockpit.'[40] Some even regarded the whole concept of the single-seater as flawed. With an astonishing lack of foresight, Group Captain Richard Peirse, the Air Staff's Deputy Director of Intelligence, had argued that the real future lay with the two-seat fighter equipped with the rear-mounted turret. 'The single-seater, however many guns it carries, is I think the least useful for a fight. The movable multi-gun, multi-seat fighter is beyond doubt the right answer. It is so far in advance of the single-seater that the latter must be considered obsolescent now.'[41] The Air Ministry went on to develop just such a plane, the Boulton Paul Defiant. It proved so hopelessly vulnerable in 1940 that it had to be withdrawn from service and its squadrons re-equipped with Hurricanes.

Thankfully, the opposition to Sorley's proposals did not prevail. On 9 August 1934 a meeting of the Air Staff, chaired by Ludlow-Hewitt, was held to discuss the replacement for the ageing Hawker Fury biplane. Despite the anxieties of Brooke-Popham, it was agreed that 'eight guns should be aimed at on the grounds of shorter time to obtain the required density and the improvement in range which was obtainable with eight guns'.[42]

The fraught arguments over fighter armament had all taken place while Camm's private venture, rejected in March, was not even under consideration by the Air Ministry. So the putative Hawker fighter, only resubmitted as a design in September, never featured in the discussion. Having decided the gun layout, the Ministry's next stage was to begin the tendering process for this new monoplane. After further consultation about the detailed requirements, specification F5/34 was finally issued in November 1934, the document stressing that eight Brownings were to be fitted. Two months later the firms of Gloster, Westland and Bristol were invited to develop designs for a prototype.

Though Hawker had not been involved in the F5/34 debate, Camm was well aware of the new specification. The call for an eight-gun fighter would later come to have a far-reaching impact on his work, for, with its thick wing, the Hawker plane was ideally placed to fulfil Sorley's vision. But by the time specification F5/34 was issued in November, Camm's initial design was already too advanced to incorporate immediately the new eight-gun configuration, and the armament he proposed was just four Browning guns, one mounted on each side of the fuselage and one in each wing. On 17 October 1934 the first drawings of the interceptor had been sent to the Hawker Experimental Shops so jigs could be prepared to build the prototype. Other progress followed rapidly. In December the Experimental Department began to construct a mock-up of the design, to be ready for inspection by the Air Ministry. That month Camm also held a meeting with Rolls-Royce, at which he learnt the encouraging news that the estimated performance of the Merlin would be even better than expected, with the engine giving 1,025 brake horsepower at take-off, only for an increase of 80 pounds in weight.

The next major hurdle was the mock-up conference with the Air Ministry representatives, held at Hawker's Kingston works on 10 January 1935. Contrary to what most aviation literature contends, the design at this stage was still known baldly as the 'Hawker High Speed Monoplane'. At the Kingston discussion the air officials made thirty-one suggestions for improvements, but most of these were highly detailed, such as a better speed indicator, a down adjustment of one inch in the pilot's seat, and the installation of an emergency exit door on the port side of the cockpit.[43] Generally, the Ministry was satisfied enough to confirm that the full manufacture of the prototype should proceed as quickly as possible. As an indicator of its support, the government drew up a new specification, F36/34, formulated solely around the Hawker design. The prototype now under construction was also given its own serial number for the first time, K5083. The sense of enthusiasm for the plane was further bolstered in February when Camm was able to send the provisional performance figures to the Air Staff. These were even better than had been expected. He reported that the F36/34 fighter might be able to attain a maximum speed of 330 mph at 15,000 feet, despite a small increase in the normal loaded weight to 4,900 pounds. One point of concern for the Air Ministry was that Hawker planned to use Plexiglas on the prototype's hood, the problem being that this tough synthetic material had been developed in Nazi Germany by the Darmstadt firm of Rohm and Hass. The Government wrote to Hawker in April 1935 to express its anxiety about the source of Plexiglas, but Hawker replied that there was no alternative. 'As there is not yet a British source of supply of material of similar transparency, the objection that you mention can no doubt be over-ruled,'[44] Hawker explained, a stance that the Ministry accepted. Fortunately, when fighter production massively increased in the late 1930s, this difficulty was overcome by manufacture of Plexiglas in the USA and Britain.

Like an outsider suddenly breaking for the front in the final lap of a race, it looked as though Sydney Camm's unheralded monoplane might win the competition to become the RAF's leading fighter. Rejected brusquely in March 1934, almost a year later it had captured the imagination of the air marshals. Then in early 1935 two separate events occurred, one technical and one political, which were to accelerate the production of this fighter. The first was a renewed intervention from Squadron Leader Ralph Sorley, who was more certain than ever of the urgent need for an eight-gun fighter. As well as visiting the Supermarine works to see the progress on Reginald Mitchell's fighter, he called at Kingston to examine the mock-up of the F36/34. He was at once struck by the aircraft's modern design, as well as its potential for accommodating his cherished octet of Brownings. He had seen the future of Britain's fighter defence, and he was certain it belonged to the Supermarine and Hawker companies, as he explained in a letter to Ludlow-Hewitt of 1 May. 'Both aircraft look to be excellent and in the hands of Mitchell and Camm I suggest they are likely to be successes,' he wrote, urging that work on the Gloster Gladiator biplane be abandoned. 'It would be a retrograde step to produce it when there are two possibles, which will do over 300 mph, due to fly before the end of 1935.' So sure was Sorley of the two types' superlative qualities that he urged the Air Ministry to put them immediately into production without even waiting for the prototypes to be flown:

I am aware that this is an unorthodox method but with the political situation as it is and the possibility of increased expansion close upon us we should take steps to produce the latest design in the shortest possible time . . . It may be said that action to tool up for these two aircraft would be unfair to other firms . . . I suggest that the situation no longer allows tender feelings for others, and we require the best aircraft that we can get at the appropriate moment.[45]

Sorley's demand for an immediate order was a step too far for the Air Ministry. The new Director of Technical Development, R. H. Verney, who had succeeded Cave-Brown-Cave, said in early May that although he appreciated the 'special circumstances' of the Hawker and Supermarine designs, he felt that, rather than take 'a production gamble', it would be better to wait until 'the aeroplanes have flown, and we know the best or the worst, as the case may be'.[46] This view was upheld by the Air Staff. But the Ministry gave a more positive response to Sorley's continued pressure for increased armament. Not long afterwards, in July 1935, the contract with Hawker was amended to include provision for eight guns, and work began on incorporating this requirement in the design. By late August a mock-up of the new installation had been completed, though it was not possible to incorporate either the guns or ammunition in the actual prototype, which by then was in an advanced state of construction and was only weeks away from its maiden flight. Despite this omission, dictated by the urgency of getting the plane in the air, the fitting of the eight guns was a relatively straightforward task because of the thickness and structure of the F36/34's wings.

Harold Tuffen, who worked under Camm in the Experimental Drawing Office, explained: 'The gun installation presented no basic problem when it came to be modified in the wing design. By happy chance, the arrangement of the two inboard diagonal rib bracing members of the outer wings enabled the gun mountings and ammunition boxes with their access doors to be worked in quite well.'[47] During the Battle of Britain, it was clear that the Hurricane's arrangement was easier to maintain than the Spitfire's, as Fred Roberts, an armourer with 19 Squadron, recorded: 'On a Spitfire, you had to take eight panels off the top of the wings and eight panels from underneath the wings. When you rearmed it, you had four flaps covering the underside of the ammunition tanks. In the Hurricane, you only had one panel covering each gun and one covering the ammunition tanks. And with the Hurricane, you could kneel on the top of the wing and rearm. On the Spitfire you couldn't. You had to get on your knees on the wet grass and take all those panels off.'[48]

The second event that helped the Hawker fighter was the introduction of greater political impetus to the policy of RAF growth. The catalyst for this new dynamic was a startling resurgence of German air power. Under the 1919 Treaty of Versailles military aviation had been banned in Germany. But the obligations of international agreements never meant anything to the Nazi regime. In February 1935 Hermann Göring, Hitler's closest ally and an air veteran of the First World War, publicly declared that Germany had created an air force. Even worse followed in March, when Hitler told the British Foreign Secretary Sir John Simon: 'We have achieved air parity with Britain.'[49] This was a wild exaggeration, characteristic of the Führer's bombast, but the claim sent a shudder through the British government. Ramsay MacDonald, normally so enfeebled and now in the twilight of his premiership, felt compelled to act. He set up a new Ministerial Committee on Air Parity in April 1935 and appointed as its chairman the tough, energetic Tory MP Sir Philip Cunliffe-Lister, the Colonial Secretary. A highly respected politician who preferred action to rhetoric, Cunliffe-Lister was to play a vital part in the arrival of the Hurricane into RAF service.

As chairman of the Ministerial Committee on Air Parity, Cunliffe-Lister immediately demonstrated his forcefulness by conducting its business in rapid time. Within a fortnight of its opening meeting on 1 May, he had already produced a powerful report advocating that the government should order another 3,800 aircraft by 1937 to meet the challenge of the Luftwaffe. Unlike the Trenchardian bomber enthusiasts, he stressed the importance of modern fighter defences. At a meeting of the Committee on 13 May, he asked Sir Edward Ellington, Chief of the Air Staff, about the progress of the Hawker and Supermarine prototypes. This was the first time that the F36/34 had been discussed at ministerial level, another sign of its increasing importance. With characteristic negativity, Ellington reported: 'Both these types could be produced within twelve months of the order being given. It was anticipated, however, that with this new type trouble must be anticipated, particularly aerodynamic troubles in connection with the controls. The Americans were experiencing considerable trouble in this matter and it was not considered safe to jig up these machines without further tests.'[50] In its submission to the full Cabinet, Cunliffe-Lister's Committee warned against overly high expectations of the two fighters, but urged that 'if the tests are satisfactory, orders could and we think should be placed'. The Cabinet endorsed both this position and the overall proposal for increased RAF numbers, now to be called Expansion Scheme C.[51]

Cunliffe-Lister's effective chairmanship meant that when Stanley Baldwin succeeded Ramsay MacDonald as Prime Minister in June 1935, he was rewarded with promotion to the post of Secretary of State for Air in the subsequent reshuffle. Immediately, Cunliffe-Lister continued in his vigorous ways, appointing as his chief adviser the Scottish industrialist Lord Weir, who, during a successful career in public life had overseen programmes as diverse as the creation of the national electricity grid and the supply of military aircraft during the First World War. Cunliffe-Lister also instituted frequent progress meetings with the Air Chiefs to keep up pressure for modernization and to reach decisions on aircraft procurement. It was this arena that would effectively decide the fate of the Hawker fighter in the coming months.

By the end of August 1935 the structure of the F36/34 prototype, complete with its Merlin engine, had been completed. The fact that it had been built in less than a year since Sydney Camm put forward the design to the Air Ministry was a tribute to Hawker's proficiency. Despite the relative simplicity of the airframe, Camm's team had to incorporate many technological innovations, such as the enclosed cockpit and the hydraulically operated retractable undercarriage and flaps. Over the next six weeks the fabric was applied to the structure, while ballast was installed in the wings to replicate the weight of the Browning guns that were still awaiting full trials. Harold Tuffen of Hawker described the sense of excitement that ran through the Kingston works as the plane took shape: 'Dramatic days indeed, as I remember the sight of the aggressive and menacing-looking machine nearing completion in the Experiment Department.'[52]

The politicians were also taking a close interest. At a progress meeting on 17 September, Cunliffe-Lister asked Sir Hugh Dowding about the 'Hawker High Speed Fighter'. Dowding replied that 'Rolls-Royce had done excellently with the Merlin engine and the machine should be flying in early October.'[53] He was being somewhat over-enthusiastic, but could report on 22 October that the aeroplane 'should be flying any day now'.[54] In fact, the very next day the prototype was taken in its component parts by lorry from Kingston to Hawker's testing and assembly facility at Brooklands in Weybridge, Surrey. There the wings were attached to the centre section. A Watts two-bladed wooden airscrew was installed. Running tests were conducted on the undercarriage retraction and the Merlin engine. The airframe was painted entirely silver, with RAF roundels inserted on the wings and fuselage. The Hawker Chief Test Pilot George Bulman did a few taxiing runs to familiarize himself with the cockpit and the closed cockpit, very different to what he had previously experienced on the company's biplanes. Just when everything seemed ready, a hitch occurred. It turned out that the Merlin had not yet completed its 50-hour provisional certificate of airworthiness test. But such was the pressure to begin the trials that Camm decided not to wait for the necessary documentation. He already had enough trust in Sir Ernest Hives's creation.

On the morning of 6 November 1935 the tarpaulins were removed and the Hawker fighter was taken out of the Brooklands hangar. It was a clear day and the silver plane glistened in the faint, wintry sun. A few of the Hawker staff whistled in appreciation at the sight of the solid yet graceful machine, ready for her first flight. 'When the design of the Hurricane had gone beyond the point of no return, I suddenly had a foreboding that it would be no good,' confessed Camm years later. He was about to find out the truth.[55]

2

'The fastest fighter in the world'

T̲HE TRIAL FLIGHTS of the mid 1930s were not the first occasions on which P. W. S. 'George' Bulman, the Hawker Chief Test Pilot, had flown a monoplane called the Hurricane. More than a decade earlier, when he was employed at the Royal Aircraft Establishment at Farnborough, Hampshire, he had been a member of the RAE aero-club, which took part in aerial displays. One of the planes built by members of the club was an extraordinary, primitive contraption with a motorcycle engine and a triangular-section fuselage. Despite its lack of power, the plane was grandly named 'The Hurricane' by the members. Bulman took it up a few times, and was almost killed on one occasion in 1923, when the engine cut out as he flew at 800 feet in a competition at Lympne in Kent. But with the skill and coolness that were to make him famous in the aircraft industry, Bulman put the plane into a vertical dive and managed to restart the engine just before he crashed into the ground.

Even in an age of colourful aviation pioneers, George Bulman stood out as an extrovert. He had won the Military Cross for his fighter exploits during the First World War, before going on to become a test pilot at the RAE and then, from 1925, at Hawker. His real first name was Paul, but as an adult he was never called that by anyone. The reason was his appalling memory for other people's names. Throughout the First World War he addressed almost everyone he met as 'Colonel' or 'General'. When peace arrived, he changed his universal greeting to 'George', so that was how he came to be known by others in response. Small, genial and self-assured, Bulman had a thick ginger moustache and a bald head, though he often wore a trilby hat, even on test flights. One post-war magazine profile paid this tribute to him: 'He worked like a Trojan turning

44

good designs into super-good flying aircraft. This good test-flying, allied to his technical knowledge and charm of manner, undoubtedly played a big part in bringing the Hawker concern to the pre-eminence it now enjoys.'[1] In fact, the Hawker company was so impressed with his technical understanding of aircraft that in June 1935 he was appointed a director, the first test pilot to sit on the board of a British aircraft manufacturer since Harry Hawker himself. One of Bulman's other qualities was his meticulous attention to detail. Throughout the development of the F36/34 he was a regular visitor to the Experimental Shop where the prototype was under construction and in the weeks before the maiden flight he had thoroughly examined the new plane.

With Sydney Camm and other Hawker executives in attendance on the morning of 6 November 1935 at the Brooklands racing circuit in Weybridge, Surrey, Bulman strode over to the silver plane. The atmosphere was one of tension mingled with excitement. Bulman was about to take a leap into the unknown, flying the first British landplane capable of travelling at over 300 mph. All the projections and estimates, the wind-tunnel results and performance figures would count for nothing if this initial flight ended in disaster. In a few neat movements Bulman lifted his diminutive physique into the cockpit. Clad in white overalls, he was for once wearing a flying helmet rather than his trademark trilby hat. Having slammed the canopy shut, he pressed the starter button on the Merlin engine. With a cough and a blast of smoke from the exhausts, the engine burst into life, the arc of the turning airscrew becoming a blur. Slowly, Bulman moved the plane forwards until it reached the end of the grass strip that lay within the racing circuit. Then he opened up the throttle and began to speed across the grass. Soon the tail came up, but the two wheels remained earthbound for a worryingly long time. Then suddenly, just as Bulman started to fear that he was running out of grass, the fighter gave a leap and was in the air. He pulled back the stick and started to climb, though on this first trip he did not retract the undercarriage because he was concerned about the reliability of the hand-pumped hydraulic jacks. For half an hour he wandered in the sky over Brooklands, revelling in the plane's easy handling.

Landing the F36/34 proved slightly more awkward. His fellow

Hawker test pilot Philip Lucas later recalled that Bulman had been 'quite astonished' at the 'low approach speed and short landing run on that first flight'. What Bulman had not experienced before, said Lucas, was the 'combined lift effect of the thick wing section and the ground cushion provided by a low wing monoplane. Later, when we learned that the use of the engine was a "must" for normal approach and landing, particularly as weight and wing loading increased, we began to appreciate the startling increase in lift which could be obtained by making use of the propeller slip-stream effect with varying degrees of throttle settings.'[2] But Bulman had still landed smoothly, appreciating for the first time, as thousands of pilots would later, the wisdom of Camm's decision to have a wide undercarriage. He taxied along the grass and onto the narrow strip of tarmac beside the Hawker sheds. As the plane came to a halt and Bulman opened the canopy, Camm climbed onto the wing to hear his initial reaction. One account held that Bulman said: 'Another winner, I think.'[3] An alternative version, based on Camm's own recollection, had Bulman telling the designer: 'It's a piece of cake. I could teach even you to fly her in half an hour, Sydney.'[4] Whatever the exact wording, Bulman's reaction was undoubtedly favourable. The Hawker fighter had passed its first test.

Over the coming weeks Bulman completed another seven flights totalling six hours, until on 18 December the Merlin engine received its formal, and belated, certificate of airworthiness. A few problems were uncovered during this period. On only the third flight, the hood broke and flew off, causing some minor damage to the fuselage, as well as sending Bulman's trilby hurtling through the air. A replacement hood with a stronger frame was installed, while Bulman was compelled to acquire a new hat. The hand-operated hydraulic pump for the retractable undercarriage also proved hard to operate, a difficulty that would not be remedied until an engine-driven pump was later introduced. Moreover, Bulman continued to be surprised by the plane's leisurely take-off. This was partly a result of the aircraft's fixed-pitch airscrew, which restricted the lift on take-off. Later Hurricanes would have variable-pitch (VP) propellers, which allowed the pilots to set them in fine pitch for take-off, providing more power, and coarse pitch for cruising, when less power but more speed was needed. But mistakenly, in December 1935, little urgency was attached to this point, and indeed Hawker believed that a variable-pitch airscrew would be heavier, alter the centre of gravity and put more stress on the engine. 'The tests carried out so far indicate that the fixed pitch airscrew will be quite satisfactory and that the VP airscrew may not be required for this aircraft,' reported the Air Ministry's Directorate of Technical Development.[5]

More worryingly, the early Merlin, despite having received official approval, was showing the first signs of trouble that would badly hit the Hurricane programme during the following year. In one flight excessive oil temperatures were reached. A replacement engine was installed, but this also suffered from magneto (the electrical generator for the ignition system) and piston failures, leading Bulman to complain of 'rough running, cutting out and oily exhaust'.[6] Some modifications were carried out by Rolls-Royce, but the Merlin was still unsatisfactory.

Yet, given the advanced nature of the aircraft, these minor faults were far outweighed by the early sense that the F36/34 could be a success. At a meeting of the Air Council in mid December, Dowding reported that the 'Hawker fighter had now completed a flight with a full load and a fixed airscrew'. All had gone well, he added, apart from the broken canopy and he hoped that 'by the New Year' the aircraft could be sent for full handling trials by RAF pilots based at the Aeroplane and Armament Experimental Establishment at Martlesham Heath, Ipswich, Suffolk.[7] The press was full of enthusiasm at the news that a new 300-mph fighter had taken to the air, its profile revealing such a dramatic contrast to the biplanes then in service. The *Daily Express* carried a photograph of the monoplane, with a caption full of breathless if inaccurate prose. 'Speed in the air! Fast machines, taking off at approx 60 mph, leave behind, at once, seagulls, with their estimated 50 mph. Now comes more speed. New single-seater Hawker monoplane, the Merlin [*sic*], has had its initial tests at Brooklands. Machine has proved the fastest fighter in the world. It is one of a number of fast experimental monoplanes being built for the RAF.'[8]

The technical press was more measured but still admiring. Barely more than a week after the first trip on 6 November, *Flight* magazine told its readers that the new fighter 'incorporated in its design every known aid to performance'. The flight tests 'are said to be entirely satisfactory. It is rather the fashion to talk of the new fighters as 300 mph machines, not because this is necessarily the figure aimed at but because it is generally held that, to be of any real use, they will have to do at least that speed. No one knows as yet, not even Mr Bulman, what the new Hawker monoplane will do, but we gather that its movement is quite perceptible.'[9] The following month *Flight* published a series of photographs of the silver prototype at Brooklands, supplemented by a generous commentary. One picture of the plane in mid-air 'indicates how carefully its designer, Mr S Camm and his colleagues have considered the aerodynamic cleanliness in order to reap the fullest advantage of the immense power output'.[10] Another trio of photos 'serve to show the flowing lines of the fuselage' and the 'sturdy undercarriage'.[11]

The favourable reaction prompted the Air Ministry to tighten the pressure on Hawker to send the prototype to Martlesham Heath for official RAF handling trials as soon as possible, especially because decisions had to be quickly reached on different aircraft types in the RAF expansion programme. The necessity to sort out the teething problems only increased the air officials' frustrations. The Deputy Chief of the Air Staff Sir Christopher Courtney, who had taken over from Ludlow-Hewitt in January 1935, stressed to the Directorate of Technical Development that production orders for some new biplanes had been suspended 'in the hope that we might be able to have monoplanes in their place'. Any contract for the F36/34 was dependent on its proving 'that it is a satisfactory product'. There was, therefore, 'no time to be lost. I hope you will impress on all concerned the urgency in this matter,' he concluded.[12] 'I agree that it is very disappointing that we have not been able to have the Hawker F36/34 Fighter at Martlesham by now,' replied R. H. Verney, the Director of Technical Development, at the beginning of January 1936. 'I have personally done all I can to impress on them the urgency of our having these tests. I issued instructions to Martlesham for the tests some time ago, so I cannot see what to do more than this.'[13]

There was some resentment, however, at Hawker, over the demands for the handover to Martlesham Heath, before the fighter had been properly examined by their own experts, as Philip Lucas, Bulman's fellow test pilot, recalled. 'We were far from happy at letting service pilots fly our precious prototype before we had time to find out about it ourselves. For instance, because of the need to nurse the engine, very few performance measurements were possible beyond snatched readings in level flight to get some idea of the suitability of the propeller and to determine the rated altitude.'[14]

Hawker had little choice in the matter. So powerful was the drive for RAF modernization that even before the Martlesham Heath trials had been completed, the government considered ordering the plane into production. It is a graphic illustration of the Air Ministry's precocious faith in the fighter, based on little more than Bulman's favourable reaction, that a major contract was under discussion within weeks of the maiden flight. One of the common myths about the Hurricane story is that Hawker unilaterally pressed ahead with preparations for manufacturing the plane, such was the firm's confident anticipation of a large order. In truth, as the official documents reveal, the Air Ministry played just as big a role in the initial drive for production. As early as mid January 1936, while the fighter was still at Brooklands, Ministry officials made an informal approach to Hawker's management to enquire about their capacity for building the aircraft.

On 6 February, the day before F36/34 was flown to Martlesham Heath, a progress meeting to discuss the RAF expansion programme was convened by Air Secretary Cunliffe-Lister, who had been elevated to the peerage as the Earl of Swinton in November 1935, partly because he wanted to concentrate on his executive work and not be bogged down by constituency or House of Commons business. Those attending the meeting at first looked at the question of bombers and pilot training, then Lord Swinton asked the Chief of the Air Staff, Sir Edward Ellington, about fighters. Ellington explained that, under the programme, at least 900 new single-seaters were needed. According to the minutes, Ellington said that 'apart from the Gloster Gladiators now on order, the only aircraft in this class which was actually flying was the Hawker F/36/34'. He mentioned that the fighter's engine was 'not absolutely right' but reported that it was 'flying very well and Flight Lieutenant Bulman, the firm's chief test pilot, said that it was very easy to handle'.

Ellington then turned to the potential for production, arising from the informal talks in January. 'Hawkers said that they could start delivery in June 1937 and rise to an output of 40 a month by August 1937 if a decision to order in quantity was given by March this year. The Chief of the Air Staff himself doubted, however, whether we should actually get more than 30 a month. He thought that we might well take a gamble on this aircraft after successful tests at Martlesham and that, in this event, an order should be placed for 600.' The balance of 300 aircraft, he argued, could go to Supermarine's new fighter, though the work there had been 'very slow', and if Reginald Mitchell's plane failed 'we should have to increase the Hawker order'. Ellington concluded his presentation by asking for 'authority to approach Hawkers straight away and put the above proposition to them'.[15]

The debate about the fighter had reached a critical stage. The plane's immediate fate was in the hands of Swinton and his Scottish adviser Lord Weir. They opted for boldness, as the minutes record. The Air Secretary 'said we should take a decision at once that the suggested ordering for 600 was a sound proposition which should certainly be aimed at if the aircraft was a success. Lord Weir agreed and said he thought it would be perfectly safe to adopt this type on a large scale.'[16]

As a result of this discussion, Sir Cyril Newall, the Air Member for Supply, visited Hawker's at Kingston on 20 February. There he saw Tom Sopwith, the company's founder, and Frank Spriggs, the managing director. As Newall later reported to a Progress Meeting on 26 February, he put to them the proposal for ordering 600 of the new fighters. They replied that 'they had already taken a gamble on "productionizing" drawings for the single seater fighter and they anticipated that the production flow should commence in June 1937, working up before very long to a production of eight a week. They felt that they would be able to produce the 600 aircraft required within the time given.'[17]

Given that the prototype had made its first flight only five months earlier, this might have seemed a commendably expeditious timetable, but the sense of urgency was now so great within the Air Ministry that some of the officials were dissatisfied when Newall relayed this news to his colleagues. Complacent in the early 1930s, Ellington now complained in the meeting that 'he could not understand why production could not commence on the single seater fighter until June 1937, seeing that the prototype was already completed and awaiting flying trials'. Newall replied that he did not think it was 'physically impossible' to bring forward the start date of production but pointed out that Hawker had a large amount of other work, including fulfilment of biplane contracts and the development of a new medium bomber and a two-seater fighter, both of which were scheduled to be part of the RAF expansion programme. In view of the RAF's priority for fast monoplanes, this explanation only caused more irritation, Weir and Swinton describing the Hawker timetable as 'unacceptable'. Then Weir made an extraordinary suggestion:

He asked whether the possibility had ever been contemplated of taking a new type of aircraft which had just been completed by one firm and handing it over to another firm for production. Would it, for instance, be possible to give the Hawker Single Seater Fighter to a firm like Bristols, and tell Hawkers that they must concentrate on putting together an improved programme of deliveries for the Medium Bomber and Two-Seater fighter?

Effectively, Weir was advocating that Hawker should lose a potentially lucrative contract before production had even started, having put so much work into the plane's development. Sir Hugh Dowding, the Air Member for Research, rightly thought that the idea was absurd. 'Such a course of action was out of the question because of the fierce jealousy it would arouse between the firms in the industry.'[18] Both the medium bomber and the two-seater fighter were later dropped, leaving Hawker able to concentrate on the single-seater fighters, but not before their heavy workload had caused more aggravation to the Air Ministry.

The next day, 27 February, Newall visited Hawker again to discuss the production programme. Frank Spriggs now told him that the company could start production on the F36/34 in April 1937, a couple of months earlier than originally suggested, and the 600 proposed planes would be built by September 1938. The Air Ministry seemed mollified by this report, Swinton describing Hawker's revised programme as 'a businesslike proposition'.[19] But then he thought of a new potential obstacle. 'Could we go ahead with the Hawker Group without waiting for the programme to be discussed with the Treasury?' he asked. The Air Ministry's Permanent Secretary Sir Christopher Bullock reassured him, stressing that 'the Treasury could not possibly raise any difficulties if it was explained to them that the aircraft we intended to order were really up to date'.[20] This was especially true because Neville Chamberlain, the Chancellor of the Exchequer, was a keen proponent of stronger fighter defences. The order for the 600 planes was therefore provisionally agreed at the beginning of March 1936.

By this stage, the Hawker fighter was undergoing its evaluation by RAF pilots. After just ten flights at Brooklands lasting eight hours, the prototype K5803 had been flown to Martlesham Heath on 7 February 1936. The aircraft still had neither its eight guns nor service equipment like the radio set, so ballast was used in their place, taking the all-up weight to 5,760 pounds. Contrary to some of the fears expressed by the Hawker test pilots, the Aeroplane and Armament Experimental Establishment gave the plane a glowing report in April after completing the handling trials. The summary stated: 'The aircraft is simple and easy to fly and has no apparent vices. All controls operate satisfactorily and are excellent at low speeds. Take-off and landing present no difficulty and in spite of the top speed, there is no difficulty in making an approach into a normal aerodrome when the flaps are down.'

Among the more specific details, the report stated that 'the aileron controls are satisfactory for a fighting aircraft', since they 'are light to handle at low speed when climbing and on the glide', and 'are effective under all manoeuvres in flight', though there was also some concern about 'their heaviness' at maximum speed level and in the dive. More praise was showered on other features of the planes. The elevator controls 'are light and effective. They give a quick response under all conditions.' The flaps were seen as 'very effective and, when down, give improved aileron control. Use of flaps makes the approach very simple and reduces flatness of glide.' The brakes were 'smooth, progressive, effective and easy to operate'. In the air, the plane was said to be stable both laterally and directionally, while it was also 'easy and normal to take off and land. There is a tendency to swing to the left when taking off but this can easily be counteracted by the rudder. There is no swing when landing.'

The undercarriage, always one of the Hurricane's strongest assets, was described in the report as 'very satisfactory, having good shock absorbing qualities and good rebound damping. The retracting gear is simple and easy to operate. The undercarriage can be retracted in about 45 seconds without undue exertion by the pilot, and it can be lowered in about 20 seconds. The indicator works satisfactorily and the wheels themselves can be seen, when up or down, through small windows in the floor. This latter is an excellent feature.' The pilot's view was generally 'good', though the report mentioned that 'there is one small blind spot aft which obscures the tail and rudder', a problem that was to cause some grievance to pilots until, much later, a rear-view mirror was installed. The cockpit was felt to be 'extremely roomy and comfortable and keeps warm even down to −50°C', something that a few Hurricane pilots, almost freezing at high altitudes, might have disputed. One significant drawback, however, was that the hood could not be kept open at over 150 mph, which meant that it would be 'quite impossible for the pilot to make an emergency exit at any speed over 150 mph'. Such a defect was 'unacceptable in a high speed fighting aircraft', and Hawker was told that the cockpit had to be modified.

Another, even bigger problem was the unreliability of the first Merlin engine, particularly its carburation, 'the running being far too sensitive to slight mixture adjustments'. Officials at Martlesham Heath recognized, however, that the Merlin was still under development and would soon be improved. 'It is understood that this engine is not of the type which will be fitted to the production aircraft.'

On the statistics of its overall performance, the Hawker prototype largely lived up to expectations. The maximum speed attained was 315 mph at 16,200 feet and the climb to 15,000 feet was achieved in 5.7 minutes. The estimated highest altitude was 35,400 feet.[21]

The favourable Martlesham Heath report fully justified the actions of the government and Hawker in preparing for full-scale production. The Air Ministry sent the firm the formal contract for 600 fighters on 3 June 1936, the largest peacetime order that any British aircraft manufacturer had ever received. Within a week, Hawker issued the first drawings to the production shops. A further symbol of the plane's growing stature came on 27 June, when the Air Ministry approved the company's proposal to call the aircraft 'The Hurricane' instead of the rather bureaucratic F36/34. The new name, commented *Flight* magazine, was 'a very suitable choice'.[22] When King Edward VIII inspected the prototype during a visit to Martlesham Heath in July 1936, he added the royal seal of approval during an informal 'christening' ceremony. Apart from the King, the public also had the chance to glimpse the RAF's exciting addition to its fleet during the Hendon Air Display in north London at the end of June. Squadron Leader D. F. Anderson, who had led the RAF team during the Martlesham Heath trials, put on an exceptional aerobatic performance, demonstrating the speed and manoeuvrability of the new fighter.

The momentum behind the Hurricane in the summer of 1936 was given more thrust by the deepening crisis into which Europe was sliding, as the megalomaniacal aggression of two dictators, Hitler and Benito Mussolini, became ever more apparent. In October 1935 Italy had embarked on its bloody attempt to create an east African empire by invading Abyssinia. Five months after this act of unprovoked belligerence, in March 1936 the Nazis undertook a remilitarization of the Rhineland, which under the Versailles Treaty of 1919 constituted forbidden territory for the German army. The tension was further worsened by the outbreak of the Spanish Civil War in July 1936, as the German and Italian dictators lent powerful military support to General Francisco Franco's fascist cause, mainly from the air. One of the most prominent weapons used by the Luftwaffe in this conflict was the Messerschmitt (Me) 109, which would become the deadly opponent of the Spitfire and the Hurricane in 1940.

The response of the British government to the gathering storm clouds was the time-honoured one: institutional change within both Whitehall and the military. The Tory Prime Minister Stanley Baldwin, one of the arch prevaricators of mid twentieth-century British politics, decided that what was needed was a Minister for Defence Co-Ordination. To this newly created post, Baldwin appointed in March 1936 the rotund Bristol lawyer Sir Thomas

Inskip, a man without any interest in military affairs. It was a typically Machiavellian move by Baldwin, for his real aim was to keep out of office Winston Churchill, then a maverick Tory backbencher and passionate opponent of the official policy of appeasing Hitler. Irresolute as ever, Baldwin feared that the promotion of Churchill would cause increased friction with the Nazi regime. Churchill's scientific adviser, Professor Frederick Lindemann, another implacable critic of Germany, called Inskip's elevation 'the most cynical thing that has been done since Caligula appointed his horse a consul'.[23] During a debate in the Commons, one backbencher, Lieutenant Commander R. T. H. Fletcher, described Inskip as 'a barrage balloon, cumbrous and not of any proven worth'.[24] The new minister, it was true, had neither a department nor power. But Baldwin miscalculated in believing his appointee to be without influence. Through his alliance with Neville Chamberlain, the Chancellor of the Exchequer, Inskip was to preside over the establishment of an effective fighter force, often in the face of opposition not just from his own Cabinet colleagues but from the Air Staff as well.

The other organizational change enacted at this time was an overhaul of the RAF's structure. Since 1925 the home air force had been under the control of the Air Defence of Great Britain, which was divided into two main components: the Fighting Area and the Wessex Bombing Area. The RAF swept away this set-up in July 1936 and replaced it with a series of specialist commands, including Coastal Command to protect the shipping lanes, Bomber Command to carry out the air offensive over the continent, and Fighter Command to ensure 'the security of the base', to use the words of Sir Hugh Dowding.[25] It was fortunate for the future of the nation that Dowding was appointed the first chief of Fighter Command, for no one had a better understanding of what was required to meet the looming threat of the Luftwaffe, from improvements in communications to better-quality aircraft.

Against this backdrop of darkening skies, Hawker and the Air Ministry pressed on with the Hurricane programme through the summer of 1936. But for all the optimism that had been generated around the new fighter, the government was worried about Hawker's capacity to deliver. By the mid 1930s, Hawker had become one of

Britain's leading aircraft manufacturers, with both an impressive record and a growing number of contracts. Reflecting its importance, the enterprise had become a public company in 1933, changing its name from H. G. Hawker Engineering to Hawker Aircraft Limited. The following year Hawker had acquired the Gloster company based at Hucclecote near Cheltenham, a move that potentially provided more capacity, though Gloster was preoccupied then by its own designs and the output of biplanes. In July 1936, at the very time when Fighter Command was created, Hawker announced an even more dramatic step: a merger with the vast Armstrong Siddeley group, which included the Manchester-based giant A. V. Roe. This amalgamation created the firm of Hawker Siddeley, whose name was to resonate until the 1970s, when it was swallowed up by the creation of British Aerospace.

Yet for all Hawker Siddeley's new industrial muscle, the Air Ministry had some doubts as to whether the firm could fulfil the Hurricane contract. A fear that the design team was overloaded was one of the reasons. R. H. Verney, the Ministry's Director of Technical Development, argued to Dowding in April that 'some better organization of Hawker's design work is necessary. The pressure on Camm is very heavy at all times; it seems to be a one-man show. Several times I have been afraid that Camm would "crack-up". But he is such a very able and keen man that he rather tends to draw everything to himself, making any schemes for decentralization rather difficult.'[26] The Air Ministry's progress meetings were regularly peppered with complaints about Hawker's supposed inefficiency. Having learnt from a report in mid June that the date for the first production Hurricane had slipped from April to July 1937, his adviser Lord Weir complained that he was 'at a loss to understand why this should be so, since so far as he could see, Hawkers would have no work to do in their preparatory departments except on this type. He wondered whether, if the firm concentrated all their energies on the single-seater fighter, they could not begin production in about ten months' time.'[27]

Later in the year Swinton himself expressed his disappointment at news that the arrival of the first production aircraft had slid back further, to September 1937, and that only 24 Hurricanes were scheduled to be produced by the end of that year. Edward Ellington, Chief of the Air Staff, agreed 'and pointed out that the firm had been given ample warning that they would be getting an order for 600 of the type. In view of this, he certainly thought they ought to have been able to offer a better programme of deliveries.'[28] The delays continued into early 1937, prompting Swinton to complain that 'he found the almost certain setback in Hurricane deliveries somewhat difficult to understand'. Having explained that part of the problem was 'the necessary jigs and tools had not yet been received', Weir said that the real difficulty was the excessive burden on Hawker Siddeley because of the Ministry's demand for other types on top of Hurricane production. Weir had 'felt for some time that this was really a task beyond their capacity,' noted the minutes. 'We had at any rate learned one lesson of value from the trouble we had experienced at Hawkers, and this was that the fewer different types we selected for our programme after 1939 the better from every point of view.'[29]

Much of this condemnation of Hawker, while it could be explained by the intense political pressure on the government to re-equip the RAF, was excessively harsh. Far from being dilatory, the firm had done a remarkable job in moving from the design proposal to the start of full production in less than two years. 'There's only one way to do a job and that's as quickly as you can!' was another of Sydney Camm's mottos, demonstrating the sense of urgency that he always tried to instil in his workforce.[30] The achievement was all the more admirable given how many innovations the Hurricane had to incorporate. Indeed, Sir Cyril Newall, the Air Member for Supply, once rightly grew exasperated at all the moaning about Hawker: 'It is probably not generally realised how extremely complicated an aeroplane the Hurricane is,' he protested.[31]

Like the Hurricane itself, Hawker Siddeley's physical organization in the late 1930s was a mixture of old and new. The Kingston plant at Canbury Park Road, the original site of Tommy Sopwith's pre-war aviation company, was a sprawling 250,000-square-foot conglomeration of premises acquired piecemeal over the firm's history. Former shops, cottages, furniture stores and even a roller-skating rink had all been converted for use by Hawker. The main building consisted of 150,000 square feet of factory space spread over three floors.

It was not a place that exuded modernity, as Graham Leggett, who began work as an apprentice with Hawker in 1937 before becoming a Hurricane pilot, recalled:

The premises at Kingston were rather primitive. The factory was somewhat dilapidated, if not over-crowded. Everything was bunched in very, very close together. All the machines were close and in fact going through the machine shops was quite hazardous. You had to be darned careful as you moved around. In those days all the metal panels which were made of duraluminium were beaten out by hand. The noise, of course, was indescribable in the 'tin-bashers' shop' as it was called.[32]

The awkwardness of the setting was also remembered by Bert Tagg, who joined Hawker in 1935: 'Internally the factory floor levels varied, requiring ramps and steps between the galleries and main areas of the first floor. The staircases were extremely steep and something of a hazard if walking down loaded with parts, which was necessary since the goods lift was slow and its use restricted.'[33] (Despite its drawbacks, the building continued to be used by Hawker Siddeley Aviation until 1962.) The atmosphere inside the Canbury Park Road site was captured by another Hawker employee of the time, Doug Halloway: 'I remember well the machine shop on the ground floor, the mass of whirling shafts with belts to each machine, which could be seen through a 15-foot square opening in the floor. The first floor was called the "rib shop" where a lot of Hurricane details were made.'

Halloway also recalled the lighter side of life in the factory: 'The tea trolleys for morning break had lovely hot doughnuts, cold cream ones and thick slices of bread and dripping. The milk cartons held about one third of a pint and when not quite empty could be a formidable missile, one of which unfortunately hit a supervisor in the chest when he came round the corner into the "rib shop".' One innocent man, unfairly fingered as the culprit, was suspended for three days without pay.[34] Tom Clare, who joined Hawker in 1928 and helped to build the prototype in 1935, remembered a tough, sometimes brutal, approach from the management: 'You did what you were bloody well told, unless you wanted the sack! Because plenty of people outside wanted your job.' But that did not stop the good humour and friendliness in the workforce: 'There was always a lark going on, a joke, somebody playing a trick on somebody, putting spurs on the back of their heels or a notice on their back. Some blokes would go up the road and find their heels were painted bright yellow. But there was always a good spirit among us! It was always friendly. Nothing vicious about it.'[35]

Once the Hurricanes had been built at Kingston, the fuselages and wings were taken separately by lorry to the Brooklands plant at Weybridge, Surrey, for final assembly and testing. The Brooklands site was more advanced, a large Erection Shop having been opened in May 1935 alongside the motor-racing track. With a floor area of 46,000 square feet, the shop had room for five Hurricanes to be progressively assembled. The completed structures were then taken to a separate Fabric and Dope Shop for the final stage of production before the planes were tested and then ferried to the squadrons. Graham Leggett gave this description of the metamorphosis of the Hurricane on its odyssey through Hawker:

> At the initial construction stage, it did not look that different from all the biplanes we had been building because the method of construction was almost identical, with steel tubes for the fuselage frame and high tensile steel, which was rolled, for the wing spars and the tail-plane rudder main spars. On top of the steel tubular construction was placed the wooden framework, which was fairly lightweight. It was attached to the steel frame with nuts and bolts. It was only when we started putting on the stringers and the fabric that it began to look like another beast altogether. The fabric people would come with their great length of stuff and simply chuck it over the top. They were dress-makers really. It would all be done by hand. The fabric would be pulled down into place and stitched together. When we put the thing up on stilts and put the undercarriage in with all the pumps and then filled it up with oil and started pumping the wheels up and down, this was an entirely new innovation. From that point onwards, it was a very different aeroplane.[36]

But Leggett felt the division between Kingston and Brooklands was 'a crazy arrangement', a point echoed by a *Daily Express* reporter, Stuart Gillies, who wrote in December 1938 after a visit to Kingston that 'the organization seemed rather disjointed. Parts made in one works have to be carted across the road to the old warehouse, where they are assembled into wings. The wings have then to be carted some miles away to the erecting plant, where they are assembled into the airplane.'[37] Despite the awkward layout, Kingston and Brooklands were working energetically on the first Hurricane production run by late 1936. But with RAF expansion still accelerating as the drumbeat of war began to sound, the Hawker Siddeley directors knew that the company needed bigger and more efficient production facilities. Supported by a loan of £30,000 from the Air Ministry, they therefore purchased a site called Parlaunt Park Farm at the Berkshire village of Langley near Slough. Construction began on the new factory in 1937, and within two years, at a cost of £775,000, the plant was completed.

At 600,000 square feet, the Slough factory was far larger than the Kingston and Brooklands works combined. Moreover, its establishment meant that Kingston could concentrate on producing parts, a task for which its makeshift structure was much better suited. Graham Leggett gave this description of the Slough plant soon after it had opened: 'It was a brand new building designed for mass production. There were almost complete Hurricanes near the door and you went down to the other end where there was a pile of steel tubes. It was totally different from Kingston. The managers had proper offices rather than pokey little cubby holes. There was a concrete floor rather than the wooden boards we had at Kingston. It was a different world.'[38] The first Hurricane came off the Langley line in June 1939, the beginning of an output run that would reach over 7,000 before the end of the war.

In addition to production anxieties, the Air Ministry in 1936 suddenly became concerned about the Hurricane's performance. After all the early confidence generated by its maiden flight on 6 November 1935 and the Martlesham Heath reports, doubts began to arise as to whether the plane was really the winner that had been suggested. There were several factors behind this mood of apprehension. One was the technological advance of the Luftwaffe, which had introduced not just the Me 109 fighter but also the new fast, twin-engined bomber, the Dornier 17. Another factor was the success of the

Spitfire, the Supermarine fighter showing a marked superiority in speed over the Hurricane. These qualms prompted a vigorous debate between politicians and officials as to whether the Air Ministry had adopted the right priorities. By June 1936, the Spitfire had been flying for three months, having made its maiden flight at Eastleigh in Hampshire, and had proved itself to be at least 35 mph faster than the Hurricane.

Lord Swinton was therefore deeply troubled. At a meeting on 16 June, he expressed his concern 'over the strategic implications' of this difference between the two fighters, given that 600 Hurricanes had been ordered compared to only 300 Spitfires. Sir Hugh Dowding tried to reassure Swinton by stressing that the Hurricane had other virtues. 'There was no doubt that it was faster than the Hawker but the view was not so good,' he said, referring to the longer nose of the Spitfire. Sir Cyril Newall, the Air Member for Supply, added with some prescience that the major disadvantage of the Spitfire was that it could not be 'so easily produced in quantity because of its stressed-skin production'. Nevertheless, he felt that because of the disparity in performance, 'Hawkers should be told that they might not be required to make as many of their single-seater fighter type.' Given Camm's reputation, it was not surprising that Swinton baulked at this idea. 'He said he was rather averse from writing Hawkers off in this way, after pressing them so hard to go ahead as quickly as possible.' In the end the meeting agreed that there should be no change in the orders for fighters until there had been a further analysis of the two types.[39]

The subsequent report from the Directorate of Technical Development gave some support to the Hurricane's case. The greater speed of the Spitfire was recognized, but it was pointed out that the Hurricane figure of 315 mph arose from the Martlesham Heath trial whereas the Spitfire's 348 mph had been measured during the firm's own tests, so the comparison was not strictly fair. Furthermore, the Hurricane had yet to be tested with its eight guns, and the plane was likely to hold an advantage over the Spitfire here. 'The four guns on each side in the Hawker wings are more closely bunched together than in the Supermarine wings and therefore any risks of inaccuracy of fire on this score should be less in the Hawker.' The better take-off and easier method of production were also points in the Hurricane's favour.[40]

At the subsequent progress meeting on 22 June, Lord Swinton said he still wanted 'to be assured that the Air Staff were prepared to accept twice as many of the type which was about 30 mph the slower of the two'. But Edward Ellington had already heard enough. He felt there was no justification for any change in orders. 'I would rather have 900 single-seater fighters, only 300 of which are of the faster type, than a smaller total number of aircraft with a greater proportion of faster aircraft,' he told Swinton. 'It is hardly possible to judge the two types properly until each has been flown by an ordinary service pilot but I don't think the gap in speed will be so great when the official Supermarine figures are known. In any case, a fighter with a top speed of 315 mph would give us a reasonable margin of speed over any known bomber.'[41] Swinton agreed that there would be no alteration in the contract. As it turned out, this was a sound move which helped to save the country in 1940. The Spitfire production run would be plagued with difficulties for the next three years, with deliveries falling far below required numbers. If greater priority had been given in June 1936 to the Spitfire than the Hurricane, the front-line squadrons would have been dangerously short of aircraft in the Battle of Britain of 1940.

The Hurricane's future was now assured, but the aircraft still needed a number of modifications before it was ready to go into active service. The most serious problem on the prototype had been the Merlin engine, which continued to suffer from internal leaks and cracking of the cylinder heads. Major J. S. Buchanan, Deputy Director of Technical Development at the Air Ministry, later described how a solution was found:

> After about 100 engines had been made an epidemic of cracks in the walls of the aluminium combined crankcase and cylinder blocks developed. Hives and ourselves had a desperate investigation into the casting procedure but after an agony of indecision for a few days we decided literally to cut the Gordian knot by splitting the one piece casting into three – crankcase and two cylinder blocks! Frantic tests of the new construction were hurried through and the trouble disappeared. Production with the drastically modified construction restarted.[42]

The new engine with the redesigned cylinder heads was called the Merlin II and became the epitome of reliability, the first in a long series of magnificently efficient Merlin power-plants that would equip the RAF's leading planes throughout the Second World War. But the development of the Merlin II further delayed production, not only because the engine itself was not available from Rolls-Royce until April 1937 but also because, with the altered shape of its cylinders, its installation required changes to several of the items on the Hurricane, including the cowlings, air intakes and header tank. 'There is no doubt that the engine changes slowed up the production contract very much more than anticipated,' Sydney Camm's project diary recorded.[43] A smoother operation was the introduction of the eight guns in the wings, after the Brownings had successfully passed their tests. In fact, when the prototype K5083 with the full armament underwent renewed trials at Martlesham Heath in the autumn of 1936, it was found that there was a marginal increase in the plane's maximum speed to 318 mph.

Other modifications included a stronger hood with locking catches to keep it open when required, an improved instrument panel and the removal of the bracing struts from the tailplane. These struts were a legacy of the Hurricane's biplane predecessors, and Camm's design staff told him that, as the tailplane had been designed and stressed as a pure cantilever structure, it did not require bracing. True to his sometimes idiosyncratic nature, Camm insisted that the struts remain in place. But when he was hospitalized with acute appendicitis in early 1936, he put one of his assistants, Roy Chaplin, in charge of the Hurricane project. Chaplin's first act was to take them out. Six weeks later, after a lengthy recovery, Camm returned to Kingston, but the struts were never mentioned again.

The only aerodynamic trouble in the Hurricane prototype gave rise both to another modification and an acrimonious dispute between Hawker and the Air Ministry. One of the key tests on any new aircraft type was to see how it reacted in a spin. Without ejector seats in those pre-jet days, it could be nerve-racking work for the test pilots, but Philip Lucas, George Bulman's colleague as a test pilot, bravely carried out the work on K5083. He later said: 'The aircraft would develop a slow, stable and rather flat spin after about three turns, with no response to opposite rudder. Fortunately, the elevators were just effective at the extreme limits of their movement and it was found that aircraft could be pitched out of the spin by coarse fore-and-aft movements of the control column.'[44] In the process, however, the plane could lose an alarming amount of height. In one spin, Lucas fell from 18,000 feet to under 2,000 feet before he was able to pull out: 'Too low for peace of mind,' he recalled.[45] Bulman felt that lives were unnecessarily being put at risk and, with the support of the rest of the Hawker board, he demanded a ruling from the Air Ministry that no spinning tests be required on aircraft weighing over 5,000 pounds. In the meantime he refused to allow any spinning of the Hurricane prototype.

But the Air Ministry refused to agree to Hawker's request. Air Vice Marshal Sir Wilfred Freeman, who had succeeded Sir Hugh Dowding as Air Member for Research and Development in April 1936, stressed that 'we wanted the Hurricane spun so that we could tell pilots in fighter squadrons what to expect, how to try to get out of a spin, if one occurred and in the last resort at what stage to abandon the aircraft'. Lord Swinton was all for holding Hawker to their contractual obligations to conduct the tests. 'If these spinning tests are provided for in the contract, and are regarded as essential for the safety of pilots, I think we ought to insist on the firm carrying them out.'[46] The impasse was resolved by the experts at the Royal Aircraft Establishment, the government's aviation research centre. They had developed a vertical spinning tunnel that could use a model to reproduce the characteristics of a Hurricane in a spin. As a result of their experiments, they found that the problem could be completely resolved by installing a small ventral fin underneath the fuselage and by extending the rudder downwards by six inches. These alternations came too late in 1937 to be incorporated on the first production Hurricanes, for Dowding, as head of Fighter Command, had agreed that the plane should be put into service as soon as possible. 'Provided the Hurricane did not spin too readily, he would like to have some delivered to the squadrons without waiting for the fillets to be fitted so he could try out certain tactical manoeuvres,' reported Freeman of his conversation with Dowding.[47] From the beginning of 1938, all new Hurricanes had the modified tail.

After all the delays and changes, the first production Hurricane came off the Kingston production line on 8 September 1937. It was then driven to Brooklands for final assembly and testing. Given the official serial number L1547, the plane had a Watts two-bladed, wooden, fixed-pitch airscrew and an all-up weight of 5,459 pounds. Throughout October most of the production testing was done by test pilot Philip Lucas, who was impressed by the improvements in the aircraft compared to the prototype. 'The sliding hood had been completely redesigned and the cockpit had a much better layout including the standard blind flying panel.' The new Merlin II engine was more powerful and efficient. Even more welcome was 'an engine driven pump for the retractable undercarriage'.[48] Lucas had one alarming moment, however, on a dank, cloudy November afternoon when he was completing a test at a low altitude. His altimeter read 2,000 feet, yet when he descended below the clouds he suddenly found himself skimming the tops of the area's wood. Most of the fabric was torn off the wings, but it was a tribute to the resilience of the Hurricane that he was able to land L1547 at a nearby airfield, where it was patched up and flown back to Brooklands the next morning. At the time, the near disaster was blamed on Lucas's inaccurate reading of his altimeter, but it was later discovered that this instrument often proved unreliable on the first Hurricanes after they had made a dive. The fault lay in the altimeter's connection to the instrument panel, a simple problem to remedy.

The squadron chosen to receive the RAF's first monoplane fighter was 111 Squadron, known as 'Treble One', whose distinguished record, stretching back to 1917, included a famous rout of the Turks in Palestine during the First World War. Based at RAF Northolt, west of London, 111 Squadron was equipped with the Gloster Gauntlet, an elegant but outmoded biplane. It was the last RAF fighter to have an open cockpit. On 15 December 1937 the squadron took delivery of its first Hurricane, and before the end of the month five more had arrived. Initially they were regarded as so sophisticated that only Squadron Leader John Gillan and two flight commanders were allowed to fly them. But then, in mid January 1938, as enough Hurricanes arrived to convert the entire squadron from using the old Gloster Gauntlet, the rest of the pilots were introduced to the new planes. Roy Dutton had his first flight on 18 January:

> I recall that this was a markedly strange experience, the Hurricane being by comparison to the ladylike Gauntlet, a large powerful, low-wing monoplane with retractable undercarriage and flaps. It may horrify the modern pilot but for the first flight each pilot was under orders to accomplish three take-offs and landings without retracting the undercarriage, and to keep the cockpit fully open. This was exciting rather than frightening, but in consequence the whole aeroplane shook like the proverbial leaf. The feel was heavy; the draught seemed in keeping with the type name of the machine and the noise, speed and sense of power exhilarating, as was the wide open view.

Dutton was allowed to fly twice again over the next couple of days, each time with the hood closed and the undercarriage retracted. 'I recall that, still not being acclimatized to the new beast, there was an impression of engine vibration and noise. The marked increase in speed in comparison with the Gauntlet also remains in my memory.' Some of his other memories were more unnerving. 'At high speed the wing gun panels sometimes partially blew out and the wing fabric distended like sausages between the ribs. On one occasion I remember being violently rotated and had some difficulty in recovering – my port undercarriage leg had extended.' With the plane's undercarriage inoperable, Dutton was forced to make the Hurricane's first belly landing, skidding along the frozen winter ground at Northolt and snapping off the propeller like a carrot. 'Such pain as I suffered, I reflected, could have been prevented had I been wearing a cricket box, for it seemed the entire force of deceleration impinged on the especially tender area of the male anatomy.'[49]

Another Hurricane novice who executed his first flight on 18 January was Ronald Brown. 'We were lined up and permitted to fly this aeroplane. We were not allowed to retract the undercarriage, nor close the hood. We were told to do three circuits and landings. It was the first monoplane I had flown. My impression was that it seemed to take the curvature of the earth to get airborne. There was no top wing to keep the sun off my eyes and it was very noisy because we had the hood open. But having said that, I think it was an easy plane to fly. I don't think anyone had any difficulty with the Hurricane.' Brown also remembered the official ban on aerobatics, which was not universally obeyed. The RAF and Air Ministry 'were scared stiff that this aeroplane would get a reputation for being difficult, too fast for people. We were not allowed to do any aerobatics until we had done 50 hours flying in the thing. Not that we took any notice. We did all our aerobatics out of the sight of the wing commander.'[50]

The arrival of the Hurricanes in 111 Squadron generated widespread excitement. Sleek, fast and powerful, the new fighters seemed the epitome of the modern age, a source of both technological fascination and pride in Britain. 'Fighter aircraft capable of speeds of 300 miles an hour are now going into service in the squadrons of the RAF. These are the Hawker Hurricane fighters,' reported *The Times* on 11 January 1938. 'The first batch of these fighters has been delivered and the rate of construction accelerated, so there will now be a steady flow of Hurricanes into certain squadrons.' The report went on to describe the plane's powerful engine, advanced undercarriage and eight Brownings 'all trained to concentrate their fire on a target at an effective range'.[51] As Ronald Brown recalled: 'The media made an absolute meal of the Hurricane. We were the wonder boys, specially chosen. The press went on about the speeds we travelled, the G we pulled and all this sort of rubbish. We got visitations practically every day from the press and the staff colleges and everyone else to see the Hurricanes.'[52]

The interest was about to become even more intense, thanks to a single electrifying event that sent the Hurricane's name soaring to a new level of public recognition.

3

'This thundering great monster'

———

S PEED WAS ONE of the obsessions of the 1930s. Ever faster movement in a decade rich in revolutionary new technology epitomized the age of modernity and the triumph of man over nature. The fascination with speed could be seen throughout contemporary culture, whether in the streamlined design of cars or the extraordinary powers of new comic heroes such as Flash Gordon and Superman, whose creators boasted that he was 'faster than a speeding bullet'. The press gloried in the constant quest for new speed records. On the railways, in 1934 the Flying Scotsman became the first locomotive to reach 100 mph. Four years later the beautiful, sleek Mallard of the London and North Eastern Railway reached 125.88 mph on a stretch of the east coast mainline, a speed that would never be surpassed by a steam train. On the seas, there was feverish competition throughout the decade to see which ocean liner would gain the Blue Riband, the prize for the fastest crossing of the Atlantic. It was a contest that came to be dominated by the rivalry between two giants of the oceans, France's *Normandie* and Britain's *Queen Mary*. The allure of speed turned daredevil Malcolm Campbell into the darling of the public as he kept pushing at the limits of velocity. The first man to drive a car at over 300 mph, he set no fewer than nine records on land and four on water.

Even the sporting arena was gripped by the fixation with pace. The Berlin Olympics of 1936 were dominated by the feats of the black American sprinter Jesse Owens, hailed as 'the fastest man on earth', whose gold medal in the 100 metres, with a world record time of 10.3 seconds, was the most eloquent possible riposte to Nazi theories about Aryan racial supremacy. International cricket during this decade was played in the long shadow cast by the notorious 'Bodyline' Ashes series of 1932–3 in Australia, when the Australians were crushed by the brutal, intimidatory fast bowling of the England attack, led by former coalminer Harold Larwood. His deliveries were once timed at over 100 mph in an experiment at the White City in London, making him one of the fastest bowlers of all time.

But the notion of speed was seen at its most thrilling in the conquest of the air. Less than thirty years after the Wright brothers' maiden flight, a plane had reached over 400 mph. This milestone was first passed in 1931, when George Stainforth flew the Supermarine S6B seaplane, winner of the Schneider Trophy, at 407.5 mph over the Solent off the Hampshire coast. Three years later another seaplane, the Italian Macchi MC72, achieved an astonishing 440 mph over the water. The development of the Macchi had been supported by none other than Benito Mussolini. Indeed, the ideology of fascism was strongly attracted by the cult of speed in the air, since the totalitarian dogma so eagerly worshipped the qualities of uncompromising action and scientific modernization. The Macchi MC72's achievement was never to be bettered by any piston-engined seaplane. For landplanes, 350 mph was first attained in 1935 by a streamlined, radial-engine monoplane built by the eccentric American tycoon Howard Hughes, who hoped to win a lucrative US Army Air Force contract from the design, though, as with so many of Hughes's projects, the large-scale order never materialized.

Yet all these record-breaking planes had been created with the specific goal of speed in mind. The position with the Hawker Hurricane was very different. It had been built for military combat, not racing competition. So its performance in terms of speed was restricted by a host of fighting requirements that added to its weight, such as guns, petrol tanks, radio equipment and the armoured bulkhead between the cockpit and the engine.

Nevertheless, in early 1938 the Hurricane performed a feat of pioneering celerity that captivated the aviation world and the British public. On 10 February Squadron Leader John Gillan of 111 Squadron, a highly experienced pilot who had served in the Mediterranean and the Far East, took off from Northolt airbase in west London on a full-power trial of the operational Hurricane. He said later that he had not been in the mood for the trip. 'I was slumbering in the ante-room after lunch – a pleasant custom I had learned in the East. It was a bitter day, a gale was blowing and the clouds were at 500 feet. There was lots of coal on the fire and I remember wondering in my sleep whether it was not one of those days when one smoked one of the fast diminishing supply of cigars one had received as Christmas presents.'[1] The telephone call then came through from the Air Ministry to confirm that the full-power trial should go ahead that afternoon. At 2.20 p.m. Gillan left his base and flew north towards the airfield of Turnhouse at Edinburgh, running into strong headwinds on the way. Having landed at 4.10 p.m., he immediately had his aircraft refuelled.

Then at 5.05 p.m., with dusk starting to creep over the Pentland Hills, Gillan took off again, this time with a powerful wind right behind him. For most of the way back to Northolt he travelled at 15,000 feet, the altitude at which the Hurricane was rated to give the best performance. In the enveloping gloom, he had to fly largely using his instrument panel. It was not a comfortable journey, as he recalled: 'At that height I had to use the oxygen apparatus and I had the smell of oil all the way. By Jove it was nasty. I was sick, very sick. I hardly noticed the landscape. I remember looking down and seeing a bunch of chimneys and the dark thread of a river. I thought, "That's Newcastle, that was." I skimmed over a few other towns and glanced down to make sure that my instruments were telling the truth.'[2] By the time he reached London, the sky was black and the outside air freezing. 'There were ten minutes of high cloud to go through when the cabin frosted up and hoar frost formed on the wings. Sometimes I felt sorry I was doing this and thought of the comfort of my men at Northolt. At other times I was glad.' Gillan then embarked on the descent. 'Coming out of the cloud at 5,000 feet, I saw momentarily a red light flashing the letter of my station.'[3] He had accidentally gone a few miles further south of Northolt airfield, but now he turned to make his landing approach. After touching down successfully, he glanced at his watch. It was 5.53 p.m. Gillan had flown the 327 miles from Edinburgh in just 48 minutes, going at an incredible 408.7 mph. In the process, he had shattered the landplane speed world record previously held by Herman Wuster, one of Messerschmitt's test pilots who had flown an Me 109 the previous November at 379.17 mph.

Sydney Camm's fighter, dismissed by the Air Ministry in January

1934, had not only broken the 400-mph barrier but had become the fastest operational military aircraft in the world. There had been a near gale-force wind behind his Hurricane, but that was scarcely mentioned by the press, which heaped praise on the new machine from Hawker. 'The plane flew more than half as fast as sound itself,' trumpeted the *Daily Mirror* on 11 February 1938. 'At such a speed a plane leaving Tower Bridge as a man stepped off the pavement in Trafalgar Square would fly over him before he had crossed the road.'[4] On the same day the *Daily Mail* gleefully pointed out that the 'latest Edinburgh-Express takes six hours' compared to the 'remarkable' Hurricane flying at 'nearly seven miles a minute'.[5] Apart from shattering the world record, what had also been significant about the flight was the endurance of the Merlin II engine, for Gillan had used take-off boost from the start until the moment he had begun his descent into Northolt. Despite the stress from remaining at 2,950 revs per minute throughout the journey, the Merlin gave no trouble, another indicator of the reliability that would later make it famous during the Second World War.

It was only a couple of months since the Hurricane had entered service, yet the plane had firmly established itself in the national consciousness. Amidst all the apprehensions about the bellicosity of the European dictators, the defences of Britain had been bolstered by the arrival of this world-beating new weapon. 'The world's fastest fighter,' proclaimed *The Times* on 4 May, explaining to its readers that the Hurricane could carry out its patrols at a cruising speed of 'fully 280 miles an hour' and with its large petrol tanks could cover over 700 miles without refuelling. 'That is a record of which no previous fighter has been capable, and marks the Hurricane as outstanding in its class in respect of duration as well as speed.'[6] A month after Gillan's flight, a reporter from *Flight* magazine visited Northolt to see 111 Squadron in action. The arrival of the 'drab but deadly looking Hawker Hurricane multi-gun, "three-hundred plus" monoplane fighters,' he wrote, was 'one of the most comforting manifestations of expansion'. There was no doubt, he continued, 'that No. 111 squadron is at the moment the most formidable fighting squadron in the world'. The *Flight* reporter was also struck by the pilots' handling of their new aircraft:

That the personal is equal to the material was readily apparent when the complete squadron demonstrated formation flying. One was particularly impressed by the very reasonable landing speed of the Hurricane, though the take-off did seem on the long side, particularly where formations were concerned. The wheels disappear without a fuss and once everything is snug the machine is fit and ready to challenge anything with wings. A demonstration by an individual machine, though not aerobatic in nature, was a revelation in manoeuvrability and awesome speed.[7]

To the envy of some others in the RAF, 111 Squadron, or 'Treble One', came to be regarded as the elite squadron in Fighter Command during 1938, rewarded by regular distinguished visitors, including King George VI, and nicknamed the '*Daily Mirror* squadron' because of all the publicity it received. Within the Air Ministry there was deep satisfaction not only at Gillan's record-breaking flight but also at the regular favourable reports he wrote about the Hurricane's performance. The aircraft was 'completely manoeuvrable throughout its whole range,' he stated in one document from January. 'Formation flying at height at speeds in excess of 200 mph is very simple,' he continued. 'The cockpit is large and comfortable and there is room for the largest man inside with the hood shut.' He also found the controls 'easily accessible and efficient', while the view when taxiing on the ground 'with the seat full up and the hood back is exceptionally good'.[8] In another report, written near the end of February, Gillan said: 'The Hurricane has proved a particularly good aircraft from the r/t [radio/telephone] point of view and considerably better results are being obtained than have ever been obtained with the Gauntlet.' Nor had any difficulty 'been experienced in maintenance in flights, though it is found that for the efficient working of the aircraft parts extreme cleanliness is essential.'[9]

In response to Gillan's praise, R. H. Verney, the Air Ministry's Director of Technical Development, told his colleagues: 'What a very welcome relief from some of the reports we are accustomed to. One begins to think we have learned something about aeroplanes. Also that Hawkers are a good firm and Camm a very good designer, not because his aerodynamics are better than anyone else's – he is not enamoured of wind tunnels – but the secret is that he gets down to details himself.'[10]

After the success of 111 Squadron's conversion to the new plane, the Hurricanes began to be delivered to other squadrons. The pilots of 3 Squadron, based at Kenley in Surrey, exchanged their Gladiators for 18 Hurricanes in March 1938. May saw a similar conversion at 56 Squadron, based at North Weald in Essex, while 73 and 87 Squadrons switched to Hurricanes in July, followed by 32 Squadron in mid September and two other units before the end of the year. Pete Brothers, later a senior commander in the RAF, gave this description of his first flight once the Hurricanes had arrived at 32 Squadron:

> I climbed into the cockpit and sat for a while finding my way around the levers and switches, then started up and taxied over the grass – we had no runways – to the boundary and took off. The big two-bladed wooden propeller gave surprisingly rapid acceleration and the solid, rugged feel of the aircraft as it bounded over the uneven surface stimulated and inspired confidence. Retracting the wheels, a novel experience, involved moving the left hand from the throttle to stick and selecting wheels up with the right hand and depressing the pump level until the wheels locked up. Now airborne, I closed the canopy, another novel experience, and, relieved of the head-buffeting slip-stream of an open cockpit, settled down to enjoy myself. Having climbed to a safe height, I tried a variety of aerobatics and was delighted by the immediate and smooth response to the controls.[11]

The sense of power in the new machines was also remembered by Douglas 'Grubby' Grice, another pilot with 32 Squadron at the time of its change from Gauntlets to Hurricanes:

> It meant flying an aircraft which at cruising speed did about 240 mph, about 100 mph faster than you were used to flying. The flaps did not worry me but what was rather startling was the Merlin engine. It was so powerful it took a bit of getting used to. We had fixed pitch pro-pellers, which meant a very long take-off run because you accelerated rather slowly. Once you were in the air it was fine. What a thrill to be flying so fast. There were no vices with the Hurricane at all. And it was so rugged. You could virtually fly it into the ground and it would just bounce up and land by itself.[12]

Not every fighter pilot was happy with the adulation that the Hurricane received. Some felt that the emphasis on the new aircraft's potency was overdone, serving to intimidate young RAF recruits.

One of the heroes of the Battle of Britain, Bob Stanford Tuck, commander of the 257 squadron, later told his post-war biographer that the attention on 111 Squadron help to create the myth of the Hurricane as 'a kind of monster to be tamed and constantly watched – a machine with a sly, malicious intelligence of its own, a killer-plane that only the dashing, devil-may-care elite were permitted to fly'. The result, said Stanford Tuck, was that the name Hurricane 'was on every schoolboy's lips and in every newspaper article on Britain's air defences. Anyone who flew it was regarded as an ace by the awed and misinformed populace.' Stanford Tuck regretted that the Air Ministry had not done more to dispel the legend of the 'killer-plane'. Such a failure, he argued, meant that 'for some years most newly trained pilots held the Hurri in almost superstitious dread, and without doubt a number of them crashed while learning to fly through lack of confidence or sheer nervousness'.[13] Stanford Tuck's claim was borne out by Dickie Martin of 73 Squadron, who felt overawed by his first experience of flying the Hurricane:

> The day came and off I started across the grass airfield, easing on the throttle. Of course with a wooden-bladed prop the take-off was very long and very slow, because the revs per minute you've got on the engine were about 1,720. The plane hardly seemed to be moving at all and I thought, 'Oh my God, I'm going to go through the hedge at the end if I'm not careful.' I started to pour on the power, with the result that the thing began to swing to the left. And when I finally became airborne I passed in front of the hangars. I can always remember frantically looking out of the right-hand side, and seeing the squadron adjutant look up from his desk in horror as my plane flashed past the window, past the hangars and disappeared across the countryside. I really was very frightened on that first solo flight in a Hurricane. It seemed absolutely weird. I felt very much out of control after flying biplanes, because all that was ahead of you was a thing like a whale's back. You seemed to be sitting on top of this thundering great monster. I was very relieved to get back on the ground again, though I did not have any trouble with the landing. For a long time I was frightened of the plane.[14]

The demands of the fast new monoplane could also stretch flying abilities to the limit, said Peter Townsend of 43 Squadron, based at

Tangmere in Sussex. 'The change from the light and agile Fury caught some pilots unaware. The Hurricane was far less tolerant of faulty handling and a mistake at low altitude could be fatal. One day a sergeant pilot glided back to Tangmere with a faulty engine. We watched him as with plenty of height he turned in – too slowly – to land. The Hurricane fell out of his hands and before our eyes dived headlong into the ground. The unfortunate young pilot died as the ambulance arrived.'[15]

But trepidation and inexperience were not the sole causes of pilots' difficulties. Inevitably there were still some technical problems to be overcome on the first Hurricanes that entered RAF service. Contrary to Gillan's experience on the Edinburgh–Northolt flight, even the early Merlin II engine was not as efficient as it became later in the war and could be prone to the phenomenon of 'surging', or unevenness in its running, which sometimes led to a sudden loss of power. D. H. Clarke, an officer with 85 Squadron in 1938, did not share the public enthusiasm for the first operational versions of the fighter:

> Believe me, at that time, they were brutes to fly. The two-bladed airscrew wasted power and made the take-off a soggy affair. The fabric-covered fuselage and wings disliked high speeds. The retractable tail-wheel frequently failed to come down, which is why they were soon fixed in the down position forever. Far worse than this was the Merlin engine, which used to cut out for no reason at all – generally at the worst possible moment. We lost lives because of this. In 1939 my Merlin cut on me, and as a result I crashed through a hedge and finished upside down in a ploughed field which was so soft my Hurricane dug itself in, wings flush with the mud. They took half an hour to dig me out. I was smothered with petrol.[16]

Peter Down, who served in 56 Squadron, also recalled that the early Merlin IIs did not always function properly:

> The main problem was that the plane would not fly in weak mixture without surging. Because the capsules in the engine – which were supposed to adjust the supply of fuel to the carburettors, making the correct atmospheric pressure with the air – tended to bounce up and down in rough weather and taking off on rough airfields, the engine tended to cut out. If it did, and you were not very high, it was a bit unfortunate. These problems were cured by our own squadron

mechanics with the aid of two representatives from Rolls-Royce. They fitted flame traps and altered the height of the cylinder blocks. Eventually the engines worked very well.[17]

Yet it would be wrong to exaggerate the troubles faced by the first Hurricane squadrons at the end of the 1930s. The plane transformed Fighter Command's capabilities, and most pilots warmed to its performance. Roland Beamont of 87 Squadron summed up the prevalent attitude among the squadrons. 'My feelings of converting onto the Hurricane were not of any great difficulty, but a feeling of exhilaration with all this power and being able to see 300 mph on the airspeed indicator very easily in a shallow dive at any point in the flight. This was a great experience for an eighteen-year-old.'[18]

The delivery of the first Hurricanes in the winter of 1937–8 coincided with a new political emphasis on fighter expansion. Until then, despite the development of the Hurricane and the Spitfire, the 'Trenchard doctrine' that favoured bombers had continued to be the dominant ethos of the Air Ministry and the senior strategists of the RAF. But the traditional theory of deterrence through the threat of a massive 'knock-out blow' against the enemy now looked increasingly threadbare as Germany rapidly built up her military forces. The real issue was Britain's ability to defend herself, not her capacity for bomber attacks. The two politicians who understood this reality most clearly were Neville Chamberlain, who had succeeded Stanley Baldwin as Prime Minister in May 1937, and Sir Thomas Inskip, the Minister for Defence Co-Ordination. Neither of them were likely warriors nor have they ever received much recognition for their actions. But together they forced through a major shift in air strategy, which would serve Britain well during the battle for national survival in the summer and autumn of 1940. Chamberlain's reputation was broken by his fruitless, at times dogmatic pursuit of appeasement with Hitler in the late 1930s and by his lack of vigour in the prosecution of the war. Yet, to his credit, he had long attached a higher priority to the creation of a strong fighter force than a bomber fleet, partly on grounds of national defence, partly through economic considerations. As he once pointed out to his Cabinet colleagues, 'one of these heavy bombers costs as much as four fighters'.[19] Inskip, too, belied his image as a parochial lawyer by directly challenging the Air Staff's bias towards bombers.

In taking on the RAF's high command, Inskip and Chamberlain were assisted by the ineffectuality of the new Chief of the Air Staff, Sir Cyril Newall, who had succeeded Sir Edward Ellington in September 1937. Newall was a pure Trenchardian who held that effective fighter defence was an impossibility, but fortunately he lacked the authority to impose his views on either the politicians or other RAF leaders such as Sir Hugh Dowding, head of Fighter Command. In fact, over his subsequent three years in office, Newall became a largely irrelevant figure. Sholto Douglas, one of his senior officers, later said that by 1940 Newall was 'an absolute bag of nerves',[20] while a front-line commander, Edgar Kingston-McLoughry, composed and circulated a memorandum that described him as 'A Weak Link in the Nation's Defences', castigating the Air Chief for his poor judgement, limited experience and irresolute personality.

One of Newall's first acts as Chief of the Air Staff in autumn 1937 was to put forward yet another expansion scheme, Scheme J, the previous four having proved inadequate in the face of the German threat. True to Newall's faith in the 'Trenchard doctrine', Scheme J concentrated on the air offensive, proposing a bomber force of some 90 squadrons, of which 64 would be the new generation of heavy bombers such as the Short Stirling. Inskip used the plan as his opportunity to strike. With his sharp legal mind, he drew up a powerful response on 9 December, in which he argued that the entire philosophy behind Scheme J was misguided. 'The role of our air force is not an early knock-out blow – no one has suggested that we can accomplish that – but to prevent the Germans knocking us out,' he wrote. Therefore, the key air battles of the early part of the war would occur not over the Reich but the south of England, and the RAF's aim would be 'to knock out as many Germans as we can'.[21] So Fighter Command, Inskip argued, had to be the government's first concern. It was a statement of policy that soon became known as the 'Inskip doctrine'. Newall was appalled at the rejection of his core belief. 'It is doubtful whether any number of fighters we could provide could impose a rate of wastage upon the enemy which he could not make good in the absence of effective counter-action against his air force and sources of supply,' he wrote to Inskip on 11 December, showing no grasp of what would actually happen in the Battle of Britain.[22] His words carried little weight. The Cabinet, led by Chamberlain, accepted the 'Inskip doctrine', and the Air Staff were ordered to come up with a new expansion scheme that put the primacy of the fighter at its core.

But it was easier for the government to call for fighter expansion than it was for the aircraft firms to deliver it. By the spring of 1938, with Hitler having annexed Austria on 12 March and beginning to make threatening noises against Czechoslovakia, the output from the English factories was seen as insufficient to meet the growing requirements of the RAF. The situation with Supermarine was desperate. Poor co-ordination with the subcontractors and technical problems in building the elliptical wings meant that not a single Spitfire had come off the production line, 'a disgraceful state of affairs' in the view of the Air Secretary, Lord Swinton.[23]

Helped by the simpler construction of the Hurricane, Hawker was doing better. Deliveries to the squadrons were running at six a week in March, though a temporary halt was caused by a brief strike at Brooklands over trade union demands for a closed shop. So alarmed was Swinton by the Spitfire crisis that in April 1938 he arranged for Hawker to be given an order for another 300 Hurricanes, taking the total number of planes due to be delivered by May 1940 to 900. He told colleagues that 'he regarded the fighter situation as serious because of the setback in Spitfires. He wished to get as many Hurricanes in 1938 and early 1939 as possible.'[24]

Yet in the fraught climate of early 1938, the overall production rate and increased orders for the Hurricane were not enough to prevent political turmoil over the supply of fighters to the RAF. Questions were asked in the House of Commons. Ministers were put under severe pressure. A Parliamentary debate on the air estimates in May brought the crisis to a head. Sir Hugh Seely, Liberal MP for Berwick and an airman himself, opened with a stinging attack on the National Government, represented on the front bench by Lord Winterton, Swinton's Deputy as Under-Secretary for Air: 'Take the Hawker Hurricane,' Seely told the House of Commons. 'Seventy or eighty MPs were asked to inspect it. There were photographs and propaganda from the Air Ministry. In June 1936, an order was given for 600. Can Lord Winterton deny that there are only twenty-eight in the service? Yet we are told that everything is all right. That machine will be out of date by the time it is in use. It is not even now in production. The squadrons where it is in service are still receiving modifications of the design.'[25] Winterton's complacent reply, in which he refused to go into detailed figures, reassured no one. As a result of the perceived ministerial failure on fighter production, both he and Swinton were asked to resign by Chamberlain, even though the Prime Minister declared in public that he was 'satisfied with the measures' that had been taken to 'overcome the difficulties that we have met and that very soon there will be a most satisfactory and remarkable increase in the rate of our production of aircraft'.[26]

Swinton's successor was the owlish, bespectacled former Health Minister Sir Kingsley Wood. An insurance lawyer before he entered politics, Wood was a dull speaker but an efficient administrator. He immediately acted on the 'Inskip doctrine' by pushing for a major expansion in fighter production. One of his first steps was to order the construction of a vast new Spitfire plant at Castle Bromwich in Birmingham. Planned to be the largest aircraft factory in Europe, it was due to turn out 1,000 Spitfires by May 1940. The new Hawker Siddeley works at Slough was another part of this formidable growth in aircraft manufacturing capacity, while the firm also instructed its subsidiary, Gloster Aircraft, to begin preparations to produce the Hurricane instead of the Wellington bomber at its Hucclecote factory in Gloucestershire.

But the biggest impetus behind an increase in fighter output arose during the Munich crisis of September 1938, when the prospect of an immediate war with Germany dramatically heightened awareness of the inadequacy of RAF numbers. Through the deal that Chamberlain and the French Prime Minister Édouard Daladier reached with Hitler on 30 September, the British Prime Minister helped to avert plunging Europe into immediate conflict. Yet the price he paid was a humiliating one. The wild enthusiasm of the London crowds that greeted his boast about 'peace in our time' could not disguise the reality that the British and French governments had shamefully colluded in the subsequent dismemberment of Czechoslovakia by the

Nazi regime in March 1939. Far from achieving a long-term settlement, the Munich agreement only strengthened Germany and sharpened the inevitability of war.

The weakness of Britain's military was one of the decisive influences behind the government's reluctance to go to war. The view that the country was too ill-prepared was also widely held outside the Cabinet, particularly in aviation circles where the slow progress of modernization was keenly understood. At the height of the Munich crisis, Sir John Slessor, the Air Staff's Director of Plans, circulated a memorandum in which he stated: 'It is probably not an exaggeration to say that it is our present inability to guarantee the security of this country against attack from the air – and that alone – which may compel us to withhold our support from the Czechs and hamstring our policy in Europe.'[27] Similarly, Sir Charles Bruce-Gardener, the Chairman of the Society of British Aircraft Manufacturers, wrote directly to Chamberlain on the eve of his fateful trip to Munich in September 1938 to warn him 'how terribly weak we still were in the air'. If war was declared, said Bruce-Gardener, the 'equipment available for the RAF, both in types and numbers, was far, far below the German air force'.[28] In fact, at the time of the Munich agreement, there were still only 5 Hurricane squadrons in RAF, with the plane accounting for just 93 of Fighter Command's 750 aircraft.

But all this was to change. Despite his public rhetoric, Chamberlain was not so self-deluded as to believe that he had really guaranteed the final settlement of Europe. Although hoping to maintain peace through his policy of appeasement, he knew that Britain would have to step up its rearmament programme. The Munich agreement bought more time for this vital task. The new Air Secretary Kingsley Wood prepared yet another, even more ambitious expansion programme, known as Scheme M, which provided for an extra 3,700 fighters by 1942, with immediate orders for half this total. Despite some grumbles from Newall, still fighting a rearguard action on behalf of the bomber, Scheme M was approved by the Cabinet. A rapid acceleration in the production of fighters was now underway.

Because of all the production setbacks at Supermarine, a large part of the responsibility for fighter output now fell on Hawker Siddeley.

The company was ready to shoulder the burden, promising the Air Ministry that it would exploit to the full the productive facilities of its substantial organization, with Hurricane output estimated to rise to 50 planes a month by September 1939. A mixture of urgency, pride and duty shines through a report sent on 26 September 1938 by Frank Spriggs, Hawker Siddeley's Managing Director, to Air Marshal Sir Wilfrid Freeman, who now carried the title of Air Member for Development and Production. Setting out the firm's immediate plans, Spriggs explained that the Hawker plant at Kingston 'will concentrate on Hurricane production, and arrange to give any advice and assistance in any other direction on the same product. The personnel will be increased as soon as available and the Slough project expedited.' He further promised that the Hawker tool room would immediately start producing duplicate tools for the Hurricane and that a complete set of blueprints and drawings would shortly be sent to the Gloster factory at Hucclecote, Gloucestershire, where work on the Wellington bomber 'will cease immediately'.

Spriggs had two other specific suggestions for speeding up output. One was to reduce the amount of scrutiny on the aircraft carried out by the inspectors from both Hawker Siddeley and from the Air Ministry's own Aeronautical Inspection Department (AID). The process, he urged, should be kept to 'a visual component inspection', eliminating 'all but a small percentage of detail'. His other proposal was to cut out 'all protective processes on metal and to substitute a coat of quick drying paint where necessary. If you could visualize the time taken and care necessary under the present procedure, I am certain you would agree at once.' Spriggs claimed that with such measures 'you would increase production by ten to fifteen per cent, and release space and labour. Needless to add, the organization is entirely at your disposal and imbued with the spirit of "get it out". Do help them if you can by stretching the red tape.'[29]

Three days later, while Chamberlain was negotiating with Hitler in Munich, Freeman wrote back to Spriggs, saying he was 'very glad to note the arrangements you have made generally'. He could not, however, agree to any relaxation of the metal anodizing or the inspection rules because he had to ensure that all production Hurricanes reached a certain standard. Moreover, some of them might be required to fight overseas, where protection of the metal would be vital.[30]

On the day that the Munich agreement was publicly announced, 30 September, Spriggs wrote again to Freeman to stress the central role that the Hurricane should play in the light of the crisis:

> The developments of the last fortnight have to my mind illustrated vividly the widespread effects of possible aerial invasion. It has made me realize that our arguments in favour of countermeasures in the past have been feeble, and more than ever am I a fervent advocate of all and any action deterrent to the invader. In this respect it appears plain that the fighter occupies the first place, and I think that the events have proved that the actions taken within the last week to expedite supplies – admirable as they are under the circumstances – could not prove really effective for several months.

Spriggs therefore suggested that the Air Ministry could raise Hurricane output by widening its manufacture to other firms outside Hawker Siddeley. 'I shall be only too pleased to encourage any other concern to have full facilities and assistance to construct the Hurricane elsewhere, and if you would like to invite any other organization to inspect the layout and productive features, we are entirely at your disposal.'[31] Although agreeing about the primacy of the fighter, the Ministry did not pursue the idea of involving other firms in the Hurricane's production. It considered that the Hawker Siddeley conglomerate was large enough to cope, particularly with the Slough and Gloster factories gearing up. But, in a move that confirmed the plane's importance, the Ministry gave Hawker Siddeley a provisional order for 1,000 new Hurricanes, by far the biggest the company had ever received. A letter from Freeman on 30 September to the head of the Treasury, Sir Warren Fisher, seeking his financial approval for this order, shows the high regard in which the Air Staff held the Hurricane at this time:

> We have considered every possible scheme by which we could increase the Fighter strength of the Royal Air Force. As you know, we have been let down over and over again on the matter of the production of the Spitfire, which is not technically clear even yet. The only alternative we have of a modern fighter is the Hurricane.

This machine is technically clear, the very best machine we have at the present time and available to get into production forthwith. In the emergency we took steps to get the whole Hawker combine on the work of jigging and tooling the Hurricane machine so that it can be produced in a minimum of time and in quantity at the Gloster works. The figure we arranged for was a minimum of 1,000 and I consider it essential that we should not have to go back on this order. I should be most grateful, as indeed would be the whole air force, if this could be sanctioned by you.[32]

Fisher agreed. One month later, on 1 November 1938, the contract for 1,000 more Hurricanes was formally sent to Hawker Siddeley.

In the aftermath of the Munich agreement the mood among the RAF was one of relief mingled with invigorated purpose. 'Thank God,' were Sir Hugh Dowding's first words on hearing the news of the settlement, having been sunk into gloom about the prospects of the British and French air forces holding back the Luftwaffe.[33] He later came to regard the year of peace after September 1938 as vital for the build-up of Fighter Command, a view shared by Sholto Douglas, a former fighter commander who was Assistant Chief of the Air Staff at the time of the Munich agreement. 'In the air in 1938, we had practically nothing. During 1939 we went a long way to catching up; and by 1940, "when the test came", as Churchill put it, we were in a position to wage successfully the most vitally important battle that has ever been fought in the air.'[34] As Hurricane production was increased, so was the delivery of the planes to the front line. By the end of October 1938, 1, 85 and 32 Squadrons had all exchanged their biplanes for Hurricanes. In the following two months 43, 79 and 151 Squadrons were similarly re-equipped.

Peter Townsend of 43 Squadron recalled the new confidence that experience on the Hurricanes brought. 'The Hurricanes completely changed our fearful mood,' he wrote. 'There grew in us a trust and affection for them and their splendid Merlin engines, thoroughbreds and stayers which changed our fearful doubts of the Munich period into the certainty we could beat all comers.' Part of this confidence stemmed from the intensive practice that the pilots underwent. 'All our flying was designed to gird us for the war which was bound to come: battle climbs to thirty thousand feet, where the engine laboured and the controls were sluggish and we inhaled oxygen which came hissing into our face-masks from a black steel cylinder behind the armoured bulkhead; air drill and practice attacks and firing our guns into the sea, where they raised a jagged plume of foam. The recoil of those eight Brownings could slow the aircraft in the climb by forty mph.'[35]

The drive to strengthen Fighter Command was accompanied by the search for further improvements to the Hurricane. The Air Staff's faith in the plane did not preclude the recognition that some of its features were inadequate, especially the fabric-covered wings, the fixed-pitch, two-bladed wooden airscrew and the absence of armour protection for the pilot. An intense effort was therefore made in the years before the war to update the aircraft. The question of producing all-metal wings for the Hurricane had been raised as long ago as 1935 because of concerns that the fabric construction would not stand the strain of high speeds. In January 1936 the Air Ministry instructed Hawker to start constructing two experimental sets of metal wings for the fighter, which would be interchangeable with the fabric ones. Sydney Camm suggested to officials that the job could be done within five months, though the Ministry's Resident Technical Officer at Kingston, B. D. Clark, felt that 'this estimate of time is, I think, a little on the optimistic side'.[36] Clark's reservations soon turned out to be correct, as the schedule slipped. There were a number of factors in this delay. First, Hawker did not initially attach a high priority to the work, largely because the fabric wing was operating successfully, even at speeds of over 300 mph. As Camm had reported at an Air Ministry meeting in February 1936, held to discuss the F36/34's wing stiffness, 'his pilot has actually dived the fighter to 330 mph without trouble'.[37] Two months later it was still the same story. 'Progress on the stressed-skin wings is still very slow. Nothing has been made up in the shops,' Sir Cyril Newall, then the Air Member for Supply, reported, blaming the firm's 'lack of enthusiasm' on the fact that the fabric wings were still performing well in tests.[38]

Financial considerations may have also played their part, as Frank Cowlin of the Directorate of Technical Development warned: 'I fear

Hawkers may be tempted to take a short view and regard it as a piece of highly experimental work which ought not to be classed with other work which is likely to show a monetary return.'[39] But the bigger problem for Hawker was that the project meant a departure from their usual method of construction. Most of the metal wing had to be planned from scratch, with the Warren bracing of diagonal girders replaced by light alloy ribs attached at right angles to the main spar. The structure was then covered with skin panels and flush riveted. Despite being significantly lighter by a margin of 70 pounds, the all-metal wing had a greater stiffness.

The work dragged on through 1936, Hawker regularly promising the Air Ministry that more urgency had been devoted to the project. 'Mr Camm now has a group of men in his Drawing Office definitely earmarked for metal wing development work and is clearly past the tentative stage of design which troubled us so much a few months back.'[40] The delays continued, however, through the early part of 1937, as Hawker had to concentrate much of their effort on turning out the first production Hurricanes. Finally, by the summer one set of metal wings had been built. Trials proved satisfactory over the following months, with the metal wings providing a significantly greater speed in the aircraft's dive, 450 mph compared to 380 mph for the fabric-covered wings, though it was found that there was little difference in the maximum speeds when flying horizontally.

Full-scale production could now proceed. With a heavy programme at Kingston, Hawker gave the job of actually building the metal wings to its Gloster subsidiary at Hucclecote in Gloucestershire, but this proved an unhappy move, as the West Country firm fell badly behind with the subcontract. As the Munich crisis escalated in September 1938, and while Hawker was planning to hand over even more Hurricane production work to the Hucclecote factory, the first production set of wings had still not appeared. Sir Ernest Lemon, the Air Ministry's Director of Production, blamed skill shortages, saying the firm was 'not in a good labour area', and he urged that subcontracting be transferred elsewhere.[41]

Given the burden on the rest of the aircraft industry, this was not a feasible proposition nor would it have saved any time. But during the autumn of 1938 the Air Ministry kept up the pressure on Hawker

Siddeley. In a letter of 1 November the RAF's Director General of Research Arthur Tedder, who was later to use the Hurricane to brilliant effect in the desert as an Allied commander in the Middle East, told Frank Spriggs at Hawker that he could 'not stress the point too strongly' that the 'change from fabric to metal covered wings on the Hurricane' was no mere 'refinement'. From an 'operational point of view, in certain circumstances a difference of no less than 70 mph is involved,' he said, so it was 'essential that every endeavour be made to introduce the stressed skin wing at an early date. Tedder concluded with the hope that Hawker would leave 'no stone unturned' in the quest to meet the RAF's operational requirements.[42] But it was not until April 1939 that the first production set of metal wings arrived at Brooklands from Hucclecote. From then on, stressed skin wings gradually became standard on all Hurricanes, but not before more than 500 of the fabric-covered types had gone into service. Indeed, many of these aircraft went on to serve in the Battle of France and in North Africa, though none fought in the Battle of Britain.

Some of the obsolete fixed-pitch airscrews also survived into 1940, despite the pre-war efforts of the government to replace them on all Hurricanes. When the F36/34 had first been designed, Hawker decided not to fit a variable-pitch (VP) propeller, because the wooden, fixed-pitch type was much lighter and was held to provide sufficient power on take-off. But once the first Hurricanes had reached the operational squadrons in early 1938, there was mounting concern within Fighter Command at the take-off distance that the plane required. Sir Hugh Dowding was one of the first to suggest variable-pitch, two-speed propellers to reduce the take-off length, but the Directorate of Technical Development initially refused to consider such a change, claiming on 5 July 1938 that there 'would be a very serious risk of over-revving engines at the cruising and maximum level speed conditions'.[43] The real answer, said the Directorate, was to alter, not the airscrews, but the length of the airstrips at the fighter aerodromes. Such a stance only provoked exasperation from Sholto Douglas, Assistant Chief of the Air Staff. He agreed that many of the fighter airfields were inadequate, but 'at the same time this is no excuse for our not doing all in our power to improve the take-off of the Hurricane. We are dealing here with human lives; and if we have fatal accidents next winter with Hurricanes at Kenley or North Weald, it is no use saying, "Oh! These aerodromes are too small." I certainly think therefore that we should go for a VP prop on the Hurricane; in fact I feel strongly about it, and I hope that its introduction will be at a very early date.'[44]

Douglas's explosion had its effect. The Air Ministry agreed to start trials with a De Havilland VP airscrew, and these showed a considerable reduction in the Hurricane's required take-off run, down from 410 yards to 250 yards. De Havilland began production of the VP airscrew for Hawker in April 1939, and by May the following year 1,250 of them had been delivered for the Hurricane squadrons. They were, however, only an interim measure, for the real advance in airscrews came with the creation of the hydraulically operated, constant-speed propeller developed by Rotol, a joint venture formed by Bristol and Rolls-Royce. The attraction of Rotol's constant-speed propeller was that the pitch was automatically adjusted to suit the speed of the aircraft, which both removed another burden from the pilot and helped with the climb. Changing from fine to coarse pitch was once described as 'rather like changing from bottom to top gear in a small four-speed car'.[45] But the Rotol invention did not become available in sufficient numbers until the eve of the Battle of Britain.

Another technical breakthrough that assisted the Hurricane's take-off and performance was the introduction of 100-octane fuel in 1939, to replace the 87-octane fuel used previously. As the historian L. F. E. Coombes explained: 'The octane number of a fuel indicates its resistance to detonation. The higher the number, the greater the resistance and therefore the higher the permissible boost pressure before detonation occurs.'[46] The 100-octane fuel significantly increased the Merlin engine's power, improving the Hurricane's rate of climb and top speed. Having seen the effect of the more advanced fuel, the government managed in June 1939 to secure supplies from the Dutch West Indies. In fact, enough was stockpiled to sustain Fighter Command right through the Battle of Britain, giving the Hurricanes and Spitfires a crucial advantage over the Me 109, because only 87-octane fuel was available in Germany. One further significant change was the introduction of bulletproof windscreens made of laminated glass that was one and a half inches thick. Experiments by the Air Ministry's Mechanical Tests Department in November 1938 demonstrated that such a panel 'stops .303 ball ammunition at ranges down to 200 yards' and 'will protect the upper half of the pilot'.[47]

While these improvements were being carried out, production continued to accelerate through 1939. The period after the Munich agreement proved crucial for the re-equipment of Fighter Command. During the third quarter of 1938, 60 Hurricanes were produced, a figure that rose to 121 in the second quarter of 1939 and 140 in the last quarter of the year. At the end of 1938, 197 Hurricanes had been built. By the end of 1939, the figure stood at 731. The growth was reflected in the size of the manual workforce at Hawker engaged on the Hurricane, expanding from 2,300 in early 1938 to almost 5,000 in December 1939. Before the Munich agreement, there had been just five Hurricane squadrons in RAF service. Within twelve months there were eighteen. Yet amidst the preparations for war, there was one highly incongruous aspect to this healthy output of Hurricanes: not all of it was devoted to the strengthening of Britain's fighter defences. While the government was urging an ever greater supply of aircraft to the RAF, Hawker was engaged in selling significant numbers of Hurricanes overseas.

This export drive was initially focused on Yugoslavia, a country with which Hawker had developed a close relationship since 1931. The Hawker Fury and the Hind, an advanced version of the Hart light bomber, were both strongly represented in the Royal Yugoslav Air Force (RYAF) in the mid 1930s. The threat from neighbouring Germany led the Yugoslav government in 1938 to order 24 Hurricanes from Hawker Siddeley, as well as concluding an agreement to produce the plane under licence in two factories at Belgrade and Zemun. The first official order for these two plants amounted to 100 Hurricanes, with an expected rate of delivery of 12 a month. One interesting version to emerge from the production run was a Hurricane fitted with a Daimler-Benz DB601 aero-engine, the only Hurricane ever to fly without a Merlin power-plant. This was the result of an experiment by the RYAF, which wanted to make a comparison with the performance and handling of the Merlin. According to some accounts, the Yugoslav pilots preferred the Hurricane with the Daimler-Benz aero-engine, which also powered the Messerschmitt 109.[48] Any thoughts of long-term Hurricane production were ended, however, by the German Blitzkrieg against Belgrade in April 1941, at which stage only 24 licence-built Hurricanes had been delivered, making a total Hurricane force in Yugoslavia of fewer than 50 planes.

Daring aerobatic displays by the Hurricane at air shows in Britain and on the continent attracted the attention of other foreign governments, desperate to modernize their forces in the doom-laden atmosphere of the late 1930s. After watching an RAF presentation in November 1938, King Carol of Romania purchased 12 Hurricanes, and the planes were delivered just days before the invasion of Poland on 1 September 1939. Similarly, the Belgian government placed an order for 20 Hurricanes in April of that year, in addition to an agreement by which the leading Belgian aircraft manufacturer, Avions Fairey, would produce the fighter under licence, though only two had actually been built by the time of the German invasion of Belgium on 10 May 1940. Turkey ordered 15 Hurricanes, which were delivered from Brooklands in September 1939, while Persia purchased 18, only one of which reached Tehran before the start of war. A small shipment of seven Hurricanes was delivered to the South African Air Force in the winter of 1938–9, the first machine assembled causing an immediate stir by flying at 335 mph from Durban to Pretoria. The Polish government purchased a single Hurricane for evaluation purposes, and the Polish air force liked the plane so much that nine more were quickly ordered in the summer of 1939. But soon after the consignment had been dispatched from Brooklands, Warsaw was in Nazi hands, so the planes had to be diverted to Gibraltar.

Hawker Siddeley's eagerness to make money from foreign sales was commercially understandable. The board was, after all, responsible to its shareholders, and Tom Sopwith's memories of bankruptcy were still less than twenty years old. Less explicable was the government's willingness to collude in the exports when the RAF was crying out for new planes. The 'Cassandra' column in the *Daily Mirror*, written by the leading left-wing journalist William Conor, spoke for many when it asked on 6 May 1939: 'The Hurricane is one of the finest fighter machines in the world. Less than four months ago the Secretary of State for Air said that we needed between five and six thousand fighter planes for home defence. We haven't got them yet, or anything approaching it. So what is the answer to selling Hurricanes to Yugoslavia when we desperately need every machine here?'[49] There were three main justifications. Firstly, the government's colossal financial burden from the costs of military expansion meant that the Treasury was desperate for foreign-currency earnings and corporation taxes. Soon after the Germans had annexed Czechoslovakia in March 1939, making a mockery of the Munich agreement, the Air Secretary Sir Kingsley Wood had introduced aircraft estimates worth £250 million, by far the biggest in history. The second rationalization was that Britain's allies and Germany's enemies needed to be rearmed to meet the Nazi threat. This was precisely the argument used by *The Times*, the most pro-government newspaper, in defending the sale of the fighters to South Africa: 'The Hurricane is a much faster type of aircraft than anything in regular use in the South African Force. It is desirable that pilots of the Union shall have some training in the types of aircraft which will have to be acquired by the Union in the event of war, and the first batch of Hurricanes will be used to that end.'[50] Thirdly, some of the foreign orders generated their own increase in production, as occurred in the licence agreements with Yugoslavia and Belgium.

Much more important was the case of Canada, whose government ordered 20 Hurricanes in the autumn of 1938. The planes were crated up, shipped to Montreal, transported across Canada and then assembled in Vancouver, the first of them going into service in February 1939. The experience gained under this contract was invaluable in encouraging the Air Ministry to reach a deal with the Canadian Department of National Defence, whereby Hurricanes for the RAF would be manufactured in Ontario by the Canadian Car and Foundry Company. Using drawings sent in microfilm from Hawker and one of the exported planes as a model, the firm, universally known as Can-Car, began to tool up for production in March 1939. Within less than a year, the first batch of 40 Hurricanes had been dispatched across the Atlantic to Britain, an achievement of outstanding efficiency. Altogether, 1,451 Hurricanes were built in Canada, more than a tenth of the entire total.

One of the key figures responsible for this success story was Elsie MacGill, Can-Car's Chief Designer and a female pioneer of aeronautical engineering. What made her rise to the top so remarkable was not just her gender but also her disability, for as a student she had contracted polio and was told that she would be confined to a wheelchair for the rest of her life. But with the aid of two metal canes and her own indefatigability, she learnt to walk again. Her leadership in overseeing the Can-Car production effort earned her the nickname 'the Queen of the Hurricanes', by which title she even featured as a wartime comic-book heroine in North America.

A primary motivation behind outsourcing some of the Hurricane's production was the fear of Luftwaffe attacks against the aircraft factories in Britain. With each passing week in the summer of 1939, such bombing seemed to become ever more inevitable, as the Nazi regime snarled at Poland. On 1 September the storm broke when the Reich's forces poured across the Polish border. Within two days, the Prime Minister Neville Chamberlain had to tell Britain that all his hopes for peace had been dashed. The nation was at war with Germany. Most of the public was full of foreboding. But among the young Hurricane pilots, there was a sense of eagerness that the conflict had finally arrived. Charlton Haw was in his RAF training unit at Hull when he heard Chamberlain's broadcast on 3 December: 'I'm afraid we let out a big cheer when we heard the news. It was a schoolboy's dream come true, flying Spitfires and Hurricanes.'[51] Harold Bird-Wilson was with 17 Squadron at Croydon in Surrey, the day war broke out: 'There was a general feeling, "Let's get on with it." There was no fear or anything like that. We felt we had one of the best aircraft in the world, the Hawker Hurricane, and we could take on the Germans. There was no worry in the squadron as regards casualties. We did not think much about the superiority of the Luftwaffe. We thought we would present them with a good fight.'[52]

4

'Real war at last'

⟐

Within three days of Prime Minister Neville Chamberlain's mournful announcement, the Hurricanes had gone into action with fatal consequences. At 6.15 a.m. on 6 September 1939 a searchlight battery on Mersea Island off the Essex coast identified a possible hostile raid at high altitude heading west of Colchester. Immediately the news was reported to the Uxbridge headquarters of 11 Group, the Fighter Command organization that covered the south-east of England. Uxbridge HQ then ordered 56 Squadron, based at North Weald in Essex, to send up a flight of Hurricanes to investigate the raid. But in his excitement at the prospect of the first combat over England, the officer in command of North Weald, Group Captain D. F. Lucking, ordered the entire 56 Squadron into the air. Moments later the other North Weald Squadron, 151, was also scrambled to intercept the enemy. With their Merlins roaring, the Hurricanes climbed through the September morning mist. As they emerged through the haze into blue sky, the pilots began the hunt for the enemy raiders.

Suddenly, a pair of fighters tore down from above, their guns blazing. Bullets ripped through the Hurricane flown by Pilot Officer Frank Rose and smoke poured from the engine, though, in an early wartime sign of the Hurricane's resilience, he managed to bring his badly damaged plane down for a forced landing in a Suffolk field. Despite the wreckage, he survived without serious injury. Another pilot was less lucky. Montague Hulton-Harrop was hit in the back of the head as shells poured into his Hurricane. He was killed instantly, his body slumping forward over the control column. His plane went into a spiralling dive and crashed into the ground on a farm near Ipswich in Suffolk.

Nineteen years old, 'tall, blond and eager', according to one of the 56 Squadron ground crew,[1] Pilot Officer Hulton-Harrop was the first RAF fatality of the Second World War. But he was not shot down by the Luftwaffe. Instead, he was a victim of fire from his own side, his death a tragic result of confusion and inexperience within Fighter Command. What appears to have happened was that as the Hurricanes of 151 and 56 Squadrons flew inland in search of the enemy intruders, they showed up as a large formation on the screens of the radar station at Canewdon on the Thames estuary near Rochford in Essex. At the same time anti-aircraft guns along the Essex coast opened up indiscriminately, further creating the illusion of an enemy attack. In the chaotic atmosphere the controllers of 11 Group thought that another enemy raid was underway, so they scrambled Spitfires from 54, 65 and 74 Squadrons to intercept. As the 74 Squadron adjutant Sammy Hoare later said, 'the picture was one of aircraft being directed and re-directed all over the sky, chasing each other and sometimes themselves'.[2]

Led by Adolph 'Sailor' Malan, a ruthlessly determined South African, the Spitfires of 74 Squadron took off first and were guided towards the Hurricanes over their radio/telephone (r/t). Malan led one section of three Spitfires, while Flying Officer Paddy Byrne, a cool Irishman, led the other. Close behind Byrne followed John Freeborn, a young Yorkshireman not yet twenty years old. As the 74 Squadron pilots caught a glimpse of what they believed to be the enemy, their adrenalin began to flow. Byrne and Freeborn maintained that they heard Malan shout 'Tally ho' over the radio, giving the order to attack. Malan later insisted he had shouted 'Friendly aircraft – break away'.[3] Whatever the truth, Byrne and Freeborn went in for the kill and were 'exhilarated' at shooting the two aircraft out of the sky. It was only when they landed that they learnt the tragedy of what had occurred. Both men were arrested and subsequently tried at a court martial for disobeying orders. Represented by the famous advocate Sir Patrick Hastings, who in wartime was employed as an Intelligence officer at Fighter Command, Byrne and Freeborn were acquitted. The incident, however, left a legacy of bitterness in 74 Squadron, for Freeborn felt badly let down by Malan.

It was never discovered what caused the initial report from Mersea

Island about the fictional enemy air raid that triggered the disaster. Sir Hugh Dowding, head of Fighter Command, maintained that it was a transport plane carrying refugees from Holland. Others said it was a Bristol Blenheim or an Avro Anson returning from patrol over the North Sea. The inability to find the cause highlighted the problem that had ultimately led to the 74 Squadron attack by Spitfires on the Hurricanes: the lack of accurate plane recognition within Fighter Command. Fortunately the Telecommunications Research Establishment, which had helped to develop radar, was at the time working on a system called Identification Friend or Foe (IFF). Through the use of an airborne IFF transmitter, an RAF aircraft could reveal its friendly intentions by sending back a coded radio signal to the radar stations. IFF was first used in January 1940, and by June all Hurricanes had a set installed.

'The Battle of Barking Creek', as it became known with tragic irony, also led to more intensive training for the radar operators, sector controllers and communications personnel in the RAF operations rooms, as well as an improved system for reporting enemy raids. If there was any beneficial legacy from the incident it lay in the greater preparedness of Fighter Command when the battle for national survival came in 1940. But 'Barking Creek' itself was not the signal for any sudden sharpening of the conflict. Just the opposite was true. In the months after the declaration of war, Britain settled into a pattern of nervous inertia, only interrupted by sporadic minor clashes with the enemy. No military assistance was given to Poland. No attempt was made by a Western power to attack Germany. When one member of the Cabinet suggested that the RAF should bomb a German armaments work, the Air Secretary Sir Kingsley Wood reacted with outrage, declaring that it was 'private property'.[4] Among the Hurricane pilots themselves, the initial exuberance on the outbreak of war soon gave way to deflation at the lack of activity. In a telling metaphor of the inaction that was to follow, the first time a Hurricane pilot used his guns was on 8 September, when Flying Officer John 'Killy' Kilmartin of 43 Squadron fired off a sustained series of bursts totalling 1,200 rounds. But his target was not the enemy. It was a stray barrage balloon that had come loose from its moorings. For most of the home-based fighter squadrons, the routine during the long winter of 1939–40 comprised convoy patrols over the North Sea and the English Channel, or endless training exercises and gunnery practice. Douglas 'Grubby' Grice of 32 Squadron, remembered his convoy duties as 'terribly dull'. He was 'never in more than a section of three aircraft, stooging up and down over a convoy, just circling around'.[5] That feeling was shared by Harold Bird-Wilson of 17 Squadron, who said that the job meant 'going round and round the ships, a boring exercise because you never knew when a German fighter would come up and have a crack at you'.[6] In fact, the few German planes that ventured over British waters were usually reconnaissance types seeking information on the strength of the home defences or convoys. Tackling them was never easy, as Eustace 'Gus' Holden of 56 Squadron recalled: 'It was a very severe winter, lots of cloud and snow. Pinning these chaps down when they were darting in and out of clouds was a very difficult task and we didn't have much success. We did fight them occasionally, but I don't remember any German being shot down.'[7]

Plunging temperatures and poor living conditions further dampened the mood within the Hurricane squadrons. The weather was so bad in the depth of winter that stations were often snowbound or enshrouded in fog. On other mornings, ice had to be swept from the fighters' wings with wire-bristle brooms, and the Merlin engines had to thaw out before there could be any flying. But some squadrons refused to remain in wintry paralysis. Peter Townsend of 43 Squadron was based at this time in the northerly station of Acklington in Northumberland, where thick snow prevented operations for a while because the wheels of the Hurricanes became clogged. With typical enterprise, Townsend thought of a way to overcome this obstacle. 'We wrenched a door off the dispersal hut, wrapped up three men in the thickest woollies and balaclava helmets, and sat them on the door. The whole lot was tied behind a tractor. Up and down it went, gradually flattening and pressing the snow into a hard surface. When the men became frozen three others took their place and soon we had a perfectly good runway. The convoys were not left unprotected.'[8]

It was Townsend who led the first attack to bring down a German plane on English soil. At dawn on 3 February 1940, he went out with the rest of 43 Squadron to fetch the Hurricanes dispersed on the far side of the Acklington airfield. 'As usual, some starter-batteries went flat and some engines had to be cranked by hand. This could at best scrape the skin off your knuckles or break your wrist through a kick-back or at worst decapitate you if you slipped forward into the pro-peller. One by one the Merlins burst into raucous life and we taxied back to the dispersal hut as the blood red sky began to mushroom in the east.' Then the men climbed out of their planes and waited for further orders. Some were dozing fitfully when the phone in the dis-persal hut rang at 9.03 a.m. A nearby radar station had picked up an unidentified aircraft about sixty miles out to sea from the port of Whitby in North Yorkshire, flying at 1,000 feet. Townsend's section was immediately told to scramble. 'Moments later I was climbing away from the Acklington airfield,' he wrote later. 'Our throttles wide open, we raced south at wave-top height, spread out in search formation.' Suddenly, above and to the right, Townsend spotted the German bomber, a twin-engined Heinkel 111. 'There was not a second to lose, for the Heinkel was just below cloud. I banked right in a climbing turn. Now the Heinkel was in my sights. My thumb was on the firing button.' Closing fast, he opened up with his Brownings. A trail of smoke began to pour from the Heinkel as it struggled towards the shore. Showing great skill, the German pilot managed to drag the plane far enough to avoid the town of Whitby, then brought it down on some farmland. Circling overhead in his Hurricane, Townsend watched the German bomber crash. 'I could see snow and mud flying up behind the Heinkel as it careered above the ground towards a line of trees. Its right wing hit one, snapping it in half. Then it slewed round and came to a rest.'9 Three of the four crew were killed. The pilot had to have his leg amputated but survived.

Less success against a Heinkel 111 was achieved by Charlton Haw of 504 Squadron, when he was scrambled for a patrol over the naval base of Scapa Flow off the north-east coast of Scotland. It was his very first experience of combat. Giving chase to the Heinkel, his sec-tion leader swooped in for the attack, followed by Haw and the other Hurricane. 'As we got close, their rear gunner opened up. It looked to me like red-hot chain links coming out of the back of it. The

German dived into cloud. We fired at it but we were too far away. As I broke away, one bullet went right through my cockpit. I came back and they were all slapping me on the back, saying how lucky I was. I was filled with a sense of excitement, not fear. As you progressed with more and more combats, you still felt that excitement. You never got used to it.' But Haw also shared that sense of boredom provoked by the Phoney War. 'There was a lot of sitting around. It was rather tedious.'[10]

Not all the Hurricane squadrons were based in Britain during these months. At the outbreak of war in September 1939, the government had sent four units to support the French on the western front. Sir Hugh Dowding, known as 'Stuffy' because of his aloof manner, was deeply sceptical about the value of this move, having faith in neither the French air force nor its organization. His disillusion had been exacerbated during a visit in early 1939 to Lille in northern France, when he had seen at first hand the shambolic nature of France's air defences. His assistant Hugh Ironside, later a distinguished Hurricane pilot himself, recounted:

> We landed at this airfield. The grass was almost knee high. Lined up along the side were a lot of incredibly old planes, including biplanes with skis between the wheels, which I didn't think even existed in France. We taxied up to a hangar and lined up there were a dozen beribboned French generals. Stuffy got out, went along the whole line saying, 'The name's Dowding.' His French was extremely limited. We got into various motor cars and went off to a large restaurant, where we had a fabulous lunch which went on for about two hours. There was an awful lot of wine, which of course Stuffy didn't touch. He hardly ate anything. I could see he was getting extremely uptight about all this. Far worse was to come. All these jolly generals packed into cars and then we went into a cellar where we sat on some hard chairs. In one corner of this large room there was a phone box and another hard chair with a French airman sitting on it. Just opposite him was a blackboard covered in squares. We sat there for some considerable time. Then the phone rang. The airman went into the box. There was a lot of 'oui, oui, oui' going on. Then he put a red arrow on the blackboard. This went on for an hour or so until the blackboard was covered with arrows of various colours. I don't think anyone knew what the hell it was all about. Going back, Stuffy never

said a word, absolutely silent. I think that's where he got his utter distrust of the French which was to show later.[11]

Nevertheless, the military requirements of the alliance meant that Dowding had no alternative but to accept the transfer of some of his forces to the continent, though the four fighter units initially sent were far less than the ten that the French Cabinet had demanded. Based at the airfield of Boos near Rouen in north-eastern France, two of the Hurricane squadrons, 85 and 87, were meant to give back-up to the ground forces as part of the Air Component of the British Expeditionary Force. The other pair of squadrons, 1 and 73, were assigned to give protection to the Advanced Air Striking Force (AASF), a group of Bristol Blenheim and Fairey Battle light bombers that was deployed to mount attacks and carry out reconnaissance across the Maginot line, the network of concrete fortifications and gun emplacements constructed by France along its border with Germany. After arriving first at Cherbourg on the north coast, 1 Squadron was stationed at the Vassincourt airfield near the north-eastern border with Belgium, while 73 Squadron was stationed further west at Rouvres near Verdun. According to Paul Richey of 1 Squadron, the arrival of the Hurricanes made an immediate impression on the French sailors at Cherbourg: 'They showed great interest in our Huricanes, marvelling at their armament and incredulous at their performance figures.'[12]

But one of 73 Squadron's young recruits, Dickie Martin, did not think much of either the strength of the force or the logistical arrangements for moving the squadron from England. 'We were a pitiful little band of chaps when you come to think of it,' he said.[13] Unlike the rest of the squadron, Martin had not flown directly to France in September 1939. Instead, he and another officer had been instructed to travel by boat from Southampton to Le Havre so they could look after all the squadron's equipment, including staff car, cranes, field kitchens and motorcycles. The ship set sail but 'seemed to be taking an amazingly long time'. Eventually, a sailor told Martin that they were heading further west for Brest, not Le Havre. Arriving in chaos at the Atlantic port, Martin had to try to shift the whole cavalcade eastwards by road. 'It was a right pantomime, because most of the drivers were reservists, hardened middle-aged chaps, bus drivers and heavy goods drivers. So they made absolute mincemeat of a couple of twenty-year-old officers.' There were constant stoppages on the way for food, cigarettes and rest. When they finally arrived, the commanding officer 'was absolutely livid with rage, sitting there unable to do anything because of lack of transport'. His mood had been further worsened after he had ordered the Hurricanes from 73 Squadron to fly over the coast as a morale-boosting exercise, only for the French anti-aircraft batteries to open fire on them. But there was one advantage to being part of the Advanced Air Striking Force. 'The landlord of the local hotel in Verdun gave us a free run of his wine cellar, much to his wife's fury.'[14]

The winter of 1939–40 was as bitter in France as it was in England. 'With the approach of Christmas, heavy and continuous rain grounded us for weeks on end and transformed the aerodrome and the area adjacent to the living huts into an unnegotiable morass. Driving, icy rain which froze where it touched, poured down every day,' remembered Roland Beamont, a pilot with 87 Squadron. In the bleakest moments 'the temperatures dropped lower, until the huts became coated with sheets of glistening ice and the doors and windows were blocked with snow'. Every morning before daybreak there would be 'a deafening roar' as the ground crews, or 'erks' as they were known, 'started up the Hurricanes to warm them and, first covering our shivering forms with layers of sweaters and leather flying suits, we floundered through the snow to our respective aircraft to supervise their running up'.[15]

Despite the conditions, the Hurricanes in France, operating from nearer Germany, inevitably saw more action than their counterparts in Britain. On 30 October, 1 Squadron claimed the first victory by a Hurricane in the war, when Pilot Officer P. W. O. 'Boy' Mould shot down a Dornier (Do) 17 over Vassincourt. His squadron comrade Paul Richey wrote this account of the combat. Having seen the Dornier, Mould 'took off without waiting for orders, pulled his plug (boost over-ride), lost the Hun, climbed to 18,000 feet – and found him. He did an ordinary straight stern attack, firing one longish burst with his sights starting above the Dornier and moving slowly round the fuselage. The Hun caught fire immediately, went into a vertical dive and made a whopping hole in the French countryside: it exploded on striking the ground.'[16] A few days later, on 8 November, 73 Squadron had its first victory as the young New Zealander Edgar 'Cobber' Kain shot down a Do 17 in a daring combat manoeuvre that began at 27,000 feet. Kain was soon to prove himself one of the most brilliant fighter pilots of the early part of the war, and by March 1940 he had become the RAF's first ace of the war by shooting down five enemy planes. 'He was a very flamboyant aviator, very determined and confident. A splendid extrovert. He was an excellent pilot and a good shot with a very good eye,' recalled his 73 Squadron comrade Dickie Martin.[17]

The Hurricane, too, was proving an effective fighter during these early skirmishes in France. Its wide track undercarriage made it ideal for the bumpy, poorly maintained grass airfields, and the erks welcomed its ability to cope with the worst conditions of that harsh winter. Reg Guppy, a ground crewman with 87 Squadron, said that waterlogged airstrips could make every aspect of aircraft handling 'one hard slog; it was common to have to literally lift the aircraft up on the backs of the erks underneath the wings to get the kites even to taxi in the mud. It was a common sight to see kites taking off more like speedboats than aircraft. I am quite satisfied that no other fighter before or since would have put up with the treatment that the Hurricane endured in France in 1939 and 1940.'[18]

As an interceptor, the Hurricane lived up to much of the pre-war promise, even though many of the planes sent to France still had the wooden, fixed-pitch propellers. Peter Matthews, a pilot with 1 Squadron, had joined the Advanced Air Striking Force at the start of the war. 'We took a heck of a long time to get to any altitude in a Hurricane Mark I, an awful long time. But the old Hurricane was a great aeroplane. It saved our lives a number of times because you could land it in a field. It was more robust than the Spitfire. I came back from a sortie filled with bullets and did not even know it.'[19] One Hurricane from 1 Squadron lost its elevator and most of its rudder after a mid-air collision with a French Morane fighter in November, yet the pilot was still able to land without any injury. Maurice Leng of 73 Squadron also recalled the aircraft's toughness. 'We often came back with strips of canvas off the fuselage, yet the plane was still flying. The Hurricane did not break up, whatever the speed – you could do 500 mph downwards. It was a bit of a warhorse but a good gun platform.'[20]

During the early campaign in France the Hurricane showed that it could be a match for the Luftwaffe's premier fighters, the Me 109 and the twin-engined Me 110, known to the Germans as 'the Destroyer'. The first Hurricane action against the Me 109 took place over Metz near the German border on 22 December 1939, as four German fighters dived on a section from 73 Squadron. Admittedly, the result went against the RAF, with two Hurricanes shot down for one German lost, but other clashes turned out to be more favourable. By the end of March 1940, five Me 109 losses had been credited to the Hurricanes of 73 Squadron, while in March and April, 1 Squadron had shot down six of them. The first, on 29 March, was a victory for Paul Richey. Flying on patrol over Metz, he spotted two Me 109s and began to climb towards them to attack. Suddenly, he saw another aircraft following behind him. 'I wasn't sure if he was friend or foe so waited to see whether he opened fire. He did, at longish range, and I twisted down underneath his nose.' Seconds later, the plane whipped past Richey's cockpit, 'so close that I heard his engine and felt the heat-wave, and I realized that he must have lost sight of me in the manoeuvre.' Richey started gaining on him as the Me 109 came out of a dive at 10,000 feet and then began a long straight climb:

> Waiting until he was in range and sitting pretty, I let him have it. My gun button was sticking and I wasted ammunition, but he started to stream smoke. The pilot must have been hit, for he took no evasive action, merely falling slowly in a vertical spiral. I was very excited and dived on top of him using my remaining ammunition. I then pulled out and saw another 109 about 2,000 feet above me. He headed for me, but knowing his speed to be superior I didn't dive away but turned on him, partly to stop him getting on my tail partly to bluff him. Either he had finished his hardware (which was unlikely, for the Germans carried 1,000 rounds for each gun to our 300) or he'd witnessed his chum's fate and wasn't feeling so brave. Anyway he beat it, and so did I at ground level.[21]

For all such confrontations, the atmosphere of the Phoney War prevailed in France almost as much as in England. The pilots of the

AASF and the Air Component of the British Expeditionary Force, which had been joined by 607 and 615 Squadrons in November 1939, spent much of their time on routine patrols or in practice. But from the start of spring 1940, there was a growing awareness that the comparative peace could not last. The Germans, stronger than ever, were bound to make a move soon. Roland Beamont of 87 Squadron had a spell in March 1940 based at a satellite station near the 'idyllic' seaside French resort of Le Touquet on the Channel coast. He and his comrades enjoyed 'a relaxed life' to 'the full, because in some way we knew that before long there would be little chance of "fun and games" and our time would be very fully occupied with other things'.[22] Back in Britain, there was also a mood of rising tension, as illustrated by a visit that 32 Squadron, based at Gravesend in Kent, received from a leading member of the government. After a morning's training, most of the men were asleep in chairs by the stove when the station commander, Dickie Grice (no relation of his namesake in 32 Squadron, Douglas 'Grubby' Grice) came in, followed by the visitor. 'We awoke as one and staggered to our feet, as we recognised the unmistakable figure of Churchill, bow-tie, cigar and all, exactly as he looked in the countless photographs we had seen,' recorded the pilot Donald 'Dimsie' Stones. Having accepted a glass of whisky, Churchill, then First Lord of the Admiralty, beckoned the men to resume their seats. One of the flight commanders, Bob Edwards, turned to Churchill and asked: 'As we are one of the squadrons on the list to be sent to France directly the war really gets started, sir, could you give us any idea when it might happen?' Churchill looked thoughtfully at his glass, then turned to the men: 'I can only think that the Boche is waiting for fine weather. Otherwise he would come through us and the French like a hot knife through butter.' There was a dead silence. Churchill finished his drink and stood up. After he had left, Edwards told the other pilots: 'What a shame, a man with his history, Marlborough and all that. Of course he's gaga – too old. We shan't hear much more of him.'[23]

Churchill was right. Hitler was about to overwhelm the Allies. But the first strike did not come in the west. On the morning of 9 April the Germans seized Denmark and embarked on a full-scale invasion of Norway. The Reich's primary aim was to secure the strategically important Norwegian ports, thereby maintaining its vital supplies of Swedish iron ore despite the British naval blockade of Germany. The Allied response was disorganized and ill-conceived. Landings were made in Norway at Aandalsnes and, further north, at Namsos, in an attempt to mount a pincer movement that would recapture the central city of Trondheim. But lacking numbers and air support, the two forces were easily beaten back by the German invaders and had to be evacuated at the beginning of May. More success was achieved around the far northern port of Narvik, where aggressive action by the Royal Navy caused heavy damage to the Kriegsmarine and left the German garrison badly isolated. Yet the Allied land operations in the area were poorly co-ordinated, allowing the Germans to re-group. One of the initial problems for the Allies was German air superiority. The only RAF plane that could reach Norway from Britain was the Bristol Blenheim, but the long journey across the North Sea would have left it with too little fuel to engage in sustained combat. The government therefore instructed that eighteen Gladiator fighters from 263 Squadron be dispatched by aircraft carrier to join the battle for Trondheim. It was also planned to send a unit of Hurricanes off a carrier into Aandalsnes, and Kenneth Cross, the commander of 46 Squadron, was taken by Sunderland flying boat to investigate the practicability of the proposed landing strip. 'I found that the strip was impossible,' recalled Cross. 'It was only 600 yards long with a steep mountain at the end of it.'[24] This was far too dangerous for the Hurricane with its leisurely take-off.

The Gladiators of 263 Squadron had to go in alone. Having landed on the frozen Lake Lesjaskog near Aandalsnes, they were an easy target for the Luftwaffe. Within a week of their arrival, every single one of them had been destroyed or rendered unserviceable, an annihilation that helped to accelerate the British army's withdrawal from central Norway. It was obvious that the Gladiator was ill-suited for this campaign. The RAF had not, however, abandoned the idea of using the Hurricane in Norway. A new plan was drawn up for Kenneth Cross's 46 Squadron to take part in the more northerly battle at Narvik, travelling across the North Sea on the aircraft carrier HMS *Glorious*. Like the first scheme, the second was something of a gamble, given that the Hurricane had never been designed to take off from or land on carriers. Nevertheless, the RAF pressed on and the resultant operation was to become one of the most daring exploits by any Hurricane squadron throughout the entire war.

In advance of the Norwegian adventure, the Hurricanes of 46 Squadron had variable-pitch airscrews fitted, while the men were given arctic clothing. Because it was thought to be impossible to land the planes directly onto the HMS *Glorious*, since the flight deck was regarded as too short, and the Hurricanes had no tailhooks to catch the ship's arrestor cable which acted as a brake on landing, they were flown by the squadron up to RAF Abbotsinch in Scotland (now the site of Glasgow International Airport), where they delicately taxied along a jetty, then they were put on barges before being sailed down the Clyde to the berth of the aircraft carrier. 'I insisted that each pilot should go with his aeroplane which was fortunate because the bargees had no idea that the wings would not take a bit of buffeting on the side of ships,' said Cross.[25] On arrival at the Clydeside, they were hoisted by crane onto the *Glorious*, which set sail the next day for Narvik.

On 26 May the carrier arrived at its destination off the Norwegian coast and the 18 Hurricanes prepared for action. 'I was the first to take off,' recalled Cross, 'which of course had never been done before from a carrier. We did not know if the Hurricane could do it or not. In fact, with our variable-pitch airscrews and the full power of the Merlin engine, they leapt off the deck without any difficulty at all.' The real problem was not taking off but landing. The airstrip that was meant to have been prepared for the Hurricanes was beside a fjord at Skanland, near Narvik, but it was little more than mud covered with coconut matting and wire netting. Cross continued: 'I landed first and as I came to a stop the wheels sank in and the aeroplane tipped gently forward. I bent about two inches of my airscrew. I was furious because it was apparent that the airstrip was unfit for landing and by this time all eighteen aircraft from 56 squadron were in the air.' The nearest airfield was at Bardufoss north of Narvik, almost 70 miles away. Seething with anger, Cross approached the reserve officer in charge 'and let him have it. Such was the strain of the times up there, with 24 hours of daylight and no respite from enemy aircraft, that the poor man burst into tears.' A successful landing, however, was made by the next plane, flown by Richard Earp, who had seen Cross's Hurricane end up on its nose. 'I thought to myself, "Oh Good Lord, what is going to happen to me now?" But I just did a normal landing.'[26] The third Hurricane pilot had an even worse experience than Cross's, digging right into the ground and then performing a complete somersault. That was enough for the commander. He climbed back into his plane, switched on his radio/telephone and ordered the rest of the squadron to fly to Bardufoss. 'It was a tribute to their ability and training that all the remaining aircraft, with very inferior maps, found their way there and landed,' said Cross, who followed the next day once his aircraft had been repaired.

The conditions at the new station were basic. 'It wasn't much of a place. There were no buildings there. We had one tent for six of us and all I had was a groundsheet and two blankets. The first bath I had out there was in a puddle of melted snow. You couldn't sleep anyway because it was daylight all the time up there. And it was terribly bloody cold,' said Richard Earp.[27] Despite the hardships of pilots, the Hurricanes proved highly effective in the air, providing welcome protection for the Allied troops and Royal Navy ships as they fought to drive the Germans out of Narvik. On 28 May, within forty-eight hours of the planes' arrival, the port had been captured. One naval officer, Captain Donald Macintyre, wrote of the gratitude felt toward the fighters: 'Anxious eyes, red-rimmed from day after day of scanning skies for enemy aircraft, saw with incredulous relief the patrol of Hurricanes circling overhead. Cheers, not unmixed with ribaldry, rose from ships' companies which had prayed so long, so fervently, so vainly for such a sight.'[28] Just as in France, the Luftwaffe quickly came to recognize the Hurricane as a tough opponent. By 2 June, nine German planes had been shot down in the air, while two Dornier flying boats had been destroyed at their moorings.

But the triumph at Narvik was short-lived. By the time the Norwegian port was taken, the Germans were pulverizing the Allies in the west, having started the invasion of France and the Low Countries on 10 May. The British government felt it could no longer sustain land campaigns in two theatres and ordered the evacuation of Norway, a decision that Kenneth Cross regarded as 'a great disappointment. We had captured Narvik and had pushed the Germans up to the Swedish border. In another two weeks, the whole of north Norway would have been ours.' From 3 June, the main task of the Hurricanes was to give cover for the troops to be transferred onto the waiting ships, a job carried out with such success that the Luftwaffe hardly intervened. On the last morning of the evacuation, some pilots from 46 Squadron chased four Heinkel 111 bombers that had been attempting to bomb their airfield. They shot down one of them, the RAF's final victory of the Norwegian campaign, though Cross's own Hurricane was hit in the attack. 'I had been unable to do up my straps because we had been in such a hurry to get to the aeroplanes. I was leaning forward, up against the windscreen, when I was hit by return fire. The back of my oil tank was knocked out and the windscreen shattered.' In retrospect, it was lucky that Cross had been crouched forward, for when he landed he found that a bullet had passed through the back of the seat where his head would normally have been. Altogether, 8 out of the original 18 Hurricanes from 46 Squadron had been lost or damaged beyond repair.

Once the evacuation was complete, Cross was told by his RAF superior, Group Captain Maurice Moore, that he could either destroy the remaining ten Hurricanes at Bardufoss or fly them up to an airfield in the extreme north of Norway, where they could be dismantled and then picked up later by a tramp steamer. Demonstrating the spirit that made him such a resolute leader, Cross declined both alternatives. To destroy ten Hurricanes wilfully was absurd, he believed, when the RAF so badly needed fighters on the western front, while the second idea was just impracticable, for there was no guarantee that a ship could be sent to retrieve the men and machines. He then made a bold suggestion to Moore: 'Couldn't we make an attempt to land back on the *Glorious*?' Moore told him that calculations done by the experts at the Royal Aircraft Establishment had indicated that the short length of the aircraft carrier's flight deck made any such attempt impossible. Using full brakes to compensate would only tip the aircraft over, he warned. Cross refused to be dissuaded. 'I believe we can do it. We could put a sandbag in the last bay of the fuselage to keep the tail down, which means that we can use full brakes.' Moore relented, giving Cross permission to try out his radical plan. The skipper of the *Glorious* was informed and agreed to co-operate. Cross decided to split the Hurricanes into two groups. The first, led by Cross's most experienced flight commander, Patrick Jameson, would comprise three aircraft. If they landed successfully, Jameson would send a radio signal back to Cross and the second group of seven Hurricanes, led by Cross himself, would follow.

In the early evening Jameson and his two comrades took off. After an hour's flight they reached HMS *Glorious*. Throttling back and flying just above stalling speed, Jameson went in first. The tail, weighed down by the sandbag, hardly bounced and he brought the Hurricane easily to a halt. The next two planes also landed without any trouble. The radio operator on the *Glorious* immediately tried to convey the news of the success to Cross but, amidst the high mountains by the fjords, the signal never reached him. Cross kept waiting through the night until 3 a.m., when he decided to take off with the remainder of the squadron. 'It was a very welcoming sight when we saw the blinking light which those carriers always had, but I didn't know then whether Jameson and the others had been successful or not. I did the first landing and it turned out to be, in point of fact, a relatively simple operation. My Hurricane stopped a little more than two-thirds up the deck. I was standing on the brakes pretty hard all the time.' The other six Hurricanes came down successfully, then all the men were given cocoa and shown to their bunks. 'The fact that we'd had no sleep for 24 hours caught up with us. Up until that moment, nobody felt the least bit fatigued when they were doing this op. Once it was over we were all exhausted and fell into the bunks.'[29]

After waking in the mid-afternoon, most of the pilots were having tea in the wardroom when suddenly the ship's tannoy blared out: 'Action Stations.' Cross assumed it was just a practice. He was tragically mistaken. HMS *Glorious* had been discovered by two deadly German battlecruisers, the *Scharnhorst* and the *Gneisneau*. Long-range salvoes tore into the carrier, setting her on fire and exploding holes in the side. Within less than two hours, with the *Glorious* listing badly, the order was given to abandon ship. Wearing their Mae West lifejackets (named after the well-endowed Hollywood actress), Cross and Jameson jumped into the sea and managed to reach a life raft.

The other eight pilots went down with the ship or were drowned in the freezing Norwegian waters. Even within the life raft, Cross's fellow survivors gradually began to die from the bone-chilling cold. It was not until three days later that the float was picked up by a Norwegian tramp steamer, Cross and Jameson being among the few men still alive. Their limbs swollen and blue from a mixture of frost-bite and trenchfoot, they were gently pulled on board and taken to the Faroe Islands. There they spent some days in hospital before returning to Britain for a long, often painful recuperation. Jameson, awarded the Distinguished Flying Cross for bravery at Narvik, recovered enough to fight in the Battle of Britain in the months ahead. Cross was given Norway's highest military decoration, the Krigskorset med Sverd (War Cross with Sword) and went on to command Hurricanes in the Middle East between 1941 and 1943.

While 46 Squadron was fighting valiantly in Narvik, other Hurricane units were facing an even sterner test on the western front. On 10 May 1940, a month after the attack on Norway, Hitler launched his invasion of the Low Countries and France, smashing through the Allied defences in a lightning attack. 'Suddenly there was a terrific "crump-crump-crump" which seemed to shake the tent,' recalled Roland Beamont, whose 87 Squadron was stationed at Senon in France near the Maginot line on that epochal morning. 'A further series of explosions sent the lamp swinging on the tent pole and a chatter of machine guns denoted that something was really going on. I got up and found a group of brilliant pyjama-clad pilots standing in the clearing, looking up at a formation of Huns through the gaps in the green spring canopy.'[30] Back in England, Donald 'Dimsie' Stones of 32 Squadron was lying in bed when his Flight Commander Bob Edwards burst into his room. 'Out you get, Dimsie – the balloon has gone up! We're off to France!' After getting up, Stones 'spent the morning bubbling with excitement as I packed for the long absence which we all expected'.[31]

Turmoil rather than excitement was a key feature of the political world on that morning, as Prime Minister Neville Chamberlain was forced to resign after the humiliation of the debate about Norway in the House of Commons over the previous two nights, when a large number of his own followers rebelled against his failing leadership.

His successor Winston Churchill formed a coalition government, with the Liberal Party leader, Sir Archibald Sinclair, taking over as the Secretary of State for Air. Eloquent, high-minded, but lacking in authority, Sinclair had served under Churchill in the Royal Scots Fusiliers during the First World War and had remained an admiring, some might say acquiescent, friend ever since. For the RAF the other key appointment in the new administration was an unorthodox one. Lord Beaverbrook, Canadian press tycoon and political maverick, took on the post of Minister of Aircraft Production, focusing all his explosive energies on increasing the output of fighter aircraft. It was a cause close to his own heart, for his son Max Aitken was a Hurricane pilot with 601 Squadron, now engaged in the Battle of France.

Immediately the German invasion of France began, the British government rushed out Hurricane reinforcements to the British air forces in France, now under the command of Air Marshal Arthur Barratt. The four squadrons in the Air Component of the British Expeditionary Force were joined by three more: 3, 79 and 504 Squadrons. Another Hurricane squadron, 501, was dispatched to strengthen the Advanced Air Striking Force, fighting behind the Maginot line further south. At the outset of the Battle of France, the RAF leaders tried to sound upbeat. 'I have never seen squadrons so confident of success, so insensible to fatigue and so appreciative of their own aircraft,' proclaimed the commander of the Air Component, Group Captain P. F. Fullard.[32] It was certainly true that many of the young Hurricane pilots were enthusiastic about the prospect of going into combat for the first time.

Ken Lee of 501 Squadron was in action almost from the moment that his unit arrived at Betheniville, near Reims. Leading a patrol from the base, Lee soon saw a large formation of Heinkel 111s: 'I was very excited about seeing them at long last after practising all these attacks for years. But I couldn't get up close enough quick enough. We'd been waiting and waiting and practising and at long last they were there.' The Hurricanes of 501 Squadron had adopted the policy of maintaining radio silence on patrol, so as not to alert the Germans to their presence. Having sighted the Heinkels, Lee alerted the rest of the squadron by waggling his wings before accelerating in pursuit of one of the bombers. Soon he had the German plane in his sights. He lowered his seat to give himself as much protection as he could from the Heinkel's rear guns, then set his own gun button to fire: 'When you fire you don't really hear anything. The aircraft shudders and you can actually notice a check in the engine speed. If you are lucky enough to knock bits off the enemy, then of course you know how well you're doing. Otherwise you want to see glycol or petrol coming out. You're after something to show that you've caused damage.'[33] On this opening day, Lee was dissatisfied that he was not able to press home his attack: 'The one that I really concentrated on started smoking from its left engine and pulling over, down to the left, but I'd fired bursts that were far too long. I had no more ammunition left. The only thing to do was to go back and refuel. No use hanging around.'

On landing, Lee found a tremendous sense of achievement running through the rest of the squadron at this successful encounter. 'I can't stress enough that we had been playing at war up to that point. I had been since January 1939 and it was now May 1940. I had done nothing but prepare for this for over a year. At long last we got them and we got away virtually unscathed. We were elated.'[34] The same exuberant spirit was reflected in a letter that Canadian pilot T. G. Pace sent to his girlfriend in Montreal, describing his efforts on that first day. 'We saw 35 Heinkels bombing a town. We waded straight in and then they saw us. Boy, oh boy, did they run? I picked out one and gave him three short bursts and down he went in flames. I saw him crash and believe me it was a satisfying sight when I think what they've been doing lately. When I landed I gave my crew the thumbs up and you should have seen them cheering and dancing. I felt glad that I didn't let them down.'[35] By the end of 10 May, the Hurricanes in France had been credited by RAF Intelligence with 49 German bombers and fighters destroyed or damaged, for the loss of 15 planes, though it later turned out that the pilots, understandably in the heat of battle, had exaggerated the amount of damage they had inflicted.

After this invigorating start, the grim reality of the conflict set in. The truth was that for all the effectiveness of the Hurricane and the bravery of the pilots, the RAF in France could do little to halt the German advance. The squadrons were grossly outnumbered, their facilities inadequate, their experience limited. There was neither radar nor any proper ground organization. Co-ordination with France's air force, L'Armée de l'Air, was woeful, partly because of the defeatist mentality that prevailed among most of the French commanders and politicians. With the odds so overwhelmingly stacked against them, the Hurricane crews quickly found that the Battle of France had turned into a nightmare of constant danger, soaring losses and draining fatigue. 'To give you an idea of the numbers we were up against,' said Dennis David of 87 Squadron, 'six of us ran into 40 Ju 87s which were dive-bombing a hospital. We shot down 14 of them and on our way back to our base, having dispersed the raid, I saw another 150 going on the same target. It was not a feeling of loss but a feeling of helplessness. How can you cope with those numbers? I remember that very clearly.'[36] Peter Down was based at Vitry, south of Calais with 56 Squadron. 'We were continually attacked and were hopelessly outnumbered. There was no organization, nothing. I don't know where the French air force was. There was one telephone that went through the local exchange and every time you were asked to take off there would be a swarm of Me 109s over the top of the aerodrome. We felt that the French were not being of any assistance at all. We were on duty day and night. We could not get much sleep, except from ten to about three in the morning, lying on boards in this hut.'[37]

Inexperience was another problem for the Hurricane squadrons, unlike the German fighter units that had fought in Poland and Spain. When 607 Squadron was converted from Gladiators to Hurricanes at the beginning of April 1940, for instance, Peter Parrott was the only pilot who had previously flown a Hurricane. 'So the squadron had only a bare four weeks with the Hurricane before we were embroiled in the most disorganized, chaotic week or ten days of action. Few, if any, of our pilots had sufficient experience on this type to be classed as operational.'[38] When Norman Hancock of 1 Squadron was posted to Boos near Rouen in May 1940, he had never flown a Hurricane, having previously been flying Spitfires in England. 'I was "shown the tits" as we said in the service, then I was given about an hour's local flying in a Hurricane. I found it a very different plane from the Spitfire but a comfortable one. On my very first patrol, a German ack-ack gun put some portion of a shell through my starboard wing without causing any damage. That was the first time someone had been intent on destroying my aeroplane and me. It was real war at last.'

Hancock's inexperience showed in his first aerial combat, when he took off from Boos to engage a large formation of Me 109s and Heinkel 111s:

> I did not see any German fighters but it did not really matter. The rear gunner of the He 111 was a damn sight better shot than I was. He hit me to such good effect that I lost my airspeed indicator and had trouble with my elevators. I was highly inexperienced and highly frightened. When I got back to Boos I had to have two attempts at landing because I could not judge the speed. I could either hit a hangar or a parked Blenheim. I hit the Blenheim and cut it in half. Thank goodness there was no one in it. My plane was bent but I wasn't. My CO came hurrying out, using a few choice words, then took me in a truck to the air shelter as the Germans had just started bombing the airfield.[39]

The RAF losses sustained in the opening days of the campaign in France were brutal. By 12 May, 96 Hurricanes had been lost, while the original bomber force of 135 planes, mainly Bristol Blenheims and aging Fairey Battles had almost been halved. Some of the encounters against the Luftwaffe had been almost suicidal, as when a force of Battles, escorted by Hurricanes, was sent on successive missions to bomb bridges spanning the Albert Canal on the River Meuse. Over two days, 80 per cent of the Battles were lost. Heavily outnumbered by the German fighters, the Hurricanes could provide little protection as the vulnerable bombers flew to their doom. Nor did the small group of Hurricanes in the Belgian air force fare any better against the might of the Luftwaffe. Imbued with feelings of superiority, Adolf Galland, the leading German fighter pilot, was scathing about the Hurricane's performance in Belgium. In his memoirs, he recalled: 'The Belgians for the most part flew antiquated Hurricanes, in which even more experienced pilots could have done little against our Me 109. We outstripped them in speed, in rate of climb, in armament.'[40]

The crucial German breakthrough on the Franco-Belgian border at Sedan, which signalled the beginning of the end for the French, was the scene of more aerial destruction. On 14 May, Prosser Hanks of 1 Squadron had just shot down an Me 109 with a skilful deflection burst and had gone into a climb when 'my aeroplane was hit by some other bugger behind me and I was suddenly drenched in hot glycol. I didn't have my goggles down and the bloody stuff completely blinded me. I didn't know where I was and somehow got into a spin. I could see damn all and the cockpit was getting bloody hot, so I undid the straps and opened the hood to get out, but I couldn't. Every time I tried I was pressed back. I started to scream then, but I stopped screaming and somehow or other I got out.'[41] This was the worst day that the RAF had yet suffered during the Battle of France. A total of 27 Hurricanes were shot down, most of them by Me 109s, and 17 pilots were killed. Squadron Leader T. G. Pace was one of those who almost died when his section tackled a group of 15 Heinkel 111s, as he explained in a letter to his girlfriend:

I got one bloke beautifully in the sights and gave him the works. He was just beginning to smoke nicely when something hit me eight times, an awful smash. One of their Heinkels had been potting at me, so I had to try and shoot him but the engine was faltering badly and then thick black smoke started pouring from under the dashboard. Mixed with it, all acrid, was the smell of glycol. I had my main oil pipe cut and a couple of 20 mm shells in the radiator. Then there were two more bangs and the wireless disappeared. I thought that the best thing to do was to force land and save the machine, or at least some of it. I couldn't see any flames so I never thought of using my parachute. I could just see through the Perspex on the left-hand side and during my various coughs and splutters, I picked a field. Just crossing the boundary, I hit a tree with my right wing. I couldn't see it owing to the smoke. There was a terrific crash, then I ducked inside the cockpit. As I hit the ground there was another crash and a sound of rending metal and a slithering sound. Then there was a terrific pop and the whole thing was a mass of flame. The sliding hood, which I had so carefully opened, shut and jammed, the gravity tank behind the dashboard exploded and spilt burning petrol on my right thigh. I tried to open the hood but couldn't. The temperature was getting a bit warm and I tried again and I succeeded in getting it open a little. I remember telling myself to keep cool, seems funny, doesn't it? I heaved at the hood and it came open enough for me to get out halfway. Then my parachute caught on the seat and I hiked myself out and landed on my right shoulder in the port petrol tank which was burning beautifully. I picked myself up after rolling off the wing onto the ground. How I did it I don't know but I walked half a mile and then came across an army motorcycle.[42]

Having been taken to hospital and then transferred to England, Pace underwent extensive plastic surgery on his burnt face and legs.

The RAF's losses meant that more reinforcements were urgently required. On 13 May another 32 Hurricanes, the equivalent of two full squadrons, were sent across the Channel. But the head of Fighter Command, Sir Hugh Dowding, who had never had any faith in the French campaign, was now alarmed at the continuing drain of his resources. As long ago as September 1939 he had warned prophetically that, in sending fighter support to the BEF (British Expeditionary Force) and the AASF (Advanced Air Striking Force), the government 'had opened a tap through which will run the total Hurricane output'.[43] The minimum number of fighter squadrons needed to defend Britain, he believed, was 52, yet the continuing dispatch of Hurricanes to the continent meant that there were now only 36. The time had come to make a stand against any more pointless waste of planes in a fight that even the French Prime Minister Paul Reynaud had admitted was all but lost. Reynaud had made an agonized phone call to Churchill at 7.30 on the morning of 15 May, telling him: 'We are beaten.'[44] The only hope, said the French leader, lay in the provision of more fighters. Churchill, who loved France as much as he loathed defeatism, was sympathetic and promised to visit Paris shortly. In contrast, Dowding was appalled at the idea of losing more of his precious fighters and argued lucidly against Reynaud's request at meetings of both the Chiefs of Staff and the full War Cabinet. As a result of his intervention, any immediate decision on Hurricane reinforcements for France was postponed until the following day, 16 May.

To emphasize his message, Dowding composed a memorandum that night for the Air Ministry, setting out the case for resisting any further dilution of his forces. It rightly became a famous document not just for the power of its simple prose but also the foresight it showed about the central role that the Hurricanes would play in the coming months. He opened by warning of the real possibility of defeat in France, which would leave the entire continent dominated by Germany. There was no doubt, he said, that in such circumstances Britain should fight on, but the country's ability to do so depended on its air defences. 'I must point out that within the last few days the equivalent of ten squadrons have been sent to France, that the Hurricane squadrons in this country have been seriously depleted.' He therefore urged the government to agree an absolute minimum strength for Fighter Command, beyond which 'not one fighter will be sent across the Channel'. Dowding concluded: 'I believe that if an adequate fighter force is kept in this country, if the Fleet remains in being and if Home Forces are suitably organized to resist invasion, we should be able to carry on the war single-handed for some time, if not indefinitely. But if the Home Defence Force is drained away in desperate attempts to remedy the situation in France, defeat in France will involve the final, complete and irremediable defeat of this country.'[45]

Yet, just as Dowding had feared, some of the politicians still clung to the notion that France might be saved with the assistance of the Hurricane. At a Cabinet meeting on 16 May, Churchill again stressed the need to respond to Reynaud's 'urgent appeal'. Churchill admitted that to send more Hurricanes from Britain 'at a time when we are most likely to be attacked ourselves' was taking 'a very grave risk', but it seemed 'essential to bolster up the French'.[46] He suggested that some of the Hurricanes could be transferred from naval protection duties at Scapa Flow in Scotland. Powerful voices were raised against his proposal. The new Air Secretary, Sir Archibald Sinclair, argued that the French were not making 'full use' of their own fighter aircraft, adding that any agreement to send more Hurricanes would be 'contrary to the advice' of Dowding, 'who was responsible for the defence of this country'. The First Sea Lord, Sir Dudley Pound, believed that the air defences at Scapa Flow had already reached 'the absolute minimum'. But Sir Cyril Newall, the Chief of the Air Staff, gave a gloomy prognosis from Air Marshal Arthur Barratt, the RAF commander in France, who emphasized the dire position of the current Hurricane squadrons and the need for more support. 'Air Marshal Barratt had reported that our fighter pilots were very tired;

they had to deal all the previous day with waves of 40 bombers every hour, heavily escorted by fighters. Squadrons of fighters were the proper counter to this form of attack but they had to operate with flights of three or five, always in great numerical inferiority. Every pilot was carrying out four or five sorties a day. The French appeared to be making little resistance on the ground.' On the basis of this information, Newall recommended 'that eight flights, the equivalent of four fighter squadrons, should be sent immediately in response to the request from Paris'.[47] Newall's recommendation was agreed, much to Dowding's regret.

Yet even this new dispatch of planes to the aid of France was not enough. Late that afternoon Churchill flew to Paris in a De Havilland twin-engined Flamingo, escorted by Hurricanes of 601 Squadron, for a meeting with the French government and military leaders. There he found a mood of despondency mixed with almost childlike faith in the Hurricane. The head of the French armed forces, General Maurice Gamelin, begged Churchill for more fighters, though in making his request, he revealed how detached he had become from military realities, for he claimed that the planes were vitally needed to stop the German tanks. The idea that the Hurricane, with its .303 calibre guns, could destroy the armour plating of a tank was ludicrous. It was not until two years later that a tank-busting version of the plane, armed with cannons rather than machine guns, went into action. The absurdity of Gamelin's stance could be seen in the recollections of the renowned Hurricane pilot J. H. 'Ginger' Lacey of 501 Squadron, who actually tried to strafe German tanks during the Battle of France. 'It was like shooting at elephants with a pea-shooter. The tank commanders did not even pay us the compliment of closing their turrets. They just ducked their heads as we came over and stuck them out again as soon as we'd gone past. The tanks rolled on completely undamaged.'[48] Nevertheless, despite its fantastical element, Gamelin's plea moved Churchill so much that he immediately sent a telegram to London, asking the War Cabinet to agree the dispatch of six more Hurricane squadrons. Such a move, he said, would galvanize the 'bravery and strength' of the French military. 'It would not be good historically if their requests were denied and their ruin resulted.'[49] The War Cabinet met that night at 11 p.m. to discuss

Churchill's telegram. Despite severe reservations, they agreed to the proposal, Neville Chamberlain, now Lord President of the Council, taking the lead. The Cabinet members, he said, knew that the battle 'might be decisive for France. They felt that they must respond to the Prime Minister's courageous leadership and had decided that everything possible must be done to give the French a chance to rally.'[50] When this news was communicated back to Paris, Churchill said that the decision had 'heartened' the French government 'to a very considerable degree'.[51] Yet the real effect of this further dispatch was mitigated by a clever stratagem from Sir Cyril Newall. He argued that because the French airfields were so poor and the facilities so limited, it would be better to operate the six additional Hurricane squadrons from England, sending them over to France at dawn and having them return to their English stations at dusk. In this way, some aid was provided to France but the strength of the home force was maintained, to the partial relief of Dowding, who was more anxious than ever about the drain on his Hurricane stock.

With a characteristic melodramatic flourish, Churchill called the War Cabinet's move 'the gravest decision that a British Cabinet ever had to take'.[52] The frenzied political importance attached to a few Hurricane squadrons might now seem ridiculously overblown. Yet the Cabinet's belief in the Hurricane's decisive influence, both in terms of morale and operations, was a reflection of the superb reputation that Sydney Camm's fighter had built up over the previous four years. More importantly, as the poetic instinct within Churchill understood, the plane was really a metaphor to describe the Allies' yearning, however desperate, to resist the German onslaught. But by 17 May, symbols of hope were not enough. The Wehrmacht, backed by the devastating power of the Luftwaffe, continued to penetrate deep into France, the French army now in headlong retreat. The Hurricane pilots still fought heroically, but they were increasingly hampered by their tiredness and the absence of any strategy or organization. On the sixth night of battle, 16 May, Gerald Edge of 605 Squadron passed out completely after landing at his base. 'I switched off the engine and the petrol. The engine was still moving. A member of the ground crew said, "Are you all right, sir? We've got a stretcher for you." They thought I had been wounded but I had just gone to sleep.'[53] The pilots sent over as reinforcements were astonished at the chaos into which the battle had descended. When Fred Rosier, commander of 229 Squadron, flew to Vitry near Arras on 16 May, he found that the senior RAF officer at the station had not arranged any billets for his men. 'The Wing Commander said he was frightfully sorry but the events over the last few days had been so tremendously hectic that they were tired out and he'd forgotten all about us. I was pretty angry as you can imagine.' Rosier then sent two of his pilots into the local village to requisition some rooms, if necessary by brandishing their revolvers. Eventually, at eleven o'clock at night, accommodation was found.

But Rosier's men were up at three the next morning and were soon scrambled, the first of five sorties they carried out that day. One mission in particular reinforced Rosier's low opinion of the French:

> There were six of us and there must have been forty to fifty Me 109s. The sky seemed full of them. It really was the most awful battle. I have no idea what victories I had but I got some bullets which went through the side of the cockpit and into the instrument panel. I landed at an airfield near Lille. It was just chaos. At Lille I found the French there with new fighters and they were not flying. They were quite friendly but I was livid with rage. They were not participating in the battle at all. The whole thing was a pretty good shambles.[54]

Pete Brothers of 32 Squadron shared this sense of frustration: 'The French air force was wholly unhelpful. I think they were demoralised. Their aircraft were totally outclassed and they had suffered so heavily in the First Word War that they were almost disinterested.'[55] Based at Biggin Hill, 32 Squadron was one of the six that operated in France during the day before returning to England at night, in fulfilment of the government's recommendation. But Brothers recalled that the arrangement only added to the confusion:

> We would take off from Biggin Hill half an hour before first light, land at primitive French bases during the day, then get back to Biggin after dark. Communications were appalling and we could not get instructions from anybody. We could not make contact with the air headquarters to find out what they wanted us to do. We were having to refuel our own planes from jerry cans and having to start them

Rugged and resilient, the Hawker Hurricane fought right through the Second World War, from the first day to the last. 'It literally saved the country,' said the great test pilot Eric 'Winkle' Brown

The Hurricane's predecessor, the elegant Hawker Fury biplane, mainstay of the RAF's fighter force in the early 1930s

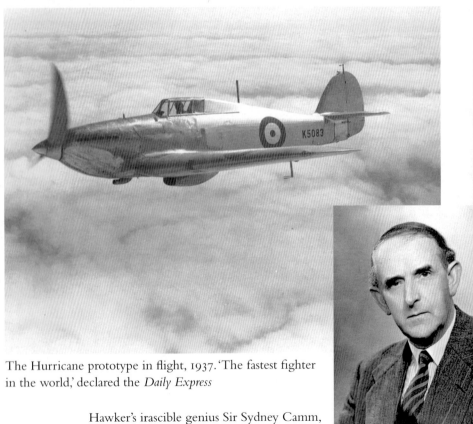

The Hurricane prototype in flight, 1937. 'The fastest fighter in the world,' declared the *Daily Express*

Hawker's irascible genius Sir Sydney Camm, the designer of the Hurricane

In December 1937, 111 Squadron, based at Northolt in Middlesex, became the first RAF unit to be equipped with the new monoplane fighter

Pilots of 87 Squadron are scrambled at their base near Lille in northern France, the first theatre in which the Hurricane saw sustained action

The finest ace of the RAF's campaign in France, Edgar 'Cobber' Kain. He was credited with the destruction of sixteen enemy aircraft and damage to one other

RAF armourers refilling a Hurricane's ammunition belts in northern France. Conditions in this theatre were primitive. 'No other fighter before or since would have put up with the treatment that the Hurricane endured,' said one crewman

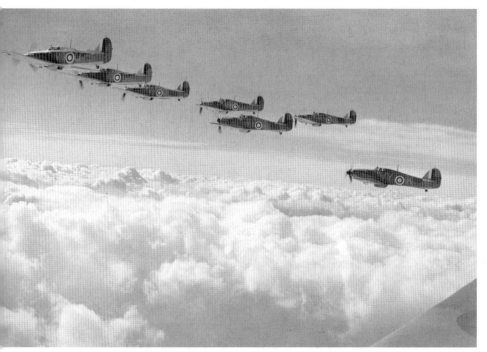

A formation of Hurricane Mark Is of 85 Squadron, led by Squadron Leader Peter Townsend, flying on patrol during the Battle of Britain. 'The Hurricane was our faithful charger and we felt supremely sure of it,' said Townsend

A Hurricane is urgently refuelled while the pilot leaves his cockpit, August 1940. 'We were sometimes going up five times a day. We had our backs against the wall,' said one pilot, recalling the pressures of the Battle of Britain

The condensation trails left by British and German planes after a dogfight, September 1940

Below: Hurricane pilots scrambled during the Battle of Britain. 'From all directions came the splutter and roar of Merlins leaping into life,' recalled one pilot

Hurricane pilots watch their colleagues taking off, late 1940

Keith Park, commander of No. 11 Group, which bore the brunt of the fighting during the Battle of Britain. His visits to the airfields in his own Hurricane were a source of inspiration to his men

Below: Sir Hugh Dowding (*left*), the head of Fighter Command, alongside the renowned legless pilot Douglas Bader (*centre*). Towards the end of the battle, they clashed over the direction of fighter strategy

Bob Stanford Tuck in the cockpit of his Hurricane. He embodied the determined spirit of Fighter Command

Possibly the greatest RAF ace of the war, Marmaduke 'Pat' Pattle, who is estimated to have shot down between thirty-four and fifty aircraft, most of them during campaigns in the Balkans, before his death in April 1941

James 'Ginger' Lacey, the highest scoring RAF ace of the Battle of Britain ourselves. We were starting these Hurricanes on handles, which meant that I would get into my aircraft and two of the chaps would wind the handles and start it and we would then leave it idling. I would get out and help start his. So it went along until we had got all twelve going. It was a scene of general chaos.[56]

The atmosphere of doom was worsened by the sight of the refugees pouring along the roads from north-eastern France in horsecarts, on bicycles or on foot, laden down with the only possessions they could carry. What made this exodus from their homes all the more pitiful was the willingness of the Germans to swoop down and strafe the long columns of innocent civilians. 'To know that the Germans were strafing these people was a double shock. We were actually scrambled to take them on,' said Harold Bird-Wilson of 17 Squadron, recalling a mission on 18 May. 'We did not find them but we found a Dornier on reconnaissance, escorted by two Me 110s. We ploughed into them and shot all three down. I had the pleasure of shooting at the Dornier and it went down in flames.'[57] Many Hurricane pilots had to endure far more one-sided combat, overwhelmed by German numbers and the lack of ground support. Fred Rosier was hit by an Me 109 in one combat and found himself jammed in a burning plane when his hood failed to open. 'I remember sinking back and thinking, "Well, that's that."' Suddenly, as his Hurricane plunged through the sky, the canopy burst open and Rosier found himself falling towards the ground. 'I suppose I instinctively pulled the ripcord. I saw that my trousers were on fire and I remember the skin leaving my hands as I tried to put the flames out.' He passed out before he landed, was taken by his French rescuers to a field hospital near Arras and was then transported to England.[58]

Another victim of fire was Brian Young of 615 Squadron, whose Hurricane was riddled with cannon shells from an attacking Me 109. 'The gravity tank was right over your knees, more or less. We did not have an asbestos bulkhead between the tank and the cockpit. It really went up very fiercely in my face and I had to get out. I saw the 109 go past as I bailed out, and I remembered to dive forward as I left so I did not hit the tailplane. I put my hand on the ripcord – I was fairly badly burnt – dropped into a cloud, then opened the parachute once

I was below it.' The parachute opened safely. After landing, Young felt machine-gun fire near his feet and a hand grenade was lobbed in his direction, causing a 'terrific explosion'. At first he thought his assailants were Germans, but then he heard English voices. Soon the British soldiers had bayonets pointing right at his nose. 'Most of my clothes had been burnt off. We had actually been down to Paris the weekend before, where we had seen girls in a show wearing nothing but boots. Well, that's rather what I looked like. So I said rather hysterically: "What the bloody hell do you think I am? A Hun dressed up as a chorus girl?"' Suffering from third-degree burns, a large wound in his side, a bullet in one arm and two in one leg, Young was taken to an emergency casualty station, where he embarked on a long, often painful recovery.[59]

Throughout the deepening crisis of the Battle of France, the effectiveness of the Hurricane remained a source of reassurance, especially because of its toughness. 'During this period I became more and more impressed by the robust qualities of the Hurricane,' said pilot Jack Rose of 32 Squadron. 'I think that some of the emergency repairs that were carried out by the maintenance crews during those few days in France would have made Sydney Camm's hair stand on end, but they worked.' On 19 May, Rose's plane was badly hit by an Me 109, but even with a bullet-riddled airframe and glycol and petrol spewing out of the Hurricane, he was able to make a successful wheels-down landing. 'When I checked the damage it seemed almost impossible that so many hits could have been registered without one passing down the centre of the fuselage and through the back of my unprotected seat. A shell from the nose cannon of the 109 had torn a gaping hole in the radiator just below me, while another had removed much of the starboard aileron. Bullets had pierced both port and starboard main petrol tanks in several places and there were a number of holes in the fuselage and wings elsewhere.'[60]

On 20 May, Derek Ward of 87 Squadron was asked to fly an operationally unserviceable Hurricane from Merville, near Lille, to RAF Debden in Essex. The plane had no gunsight and no functional instruments except the compass and the oil and petrol gauges. Soon after take-off, Ward saw that the engine was overheating, yet he was still able to attack two Dornier bombers by 'pointing my guns in the general direction of the enemy aircraft'.[61] After this confrontation, he was forced to land at Abbeville, near Amiens, to check the engine. As he taxied into the aerodrome, he found that he had a puncture in the starboard-wing tank, from which petrol was spraying out. Showing the resourcefulness so typical of the fighter crews, he 'stuck a bayonet several times into the starboard tank to empty it', then persuaded two airmen to fill the port tank. Ward got airborne again and made it back to England, even giving a burst on the way to a passing Me 109 that was escorting some German bombers. On another occasion, ground crews used some unorthodox improvisation to get a damaged Hurricane airborne. The plane took off from Merville, recalled Louis Strange of 24 Squadron, 'with a good many bullet holes in it, the variable-pitch airscrew tied to fine pitch with a bit of copper wire and a piece of telephone cable back to the cockpit to enable the pilot to change pitch by breaking the copper wire with a good tug'.[62]

But no amount of innovation could hide the reality that the air campaign had failed in its objective to resist Germany. After less than two weeks of fighting, Holland, Belgium and France were all within the Reich's grasp. It was impossible for even the most courageous pilots to avoid a feeling of despondency as the Luftwaffe gained superiority through sheer weight of numbers. Paul Richey, who had been serving with such distinction in France since September 1939, later wrote how the pressure had infected the whole of his 1 Squadron. 'Our nerves were getting somewhat frayed and we were jumpy and morose. Few of the boys smiled now – we were no longer the merry band of days gone by.' Richey himself had been shot down in a twisting, turning dogfight over Sedan on 15 May:

> I was flying down head-on at a 110 which was climbing up to me. We both fired – and I thought I had left it too late and we would collide. I pushed the stick forward violently. There was a stunning explosion right in front of me. For an instant my mind went blank. My aircraft seemed to be falling, limp on the controls. Then, as black smoke poured out of the nose and enveloped the hood, and a hot blast and a flicker of reflected flame crept into the dark cockpit, I said, 'Come on – out you go!', pulled the pin out of my harness, wrenched open the hood and hauled myself head first out to the right.

Richey landed successfully, but was haunted for days afterwards by the incident, becoming jumpy and snappy, often on the verge of tears. His sleep was haunted by terrible nightmares of being shot down: 'I shall never forget how I clung to my bed-rail in a dead funk.'[63]

The tide had turned decisively against the RAF. On Saturday 18 May 1940, at least 33 Hurricanes were shot down or crash-landed in France as a result of combat, with seven of their pilots killed. The Luftwaffe also lost 46 planes that day, but with their overwhelmingly superior numbers they could easily sustain such damage. The RAF could not. The next day, Sunday 19 May, another 35 Hurricanes were lost. By now, with the French in headlong retreat, the Germans had almost reached the Channel around Calais. From Monday 20 May, the few Hurricanes that were left in the Air Component of the British Expeditionary Force began to be pulled back to England, an operation that was completed the following day. Dowding's despair at the futility of sending more Hurricanes across the Channel had largely been justified. Just three squadrons of the Advanced Air Striking Force remained further south around Paris. Altogether, after the ten days' fighting so far, of the 261 Hurricanes in the Air Component, 195 were now out of action: 75 of them had been shot down and 120 rendered unserviceable through damage. Just 66 Hurricanes had returned to Britain. Yet the sacrifices had not entirely been in vain. The Luftwaffe admitted that 299 of its planes had been shot down and 65 seriously damaged. When the two forces were to meet over English soil in a few months, the German losses would be devastatingly higher.

5

'A mad struggle for survival'

———

THE CAMPAIGNS IN Norway and France may have been failures, but they provided invaluable lessons for Fighter Command. One of the most vital was the importance of an effective organization to ensure that the fighters could track the enemy, something that had been badly missing on the western front. 'There was no Intelligence, no early warning,' said Fred Rosier of 229 Squadron. 'Communications were also non-existent so you had no idea when you were going to be attacked. It was as though you were operating blindfolded.'[1] But the position was very different in England. Fighter Command had already developed a sophisticated, robust control system geared towards providing pilots and stations with precisely this sort of information about the enemy's movements. The system was the masterpiece of Sir Hugh Dowding, who, unlike other RAF leaders of the 1930s, had recognized the necessity of building a fighter defence network that exploited the latest technology.

Stubborn and introverted, Dowding was an unlikely revolutionary. He was born in 1882, the son of a schoolmaster from Scotland, and all his life he retained a somewhat Victorian, puritan air, hence his nickname 'Stuffy'. During the First World War, in which he served as a fighter pilot and officer in the Royal Flying Corps, his remoteness was taken by the RFC's commander Hugh Trenchard for a lack of aggressive spirit. 'A dismal jimmy' was one of Trenchard's insults,[2] an opinion shared by Dowding's fellow officer, Duncan Grinnell-Milne: 'He was too reserved and aloof from his juniors; he cared too much for his own job, too little for theirs. He was not a good pilot, seldom flew and had none of that fire which I then believed and later knew to be essential in the leader of a good squadron.'[3] Dowding's introspection was deepened by personal tragedy soon after the First World War, when his young wife Clarice died suddenly, leaving Dowding to bring up their infant son on his own. A lonely widower, he lived for most of the remainder of his RAF career with his sister Muriel, an arrangement that did nothing to counter his natural unsociability. Hugh Ironside, his assistant at Bentley Priory, Fighter Command's headquarters at Stanmore in Middlesex, later recalled that he was a 'very shy' and 'very private chap'. One of Ironside's jobs was to organize occasional sherry parties which Dowding, purely out of a sense of duty, felt that he should host at his official residence. 'It was really gruesome. Nobody wanted to attend because it really was terrible. Stuffy would have one sherry. There was an ancient gramophone on which he would play some ancient tunes. After a time, I found it most difficult to get anyone to come. He had no small talk. He was always thinking about waging war . . . It was difficult to engage him in conversation. It was hard-going unless it was a matter in hand, such as how many guns we should have on our fighters.'[4]

Yet it was Dowding's remorseless concentration on his work that yielded such dramatic results for Fighter Command. He may have been conventional in his manner but he never was in his thinking. During the First World War, he had been an early advocate of radio communication between pilots and ground controllers. It was this technocratic vision, combined with his gift for administration, that helped him rise up the RAF hierarchy in the interwar period. Even Trenchard had the grace to admit: 'I don't often make mistakes about people, but I made one about you.'[5] In the 1930s, first as Air Member for Research and Development, then as head of Fighter Command, he presided over the transformation of the RAF's defences. The drive to introduce fast monoplanes was partly as a result of his influence. Just as significant was his creation of the fighter control organization, which rightly became known as 'the Dowding system'. The key element of the system was radar, or 'radio direction finding' as it was originally called, which enabled the RAF to plot the course of incoming enemy raids.

Radar had first been developed by the brilliant Scottish scientist Robert Watson–Watt, a radio expert at the National Physical Laboratory at Teddington in Middlesex and descendent of the pioneer of steam power, James Watt. In February 1935 Watson-Watt sent the British government a report of his studies into methods of locating aircraft by radio waves. The chairman of the Aeronautical Research Committee, Sir Henry Tizard, was intrigued, as was Dowding. They quickly instructed Watson-Watt to organize a full-scale demonstration to prove his theories. The experiment, held two weeks later held at Daventry, Northamptonshire, was a gratifying success, as the flight of a Handley Page Heyford bomber gave a clear signal to a cathode-ray receiver on the ground. The government now moved quickly. Further experiments were held with bigger equipment at a longer range, while construction began on a chain of coastal radar stations around the south-east of England. By early 1940, 32 of these stations had been constructed, stretching to northern Scotland and Cornwall in the west, each consisting of a 350-foot transmitter aerial mast, a 250-foot receiver mast, and a brick block housing the operators and radar display screens.

Radar was the lynchpin of the Dowding system, but on its own it was not enough. The chain of home radar stations could detect incoming aircraft over the sea, but they could not tell their type nor operate inland. For this information, the RAF relied on the 30,000-strong Royal Observer Corps, whose members kept watch on the skies from a network of 1,000 posts across the country. The observers, 4,000 of whom were women, used binoculars and sextants, simple equipment compared to the radar, but adequate for the task of ascertaining further details of enemy formations. The data from the radar stations and the Royal Observer Corps was continually fed to Bentley Priory at Stanmore, from where it was disseminated to fighter groups and sectors.

The structure of Fighter Command was another reflection of Dowding's organizational flair. The command was geographically divided into four groups, by far the most important of which was 11 Group, which covered London and the south-east of England, the prime target for any German attack. The commander of 11 Group was Keith Park, a tough, sometimes prickly New Zealander who was adored by his men but regarded with suspicion by some of his fellow military chiefs because of his perceived vanity. Throughout his time in charge of 11 Group, Park made regular visits in his own Hurricane to the stations in his group so he could keep personally in touch with the operational front line. Comparing Dowding and Park, Christopher Foxley-Norris, who served with 3 Squadron during the Battle of Britain, had this analysis: 'Dowding was absolutely outstanding, but not in an inspirational way. His leadership was superb in terms of husbanding his resources. He was a sort of father figure and we felt that as long as he had his hand on the tiller, all was going to be well. Keith Park was a far more direct and inspirational man and you did see quite a lot of him. He used to come into the airfields in his Hurricane and he inspired a great deal of confidence.'[6]

The other three Fighter Command groups were 10 Group, under the leadership of the South African Quintin Brand, covering the west of England and south Wales; 12 Group, commanded by Trafford Leigh-Mallory, in charge of the Midlands and East Anglia; and 13 Group, led by Richard Saul, whose command embraced the north of England and Scotland. Brand and Saul were men of instinctive loyalty to their superiors, but Leigh-Mallory, the brother of the famous mountaineer George Mallory, was a more difficult character. Ferociously ambitious with a streak of pomposity, Leigh-Mallory had his own ideas as to how the Luftwaffe should be defeated and became increasingly antipathetic towards both Park and Dowding as the Battle of Britain intensified.

Every Group was then further subdivided into sectors, which usually controlled between two and four squadrons. Each squadron generally had between 12 and 16 aircraft, three fighter squadrons making up a 'wing'. The nerve centre of the Dowding system was Fighter Command's headquarters at Bentley Priory, an elegant eighteenth-century mansion, where a large two-level operations centre had been carved out of the basement and ballroom. Along numerous secure telephone lines, information poured from the radar stations and observers into the Filter Room, where the details were checked and processed before being passed on to the Operations Room nearby. Here the aerial movements were plotted on a large map with counters marked 'F' for friendly, 'H' for hostile or 'X' for unknown, each one colour-coded to show the time it was placed. As the action unfolded, WAAF (Women's Auxiliary Air Force) personnel and airmen, like croupiers in a casino, used long rakes to shift the counters around the map table. On a mezzanine balcony overlooking this scene, Dowding and other senior officers could study the progress of the conflict, the plots giving them a comprehensive visual picture of what was happening in the air. The atmosphere was tense and determined, but never frantic. Throughout any combat, instructions, bulletins and reports were constantly fed to the fighter groups by telephone and teleprinters.

Each Group headquarters had its own Operations Room, as did each sector. Having received instructions from their Group, the sector controllers had the responsibility of giving their squadrons the order to scramble. They stayed in contact with their pilots by radio/telephone once the planes were airborne, using the information from plots to direct the fighters towards the enemy target. Hurricane pilot Ray Holmes of 504 Squadron wrote of how impressed he was by his controller on his very first combat flight over the Moray Firth, having been vectored onto the path of a German bomber at 15,000 feet. 'I marvelled at the accuracy of the radar that had plotted the height and course of this aircraft so exactly, almost bringing us onto a collision course.'[7] Indeed, such was the efficiency of the system, it has been estimated that on occasions Fighter Command achieved enemy interception rates of 80 per cent, while the time taken from detection of the enemy to getting the fighters airborne was an average of just six minutes. For all its complexity, Dowding's structure was so well conceived that it was straightforward to manage, with information flowing freely across the network. When the American military attaché Raymond Lee visited Bentley Priory in 1940, he was almost lost in wonder at what he saw: 'I had no idea that the British could evolve and operate so intricate, so scientific and rapid an organization.'[8]

But even the finest system would have been useless without sufficient fighters. Fortunately, by the summer of 1940, Hurricanes were emerging from the Hawker factories in reassuring numbers. In the first three months of the year 206 planes were produced, in the next three months 421. By the beginning of June 1940 a total of 1,358 Hurricanes had been made. The rate of deliveries from the Gloster factory in Hucclecote, Gloucestershire, so beset with problems in the late 1930s, passed 100 a month at the end of May 1940. As output increased, the plane continued to undergo modifications, some of them inspired by the experiences of fighting in France and Norway. Mirrors were fitted to the top of windscreens to give the pilots a better rearward view, an innovation that was first adopted by 229 Squadron under the leadership of Fred Rosier, as pilot George Johns recalled: 'Most of our Hurricanes did not have rear mirrors. When we were at Northolt, I said to Fred Rosier, who had been shot down over France but had now recovered, "We can buy mirrors at the local garage." Fred agreed. We had a very good flight sergeant then who leapt into his car, went down to the garage and bought them. That afternoon they were screwed into the tops of the canopies. They were invaluable really. They became a standard fitting.'[9] The programme to finish installing De Havilland two-pitch airscrews was accelerated, and from May 1940 all new production Hurricanes were fitted with Rotol constant-speed propellers. The Air Ministry decided that the undersides of all planes should be painted duck-egg blue, abandoning the practice sometimes used in France of having the underneath of one wing black, the other white. 'We stood out like flying chequer-boards,' complained Paul Richey, whose own 1 Squadron independently adopted a blue scheme on seeing that the undersides of the German Me 109s were painted this way.[10]

Richey also claimed that his unit was instrumental in a more important change: the introduction of armour plating at the back of the pilot's seat. It was true that, unlike the RAF's light bombers, the only armour on many of the Hurricanes in France was a thick cowling over the petrol tank, leaving the pilots vulnerable to an attack from astern. According to Richey's account, 1 Squadron asked the government for more protection, but the Air Ministry 'refused our request because the experts maintained that back armour would affect the Hurricane's centre of gravity and lead to flying difficulties'. Richey's squadron commander 'Bull' Halahan was so furious at this rejection that he found a wrecked Fairey Battle bomber, ripped out its armour and had it put in his own plane. In Richey's version of events, Squadron Leader Halahan then had this Hurricane flown by one of his pilots to the Royal Aircraft Establishment at Farnborough, Hampshire, where its ease of handling left the experts 'convinced and back armour was henceforth fitted as standard equipment to RAF fighter aircraft'.[11]

Yet this was hardly the whole story, as the official archives reveal. It was true that the Air Staff had once held out against the installation of back armour. Fascinatingly, the senior officer behind this policy was none other than Dowding himself, for once not displaying his customary wise technical judgement. During a meeting held at Hawker offices on 21 July 1938 to discuss pilot protection in the Hurricane, he argued that 'the modern view on air fighting tactics was to have the fighting aeroplanes protected in front of the pilot as a defence against fire from ahead. The superior speed of the fighter aeroplane would render it less vulnerable to attack from the rear. Armour plate other than in front of the pilot would be too heavy to contemplate to give effective protection.'[12] It was an extraordinary statement, subsequently contradicted by all fighter experience during the war. In fact, the vast majority of kills during the Battle of Britain were made from within fifteen degrees of dead astern. But by mid 1939, months before the war started, the policy had changed, and the Air Ministry decided that an armour plate might be needed for fighters sent on service to the continent, though it would 'have to be detachable because it will not be needed for home defence purposes'.[13] Hawker had soon mocked up such a plate, four millimetres thick, and the design was shown to the Air Ministry. Contrary to Richey's version, the Ministry was quite satisfied, as it stated on 29 August: 'There should be no difficulty in fitting this armour in the service and the design of the plates is extremely simple.' Nor was there any problem with the centre of gravity, which remained 'within accepted limits'.[14]

By September 1939 the mood was shifting in favour of permanent back armour on all Hurricanes. One of the strongest proponents of this change was Sholto Douglas, Assistant Chief of the Air Staff, who demanded that the necessary orders be placed for sufficient rear-armour sets. With words that reflected tactical realities if not faith in the Hurricane, he warned on 25 September: 'It is possible that the Germans may escort their bombers with fighters. The Hurricane is on the slow side, and may conceivably be attacked from the rear in certain circumstances.'[15] Douglas convinced his colleagues. On 20 October the Air Ministry instructed that 'back armour shall be fitted on all Hurricanes.'[16] The order, however, came too late to apply to all the Hurricanes in France.

Protection from enemy bullets was one matter; protection from fire was another. The tendency of Hurricanes to burst into flames was probably its worst physical weakness, causing much anguish to its pilots, who talked of the phenomenon of 'Hurricane burns'.[17] Battle of Britain hero Tom Neil of 249 Squadron wrote that 'a fire in a Hurricane caused by blazing fuel presented the pilot with a desperate and fearful crisis. In a matter of two or three seconds, the aircraft became untenable and the act of opening the cockpit hood for the purpose of bailing out had the effect of drawing the flames into the pilot's face.'[18] The dashing US pilot and former Olympic bobsleigh champion Billy Fiske was one of many who succumbed to this terrible end. After he somehow landed his badly damaged, smoking Hurricane following an attack by an Me 109, he had to be hauled from his cockpit by a nursing orderly, Jeffrey Faulkner, who later recalled: 'His burns were really horrific. When we took off his gloves, the skin just sort of fell away from his hands.'[19] Fiske died soon afterwards in hospital.

Hawker had tried to tackle the problem of fire by fitting the two wing tanks with a sealant called Linatex, but this material had not been applied to the gravity tank, containing 28 litres of fuel, in front of the fuselage, partly because the tank was difficult to remove and partly because it was thought to be relatively safe, sandwiched between two bulkheads. The experience of combat showed how mistaken this approach had been. Dowding ordered a retrospective sealing of all Hurricane gravity tanks with Linatex, and Hawker completed the job by turning them round at the rate of 75 a month. Yet many pilots felt that the real blame for the fires lay with the two wing tanks, which each contained 35 gallons of fuel. Tom Neil himself felt that this pair of tanks were 'the culprits. Not only were they easier to hit and puncture – the reserve tank was largely shielded by the engine, the pilot and the armour plate – but there being no blanking plates between wings and fuselage, the blazing fuel was drawn into the cockpit by the natural draught pattern.' All fighters, wrote Neil, 'were susceptible to the fire hazard; the Hurricane was perhaps worse than some.'[20] But short of completely redesigning the Hurricane, there was little that could be done, so the plane was left with 'two wells of highly combustible liquid sloshing about asking to be ignited by a passing cannon shell'.[21]

Another vital lesson of the French campaign in 1940 was that the Hurricane's eight .303 Browning guns were only effective at close range. When the .303s had first been introduced in 1935, conventional wisdom in the RAF held that the gunfire should be sprayed at its target from about 600 yards. The theory was that, because of poor marksmanship by inexperienced pilots, a wide-spread pattern was needed to ensure that at least some of the bullets hit the enemy. By 1939, however, it was recognized that this method would provide an insufficiently lethal density of fire. Dowding therefore decided that the guns should be aligned or 'harmonized' so that the bullet streams would converge at around 400 yards, this cone of fire becoming known as 'the Dowding spread'. But pilots soon learnt that a distance of 400 yards was still too far away to cause real damage. Even before the war began, Paul Richey's 1 Squadron conducted experiments in harmonizing their Hurricanes' guns at a range of just 250 yards. 'Our shooting results on towed targets showed we were right – we shot them clean away time and time again. Action in France had now proved the point.'[22] Those who adhered to 'the Dowding spread' paid the price, as Ken Lee of 501 Squadron found out. 'It was a bitter mistake. We were sticking with the drill when we should have been closing in.'[23] By the time of the Battle of Britain in the summer and autumn of 1940, harmonization at 250 yards was becoming standard across Fighter Command, thanks partly to the influence of the bullish fighter leader Harry Broadhurst, who had served with the Air Component in France and then in January 1940 had taken charge of training in Park's 11 Group.

The actual process of harmonizing the guns was described by Hurricane pilot Donald 'Dimsie' Stones of 32 Squadron:

The practice was to align one's guns on markers painted on a hangar door while the aircraft was jacked up in a flying position. An optical instrument called in typical RAF manual jargon 'Mirror, bore, reflecting', was inserted into the breech of each gun, which was then adjusted on its mounting in the gun-bay of the wing and aligned to markers on the hangar door. Depending on the range and cone of fire desired by the pilot, the guns were then tightened and locked in that position.[24]

Yet harmonization could not solve the essential problem that the Brownings lacked a deadly punch in combat. The guns had seemed almost revolutionary when first proposed by Squadron Leader Ralph Sorley in 1935, but by 1940 they were inferior to the cannons installed on the German fighters. The Hurricane's eight Browning .303s carried 2,660 rounds in total, enough for fourteen seconds of firing, but the bullets were only 7.7 mm in calibre, the same as used by the British army. As a result, a Hurricane pilot often had to give a prolonged burst, using hundreds of rounds, to have an impact, particularly against bombers with their heavy armour plating. 'I lost count of the number of times we sat behind bombers and saw our bullets exploding on them with apparently nothing happening,' recalled John Ellacombe of 151 Squadron.[25] In contrast, the Me 109 had not only two machine guns above the engine but also two wing-mounted Oerlikon cannons, which could destroy a fighter with just a couple of their explosive 20-mm shells. It has been estimated that a three-second burst from a Hurricane weighed thirteen pounds, whereas the same from an Me 109 weighed eighteen pounds. Such a disparity left the Hurricane at a serious disadvantage in high-speed combat, when fighters might have the enemy in their sights for just a few seconds.

Aware of the weakness of the Brownings, the Air Ministry had embarked on an experimental programme to provide cannons in the fighters. A trial installation of a Hurricane with four 20-mm cannons in its wings was held in June 1940, but it was not until February 1941 that all the production and engineering problems were overcome, enabling this type to go into service. There were, however, other measures taken that compensated for the inferiority of the .303s. One was the provision of an efficient reflector gunsight, which from 1939 began to replace the traditional ringsight used on the first Hurricanes. The 'GM2 reflector sight', as it was called, worked by projecting a circular image, with a dot at its centre, onto a glass panel fitted in front of the windscreen, the dot representing the line of fire. The pilot could adjust the diameter of the projected image in proportion to the wingspan of the target, larger for bombers, smaller for fighters. This helped him judge the range from which he was firing. It is a rich irony that many of the GM2 sights fitted to Hurricanes during the Battle of Britain were actually built in the Reich. The reflector sight had originally been developed by the Glasgow optical engineers Barr and Stroud, but as the RAF expansion programme intensified in the late 1930s, the company found it impossible to keep up with demand, even with twenty-four-hour working. The government therefore reached a deal with the Austrian firm, C. P. Goerz of Vienna, to produce the GM2 under licence. When Austria was absorbed into Nazi Germany by the *Anschluss* in March 1938, the British Air Ministry feared that production would cease. But C. P. Goerz honoured their contract, and no fewer than 700 Austrian-made reflector sights were supplied to the RAF, before another British manufacturer, the Salford Electrical Company, began making and supplying them from January 1940.

Another welcome advance was found in the type of ammunition used by the fighter pilots. A Belgian inventor living in Switzerland called Mr de Wilde had come up with a new bullet in 1938, and in December that year the Air Ministry was sufficiently impressed to buy the design. Less taken with the product was one of the Royal Arsenal's explosive experts, Major C. Aubrey Dixon, who pointed out that the de Wilde bullets had to be hand-made rather than mass-produced, greatly reducing their wartime potential. He therefore invented his own ammunition, though for reasons of military secrecy he retained the name 'de Wilde'. Dixon's version went into production in May 1940 and was an instant success with pilots, who liked both its explosive power and the way the flashes from its impact could guide their aim. In terms of ammunition, one of the virtues of the Hurricane was that it was easy to rearm, as John Ellacombe of 151 Squadron recalled: 'You had two batteries of four guns and it used to take about three minutes to open the top, take out the old thing and put in the new complete set with all the ammunition. It was superb. This was an advantage over the Spitfire, which took about eight or nine minutes to rearm.'[26] After cleaning and reloading the Brownings, the last task the armourers performed was to put bright red fabric patches made from sticky tape over the gun ports. In combat, the bullets simply ripped through the fabric. There were two purposes behind these patches: first, to prevent moisture from entering the open ports, causing the gun breeches to freeze, and second, to show that the fighter was ready for action again.

For all their disadvantages, the Brownings were still a potent weapon when unleashed. Ray Holmes of 504 Squadron wrote a vivid description of firing his guns for the first time as a trainee on the Hurricane, when he was sent on a trip over the sea off Scapa Flow to practise blasting away. 'The racket as each gun hammered out its twenty shells a second was deafening, even above your engine noise and with our helmet covering your ears.' The effect of the shooting on the controls, Holmes said, was 'unexpected':

> When a single round is fired from a rifle the recoil as the bullet leaves the barrel jerks the butt into the marksman's shoulder. This recoil is used in the machine gun to throw back the breech block and eject the spent cartridge case. On the way forward again it grabs a new round from the ammunition belt, rams it into the barrel and fires it. This process is repeated twenty times a second in each of the eight guns, until the pressure is removed from the firing button. This recoil, although absorbed to some extent by the gun itself, still gives a pronounced braking effect to the aeroplane, slowing it down noticeably and making the nose sink. The sinking effect, when only 100 feet above the water, can be disturbing.

Holmes was also surprised to see the effect of the bullets on the water. 'After a lull of perhaps a second while bullets are speeding to their target, there is a seething and frothing of the water ahead as though a school of enraged sharks has suddenly surfaced. A second later you have skimmed over the maelstrom.'[27]

One lesson that failed to be learnt during the early Hurricane campaigns was that the RAF's tactics were totally inadequate for modern warfare. Even after all the experience of the aerial combats over France, many strategists at the Air Ministry still clung to the traditional approach left over from the 1930s, whereby fighters had to fly in tight formations, then line up to attack the enemy through certain prescribed, regimented manoeuvres. These orderly, meticulously choreographed patterns, known as Fighter Area Attacks (FAA), bore no relationship to the chaotic, frenzied world of monoplane dogfights. As the Battle of Britain pilot George Unwin put it, they were 'more suited to the Hendon aerial display' than fighter action.[28] So rigid was this policy that the RAF had a manual, taught to all new recruits, setting out in detail the six different types of Fighter Area

Attacks. In Fighter Area Attack Number One, for instance, a section of fighters would neatly move into line astern above a lone enemy bomber and the planes would then take it in turns to fly down and open fire. Alternatively, Attack Number Five stipulated that the section should move into line abreast to take on a group of enemy bombers. What was entirely missing was any recognition that the RAF might also come under fire from enemy fighters. This was because the FAA manual was developed when it was still considered that the main duty of the RAF's interceptors would be to tackle bombers from Germany, which would be unescorted because the Luftwaffe's fighters would not have the range to reach Britain. It was the same reasoning that had led Hugh Dowding to reject back armour in 1938, though the fall of France and the Low Countries in 1940 made a nonsense of such logic, bringing the Luftwaffe fighters within less than 30 minutes of the British bases. Yet still the official adherence to Fighter Area Attacks persisted through 1940. They continued to be taught by some units as late as 1941.

The inherent inflexibility of Fighter Area Attacks was compounded by the RAF's attachment to the 'vic' as the basic element of a fighter formation. The 'vic' comprised three planes flying in a V, with the section leader in the centre and two wingmen in echelon on either side. In theory this layout provided all-round cover, but in practice it meant that the two rear pilots tended to be watching their leader rather than searching the skies for the enemy. The Germans, exploiting their experiences from the Spanish Civil War of 1936–9, adopted a much more flexible approach. The essential unit of their formations was the *Rotte*, in which a pair of aircraft flew in line astern about 200 yards apart. Two *Rotten* often combined together to form a *Schwarm* of four aircraft. 'The Germans were all flying loose pairs, which were far more effective,' wrote Ken Lee of his experiences with 501 Squadron in 1940. 'I'm sorry to say I do think our training and our theory were poor. We'd have done much better if we'd taken notice of the tactics the Germans used in Spain . . . the theory that we had been spoon fed was wrong.'[29] Eventually, the RAF's fighter squadrons began to use a similar arrangement, known as the 'finger four' because of its resemblance to the digits of an outstretched palm, with the leader representing the second, or longest, finger, two other pilots on either side, and the final man taking up the position known as 'tail-end Charlie' or 'arse-end Charlie'.

But such methods did not become universal until after the Battle of Britain, much to the anger of some Hurricane pilots such as Kenneth McGlashan of 245 Squadron: 'Our compact little Vs were ideal for airshows, not modern combat. Be it fighter-to-fighter or attacking bombers, fighting at such close quarters increased the risk of collision and committed us to slow steady movements, which made us vulnerable targets.' In contrast, McGlashan continued, the German fighters 'swept round the sky in an unrestrained, fluid motion. They were constantly able to check their tails for any approaching fighters and were not locked into any predictable manoeuvres. They would fill the sky with a gaggle of pairs, making them efficient predators and difficult prey. It was a bloody lesson learnt the hard way to an extreme and too many men died at the hands of an antiquated strategy.'[30] Indeed, the legless fighter ace Douglas Bader complained bitterly about the failure of the RAF to change tactics after the Battle of France. 'One would have thought that the views and experiences of these pilots would have been passed on to the Hurricane and Spitfire pilots of England-based squadrons,' he wrote, but 'not a bit of it.' Bader thought this showed 'a total lack of understanding of basic operational needs by the non-operational, non-flying officers and personnel at headquarters'.[31]

The failure was all the more reprehensible because the RAF fighters had remained in ferocious combat with the Luftwaffe in the days immediately after the completion of the withdrawal of the Air Component from northern France on 21 May 1940. The three battered Hurricane squadrons of the Advanced Striking Force were still clinging on, while most of the Hurricane force from 11 Group were engaged in trying to provide cover for the evacuation of a major part of the British Expeditionary Force trapped at Dunkirk, east of Calais.

The great exodus from Dunkirk began on 26 May, with British military leaders holding out little hope of success. 'Nothing but a miracle can save the BEF now,' wrote Alan Brooke, commander of II Corps.[32] As the exhausted soldiers poured into the town and onto the beaches, the Luftwaffe began its heavy bombardment of the area, sending a huge pall of black smoke into the sky. 'I guarantee unconditionally that not a single British soldier will escape,' Reichsmarschall Hermann Göring told Hitler,[33] having taken full responsibility for the destruction of the British forces. Due to the heavy losses in the French campaign, Keith Park had only around two hundred serviceable fighters, including some ineffective two-seater Defiants, with which to provide protection for the navy; nor could he use Fighter Command's control system to run operations. All he could do was mount as many daily patrols as he could over the Channel, though the shortage of fighter numbers meant that there were large gaps in the air cover, which were ruthlessly exploited by the Luftwaffe.

Stretched to the limit, the Hurricane squadrons had to fly over six sorties a day, at constant risk of being shot down over hostile territory. 'We had moved to Biggin Hill right at the beginning of the Dunkirk campaign and set off at ten o'clock. We had done three trips to Dunkirk by ten o'clock and lost eight aircraft. I think it was the worst period of the war for all of us. We were absolutely tired out by the end of Dunkirk,' said Richard Mitchell of 229 Squadron. 'We were so weary that we were a liability flying aeroplanes. Most of us rarely reached Dunkirk because we were attacked on the way there. We had great difficulty with just plain ball ammunition. With that, you had to hit something like an oil pipe to do real damage. When we got the de Wilde ammo later, things began to happen.' The only solace for Mitchell was the Hurricane itself. 'I had great confidence in it. It was a marvellous plane in that it was so rugged. You could turn it on a sixpence. The 109s were faster and their guns were bigger and better but we could turn inside them.'[34] For George Johns, one of Mitchell's comrades in 229 Squadron, the worst problem was the fuel capacity. 'We did not have the endurance in our Hurricanes to get very far in Dunkirk. We were flying at the extreme range. It was a question of trying to get back before we ran out of fuel. I can remember a chap landing on the runway at Biggin Hill and his engine just stopped. He was out of fuel completely.'[35]

On the first day of the battle at Dunkirk, Peter Parrott of 145 Squadron was one of the many Hurricane pilots whose plane was hit by enemy fire. Flying number two in the last section of his squadron, he was making a stern attack on a Heinkel 111 when the German rear gunner opened fire on him. 'I had just got one of its engines smoking when he put two bullets into me. One hit the wing and one hit the front water jacket on the Merlin and I immediately had a cockpit full of glycol steam.' With the Hurricane losing height and the engine running rough, Parrott had to turn round and fly back to England. Having crossed the coast at just 1,500 feet, he had to make a forced landing in a field in Kent, the Hurricane coming 'to a standstill pretty quickly'. Unfortunately, he killed a few sheep in the process, much to the fury of their owner, a local farmer. 'Who's going to pay for these sheep then?' he asked. 'The Air Ministry!' replied Parrott.[36]

The scene at Dunkirk was one of devastation and fear, yet the British troops never panicked, even as they were strafed and bombed by the Luftwaffe while they waited patiently to board the rescue ships. 'I had a good view of the beaches,' recalled Geoffrey Page of 56 Squadron. 'It looked like masses of ants on the sands. I felt desperately sorry for the troops down below.'[37] Flying regular patrols in daylight hours over the French coast, Harold Bird-Wilson was another witness to the evacuation. 'They were big beaches at Dunkirk and there were strings coming from the sand dunes and the strings were people, soldiers lining up and going down to the water's edge. There was a general shambles at the sand dunes. We were greatly shocked at the number of troops coming through.'[38]

Even some of the German attackers felt sympathy for the British army in its raw vulnerability. Captain Paul Temme, who flew with his guns blazing at just 300 feet over the snaking queues of soldiers, felt that it was 'just unadulterated killing. The beaches were full of soldiers. I went up and down "hose-piping". It was cold-blooded, point-blank murder.'[39] But despite their vastly superior numbers, the Germans did not have the air battle all their own way. Throughout the nine days of the evacuation, they encountered aggressive opposition from the RAF. For the first time during the war, the Luftwaffe was put under severe pressure as 11 Group threw all its resources into the fight to protect the convoys and the beaches. A Junkers (Ju) 88 pilot, Oberleutnant Jocho Helbig, later said: 'We called it "the Hell of Dunkirk". We met terrific resistance from the British fighters and the battleship AA (anti-aircraft fire). It was the turning point. Now we knew what the enemy's mettle was like.'[40]

According to Keith Park's own analysis of the Dunkirk campaign, 11 Group mounted 2,739 sorties, involving 4,822 hours of flying, and destroyed 258 German aircraft, with 119 damaged. The RAF paid a heavy price for this pugnacity. A total of 87 RAF pilots were reported to have been shot down during the battle.[41] But none of the German fighter pilots could now doubt that the days of easy victories were over. 'We had been briefed about the quality of the British pilots and their aircraft and expected a hard fight,' wrote Ju 88 pilot Ulrich Steinhilper. 'Indeed, when we first saw their Hurricanes and Spitfires attacking our Stukas, it was immediately clear that we were up against a very tenacious opponent.'[42]

That spirit of tenacity was epitomized by a patrol carried out on 1 June by 43 Squadron Leader George Lott, who ended up in a series of gruelling dogfights. 'I found myself alone amidst what seemed like hordes of Huns in a matter of seconds. They came from all directions and I had a mad struggle for survival. First one and then another would get on my tail; twice I was down to 3,000 feet and twice back up to 17,000; twice I flicked into a spin. Not once did I get a chance to shoot back.' There followed a brief lull in the action, then Lott managed to get on the tail of an Me 110, which was diving gently:

> Steady and straight he flew, and I gained a little. I put the bead of my reflector sight slap on him; I was thinking most extraordinarily clearly for some reason and calmly and methodically lifted the sight just a little to allow for the longish range. It was about 400 yards. Firmly I pressed the firing button and almost immediately first one engine and then the other poured black smoke. I kept the button pressed for a long burst with the sight remaining rock steady.

The stricken German fighter plunged into a cloud as Lott pulled away. 'I was steaming and my hands were shaking a little, and I decided that I learned enough for one day and set off for home.'[43]

By far the easiest target for the Hurricanes was the Ju 87, gull-winged Stuka, whose screaming, almost vertical dives had struck such fear during the Blitzkrieg assaults on Poland and the western front. But their slow speed when flying level or coming out of a dive made them easy prey for the RAF fighters, as Geoffrey Page of 56 Squadron recalled: 'In our Hurricanes, by throttling back the engines, we could sit behind the Stuka. There was the poor rear gunner with one little pop gun to defend his aeroplane and we were sitting there with eight machine guns. I'm not proud of the fact that we just knocked them off like skittles.'[44] Even the Luftwaffe fighter leader Adolf Galland, so scathing about the Hurricane's performance in the Battle of France, was forced to admit that the British fighters at Dunkirk 'made a great and successful effort to provide air cover for the remarkable evacuation operation'.[45]

Those words expose the injustice of the vociferous complaints about the RAF from the retreating troops at Dunkirk. 'What was the bloody RAF doing?' was the question asked by so many soldiers, struggling to cope with the bombardment.[46] Sergeant Major Martin McLane of the Durham Light Infantry spoke for most his comrades when he said: 'The RAF did a very poor job of defending us. The Germans were working in close co-operation with their aircraft. When they wanted support, they called in their dive-bombers and their fighters who strafed and bombed us to clear the way. And what support did we have? We had no damn thing at all. Not a bloody thing. We were just left to God and good neighbours.'[47] Such bitterness might have been natural, given how defenceless the men must have felt on the beaches of Dunkirk, but it took no account of how hard the RAF fought against savage odds, constantly outnumbered, without radar and still hampered by outmoded tactics. Furthermore, many of the combats took place inland over France, far from the eyes of the troops, while even those that occurred above Dunkirk were often fought at over 15,000 feet, beyond the thick fog and smoke that hung over the port.

Nevertheless, the resentment felt by the troops was deep. Some airmen were verbally abused by soldiers when arriving at ports or stations; others were physically attacked in pubs when the beer started flowing. The anger also manifested itself in the middle of the battle. 'One of our chaps was shot down by a Ju 88 and landed by parachute near the beach,' remembered Harold Bird-Wilson. 'He made his way towards the boats, but an army officer told him, "The boats are for the army, not the RAF." He had to fight his way on board. The very next morning he was on patrol again over Dunkirk.'[48] When Douglas 'Grubby' Grice of 32 Squadron was shot down near Rouen and successfully bailed out, he was confronted by two army privates as he marched northwards. 'They barred my way and said, "Where the fucking hell have you air force chaps been?" They were really quite aggressive. I said: "We've been here. I was shot down." That made a difference. They realized I had been in action.'[49]

The feelings of hostility were not all on the army side either. According to Tom Neil of 249 Squadron, parts of the RAF 'had little more than contempt for the "brown jobs". Among other more wounding epithets, some pilots scathingly referred to the soldiers as the "Dunkirk Harriers".'[50] The fractious relationship between the army and the RAF continued long after Dunkirk was over. It was not until the campaign against Field Marshal Erwin Rommel in late 1942 that a fruitful army co-operation with the fighter force was established.

Without the attacks by the Hurricanes and Spitfires on the Luftwaffe, the evacuation from Dunkirk could have been a blood-soaked disaster for the army. Instead, it became 'a miracle of deliverance',[51] to quote Winston Churchill's phrase when addressing the House of Commons on 4 June 1940, the day after the completion of the evacuation. Under Operation Dynamo, an armada of naval ships, commercial vessels and even pleasure cruisers had brought back no fewer than 338,000 Allied troops from France. In the same Commons speech the Prime Minister gave special credit to the RAF, claiming it had achieved victory in 'a great trial of strength' against the German air force. The Germans 'tried hard and they were beaten back; they were frustrated in their task. We got the Army away.' He lavished further praise on the fighter crews: 'All our types − the Hurricane, the Spitfire and the new Defiant − and all our pilots have been vindicated as superior to what they at present have to face.'[52] Such a statement was a classic piece of Churchillian exaggeration, especially about the woeful Defiant, but without his optimistic boldness Britain may well have been doomed in 1940.

Indeed, at the very start of the Dunkirk evacuation, some of the old guard of Tory appeasers, led by Lord Halifax, were pressing for a peace settlement by opening a secret negotiating channel with Mussolini. Barely a fortnight into his Premiership, Churchill immediately had to crush such defeatism at the heart of his Cabinet. Negotiations were an impossibility, he argued, because they would mean the end of British independence and the beginning of Nazi mastery in Europe. The only way to deal with Hitler, said Churchill, was 'to show him that he could not conquer this country'.[53] But it would take another, more epic, clash between the RAF and the Luftwaffe a few months later before all such pusillanimous talk was abandoned.

Even after Dunkirk there were still in France around 30 Hurricanes from the Advanced Air Striking Force (AASF), which tried to provide support to the other Allied armies retreating westwards and to the south of Paris. With the French government having all but conceded defeat, the situation for the Hurricane pilots was truly desperate, yet they continued to take heroically to the air, sometimes inflicting significant damage on the Luftwaffe.

Back on 27 May the fighters of 501 Squadron had taken part in one of the most astounding Hurricane triumphs of the entire war. On patrol near Rouen, they sighted 24 Heinkel 111s escorted by 20 Me 110s. Immediately, the Hurricanes went on the attack, with Eustace 'Gus' Holden, now in 501 Squadron, leading:

> I said over the r/t, 'Select one and kill it.' That is exactly what we did. I got behind mine and at 300 yards fired a burst. Nothing happened for a few seconds, even though I knew I had hit him right in the heart of the aeroplane. But then his left wing started to drop. He ploughed on, turning slightly left. Then he went into a steep dive and crashed. I had obviously killed the pilot. I went round and I counted twelve fires on the ground. We had almost got the lot. It was an extraordinary performance.[54]

Altogether Holden's squadron claimed 14 Heinkels and 1 Messerschmitt. But such victories became rare as the pulverizing German war machine rolled on through France. The Hurricane squadrons kept having to move backwards from one wrecked airfield to another. Equipment was in short supply, conditions desperate. For Norman

Hancock of 1 Squadron, there was 'nothing but retreat, anxiety, lack of knowledge as to what was going on and non-existent communications'.[55] Holden's glorious achievement in 501 Squadron offered little respite from the pressure, as he recalled. 'Our airmen had a pretty rough time. Sleeping accommodation was bizarre to say the least. We had tents and very little else. I remember one occasion when our French liaison officer told us that the local water had been pronounced unfit by the local medical officer and we ran out of milk quite quickly. So the French liaison officer got into a wagon and came back loaded up with champagne. We found we flew quite well with champagne.'[56] At one stage a pigsty had to serve as accommodation for Dennis David of 87 Squadron. 'There was no room at the local hostelry, so I just lay down on the straw, fully clothed. I remember being very, very tired. I could have slept anywhere. We did not have baths. We ended up scruffy and that did not do a lot for morale.'[57]

The wretchedness of this period was symbolized by the tragedy that befell the brilliant RAF ace Edgar 'Cobber' Kain of 73 Squadron, whose exploits had made him the darling of a British press eager for the occasional gleam of good news amid the darkness of retreat. The recipient of the DFC (Distinguished Flying Cross) in March for a heroic action when he shot down an Me 109 despite severe damage to his own Hurricane, Kain was credited with the destruction of 16 enemy aircraft and damage to one other. On 6 June he received the news that he was being transferred back to England, and the next morning he took off from his base at Echemines, south-west of Paris. A mood of celebration was mixed with his usual exuberance as he roared over the airfield in one of the last wooden-bladed, fixed-pitch Hurricanes. Flying at low level, he performed a couple of flick rolls, then tried a third, only to misjudge his altitude and plough into the earth. As the Hurricane exploded on impact, Kain was hurled over ninety feet away. He died the moment he hit the ground.

The final duty of the Hurricane squadrons in June 1940 was their attempt to provide some cover for the evacuation of the smaller part of the BEF and other Allied troops and civilians from France's north-western and Atlantic ports. Because of the limited numbers of

available planes, the British government decided to send over temporarily to Normandy two more Hurricane squadrons, much to the
fury of Hugh Dowding, who feared Fighter Command's resources
were being drained away in another fruitless operation. At a Cabinet
meeting on 3 June, he spoke forcefully against any further dispatches
of Hurricanes and, during his intervention, even stood up to walk
over to Churchill, prompting Lord Beaverbrook, the Minister of
Aircraft Production, to think that Dowding was about to resign. The
truth was less dramatic. In fact, Dowding placed in front of the Prime
Minister a graph, produced by the research section of Fighter
Command, which showed the heavy Hurricane losses in France.
According to Dowding's account: 'I laid the graph on the table
before him and said: "If the present wastage continues for another
fortnight, we shall not have a single Hurricane left in France or this
country." '[58] Dowding's figures persuaded the Cabinet. No more
fighters were sent.

The few Hurricanes still left in France were unable to prevent the
worst maritime disaster in British history, which took place near the
western French port of St Lazaire on the afternoon of 17 June.
Anchored off the coast that day, among the other vessels of the
evacuation fleet, was the troopship *Lancastria*, a 16,000-ton former
Cunard liner which had embarked between 4,000 and 8,000 troops,
RAF personnel and refugees. Suddenly, at 4 p.m., a group of six Ju
88s appeared in the sky above the fleet, pursued by a flight of
Hurricanes from 1 Squadron. One of the fighters, flown by Norman
Hancock, went after the Junkers bomber that was heading towards
the *Lancastria*. 'I followed it for a hell of a way but with no success.
My shooting was not good,' recalled Hancock. Having avoided the
Hurricane on its tail, the Ju 88 went into a dive and released its
bombs. Four of them scored direct hits on the ship, the noise of their
impact sounding 'like someone bursting a child's tin kettle drum with
a hammer', according to one sailor on board.[59] Within two minutes
the *Lancastria* was listing heavily. 'I did not see the bombs hit but
I saw the ship starting to go down. Circling the troops afterwards, I
threw my Mae West down to them. I did not realize at the time what
a tragedy it was,' said Hancock.[60]

There were 2,477 survivors from the *Lancastria*, but because of the chaotic scenes at the embarkation, it was impossible to work out exactly the true death toll. One Admiralty report conservatively put it at 2,823; others have put it much higher, possibly over 5,000. Yet even at the lowest estimate, the sinking of the *Lancastria* incurred the greatest loss of life at sea that Britain ever suffered in one incident, worse than the catastrophes of the *Titanic* in 1912 and the *Lusitania* in 1915 combined.

The next day, 18 June, the last of the Hurricanes on the continent were recalled to Britain. Despite the *Lancastria*, the evacuation from north-western France had been almost as successful as from Dunkirk, with 192,000 troops and civilians saved. Yet the price paid by Fighter Command on the western front had been a heavy one. Since 10 May, 477 fighters had been lost over France and the Channel, 386 of them Hurricanes. One-fifth of the professional peacetime pilots were either dead or disabled, with the result that almost half of the pilots left in Britain were newly trained and lacking in experience. But the Germans had not escaped lightly. The Luftwaffe had lost 1,284 aircraft in battle, the great majority of them to the Hurricane. A total of 129 German officers and almost 600 men from other ranks had also been killed, a rate of attrition that not only exposed the myth of Nazi superiority but would also be unsustainable if suffered in a longer campaign.

That same day of 18 June 1940, just as the Hurricanes returned home, Winston Churchill stood up in the House of Commons to deliver the finest of all his wartime speeches, a beautifully crafted piece of rhetoric that combined history, romance, patriotism and defiance in an inspirational appeal to the British people:

> What General Weygand has called the Battle of France is over. I expect the Battle of Britain is about to begin. Upon this battle depends the survival of Christian civilization. Upon it depends our own British life and the long continuity of our institutions and our Empire. The whole fury and might of the enemy must very soon be turned on us. Hitler knows he will have to break us in this island or lose the war. If we can stand up to him, all Europe may be free and the life of the world may move forward into broad sunlit uplands. But if we fail, then the whole world, including the United States, including all that we have known and cared for, will sink into the abyss of a new Dark

age made more sinister, and perhaps more protracted, by the lights of perverted science. Let us therefore brace ourselves to our duties, and so bear ourselves, that if the British Empire and its Commonwealth last for a thousand years, men will still say, 'This was their finest hour.'[61]

6

'Our air force is sublime'

⬥

THE IMAGERY AND sounds of the Battle of Britain still resonate today, decades after the conflict was over. We picture dashing young pilots, defying the odds against them, as they speed across the blue summer skies towards the intruder above southern England. In our mind's eye we see a German fighter go into an uncontrollable spin, smoke pouring from its bullet-riddled engine, the plane emitting a deathly high-pitched scream at it plunges to earth. The reassuring roar of the Merlin engine echoes across the rolling hills of the Sussex downs. Airmen doze in deckchairs outside their dispersal huts, the mellifluous voice of Vera Lynn wafting from a nearby wireless. Suddenly the call to 'scramble' sends them racing over to their Hurricanes as determined ground crews start up the engines. Meanwhile, a crashed German bomber lies in a Kent field, its airscrews bent at right angles, a member of the Home Guard proudly standing watch by the wreckage. In an underground Operations Room attractive WAAFs, wearing headphones and solemn expressions, use their long-handled rakes to push markers across the map table as another raid unfolds. From the House of Commons chamber, Churchill's whisky-soaked growl rouses a nation to resistance at its moment of darkest peril.

The Battle of Britain continues to have such resonance because the campaign so magnificently fused an epic quality with a moral purpose. It represented the classic fight between good and evil, between freedom and tyranny, between survival and subjugation. It was the ancient myth of St George slaying the Dragon made real: the Arthurian legend translated into the modern world, with the Knights of the Round Table cast as the selfless RAF pilots and the sword of Excalibur as the fighter force. It was the embodiment of the inspiring parable of David against Goliath: the hero who triumphs by cunning and fortitude against a much larger opponent. Though the battle was waged with the very latest technology, some of the duels in the air almost had the character of medieval chivalry. There was a moral purity about the individual combats, in that civilians' lives were rarely put at risk. The horrors of total war, reflected at their worst in the mass indiscriminate killing visited upon Coventry, Dresden or Hiroshima, were entirely absent. Nor did the pilots, for all their spectacular bravery, have to suffer anything like the grim experiences and dwindling odds of survival endured by First World War troops at the Somme or the Lancaster aircrews during the bombing offensive against Berlin in the black winter of 1943–4. The Battle of Britain also stirred the deepest patriotic spirit, for it was the first time since the Spanish Armada of 1588 that a continental foe had attempted a major military offensive against the island.

As with so many of the glorious episodes in our national story, there was an element of myth-making about the battle, not least because of Churchill's own account in his war memoirs. The superiority of the German aircraft numbers was often exaggerated. Equally, the numerical strength of Fighter Command has sometimes been understated. Hitler's invasion plans were tentative and opportunistic, for his real long-term target had always been Russia. Germany had shortages of landing crafts, barges and troopships, while the Norway campaign had inflicted crippling losses on the Kriegsmarine, leaving it vulnerable to the Royal Navy if a Channel crossing were to be made. Indeed, some historians, notably Derek Robinson, have argued that the British naval threat was as important as the RAF in forcing Hitler to abandon his plans for invasion.[1] Nor did aerial power prove as all-dominant in the war as the fearful prophecies of the 1930s had suggested. The night-time Blitz in the winter of 1940–1 did not come near to breaking Britain, while Malta survived in early 1942 despite overwhelming German air supremacy. Yet it would be wrong to downplay the enormous significance of the Battle of Britain. Until this moment, the fearsome German war machine had seemed unbeatable, forcing most of western Europe and Scandinavia under its grip. The RAF, however, had defeated an air force more than twice its size. After the autumn of 1940 the belief in Nazi invincibility was destroyed. Fighter Command's resistance ensured that Hitler's war changed from one of conquest to one of struggle. Thrown back in the west, he faltered in the east. Saved by the RAF, Britain became the engine room of resistance to Germany, hammering its industries from the air, sending convoys to Russia by sea.

After the war, the German general Gerd von Runstedt was asked in a television interview if the turning point in the conflict had been the Battle of Stalingrad. 'Oh no, it was the Battle of Britain,' he replied. 'That was the first time we realized we could be beaten and we were beaten and we didn't like it.'[2] Moreover, the Battle of Britain was unique in being by far the greatest single aerial engagement that was ever fought. As the Swiss historian Dr Theo Webber put it: 'Fighter defence achieved here a qualitative peak of striking power and efficiency which is unique in the history of air warfare and will probably remain so.'[3]

The Hurricane was at the centre of this victory. It was the plane that made up most of Fighter Command's force throughout the battle, inflicting more damage on the Luftwaffe than all other aircraft types put together. In the folklore of 1940, the more glamorous Spitfire has long overshadowed the Hurricane, but this has done an injustice to the role of Sydney Camm's fighter, without which the battle could never have been won. Despite the heavy losses suffered during the Battle of France and Dunkirk, the Hurricanes were still numerically the leading type on the eve of the hostilities over Britain, thanks partly to the high rates of production from the Hawker factories. On 1 July Sir Hugh Dowding, head of Fighter Command, had at his disposal 58 squadrons. These comprised 29 squadrons of Hurricanes, including 347 serviceable aircraft, and 19 squadrons of Spitfires, with 199 aircraft. Altogether, including non-serviceable aircraft, Fighter Command had 754 single-seater fighters. The other 10 squadrons were made up of Bristol Blenheims and Boulton Paul Defiants. Fifty-four per cent of the entire operational strength of Fighter Command, therefore, lay in the Hawker Hurricane. Within the crucial 11 Group in London and the south-east, the Hurricanes outnumbered the Spitfires by more than two to one, making up 17 squadrons compared to the Spitfires' 8. That distribution was reflected in the German losses: for every two Luftwaffe planes brought down by Spitfires during the Battle of Britain, three were destroyed by Hurricanes. Those figures led Dowding himself to give this verdict: 'The Hurricane was a jolly good machine, a rugged type, stronger than the Spitfire.'[4] It was a view shared by one of the great Battle of Britain pilots, Peter Townsend: 'We thought they were great and we would prove it by shooting down one thousand Luftwaffe aircraft in the battle.'[5]

Like some post-war commentators, however, the Germans were dismissive of the Hurricane, an attitude of contempt that helped to breed complacency in the Luftwaffe fleets. This disdain ran right through the German air force, from the senior commanders to the aircrews. A comparison by Luftwaffe Intelligence made in July 1940 stated that '40 per cent of the RAF's fighters are Spitfires, the rest are Hurricanes. Of the two models, the Spitfire is the better one. In view of their still missing cannons and their fighting characteristics, both models are inferior to the Me 109.'[6] A more detailed analysis of the two British fighters was produced by the German ace Werner Molders, veteran of the Spanish Civil War and the first wartime pilot to be credited with 100 victories. During the fall of France, the Germans had captured several intact Hurricanes and Spitfires, and Molders, with his unique expertise, was asked to test fly both types. 'The Hurricane is a bit of a tugboat with a retractable undercarriage,' he wrote in his report. 'In our terms both are very easy to fly, the Hurricane being particularly good natured, steady as a rock in the turn, but well below the Me 109 when it comes to performance. It's heavy on the rudder and the ailerons are sluggish. Take-off and landing in both types is child's play. The Spitfire is one class better, very nice to the touch, light, excellent in the turn and almost the equal of the 109.'[7] Another German airman, Johannes Steinhoff, was even more scathing: 'The Hurricane was a big disadvantage to you, the rate of roll being bad – we were lucky to meet Hurricanes.'[8]

But this Teutonic derision was not entirely rational. Part of it stemmed purely from poor aircraft recognition, whereby many Luftwaffe pilots were inclined to regard all fast RAF monoplanes as Spitfires. Throughout the Battle of France, German airmen frequently talked of being hit by Spitfires, though the Hurricane was the only single-seater RAF fighter to serve in that theatre. This outlook in turn fuelled a form of Spitfire snobbery, in which the German airmen were too ignorant or contemptuous of the Hurricane to believe they could have been shot down by such a mediocre plane, so they ascribed their defeat to the Spitfire. Peter Townsend came across this mentality in April 1940 after his squadron hit a Heinkel 111, which subsequently crash-landed at his airbase of Acklington in Northumberland, with the crew surviving. 'Later they insisted that a Spitfire had attacked them. It was the first sign of the Luftwaffe's "Spitfire Snobbery". There were no Spitfires within miles,' said Townsend.[9] Squadron Leader Bob Stanford Tuck of 257 Squadron once shot down a Luftwaffe fighter near his airfield at Debden in Essex and subsequently met the pilot who had crashed. The German congratulated him on the excellent qualities of the Spitfire, only to be told to his astonishment that he had been brought down by a Hurricane.

What the Germans failed to recognize were the powerful virtues that made the Hurricane the ideal complement for the Spitfire in the crucial months of 1940. The Hurricane certainly was inferior to the Supermarine fighter in several respects. It was slower, took longer to climb, was less responsive on the controls, had a lower ceiling and less potential for development. Even in 1940 the Spitfire was at least 30 mph faster at cruising speed and 70 mph faster in the dive than the Hurricane, a gap that kept widening through the Spitfire's constant redevelopment. With its solid appearance, the Hurricane was less elegant and aesthetically appealing than the Spitfire, another reason why it did not attract the same public attention. It was a substantially bigger plane, with a length of 31 feet 4 inches and a wingspan of 40 feet, compared to the Spitfire's length of 29 feet 11 inches and wingspan of 36 feet 10 inches. The Spitfire's elliptical wing, the cause of so many production problems, was also much thinner.

Sydney Camm himself once expressed his regret that the solidity of the Hurricane's thick wing had inhibited its performance: 'Bulman [the Hawker Chief Test Pilot] and I had decided that strength should be an important factor in this ship, but I always had one regret. I wished the wing had been thinner. If we had had more time it would have been the greatest aircraft of all time.'[10] But it was because the Hurricane had been developed quickly and, with its traditional design, could be produced rapidly that it was so invaluable to the RAF. Without the fighters pouring out of Kingston, Slough and Hucclecote, Fighter Command would have been in desperate trouble, especially since the huge Spitfire factory at Castle Bromwich in Birmingham, erected with such a fanfare in 1938, had not turned out a single plane by June 1940 as a result of gross mismanagement and union intransigence.[11]

Indeed, the ease of manufacturing Camm's fighter was a crucial factor in the nation's survival, given that the Spitfire took almost twice as long to build as the Hurricane. It has been estimated that 170,000 man–hours of design, development and construction were needed to get the Hurricane ready for squadron service, compared to 300,000 man-hours for the Spitfire. As the historian L. F. E. Coombes has pointed out, the Hurricane took 60 design hours for each pound of its weight, compared to 150 for the Spitfire.[12] Camm's retrospective wistfulness also ignored some of the advantages of the Hurricane's wing design. Its thickness and size meant the wing loading on the Hurricane was lower than on the Spitfire: 24.1 pounds per square foot on the former, 26 pounds per square foot on the latter. This difference gave a turning radius of 800 feet for the Hurricane, compared to 880 feet for the Spitfire, making the Hawker fighter highly effective in a dogfight, contrary to what the Luftwaffe claimed. Furthermore, many pilots felt that the Hurricane's wing meant that it was more stable when firing, a view propounded by the famous disabled fighter pilot Douglas Bader, who flew both Hurricanes and Spitfires before being shot down over France in 1941. Writing of his experiences in the Hurricane, he said: 'Best of all, it was a marvellous gun platform. The sloping nose gave you a splendid view forward, while the eight guns were set in blocks of four in each wing, close to the fuselage. The aeroplane remained rock steady when you fired.' In contrast, he wrote, the Spitfire 'was less steady when the guns were firing because, I have always thought, they were spread further along the wing, and the recoil effect was noticeable.'[13]

Fascinatingly, this was a verdict shared by Supermarine engineer Eric Davis, who worked with Reginald Mitchell on the design of the Spitfire. When Davis first saw a Hurricane stripped of its fabric, he thought to himself: 'My word, isn't it crude.' But the onset of war made him change his mind: 'In many respects the Hurricane was better than the Spitfire because all the guns were mounted on a special platform in the middle of the plane. The result was that they could concentrate much better on the enemy than the Spitfire, with its guns spread along the wings. The Spitfire, with its wing bending, was not such a good platform as the Hurricane.'[14] An unsentimental view came from Roger Wilkinson of 3 Squadron: 'The Spitfire was a beautiful aircraft, no doubt about it. But it was a Rolls-Royce. The Hurricane was a tank. Which would you rather go to war in? The gun platform was much better on the Hurricane because the guns on the Spitfire used to wobble about and scatter the bullets.'[15]

In addition, the solidity of the wing assisted the job of the armourers and maintenance crews, an attribute that the Supermarine chief test pilot Jeffrey Quill admired: 'You could lower the undercarriage on a Hurricane and take the wings off because the undercarriage was in the centre-section. So you take the wings off, put the tail up on a three-ton lorry and tow it along the road. You couldn't do that with the Spitfire. If you took the wings off, it took the undercarriage off as well.'[16] With its wide track undercarriage, lack of vices and intrinsic strength, the Hurricane was the ideal plane for raw recruits, a priceless asset during the Battle of Britain when the demand from the operational squadrons for new fighter pilots was so high. 'If you couldn't fly it, you shouldn't really be in the air,' thought Frank Barber, who served the RAF in both types. 'The undercarriage was so strong and so well constructed that you could drop them in very carelessly and get away with it.'[17]

The Hurricane's forgiving nature meant that even the most inexperienced airmen could usually handle it, whereas the Spitfire took more skill. According to the American fighter pilot James Goodson, who joined the RAF in 1939 through his repugnance toward Nazism: 'I think most pilots, when they switched to Spitfires, were disappointed. They had heard so much about it. But it was difficult to land because it was so sensitive, whereas with the Hurricane you could be ham-fisted and still land. With the Spitfire, you moved that stick just a fraction of an inch and the thing would immediately respond. Therefore you could always tell a pilot who had just gone from Hurricanes on to Spitfires by the way he landed. The aircraft was on one wheel, then the other, then ballooning up and down again because he was over-controlling.'[18] The simplicity of flying the Hurricane was highlighted on one occasion during the Battle of France when a new pilot, Johnny Gibson, arrived at 501 Squadron, as Ken Lee recalled: 'He hadn't ever seen a Hurricane. He'd only flown biplanes. The CO told him to go and have a little ride in a Hurricane on his own. Remember this was not a proper airfield, this was a piece of "ploughed land". He took it off perfectly, came back and landed it perfectly. Never having seen one before!'[19] Donald 'Dimsie' Stones of 32 Squadron wrote that he found the transition from the Harvard, one of the RAF's main trainers, to the Hurricane 'quite painless'. The first time he climbed into the cockpit his first impression was that 'it was larger than I had expected' and he was also struck by the smell: 'Every aircraft type has its own smell and to me all Hurricanes smelled of rubber and some sort of disinfectant containing alcohol which I always put down to glycol coolant and not – please God – to petrol leaking from the reserve tank immediately in front of the pilot.' The first flight itself was 'thirty-five minutes of pure joy'. On take-off he had noticed 'that the nose pitched up and down more than I expected but I soon got used to it and smoothed it out. The pre-take-off butterflies had gone, replaced by tremendous exhilaration – I was flying a Hawker Hurricane, the RAF's main fighter, and the power of it I could feel in my hands, feet and backside.'[20]

After a spell flying Westland Lysanders with RAF Army Co-Operation, Christopher Foxley-Norris transferred in July 1940 to a fighter training unit at Aston Down, where he was immediately at ease with the Hurricane. 'It's very often an instinct with an aircraft. You get into one aircraft and it gives you enormous confidence and you get into another and it doesn't. The Hurricane was very stable and at the same time manoeuvrable. If you didn't want it to turn it was absolutely rock steady. If you did turn, it was very manoeuvrable, more manoeuvrable than the 109.'[21] For Ray Holmes of 504 Squadron, his first flight in the Hurricane was 'one of my most exciting moments of the war'. Like Johnny Gibson of 501 Squadron during the campaign in France, Holmes had never even seen a Hurricane before he was asked to get airborne in one. But that first trip, which took place from Wick airfield, Scotland, in June 1940, left

him glowing with triumph. 'I was the master of my very own aircraft
. . . She handled so beautifully that I was soon at home with all the
normal manoeuvres of turns, stalls and spins . . . To bank the Hurricane
was as easy as turning a car's steering wheel. The control column was
cunningly geared and a gentle heave had the aircraft on its side in an
instant. Slow rolls, barrel rolls, rolls off the top of the loop all came so
easily. The surge from its powerful engine climbed you vertically in
fine pitch at 3,000 revs as though heading for outer space.' The landing was just as uncomplicated: 'With a little speed in hand she sat on
the runway smoothly and steadily at 68 mph and ambled to a docile
halt. The Hurricane and I were going to be good friends.'[22]

One of the paradoxes of the Hurricane was that its structure, a
legacy of the vanished biplane era, gave it an impressive resilience
in the new age of advanced technological warfare. In fact, many
pilots believed that it was even more robust than the all-metal
Spitfire because shells would often pass right through the fabric
rather exploding on impact. The toughness of the Hurricane
became legendary within the RAF during the war. The respect that
the plane inspired was shown in these words of Ben Bowring of
111 squadron:

> I liked it better than the Spitfire. I flew quite a lot of Spitfires, but as
> a general-purpose aircraft the Hurricane would beat the pants off the
> Spitfire. It was the plane that won the Battle of Britain. It could take
> a tremendous number of bullets, because it was made of wood and
> fabric. It would keep flying almost after it was destroyed. If you put a
> Spitfire and a Hurricane dogfighting together − not a question of
> speed or climb − the Hurricane would do better than the Spitfire.[23]

Bowring was once flying his Hurricane over Scapa Flow when
he went into a dive so violent that the wing was wrenched out of
alignment. In such circumstances, most other aircraft would have
disintegrated, yet Bowring's Hurricane remained airborne and he
was even able to land. 'That aircraft's a bloody miracle,' he said after
jumping out.[24] Bob Stanford Tuck felt the same when he was
attacked on a routine patrol over Southampton in June 1941. 'The
radio went dead and my speed was falling off rapidly. Oil and glycol
were drenching my legs. The plane stumbled on. My God, the

punishment those Hurricanes could take. The airframe could stand almost anything.' But the damage was too much even for Tuck's valiant fighter and he had to bail out into the sea, fortunately to be rescued by a coal barge.[25] During the Battle of Britain in July 1940, Eric Seabourne of 238 Squadron was hit by several Me 110s over Portland in Dorset. 'Large holes started appearing in my port main frame and I could feel the bullets hitting the armour plating behind my seat. It was time to get out of the way so I stuffed the nose down and achieved a magnificent speed of over 400 mph going straight down.' To his horror, Seabourne found that he could not get out of the dive. Nothing happened when he heaved and tugged at the control column. 'So I started winding the tail trim back, something we had been told never to do. But it worked and I came out in a beautiful gentle curve and I was flying again straight and level.' Seabourne throttled back and landed at his base of Middle Wallop in Hampshire. 'My aircraft had rather a few holes in it and needed a complete new wing. The engineer officer said it was amazing that the wing hadn't pulled off in the dive as two armour piercing bullets had lodged in the main spar.'[26]

Equal surprise was shown by engineers when Tom Neil of 249 Squadron was instructed to fly a Hurricane to an RAF Maintenance Unit at Henlow in Bedfordshire. 'I assumed it to be for a major inspection and gave it no more than a cursory glance.' When Neil landed at Henlow after flying without incident, he was approached by a sergeant, who expressed his astonishment. Neil asked why and with a shrug, the man said, 'It's an absolute wreck, that's why. One of the main fuselage members had been shot clean through. We expected it to come by road.'[27]

The sturdiness of the Hurricane also made it comparatively straightforward to repair, another crucial factor in the Battle of Britain when resources were under pressure. 'It was a rugged old thing,' said Dennis David of 87 Squadron. 'To repair a hole in the back of the Hurricane only needed a bit of dope fabric whereas on the Spitfire a panel had to be beaten in and riveted.'[28] If the Hurricane's damage was too severe to be repaired by the ground crews at an airfield or if the plane had come down in open country, then the plane would be taken by road to a depot run by the Civilian Repair Organisation, a large network of contractors and engineering companies overseen during the Battle of Britain by that managerial dynamo Lord Beaverbrook, the Minister of Aircraft Production. Once the Hurricane had been brought into a CRO unit, the damage would be assessed; then an order would be sent to Hawker Siddeley for the necessary parts. Like the Dowding system, the CRO was a masterpiece of administrative efficiency, embracing no fewer than forty-three different companies around the country, while there were also mobile CRO contractors that carried out repairs at the Fighter Command airfields. Among the firms that worked on the Hurricane were Taylorcraft of Rearsby in Leicestershire and David Rosenfield Limited, based at Barton near Manchester.

By mid July 1940 the CRO was returning aircraft to operational service at a rate of 160 a week. It has been calculated that 35 per cent of all the fighters issued to squadrons during the Battle of Britain were repaired aircraft. No fewer than 60 per cent of Hurricanes that crashed on British soil ended up back in service, the other 40 per cent serving as a useful supply line for components. Altogether during the war, 4,000 damaged Hurricanes were put back into service by the CRO, a remarkable achievement that not only lessened the impact of the Luftwaffe but also highlighted the durability of Sydney Camm's design.

The Hurricane was at its absolute operational peak in 1940, when it acted as the nation's saviour. Available in the numbers that were required, attuned to the needs of the RAF pilots, strong in attack, resilient in defence, the fighter was indispensable during the months when Britain's independence was under threat. It was this reality that led many pilots to decry any attempt to devalue the Hurricane's contribution to the battle of 1940, even if they recognized that over the span of the war the Spitfire was ultimately the greater fighter. 'Statistically speaking, the Hurricane did more damage to the enemy than the Spitfire did,' said Jeffrey Quill, who temporarily left his test-pilot duties at Supermarine to fight in the Battle of Britain. 'The Hurricane was a wonderful plane. I held the view that it took both the Hurricane and the Spitfire to win the battle and neither of them would have succeeded on its own. I personally have never liked people becoming very partisan about the Hurricane or the Spitfire.

Both the Spitfire and the Hurricane won the Battle of Britain and they should both be given credit.'[29]

The battle in which the Spitfire and Hurricane covered themselves in glory officially started, according to the retrospective judgement of both the British government and historians, on 10 July 1940 – though the Germans had mounted raids on the English coast and Channel shipping from almost the beginning of the month, while small groups of bombers had been making night attacks since the fall of France, though these were largely ineffectual. On 2 July Hitler, now recognizing that Britain under Churchill would not meekly surrender, authorized the three armed services to start drawing up formal plans for an invasion across the Channel. As a preliminary to the invasion, the Luftwaffe was given an operational order that aimed to bring the country to the brink of collapse through the pursuit of two related objectives: first, the destruction of the RAF's fighter force, and second, the closure of the English Channel to shipping, which would strangle Britain's imports. By 11 July the German Chief of Staff Alfred Jodl had drawn up the first outline for the assault, which gave the key duty of securing the sea route to the Luftwaffe because of the weakness of the Kriegsmarine. 'In the Channel, we can substitute command of the air for the naval supremacy we do not possess and the sea crossing is short there. The landing must therefore take place in the form of a river crossing in force on a broad front. The role of the artillery will fall to Luftwaffe. The first wave of landing troops must be very strong and, in place of bridging operations, a sea lane completely secure from naval attacks must be established in the Dover Straits.'[30] The plan envisaged the German army invading Britain in two waves totalling 260,000 men, supported by 34,200 vehicles, 57,500 horses and 26,000 bicycles.

At the beginning of July 1940 the Luftwaffe was by far the strongest air force the world had ever known. It possessed no fewer than 4,074 aircraft, more than twice the RAF's total strength of 1,963 planes. The vast German aerial armada include 1,107 single-seater fighters, a much greater total than Fighter Command's 754 Hurricanes and Spitfires. There were also 1,380 bombers, 357 two-seater fighters and 428 Stuka dive-bombers. The most formidable fighter was the Me 109, designed by the erratic genius Willy Messerschmitt. Like the

Hawker Hurricane, the Me 109 was a plane that was initially unwanted because the head of the Reich's Aviation Ministry, Erhard Milch, loathed its creator, a hostility that stemmed from a tragedy in 1931 when one of his closest friends was killed in a plane designed by Messerschmitt. Seething with bitterness, he tried to block the progress of the Me 109, only failing because of the vocal support given to the fighter by Ernst Udet, a daring First World War ace who had become head of the Luftwaffe's Technical Department and was close to Hermann Göring. Ironically, the Me 109 prototype was fitted with a Rolls-Royce Kestrel engine because German aero-engines were incapable of producing sufficient power until the arrival of the Daimler-Benz 601A in late 1937. Fast, well-armed, manoeuvrable, the Me 109 was one of the finest of the new generation of mono-plane fighters, though it had major defects. Unlike the Hurricane, it had a narrow undercarriage, which caused a high accident rate among its pilots. Moreover, its armament could be unreliable, especially the cannon that operated through the hub of its airscrew. It was also a smaller, slightly more delicate aircraft than both the Hurricane and the Spitfire, with a total wing area of 174 square feet, whereas the Hurricane's was 258 square feet and the Spitfire's 242 square feet.

The hugely experienced test pilot Eric 'Winkle' Brown, who flew almost every type of aircraft during the war, later said of the Me 109: 'I certainly did not think it was a great aeroplane. I think it was a wonderful workhorse in the war, as a fighter aircraft, but it had some nasty handling characteristics which were a disadvantage in combat. It was a very claustrophobic aircraft to fly, tight in the cockpit, and it was not an easy plane to land in bad weather.'[31] An interesting experiment to compare the performances of the Me 109 and the Hurricane was conducted just before the Battle of France on 2 May 1940, after an intact Messerschmitt fighter was captured by the British forces. Held at an airfield near Orléans, the trials consisted of climbs to 15,000 feet and mock dogfights.

The subsequent report, produced by 'Bull' Halalan of 1 Squadron, brought some reassurance to those who feared that the Hurricane might be badly outclassed in combat. 'Both the take-off and the initial climb of the Me 109 was better than that of the Hurricane, in spite of the fact that the Hurricane was fitted with a constant-speed airscrew and full throttle and full revs were used,' opened the account. But its tone became more positive: 'At 15,000 feet the aircraft separated and approached one another head-on for the dogfight. The Hurricane did a quick stall turn followed by a quick vertical turn and found himself on the 109's tail. The pilot of the 109 was unable to prevent this manoeuvre succeeding. From that point the Hurricane pilot had no difficulty in remaining on the tail of the 109.' Halalan concluded:

> The Me 109 is faster than the Hurricane by some 30 to 40 miles an hour on the straight and level. It can out-climb and initially out-dive the Hurricane. On the other hand it has not the manoeuvrability of the Hurricane, which can turn inside without difficulty. After this clear-cut demonstration of superior manoeuvrability there is no doubt in my mind that provided Hurricanes are not surprised by 109s, that the odds are not more than two to one and that our pilots use their heads, the balance will always be in favour of our aircraft, once the 109s have committed themselves to combat.[32]

Before the Battle of France the RAF had actually feared the Luftwaffe's other Messerchmitt fighter, the two-seater Me 110, more than the Me 109, partly because of the ferocious image that the Germans had given it, reflected in its nickname, 'The Destroyer'. But such anxieties were soon allayed in battle, where the Me 110 proved vulnerable because of its wide turning circle and poor acceleration. After 1 Squadron had shot down several of them at the end of March, a squadron report concluded, 'as a result of this combat it may be stated that the Me 110, although very fast and manoeuvrable for a twin-engined aircraft, can easily be outmanoeuvred by a Hurricane'.[33]

In contrast to the RAF, where the divisions in the command structure reflected different operational purposes, such as fighters, bombers, transport and training, the Luftwaffe was arranged in air fleets, each of them like an individual air force with its own self-contained organization and full range of aircraft types. For the Battle of Britain three fleets, or *Luftflotten*, were involved: Luftflotte 2, under Albert Kesselring, was based in the Low Countries and was given responsibility for attacking eastern England; Luftflotte 3, under Hugo Sperrle, described by Hitler as one of his 'most brutal-looking generals',[34] was based in northern France and charged with breaking western England's defences. The third fleet, Luftflotte 5, commanded by Hans-Jurgen Stumpff, was quartered in Norway and Denmark, ready to attack the north of England and Scotland.

The overall commander of the force, Hermann Göring, could not have been more different to his opposite number in Britain, Sir Hugh Dowding. Ruthless, charming, dynamic and cultured, he was a man of extravagant tastes and appetites, whose lust for power was matched by his devotion to luxury. A highly decorated flying veteran of the First World War, he was perhaps Hitler's closest ally, having joined the Nazi Party in 1922. It was this early involvement in extremist politics that led for a time to his chronic addiction to morphine, for Göring was given the drug after he was badly wounded during the notorious Munich putsch of 1923. After several stays in mental institutions, during which he was sometimes held in a straitjacket, he eventually conquered the habit through his own sheer willpower. As he grew ever more influential in the Reich during the 1930s, he increasingly wallowed in pantomime imperial grandeur. As well as castles, fine-art collections, retinues of servants, town houses and hunting lodges, all acquired through his corrupting greed, he had his own magnificently appointed private train, which included finely furnished bedrooms, guest cars and even a cinema. His self-indulgence was further reflected in his corpulent figure, weighing over 20 stone, and in his fondness for gaudy costumes, ranging from an all-white Air Marshal's uniform, bedecked with medals, to a theatrical hunting ensemble complete with green leather jacket and feathered hat.

Göring was also the opposite of Dowding in his thinking about air strategy. Describing himself, with typical egotism, as 'the Iron Man', he believed simply in using overwhelming force in the air. He had little interest in technology or organization, one reason he consistently underestimated the sophistication of radar and the Dowding system. Again, unlike the British, he never put any effort into the development of a four-engined strategic heavy bomber, an omission that seriously weakened the impact of the Luftwaffe during the Blitz.

For all his many intellectual and moral failings, Göring was a shrewd political operator, brilliant at exploiting his closeness to the

Führer. It was due in part to his influence that the Luftwaffe was such a colossal force in mid 1940 and was seen as the prime weapon in achieving the Reich's goal of bringing Britain to her knees. The Luftwaffe was 'at its zenith' when the battle started, according to Werner Kreipe, a senior officer in Luftflotte 3: 'The pilots were highly skilled. Their morale was very high and they were confident of victory.'[35] In accordance with Hitler's order of 2 July for an invasion across the Channel, the Germans began to probe the RAF's defences. On 3 July they dispatched 50 aircraft across the Channel, a quarter of them reconnaissance planes, the rest being bombers and their fighter escorts. Fifteen British civilians were killed when bombs fell on Guildford in Surrey, while the Fighter Command controllers sent up no fewer than eight squadrons to counter the attacks, shooting down five German aircraft. This was the pattern for the next few days, as numerically light, though sometimes lethal, German raids were flown over southern England or against shipping convoys. Eight Hurricanes from 79 Squadron, scrambled from Hawkinge in Kent to intercept two groups of Dornier 17s on the afternoon of 4 July, found themselves bounced by the Me 109 escorts. One pilot was shot down and killed over Dover as the rest of 79 Squadron was driven away. Three days later 79 Squadron lost another two pilots over Kent when free-hunting Me 109s swooped down on its Hurricanes. The exhausted and depleted unit, which had been in action continuously since the French campaign, was sent up to Sealand in Flintshire to re-group. The British public was also suffering. The night of 6–7 July saw sixty-two people killed in scattered attacks on Surrey and Hampshire.

The intensity of action increased from 10 July, the day subsequently designated as the start of the Battle of Britain by the Air Ministry, for the purposes of awarding campaign medals. At first, it seemed that this would be another routine day of skirmishes, but in the early afternoon the radar stations revealed a large build-up of enemy aircraft over Calais. The target was all too obvious: a major convoy, code-named Bread, heading westwards, which was escorted by just six Hurricanes. As soon as the extent of the enemy formation became clear, further reinforcements were dispatched from the southern airfields, including the Hurricanes of 111 Squadron based at Croydon in south London.

The RAF fighters soon found themselves confronted with a substantial German formation, made up of 26 Dornier 17s, 24 Me 109s and 40 Me 110s, acting as fighter-bombers. Despite being heavily outnumbered, the Hurricanes tore into the enemy using an extraordinarily brave but dangerous tactic. Contradicting all their training in Fighter Area Attacks, they flew in their vics head-on towards the Germans. The closing speeds were over 500 mph. The risk of collision was great. But the method caused terror in the German pack, which broke up in disarray. 'It was an effective way of doing it, but by golly, you had split seconds. It was so effective because it scared the living daylights out of them,' recalled Ronald Brown of 111 Squadron. 'You're flying along, minding your own business and three Hurricanes come blazing at you and there is nothing between you and them but Plexiglas. Under ideal conditions it was an effective way of attacking a bomber but you had so little time to get a bead on him and break clear. And of course you never knew if he was going to break up or down.'[36]

In fact, one Hurricane, flown by Tom Higgs of 111 Squadron, collided with a Dornier 17 and began to spin towards the sea. He was seen bailing out, but no rescue launch could find him and his body eventually washed up on the Dutch coast. The Hurricanes' unorthodox aggression ensured that just one of the ships in the Bread convoy was sunk. Other German raids on this day, 10 July, proved more successful. A force of 70 bombers managed to evade radar in the west of the country and launched heavy attacks on Swansea in south Wales and Falmouth in Cornwall, killing thirty people and causing damage to railways and shipping without any losses in return. But altogether, this first day of battle had been an uplifting success for Fighter Command, which had destroyed ten Luftwaffe planes and damaged six more, while only losing one Hurricane in the process. Put under pressure for the first time, the fighter control system had generally stood up to the test, as fighters in 11 Group were scrambled in time to meet the enemy. Furthermore, the weakness of the Me 110s had been confirmed. As soon as they had come under attack from the Hurricanes, they had gone into a tight defensive circle, covering each other's tails.

For the rest of July, the German attacks concentrated largely on shipping and southern coastal targets, though their operations were often hampered by changeable weather. Under political pressure, Sir Hugh Dowding was required to provide cover for the convoys travelling through the English Channel, something he was reluctant to do because the concept of standing patrols was the very antithesis of his strategy. His fundamental aim throughout the Battle of Britain was to conserve his resources as far as possible. This meant avoiding large set-piece air battles, in which a significant part of his force might be wiped out in a single afternoon, or lengthy patrols that drained away petrol and his pilots' energies without necessarily inflicting any damage on the enemy. The central purposes of the Dowding system were to ensure the concentration of force where it was needed most and to maintain the strength of the front-line squadrons. He knew in July, as the Germans conducted what became known as 'the Channel War', that the great trial over English soil would come soon. He would need every man and plane for that struggle. The longer Fighter Command lasted, the greater the chances of national survival, for by October, with winter approaching, it would be too late for Germany to mount an invasion.

Because Dowding only committed the minimum possible fighter protection to the convoys, the Luftwaffe came to enjoy daylight superiority over the Channel by the end of July. Four Royal Navy destroyers had been sunk and merchant vessels were under constant threat. Yet this apparent triumph was something of an illusion, because shipping could still travel along the route in little fear at night. Just as importantly, even though Fighter Command had refused to throw its full weight into the engagement, the Hurricanes and Spitfires inflicted much greater losses on the German air force than they themselves suffered. During the whole month of July the Luftwaffe lost 218 planes, compared to 115, including 47 Hurricanes, on the RAF's side, an augury of things to come. The lumbering Stuka dive-bomber again proved particularly vulnerable to the British fighters, as Barry Sutton of 56 Squadron found when he was scrambled on 25 July to attack a group of Ju 87s that were menacing a convoy. On seeing the Hurricanes arrive, the Stukas dived and tried to head back to France. But Sutton, who had only recently entered operational service, quickly had one of the German aircraft in his sights. 'The worst shot in the world couldn't have missed. In less than a second it was all over. It plunged like a stone and made a little splash. Something wound up in my stomach. It was my first Hun but there was no feeling of elation. I was conscious of a sickly, nauseating wave of sympathy for the wretched men I had sent to their doom.'[37]

Geoffrey Page was another member of 56 Squadron who experienced his first combat during the 'Channel War' or *Kanalkampf* as the Germans called this stage of the battle. 'Six of us were scrambled and, as we climbed, we were told that 20 bombers were coming in to attack a convoy, with about 60 fighters above them as escorts,' he recalled. Three of the Hurricanes were ordered to go for the bombers, the other three, including Page's, to attack the fighters. 'I suppose with hindsight I should have been scared stupid, but I was so busy getting my aircraft ready – for example making sure that the safety button on the guns was on "fire" and generally trimming up the aircraft for combat. Suddenly there was this enormous swarm of aircraft above us.' Initially, Page only saw some Me 110s:

> I had a quiet chuckle to myself when the Me 110s went into a defensive circle to protect themselves from an attack by just three Hurricanes. I dived into the circle, firing rather wildly through absolute inexperience. Then the 109s came down on us. There was this phenomenon, which I saw again and again during the war, that when you have a dogfight, there are so many aeroplanes and then suddenly it is as if the Hand of God had wiped the slate clean and there is nothing else in the sky. I suddenly found myself alone except that in the distance there was one speck of an aeroplane, circling. He was turning towards me. We approached each other and then I realized it was a Me 109. So we did the equivalent of tilting at the lists in medieval times. We just attacked each other head on. I could see the little white dots on the leading edge of his wing as he fired. I was feeling stubborn that morning so I did not budge. He flashed over the top of me and I returned to base and landed.

Page told his CO that he was not sure whether he had hit the Me 109, but seventeen years later a researcher sent him a cutting from a German newspaper showing a Luftwaffe pilot standing beside the wreckage of the same Messerschmitt in a field in northern France. 'So I got a confirmed kill seventeen years later.'[38]

Despite Dowding's caution, the Channel war placed a severe strain on the squadrons of Fighter Command. Eighty pilots, including some of the most experienced commanders, had been killed or seriously injured. Often over 500 sorties a day were flown. On 19 July no fewer than 701 sorties were carried out as the Germans unleashed some of the biggest raids yet. That day the RAF lost ten fighters compared to just four Luftwaffe aircraft destroyed, prompting Göring to boast of inevitable victory in the coming battle over southern England. 'Think now of all the bombers we can parade in the English sky. The few RAF fighters will not be able to cope.'[39] 11 Group pilots grew weary at the long hours, the constant pressure of dangerous missions, the pre-dawn rises to be at readiness for the first scramble. The stress could affect their flying, as Douglas Grice of 32 Squadron candidly admitted in recalling a sortie over the east Kent coast. Flying over Deal harbour, he suddenly saw three Me 109s on his tail. 'For the first time in my operational life, I froze. It was the most extraordinary feeling. I couldn't move, except that my hand was still on the stick and I was doing gentle banks left and right. I was looking straight ahead, motionless apart from that. Of course the inevitable happened. There was one very large bang. My engine stopped. I realized I had no rudder control and no left-hand aileron control.' But with the plane in its stricken state, he still managed to make a belly-landing on the links at Sandwich Golf Club in Kent. Having climbed out of the cockpit, he inspected the aircraft. 'The shell that had gone through my port wing-root and stopped the engine was a solid shell. How it missed my back, God knows. The shell that hit my tail was an explosive shell and had severed the rudder controls and half severed the elevator controls. I was lucky to get down.'[40]

Peter Townsend, now in command of 85 Squadron, was not so fortunate when he was in a fight with a Dornier 17 at 8,000 feet over the North Sea. In thick, dark clouds he had been guided to the target by 'the miracle of radar', but could 'only dimly see the Dornier through my rain-washed windscreen. I opened up the hood and slanted my head out into the battering slipstream. It helped a bit. Another hundred yards and I would have to risk a pot shot.' Despite the foul conditions Townsend was seen by the Dornier, whose rear gunner immediately opened fire. Feeling that the bomber was still out of his effective range, Townsend bravely drew closer, then pressed the gun button. Pieces of metal and fragments flew from the Dornier, but still the rear gunner kept on firing at Townsend. 'Suddenly there was a bright orange explosion in front of me,' he said. His engine had been hit. With no power, he could only glide down through the rain clouds. 'The sea was waiting for me. It was the minute of truth: life or death.' He stood in the cockpit and then bailed out head first. 'I was falling on my back, in total silence, my feet pointing at the sky, when I pulled the ripcord. The parachute canopy cracked open and the harness wrenched my body from its headlong fall. Far below I could see my Hurricane diving vertically towards the sea to disappear in an eruption of spume and spray.' Soon after he had landed in the sea, Townsend was picked up by a little boat sent out by a passing trawler which had seen him come down. One of the sailors pulling him from the water shouted: 'Blimey, if he ain't a fucking Hun.' From Townsend, there was only one possible answer: 'I'm a fucking Englishman.'[41]

Accidents rather than the Luftwaffe were to blame for some of the deaths that befell Fighter Command during this period. Between 10 July and 11 August no fewer than 47 RAF fighters were destroyed in accidents, and another 68 were badly damaged. Inexperience, poor judgement and bad weather all played their part. Teddy Donaldson of 151 Squadron based at North Weald in Essex witnessed one such tragedy, due to overconfidence by his fellow pilot and close friend Jack Hamar. In limited visibility 151 Squadron had been scrambled on 24 July, after an unidentified aircraft had been spotted over the Suffolk port of Felixstowe. Almost as soon as the Hurricanes were airborne, the message came through from the Group controller that the plane was in fact friendly:

> We turned round, and flying slowly at 120 mph and only some 60 feet above the ground, I waited for North Weald to reappear, which it did in a few minutes. I ordered Jack to break. To my horror, he broke upwards and commenced an upward roll. In a Hurricane it was impossible to carry out such a manoeuvre at that low speed. As I saw him start his right-handed roll, I screamed, 'Don't, don't' down the r/t, but it was too late. Jack stalled and hit

the deck upside down. I was on the ground and beside him within seconds. Jack had his hood open to improve the visibility in the awful weather conditions, which had caused massive head injuries. I was devastated. I absolutely loved the man.[42]

Only the day before, the RAF had announced the award of the Distinguished Flying Cross to Hamar for his gallantry in the air.

Traumatic and exhausting though the Channel War had sometimes been, it was only a prelude to the far greater struggle that lay ahead. By mid July, Hitler's determination to crush Britain had magnified. Accordingly, he issued Directive No. 16, which opened: 'As England, despite the hopelessness of her military situation, has so far shown herself unwilling to come to any compromise, I have therefore decided to begin preparations, and if necessary to carry out, an invasion of England. The aim of this operation is to eliminate Great Britain as a base from which the war against Germany can be fought, and, if necessary, the island will be completely occupied.' The planned operation was named *Seelöwe*, or Sealion. Two days later, in a typically bombastic speech at the Reichstag, Hitler urged Britain to come to her senses and avoid annihilation by reaching a settlement. 'A great Empire will be destroyed, an Empire which it was never my intention to destroy or even harm,' he fulminated, mixing threats with hollow pleas. 'I consider myself in a position to make this appeal since I am not the vanquished begging favours, but the victor speaking in the name of reason.'[43] Inspired by the RAF's defiance, the British were in no mood to listen to Hitler's so-called 'appeal to reason'. The angry mood was summed up by the *Daily Express* journalist Sefton Delmer: 'Let me tell you what we here in Britain think of this appeal of yours to what you are pleased to call our reason and common sense. Herr Führer and Reichskanzler, we hurl it right back at you, right in your evil-smelling teeth.'[44]

The British refusal to surrender led Hitler to hold a series of conferences with his military chiefs during the last week of July, during which they worked out more details of Operation Sealion, with the Luftwaffe again given the central role. At one stage Hitler sent for Hugo Sperrle, the commander of Luftflotte 3, and demanded 'the violent and maximum commitment of the Luftwaffe against

Britain'.[45] The Führer and High Command agreed that the full air assault on England should be launched on 5 August or the soonest possible date after that, weather permitting. The plan for the offensive was set out in Directive 17, issued from Hitler's headquarters on 1 August. 'In order to establish the necessary conditions for the final conquest of England,' the Directive stated, 'the German air force is to overpower the English air force with all the forces at its command, in the shortest time possible. The attacks are to be directed primarily against flying units, their ground installations and their supply organizations.' The document then instructed that 'after achieving temporary or local air superiority, the air war is to be continued against stores of food, and also against stores of provision in the interior of the country'. In even more sinister language, Hitler reserved 'to myself the right to decide on terror attacks as measures of reprisal', a move that would ultimately have fateful consequences for the Luftwaffe.[46]

On the day that Directive 17 was issued, Göring met his senior Luftwaffe commanders at The Hague in the Netherlands. Clad in his white uniform, the Reichsmarschall was in ebullient form, confident of impending victory and delighted at the trust that Hitler had placed in his force. 'Now, gentlemen,' he declared, 'the Führer has ordered me to crush Britain with my Luftwaffe. By means of hard blows, I plan to have this enemy, who has already suffered a decisive moral defeat, down on his knees in the near future, so that an occupation of the island by our troops can proceed without any risk.'[47] Göring believed that the RAF would be beaten within a few days or a fortnight at the most, provided the weather was good. The mighty offensive, called *Adlerangriff*, or Attack of the Eagles, would be launched on 10 August with three successive massed waves of attacks by Luftflotte 2 and 3, followed the next morning by a heavy assault from Luftflotte 5 based in Scandinavia. Echoing the theme of soaring Nazi confidence, the start of the campaign was to be entitled *Adlertag*, or Eagle Day. Göring's belief that the RAF was about to crumble ran right through the top ranks of the Luftwaffe. 'The situation as it presents itself against Britain is as favourable as can be. What will happen when the German air force employs its whole strength against England? The game looks bad for England and her geographical and military isolation,' said General Erich Quade, commandant of the Luftwaffe staff college.[48]

One key reason why the Luftwaffe was so confident was the gross underestimation by German Intelligence of the strength of Fighter Command. The campaigns over Norway, France, Dunkirk and the Channel were thought to have reduced the RAF to less than 500 fighters. But this neither took account of Dowding's careful husbandry of his resources, including the creation of large fighter reserves outside the southern England, nor the great expansion in aircraft production under Lord Beaverbrook's vigorous leadership. July alone saw more than 300 Hurricanes manufactured by Hawker and its Gloster subsidiary. At the end of the month Fighter Command's total strength, including reserves, was 964 planes, with 527 Hurricanes and 321 Spitfires making up the majority.

During the first week of August an eerie lull descended after the ferocity of the *Kanalkampf*. On several days there were no German raids at all. A mood of deepening tension gripped the RAF and the government. 'It's too quiet,' said Keith Park, commander of 11 Fighter Group, to Dowding, 'At least I've managed to re-establish my airfields but the blighters are up to something.'[49] Across the Channel, the front-line Luftwaffe pilots welcomed the respite but sensed that the time for greater action was looming. As Hans Joachim Jabs of 27 Fighter Group recalled: 'All of us had a gut feeling that something was now about to break. During the previous month we had all been engaged in heavy combat, but by the end of the month all operational missions became few and far between, many squadrons only going out on spasmodic attacks. We enjoyed the comfort and relaxation of that first week in August. We almost behaved as if there was no war on, although many asked the question . . . why?'[50]

The answer became clear on 8 August, when Göring issued his official order to the Luftwaffe telling them that Eagle Day was imminent. 'Within a short period you will wipe the British Royal Air Force from the sky.'[51] In fact, 8 August saw the first gusts of the breaking storm as the Luftwaffe mounted one of its largest operations of the war so far. Mistakenly taking advantage of the lull, the British merchant navy had sent a huge convoy of 25 ships, code-named Peewit, through the Straits of Dover towards the Atlantic. But

German radar, newly installed near Calais, picked up the movement along the Channel. That morning 57 Stukas, accompanied by 20 Me 110s and 30 Me 109s, took off to attack the convoy near the Isle of Wight, whose own radar station at Ventnor spotted the large German formation. Four squadrons of Hurricanes and Spitfires were immediately scrambled and a huge dogfight ensued, involving over 150 aircraft. As so often before, the RAF fighters were heavily outnumbered. It was 'a raid so terrible and inexorable that it was like trying to stop a steam-roller,' said 43 Squadron's Frank Carey, an exceptional pilot who had shot down 14 German planes during the Battle of France.[52] Despite the odds against them, the RAF pilots fought intrepidly. Though the Peewit convoy was badly mauled, the Luftwaffe lost 10 Stukas, 8 Me 109s and 4 Me 110s, as well as having another 12 aircraft badly damaged.

Flight Lieutenant Kenneth Grundy of 257 Squadron was one of the victorious Hurricane airmen, as recorded by the stark prose of his combat report. Patrolling at 14,000 feet, Grundy manoeuvred behind an Me 109 and then gave two bursts of fire from 250 yards:

> I observed Me 109 to be hit and dive in a gentle turn, disappearing into the sea with a trail of black and white smoke behind. Meanwhile, an Me 109 had got on my tail and I saw tracer bullets passing my right. After making sharp left turn through 300 degrees I found opportunity for two bursts of deflection shots on Me 109 turning outside me. This aircraft I observed to be hit in the starboard wing, emitting a white trail of petrol or smoke. It immediately turned on its back and dived steeply but still under control. I followed for approximately one minute, but turned back to rejoin my section.[53]

Another Me 109 fell victim to Eric Seabourne of 238 Squadron:

> I slipped in right behind him and followed right below him at about two or three hundred yards' distance. He didn't move. He just flew absolutely straight and level; it never varied a bit. So I set up my gun sight and lined him up. Still nothing happened so I got a bit closer. Still he went on straight and level. So I just eased the nose up till he absolutely filled the gun sight and then put my thumb on the button and kept it there. Large pieces flew off his aircraft all over the place and he went down in a vertical dive.

Moments later Seabourne saw the Me 109 plunge into the sea with 'an enormous explosion'.[54] Fighter Command did not escape without its own heavy casualties. Thirteen Hurricanes were lost, four more were damaged, one Spitfire was destroyed and twelve pilots killed. Nevertheless, the day's effort provided further encouraging signs that the Dowding system could respond swiftly to large German formations, and that the Hurricane could hold its own in combat. News bulletins about the action heartened a nation increasingly feeling itself under siege. That astute observer of the political scene, the effete Tory MP Henry 'Chips' Channon, noted: 'A great air battle over the Channel, and a vast number of German aeroplanes have been brought down over the coast! Our air force is sublime.'[55]

The attack of 8 August was not a carefully planned precursor to *Adlerangriff* but rather a purely opportunistic strike when the Peewit convoy had been identified. Understandably, however, Fighter Command saw it as the start of the major German assault, having been warned by Intelligence, using the Ultra code decrypts from Bletchley Park in Buckinghamshire, that Eagle Day was imminent. 'Members of the Royal Air Force, the fate of generations lies in your hands,' proclaimed the battle order that evening.[56] In fact, the launch of the mammoth offensive, which was meant to strike such fear into the hearts of the British, descended into a cocktail of frustration and confusion. First of all, because of poor weather, Göring had to postpone *Adlertag* from the chosen start of 10 August until the 13th, much to the annoyance of the Führer. Then, on 12 August, a concerted attempt by the Luftwaffe to blind Fighter Command in advance of *Adlerangriff*, by smashing the Chain Home radar stations along the south coast, ended in failure, partly because 11 Group again put up powerful resistance, partly because the buildings and aerial towers proved surprisingly resilient and easy to repair. Only Ventor on the Isle of Wight was out of action for more than a few hours and even it was operating again within less than three days. Once more, at the end of another major confrontation, the balance was against the Germans, as they lost 27 aircraft compared to the RAF's 21.

Adlertag itself, on 13 August, started badly for the Luftwaffe, when drizzle and fog over southern England persuaded Göring to postpone the assault yet again. But due to a breakdown in communications, his message never reached two large formations of Dorniers from Kesselring's Luftflotte 2, which flew on to England without their fighter escorts. Though they successfully bombed the coastal bases of Eastchurch and Sheerness, they were heavily attacked by the RAF fighter squadrons, losing five of their number. Another group, comprising Ju 88s, also never received Göring's instructions and were so harried by the fighters, including Hurricanes from 43 Squadron, that they completely missed their targets. The weather had cleared sufficiently in the afternoon for the massive, concentrated attacks to be mounted by Luftflotte 2 and 3 against the airfields and radar stations, but again Fighter Command coped superbly. Despite mounting almost 1,500 sorties, compared to the RAF's 700, the Luftwaffe suffered badly again, losing 44 aircraft to Fighter Command's 13. What was meant to be a day of triumph had turned into a definite defeat.

Stung by its losses, the Luftwaffe mounted only a few minor raids the next day. Meanwhile the British government and the public were filled with both jubilation and relief that Fighter Command had come through its sternest test. 'This is indeed a victory and will do much for public morale,' Churchill's private secretary Jock Colville wrote in his diary. 'The Germans can hardly sustain their present losses and it looks as if the tide may be turning.'[57] Colville's perception of the public mood was right. This note by a Mass Observation researcher was typical: 'More news of air raids; the number of enemy planes brought down is rapidly rising. I hear expressions of our splendid boys – what would we do without our air force.'[58]

The following day, 15 August, brought even greater setbacks for the Luftwaffe. For the first time Hans-Jurgen Stumpff's Luftflotte 5, led by 72 Heinkels, went into action, attacking Scotland and Yorkshire. But they lacked effective escorts, since the distance across the North Sea was too far for the Me 109s, while German Intelligence failed to recognize that Dowding had placed large fighter numbers in 12 and 13 Groups, with the result that the strength of the northern defences came as a shock to Stumpff's men. Twenty per cent of the Luftflotte 5 raiders were wiped out in action, with 81 crew members killed.

More success, however, was achieved by the two other German

air fleets that attacked from across the English Channel. The largest force yet assembled, comprising 800 bombers and 1,000 fighters, targeted airfields, industrial sites and ports in southern England across a front 500 miles wide. So many plots appeared on the home radar screens that the operators could not distinguish between the incoming formations. A *Daily Express* reporter, watching the vast horde of German aircraft approaching over the coast, wrote that the numbers were so great as 'to make an aluminium ceiling to the sky'.[59] Fighter bases ranging from Croydon in south London to Martlesham Heath in Suffolk were badly hit, as were the Shorts bomber factory at Rochester in Kent and the radar station at Foreness near Margate, also in Kent. But even in the face of this unprecedented onslaught, the fighter pilots remained undaunted, hurling themselves at the enemy despite their much smaller numbers. Even under extreme pressure the Dowding system continued to operate effectively. By now, the controllers had developed the general policy of sending the faster Spitfires towards the German fighters and the slower Hurricanes towards the bombers, though in practice the turmoil of combat often rendered such demarcations meaningless.

Confronting a pack of raiders over Martlesham Heath, for instance, Hurricanes from 1 and 17 squadrons took on both the Me 110s and the Me 109s. The spirit of Fighter Command was vividly captured in the account told by Roland Beamont of 87 Squadron based at Exeter in Devon, who took part in a savage dogfight over Portland. The squadron had just nine Hurricanes operational that day, but did not hesitate to go on the attack against a German formation of more than 150 aircraft, as Beamont explained:

> The controller said, 'Bandits, twenty miles ahead, you should see them directly.' Almost immediately the blue sky began to turn into a mass of little black dots. It could only be described as a beehive. Our CO continued to lead us straight towards it. I wondered what sort of tactics he would employ: dive out of the sun or come from behind. While I was thinking, it became apparent that he was not going to do anything like that. He bored straight through the middle of this lot, until we seemed to be going into the biggest formation of planes you ever saw. Then he said, 'Target ahead. Come on, chaps, let's surround them.' There were just nine of us.

Without a hint of panic, the Hurricanes tried to choose individual targets within the mass of planes:

> I fired at a Ju 87 at point blank range. I hit it. I could see my tracers going into it, then I rolled away from it as I went by because I was going much faster than the Ju 87. While I did that, I came under attack from a Me 110, doing a zoom climb, firing straight up at me. He missed me. I rolled away from him, and straight behind one of his mates. I fired a long burst and his port engine started to stream smoke and fire. There was a lot of activity behind his tail so I went into a very tight, diving turn until I was free of all the other aeroplanes. I levelled out and then climbed back up. As often happened in that sort of confused fight, there was no sign of any other Hurricane. I could see a formation of aeroplanes in the distance, which was probably the rest of the enemy heading off back across the Channel, and two or three streaks of smoke in the sky where there were burning aircraft. By then I was over Lyme Bay. I could see great boils in the water where either bombs or aircraft had gone in. There was nothing else to do but go home.[60]

The sort of astonishing bravery exhibited by the men of Fighter Command that day could come at a high price, as Douglas Grice of 32 Squadron found when he was shot down during a dogfight over the Essex port of Harwich:

> I was flying what the RAF called Arse-End Charlie, weaving like mad and looking all around me. Suddenly, out of the corner of my eye, I saw a flash over my left wrist. The next moment, the cockpit was in flames. The heat was enormous. I did two things absolutely instinctively. My left hand had gone to the handle of the hood and my right hand to the pin of my parachute harness. I was pulling with both hands. The next moment I was out in the open air. I had made no attempt to jump from that aircraft. What I think happened was that I was doing a left-hand turn and my aircraft had gone on turning on its back and I had just fallen out.

Once he came down in the sea, Grice tried to blow up his Mae West lifejacket. 'I wasn't terribly successful because something seemed to have happened to my face. There were bits of skin flapping around my eyes and my mouth felt very uncomfortable. I realized I'd been burnt.' He was picked up by a rescue launch and then taken to a naval hospital, where a surgeon cut away the loose pieces of skin. His face was then put in a mask. A few days later part of the mask was removed around the eyes and Grice caught a glimpse of himself in a mirror. 'There I was, purple, with this terrible-looking mask. Talk about Frankenstein. I really was a sight.' Soon afterwards he was visited by the pioneering plastic surgeon Dr Archie McIndoe, whose clinic at East Grinstead in West Sussex was achieving remarkable results with revolutionary skin-graft techniques. 'Quite shortly, I'm going to have to take a piece of your bottom,' said McIndoe breezily. But such a drastic procedure was never required because Grice's face began to grow a new skin on its own. As McIndoe told him: 'You're one of those lucky chaps who isn't going to need me. The main reason is that you came down in the sea and we've learnt that a brine bath is the best initial treatment for bad burns.' Eventually, the only legacy of Grice's experience was a red line around his face where the mask had been.[61]

The Germans flew over 2,000 sorties on 15 August, a figure that was not to be surpassed for the remainder of the Battle of Britain. But the day had been a disaster for them, becoming known within the Luftwaffe as 'Black Thursday'. They had lost 75 aircraft to the RAF's 34, two of which were destroyed on the ground. The attempt by Luftflotte 5 to devastate the north of England and Scotland had backfired and never again would that fleet mount another major raid during the battle. Over the coming weeks its aircraft were transferred to the other Luftflotten on the Channel coast. Within the senior ranks of the Luftwaffe there was dismay at how badly mistaken the predictions of the RAF's weakness had been. 'We thought that the propaganda about England being unprepared was wrong and it annoyed us. We found the English well-prepared and our job was not an easy one. We were not hopeful of victory,' wrote the German fighter ace Adolf Galland.[62]

For the RAF, 15 August had been a vindication of the Dowding system and the men and machines of Fighter Command. During the day Churchill had visited its headquarters at Bentley Priory, to watch the action unfold in the main operation. That evening, his warrior impulse still quivering with excitement, he told his colleagues that he had just witnessed 'one of the greatest days in history'.[63] The press joined in this mood of celebration, feeding the public wildly inflated figures of the RAF victories. *The Times* described how, in the battle over Kent, 'the Hurricane pilots swooped down on the Nazi airmen and in the general melee that followed completely broke up the enemy formation'. The paper had further enthusiastic coverage of the action over Portsmouth in Hampshire and the Yorkshire coast, where the air 'was filled with diving and zooming aircraft' as the Hurricanes attacked the Me 110s. Fighter Command, concluded the report, had again broken its record: 'One hundred and forty-four enemy aircraft were destroyed – the greatest total of any single day of the war.'[64] It was almost double the real total, but in a fight for national survival the exaggeration was forgivable.

More than six years earlier, the Hurricane design had been rejected by the British government. Now it was the mainstay of the nation's defence. As the aviation historian Francis Mason later put it: '15 August was the day that justified the Hurricane. It was then that almost every Hurricane squadron – built up and nurtured over the past three years – went into action to defend this country against the heaviest attack that Germany could mount.'[65] But darker times lay ahead for the fighter squadrons as the Battle of Britain approached its climax.

7

'The sky seemed full of Hurricanes'

E VEN IN THE First World War's new age of aerial adventure, Welshman Ira 'Taffy' Jones stood out for his boldness. Having only become a pilot in 1917, he had shot down thirty-seven German planes by the end of the conflict. This record included an exceptional spell of eleven days in the summer of 1918, when he destroyed six enemy aircraft, earning the DFC in the process. Though he was in his mid forties at the outbreak of the Second World War, his audacity had not faded over the two intervening decades. As an officer with Training Command in Swansea, he was once flying an unarmed aircraft, which was towing a target for trainee pilots, when he spotted a Ju 88. Instinctively he gave chase and opened fire with his Very pistol, a type of flare gun. That was enough to send the bomber hurrying away from the coast. But Taffy Jones knew that fear was an integral part of air warfare, as he told the trainees under his instruction. One of his lectures during the late 1930s was recalled by Pete Brothers, a renowned Hurricane pilot who won the DFC in 1940 and later became Director of Overseas Operations for the RAF: 'He stuttered terribly. And Taffy warned us that there was going to be a war and we were going to be in it. And – I make no apology for his language – this is how he put it, he said, "When you g-get into your f-first f-fight you'll be f-fucking f-frightened. Never f-forget that the c-chap in the other c-cockpit is t-twice as f-fucking f-frightened as you are."'[1]

The life of any Battle of Britain airman was filled with mortal danger. During a combat he might be killed directly by the enemy's shells, which could even pierce armour plating at a range of less than 200 yards. Bullets might hit his fuel tanks or oxygen bottle, causing his plane to explode in a ball of fire. His controls might be shot to pieces, sending the aircraft into an uncontrollable spin. His engine might fail. He might find it impossible to open the hood if he had to bail out, a particular problem with the early Hurricanes. Even if he escaped, his parachute might not open or he might come down in the freezing sea and die of hypothermia before he could be rescued. In August alone, eighty-five Hurricane pilots were killed and another sixty-eight badly wounded. The grim shadow of death could not be avoided. For many it loomed ever larger as the battle dragged on for week after week. Harold Bird-Wilson of 17 Squadron candidly remarked in a post-war interview:

> You read many stories nowadays of pilots saying that they were not worried when they saw little dots in the sky which gradually increased in numbers and grew in size as they came from the French coast. I maintain that if anyone says that he was not frightened or apprehensive on such occasions then he is a very bad liar. You cannot help but get worried when you look around you and see eleven other aircraft and you look ahead of you and see hundreds of aircraft coming towards you, whether they be fighters or bombers. I don't believe that any man is that tough. I openly admit that I was worried, frightened at times. As the battle went on and on, we were praying for bad weather. We prayed mighty hard. Fatigue broke into men's mentality in the most peculiar ways. Some got the jitters and facial twitches. I had nightmares at night. I admit that I used to wake up in the dispersal hut, sleeping within 25 yards of my aircraft, after imagining that I'd been night-flying my Hurricane. This went on for a long time.[2]

Yet, for all such fears, Bird-Wilson could hardly have had a more heroic war record. Having survived a horrendous pre-war accident, which left his face so badly damaged that it had to be rebuilt by Dr Archie McIndoe at East Grinstead, Bird-Wilson, still aged only twenty, shot down six enemy aircraft during the Battle of Britain before he himself became the German ace Adolf Galland's fortieth victim in a dogfight over the Thames estuary. Badly wounded and burned, Bird-Wilson managed to bail out of his flaming Hurricane and came down in the water, from where he was picked up by a rescue launch. After a period of hospitalization, he returned to active service in November 1940. With some shrapnel still lodged in his head, he went on to claim another five victories during the war.

Equally inspirational was the record of Dennis David of 87 Squadron, who shot down eleven German aircraft during the Battle of France in May and June 1940, won the DFC and then, during the second week of August, destroyed another four Luftwaffe aircraft. Like Bird-Wilson, he was honest about his sense of disquiet. 'The fear is there. There is no real man who is not frightened, although once the battle started you were so busy, you did not have time to think. I'll always remember the smell of cordite. When the enemy is shooting at you, you can actually smell hot lead. That shows you how close combat was. It was a horrible feeling. Hot lead smells, and to smell that in the cockpit was quite something.'³

Occasionally, men would buckle under the strain, unable to cope with the constant, pounding tension. Anger could play as big a part as fear in such cases. Squadron Leader Gerald Edge of 605 Squadron had an astonishing experience during the Battle of Britain at the hands of one of his comrades, a Pole named Wlodzimierz Samolinski, who said that his mother and sisters had all been raped by Russians during the collapse of his country. On a clear morning the two men were flying on patrol, Samolinski about 50 yards on Edge's starboard beam:

> After about half an hour he gave the sign that he wanted to change sides. I was very glad to agree, as it can get tiring looking round from that one position. He came in. I saw his wing about 15 feet below me. As the wing disappeared, my plane was suddenly filled with incendiary bullets. According to the Observer Corps, there was no other aircraft around there. The burst came through and immediately I went on fire. I dropped in the Channel. I don't know what happened to him. He just must have cracked. He never came back.⁴

From April 1940 the RAF officially classified cowardice as 'lack of moral fibre' (LMF), an extremely serious offence which could result in a pilot being stripped of his rank, demoted to menial duties or expelled from the air force. Teddy Donaldson of 151 Squadron had one such case during the Battle of Britain. 'He came and admitted to me that he was terrified. I noticed it before he told me, because he had too many engine failures. He would just disappear in the middle of the battle and go home.'⁵ But the RAF, though aware of the need to maintain discipline, could also be sympathetic, certainly more so than the First World War generals with their infantrymen. Peter Brothers recalls one pilot in his squadron who started to become physically ill at the thought of combat. 'He had reached the stage where he had got beads of perspiration on his head. He was sitting at dispersal with us and I thought he must have got pneumonia. He looked hot and his hands were shaking, so I sent him off to a doctor.' The message came back that he was not to fly again. 'He subsequently became a test pilot testing rebuilt aircraft and had a ghastly crash, badly smashed up, but he went back to it. He had a lot of guts, but not the sort of guts to face the enemy.'[6]

Given the pressures on the airmen, it is a reflection of their toughness that there were not more cases of breakdowns or flinching in the face of the enemy. The incidence of LMF was extremely rare, and in the whole of the RAF it stood at a rate of just 0.4 per cent during the war. What was more striking, however, was the willingness of the vast majority of pilots to overcome their natural fears and keep on flying. Even men whose taut nerves meant they suffered spasms of vomiting before every sortie continued to fight. Indeed, for all the stress that individuals were under, morale in Fighter Command rarely faltered during the Battle of Britain. 'If people were frightened or tired or neurotic or disillusioned or despondent, there was an unwritten rule in Fighter Command that you did anything rather than show that,' said American pilot James Goodson.[7] The culture of Fighter Command sustained morale by downplaying the drama and the intensity of the fight, thought Roland Beamont of 87 Squadron. 'Apprehension or bragging were laughed out of court. No matter where you were, there was this extraordinary spirit. One of my greatest recollections of that time was the laughter. There was a release of tension in seeing the funny side – perhaps some might say a bit of hysterics – but it never occurred to us like that.'[8]

No two men captured that spirit better than James 'Ginger' Lacey, the highest-scoring ace of the Battle of Britain, and Douglas Bader, who overcame major disabilities to lead a Hurricane squadron from June 1940. The son of a Yorkshire cattle dealer, Lacey claimed that his brilliant marksmanship was due to his childhood experience of shooting rabbits on the Dales. Known at school as Ginger because of his shock of red hair, he found that the nickname stayed with him for the rest of his life. In his youth he trained as a pharmacist, but his heart was always in flying and in 1936 he joined the RAF Volunteer Reserve, becoming an instructor with Yorkshire Airways Limited two years later. When war broke out he was called up to 501 Hurricane Squadron as a sergeant pilot and soon impressed colleagues with his resoluteness, excellent shooting and sharp eyesight. During the Battle of France he had five victories, including an incredible performance on the morning of 13 May when he shot down three German aircraft before breakfast, an achievement for which he won the Croix de Guerre. This superb record continued during the Battle of Britain, in which he was credited with eighteen victories.

Lacey's most famous victory came on 13 September. Flying on patrol over Kent, he spotted a lone Heinkel 111 and dived down on it. The German bomber was badly damaged, but gave enough return fire for Lacey's Hurricane to take some shells in its radiator, forcing him to bail out. He came down near Leeds Castle, having suffered only minor injuries. As it turned out, Lacey's target was reported to be the plane that had earlier dropped bombs on Buckingham Palace, so by royal association he instantly became a celebrity in the press, though the historian Stephen Bungay has cast some doubt as to whether the Heinkel that Lacey hit was really the Palace attacker.[9] His escape over Kent pointed to another of Lacey's vital attributes as a fighter ace: his good luck. During 1940 he had to resort to his parachute several times, once crash-landed in a bog and on another occasion, after his engine was hit by enemy fire, he had to glide his stricken Hurricane down into Gravesend airfield in Kent. 'They are shooting me down too often,' he noted laconically in his logbook following one such incident.[10]

Later in the war Lacey flew Spitfires in the Burma campaign, taking his total number of victories to twenty-eight. Boyish-looking, modest but independent-minded, he had the kind of humorous perspective that was typical of the RAF. Asked about which of the two fighters he preferred, he replied: 'I'd rather fly in a Spitfire but fight in a Hurricane – because the Hurricane was made of non-essential parts. I had them all shot off at one time or another, and it still flew just as well without them.'[11]

Aged over thirty at the time of the Battle of Britain, Douglas Bader was far older than Lacey and most other airmen in Fighter Command. Like that other stubborn but heroic pilot, the Dambusters' leader Guy Gibson, Bader was the son of a civil engineer working in India and was educated at St Edward's School, Oxford. A brilliant student at the training college of Cranwell, where he was described as 'plucky, capable and headstrong', Bader was commissioned in the RAF in August 1930.[12] Such was his dedication to flying that he neither smoked cigarettes nor drank, for he reckoned that either activity could affect his health and concentration. But one year later, when he was still only twenty-one, his impetuosity almost cost him his life. Practising in a Bristol Bulldog biplane over Woodley airfield near Reading, he made a tragic error at low level and allowed the left wing tip to touch the ground. Immediately the Bulldog went out of control and disintegrated on impact with the ground. Dragged from the wreckage, Bader hovered between life and death in intensive care at Reading infirmary, his body in deep trauma after both his legs were amputated. Only his monumental willpower pulled him through. At one stage he dimly overheard a nurse whisper to a colleague: 'Quiet, there's a boy dying in there.'[13] This was the moment when he galvanized himself to start his recovery. The same iron will was demonstrated when he taught himself to walk on his artificial legs without the aid of a stick, though his brusque impatience could sometimes be trying for the nursing staff. 'Take it easy – and I do wish you wouldn't use that appalling language,' said one.[14] He might have learnt to walk again, but the idea of renewing a career with the RAF was out of the question. Much to his frustration, he had to take a clerical job in the City.

War brought Bader his liberation. With the RAF crying out for experienced pilots, he was re-engaged in November 1939, flying Spitfires at first, then, from June 1940, leading the Hurricane 242 Squadron based at Duxford in Cambridgeshire. During the Battle of Britain he scored eleven kills in his Hurricane, plus one other probable. It was a plane that he held in deep affection, as he later wrote: 'I grew to love it. It was strong, highly manoeuvrable, could turn inside the Spitfire and of course the Me 109.'[15] Ironically, Bader's severe physical handicap may have helped him in combat. The tremendous gravitational, or G, forces generated by aggressive manoeuvres drained the blood downwards from the head to other parts of the body, chiefly the legs, causing pilots to lose their vision and their ability to move the controls, a process known as 'blacking out'. Without his legs, Bader took longer to be affected by G forces and therefore had an advantage over his opponents. But he was not a faultless pilot. To the amusement of his squadron, he once crashed on take-off when he forgot to put his airscrew in fine pitch rather than coarse.

Nor was Bader universally popular. His relentlessly driven, self-centred personality could grate on others, though most were willing to forgive him, knowing that without his obstinacy he would never have taken to the air again. 'I got used to his rather gruff and egotistical attitude towards life. He was not only a successful person but a difficult one. A hero has to be to get through,' said fellow Hurricane pilot Ben Bowring.[16] Bader's remorseless optimism and contempt for Germany was also the attitude that was needed when the nation was in peril. On one occasion, after listening to a young comrade agonizing over the sight of a Messerschmitt pilot being burnt to death, he said without a shred of sympathy: 'No one asked the buggers to come over here.'[17]

It was another tribute to the Hurricane that both the Battle of Britain's highest-scoring ace, James 'Ginger' Lacey, and the RAF's most famous pilot, Douglas Bader, flew the plane during the conflict. Similarly, the only Victoria Cross won throughout the battle was awarded to a Hurricane pilot, Flight Lieutenant James Nicholson of 249 Squadron, who showed death-defying selflessness when he went into his very first combat against the Luftwaffe over Southampton in Hampshire on 16 August. 'I had never fired at a German in my life and I was longing to have a crack at them,' he wrote. He soon had his wish. Climbing to 18,000 feet, he was suddenly hit by four cannon shells from an Me 110. 'The first shell tore through the hood over my cockpit and sent splinters into my left eye. One splinter, I discovered later, nearly severed my eyelid. The second cannon shell struck my spare petrol tank and set it on fire. The third shell crashed into the cockpit and tore off my right trouser leg. The fourth shell struck the back of my left shoe and made quite a mess of my left foot.' With his Hurricane in flames, Nicholson prepared to bail out. But then the Me 110, carrying out a steep turn, came into his gunsight. Ignoring his own agony from the fire, Nicholson sank back into his bucket seat. 'I pressed the gun button, for the Messerschmitt was in nice range. I plugged him first time and I could see my tracer bullets entering the German machine. He was going like mad, twisting and turning as he tried to get away from my fire. So I pushed the throttle wide open. Both of us must have been doing about 400 mph as we went down together in a dive.' As Nicholson kept firing, his left hand remained on the throttle to keep it open. The hand 'seemed to be in the fire itself and I could see the skin peeling off it. Yet I had little pain.' After a final burst, Nicholson saw the German plane falling from the sky. Then he pulled back the hood, undid his straps and bailed out.

Somersaulting downwards, he fumbled for the ripcord with his mutilated hand. Almost as soon as the parachute opened, another Messerschmitt came hurtling past. 'I decided to pretend I was dead, and hung limply by the parachute straps. The Messerschmitt came back once and I kept my eyes closed but I didn't get the bullets I was half expecting.' As he floated down, Nicholson looked at the extent of his injuries. Blood was pouring from his left foot. The bones on his left hand were showing through to the knuckles. His right hand was badly burnt too. 'I began to ache all over and my hand and leg began to hurt a lot.'[18] His ordeal was not over. Heading towards an open field near the village of Millbrook in Hampshire, he was shot at from the ground by a member of the Home Guard who mistook him for a German, despite Nicholson's shouts that he was from the RAF. Some of the pellets from the antiquated airgun lodged in his backside, adding to his agony. Luckily, a butcher's boy had witnessed the aerial duel and Nicholson's descent. He cycled furiously to the scene, where he first punched the Home Guardsman, then arranged for help to be brought for the badly injured pilot. After a spell at the RAF hospital in Halton, Buckinghamshire, Nicholson began a lengthy convalescence at the Palace Hotel in Torquay, Devon. During his stay there, he received the news that he had been awarded the Victoria Cross, part of his citation reading: 'This incident shows that he possesses courage and determination of a high order. By continuing to engage the enemy after he had been wounded and his aircraft set on fire, he displayed exceptional gallantry and disregard for the safety of his own life.'[19]

Nicholson was characteristically modest about the award, as one of his fellow Torquay convalescents, William Walker, recalled: 'At first Nick got into trouble for being improperly dressed, because he refused to stitch the maroon ribbon to his tunic. In the end I think he adopted the attitude that he was accepting the medal on behalf of us all. He was a very good sport, in fact.'[20] Nicholson recovered sufficiently to return to active service, serving with the RAF in India. Tragically, he was killed in May 1945 when an RAF Liberator bomber in which he was flying as an observer crashed in the Bay of Bengal after catching fire. His body was never recovered.

On the day that Nicholson brought down the Messerschmitt, 16 August, Winston Churchill visited Keith Park's 11 Group headquarters at Uxbridge. From the gallery in the Operations Room he watched with a mixture of alarm and admiration as Park sent up his squadrons to confront more huge raids by the Luftwaffe, which flew 1,715 sorties against southern England that day. As he left for Chequers that evening in the back of his official car, Churchill turned to his Chief of Staff Sir Hastings Ismay and said: 'Don't speak to me; I have never been so moved.'[21] The Prime Minister stared out of the car window into the black night, apparently lost in thought. Then, a few moments later, he broke the silence: 'Never in the field of human conflict was so much owed by so many to so few.'[22]

Four days later Churchill repeated those words in one of his great set-piece orations at the House of Commons dispatch box. Taken up by the press, the phrase 'The Few' at once resonated with the public, embodying the sense of gratitude and adoration felt towards the heroes of Fighter Command. 'My uniform has become the key to hospitality everywhere,' wrote the American Art Donahue in a letter home. 'These people almost worship the RAF pilots. Conductors on buses and policemen in the streets just fall over themselves to help me find my way about.'[23] Pete Brothers remembered rarely having to pay for a drink during the Battle of Britain: 'When you had a night off and went up to London, someone insisted on paying for your meal or sending over a bottle of wine. Quite incredible.'[24] Contrary to some post-war myths, most of 'The Few' were not insouciant ex-public schoolboys with handlebar moustaches. In fact, of the 3,000 pilots who took part in the Battle of Britain, only 200 had been to private schools. Class consciousness was less powerful and social hier-archies less rigid than in other services, partly because the RAF was little more than twenty years old. Men hailed from a wide variety of backgrounds. Bob Stanford Tuck, born into a Jewish family from Catford, London, had served in the Merchant Navy before the war. The leader of 151 Hurricane Squadron, Victor Beamish, an ex-rugby-playing Irishman who exuded aggression, had graduated from RAF Cranwell in Lincolnshire as early as 1923.

Around a fifth of the pilots in Fighter Command were born overseas, either within the British empire or in nations conquered by Germany, especially Poland and Czechoslovakia. So large was the number of Polish recruits that two separate Hurricane squad-rons were created for them, 302 and 303 Squadrons, both of which established reputations for unrivalled ferocity in combat. 'The Poles were great but they felt very differently from us. They really felt that they had to kill Germans. They had much more of a killer instinct,' recalled Peter Matthews of 1 Squadron. Once, on a brief spell of leave during the Battle of Britain, he saw the Hurricanes of 303 Squadron firing at Germans who had bailed out and were coming down in their parachutes, conduct that ran against the traditional code of the RAF. 'They owned up to it. They said that the only good German was a dead German.'[25] The deadliness of the Polish fighter pilots was highlighted by 303 Squadron's record of forty-four kills, making it the leading Hurricane-equipped unit of the Battle of Britain.

The bravery shown by 'The Few' was all the more impressive, given the exhaustion the pilots and ground crews had to endure because of the long hours and continual action. 'We were sometimes going up five times a day,' recalled Brian Considine of 238 Sqaudron. 'We had our backs to the wall. The fatigue was terrible. I think I lost a stone in weight over that period.'[26] Gus Holden of 501 Squadron once went home on leave, climbed straight into bed and slept round the clock for over twenty-four hours. The early starts in the Hurricane squadrons were one reason for this tiredness. During the hectic months of August and September 1940, the day for many pilots could begin well before dawn, as they were woken up in their living quarters before reporting for operational duty at their dispersal huts on their airfield. Most crews had their accommodation at their stations, but some, like those Hurricane units based at Croydon, outer London, had to use nearby private rented rooms. Ray Holmes of 504 Squadron, which used the Hendon airfield in north-west London during September 1940, had this memory of those early mornings. 'We would hear the horn of the Humber brake when it was still dark about 5 a.m. We would struggle, befuddled with sleep, into our clothes, and stumble out to the brake, which shot off to the Officers' Mess.'[27]

Pilots generally wore ordinary service uniforms, sheepskin-lined flying boots, leather gauntlets and silk scarves to stop their necks being chafed by the constant turning in combat. As winter approached, they donned the famous Irvin fur-lined brown leather flying jackets which came to be so closely associated with wartime RAF, though Leslie Irvin, the garment's designer, was actually an American and former Hollywood stuntman. The pressures of war could bring with them peculiar sartorial unorthodoxies. 'Some pilots scrambled in their pyjamas or with their trousers over their pyjamas,' recalled Harold Bird-Wilson of 17 Squadron.[28] After breakfast the pilots would be driven out to dispersal, where they would carry out checks on their aircraft and equipment, complete the necessary paperwork and warm up the engines. 'It was check helmet, parachute and map, and don Mae West. Then sign Form 700 certifying that your aircraft is serviceable for fuel, guns, radio and airframe. Out and into it to start and warm up the engine. After a check for rev drop on either magneto and a test of hydraulics and electrics, it was back to dispersal,'[29] said Ray Holmes. As they finished their checks on the Hurricanes and returned to their dispersal huts, most airmen placed their parachutes either in the cockpit or on the wing, ready for the first scramble.

The actual process of starting the Hurricane's Rolls-Royce Merlin engine was described by the Hawker test pilot Bill Bedford. This involved:

unscrewing the ubiquitous Ki-Gass priming pump, pushing its plunger in and out and thus passing neat fuel into the power-plant. One-and-a-half to two pumps of the Ki-Gass was usually adequate to coax the Merlin into life, depending on the weather temperatures, and one would keep the device open just in case more neat fuel was needed until the engine ran smoothly. With the fuel flowing and ignition switches on, you simultaneously pressed the starter-motor and booster coil buttons – actions which were soon followed by a marvellous crackle from the engine as it barked into life.[30]

Once satisfied that the Merlin was running well, the pilot had to carry out other checks, as Graham Leggett of 46 Squadron recalled. 'You did pre-flight checks on the landing flaps, the lever for the under-carriage and the lever for the variable-pitch airscrew. You checked the buttons on the temperature and fuel gauges, making sure you had a full load of petrol. You trimmed the aircraft, which meant taking the weight off the control surfaces by a couple of wheels. You made sure that the gun button was locked in the safe position. There was also a flap behind the radiator which you could raise or lower to control the amount of air passing through it. Those were the checks so that at scramble all you had to do was run out and jump in the cockpit.'[31]

After returning to their dispersal huts, the pilots might have tea or a second breakfast. Then they would wait for the order to scramble. Some might sleep, others might play cards or cricket. What they almost all came to dread was the shrill sound of the ringing telephone, which could signal the start of the day's first sortie. 'You were at a high nervous pitch. Every time the phone rang you got an unpleasant butterfly feeling in the stomach,' said Francis Twitchett, who flew with 43 Squadron in the Battle of Britain.[32] Sometimes the call might be about some administrative banality or news that the NAAFI (Navy, Army and Air Forces Institute) cart was on its way with more refreshment. But at other times it would be the instruction to become airborne. Immediately there would follow a frenzy of activity as the men rushed to their Hurricanes. It was a matter of pride for most squadrons that they had reduced the schedule before take-off to a minimum. Kenneth McGlashan of 245 Squadron habitually tried to doze while waiting at readiness, but the moment he heard the word 'scramble':

I'd fly to my feet. At this time there was absolutely no fear as I ran to my aircraft, concentrating on not tripping over. Climbing into my cockpit, plugging in the r/t, strapping on my helmet, parachute and safety straps. With a thumbs up to the ground crew, magnetos on, battery OK and a press of the starter button the Merlin would shake and explode into life. Gauges would come to life and I'd wave away the battery cart and chocks; we'd be on our way. From slumber to slipstream in less than two minutes.[33]

Some pilots, out of necessity or superstitious ritual, urinated on the tailwheel before climbing into the aircraft. Often, to speed up the scramble, the fitters themselves started the Merlins and then assisted the pilots by strapping them into their cockpits. A graphic description of the scene at 504 Squadron's base was provided by Ray Holmes:

There was surprisingly little panic. The odd lighted cigarette may have been flung into a chair, or poker dice scattered around the floor in the rush to get out of dispersal, but nobody lost his head. The ground crews were superb. From all directions came the splutter and roar of Merlins leaping to life. How those boys had got to the aircraft ahead of us was a mystery. The din mounted as twelve engines thundered their eagerness to be away. Dust clouds and the occasional forage cap or empty oil tin caught in the slipstreams, went swirling across the airfield. Each pilot, goggles pulled down, peered through the dust storm to follow his leader as the twelve raced to the runway.[34]

Gathering speed as they hurtled over the grass, their Merlin engines at a deafening roar, the Hurricanes became airborne at around 350 yards. As well as pulling back the column to begin the climb, each pilot now had the job of retracting the Hurricane's undercarriage and flaps, which were operated by a set of levers in an H-shaped arrangement on the right-hand side of the cockpit. According to Pete Brothers, this required 'seconds of feverish, yet totally co-ordinated hand movement'. It was 'a tricky procedure' that could only be performed by the pilot switching his right hand from the control column onto the up levers for the undercarriage and flaps. At the same time his left hand, normally used for the throttle, had to hold the stick. 'You could always tell a Hurricane pilot was "cleaning up" his machine as it tended to porpoise whilst being flown by the "throttle hand". Some pilots mastered the technique of seamless flight with both hands but most tended not to bother,' said Brothers.[35] The complexity of this movement meant that it was vital for the friction nut on the throttle to be tightened before take-off. If this was not done, explained Hawker test pilot Bill Bedford, then as the pilot flew with his left hand, 'the unrestrained throttle would come back to the closed position and the aircraft would lose height just when you really didn't want it to'. Many pilots were caught out like this, said Bedford, 'as they fought to tighten up the nut in mid-air, whilst trying to retract the gear and control the Hurricane with the same hand. Worse still, some pilots subsided ignominiously back to earth with the undercarriage only partially extended.'[36]

One feature of the throttle that was beneficial to the pilot was its ability to provide an emergency boost of 12 pounds per square inch from the Merlin, an asset that was particularly useful for the Hurricane in combat against the faster Me 109. But the use of boost, known as 'pushing through the gate', could only last a maximum of five minutes because of the overload on the engine. Early in the Battle of Britain, Sir Hugh Dowding sent a memo to all his fighter groups complaining that pilots were 'overstepping the engine limitations' by resorting to the emergency boost 'with little excuse on every occasion', and the result was that there had been 'an increase in the number of engine failures'.[37]

Once their planes were climbing, the Hurricane pilots were guided towards the target by the ground controllers, whose instructions employed simple coded phrases like 'bandits' for the enemy or 'angels' for each 1,000 feet in altitude. In the air, said Teddy Donaldson of 151 Squadron, 'it was a matter of steering the course until the next message was received. "Bandits approaching you from the south, same altitude." Then silence. Then "Bandits 100 plus." Then one's eyes got like organ stops with staring until every enemy was placed.'[38] Once the Germans were sighted, the squadron leader shouted the old hunting cry of 'Tally ho' over the r/t, the cue for an attack to commence. Most of the Hurricane pilots had full confidence in the effectiveness of the Dowding system. As Ray Holmes put it, 'whenever we were given a course to steer, it always took us straight onto the bombers. If we hadn't had radar, we'd have had squadrons flying around uselessly, whereas radar always took a squadron to an interception.'[39] But that was not a universal view. One rare voice of dissent came from Peter Down of 56 Squadron, who was 'never a great believer in the idea that ground control was really much help or that radar was any good. It was much easier to find the enemy by watching the ack-ack shells bursting or following the vapour trails. You knew exactly where to go before the Ops room came on to you. That method worked.'[40]

Whatever the qualities of the control system, a major problem facing any Hurricane pilot was the plane's weakness in the climb. Recalling his fights against the Luftwaffe in August 1940, Ken Lee of 501 Squadron said that the Germans invariably seemed to be above him. 'It was a long, long climb, pushing, trying to get there. It's only four or five miles different in the speed, especially when you're climbing and they're going straight and level. You're not closing fast, so that's the waiting period, the time to get close enough to do the damage. The luxury of being able to dive in from above them was unheard of except in those early days in France when we did find them in all kinds of compromising situations.'[41] Some Hurricane pilots tried to compensate by climbing more steeply, but this only diminished the rate of acceleration while also harming the engine, as Dowding warned in another of his complaints: 'A less steep angle with a forward speed of 150 to 180 miles per hour will not affect the rate of climb materially, and will prevent the engine overheating with the subsequent liability of engine trouble.'[42] The difficulties of the climb were exacerbated by the Hurricane's lack of any rudder bias, which meant that a pilot had to keep his leg fully extended on the rudder during a full-throttle climb or rapid descent to counteract the effect of the engine torque pulling the aircraft to the left. Tom Neil of 249 Squadron felt this was 'a thoughtless and irritating omission' in the design of the Hurricane, adding after one gruelling mission in September that 'if this business went on indefinitely, they would have to breed pilots with one leg longer than the other'.[43] Ironically, Douglas Bader, the one man in Fighter Command who due to his handicap could have artificially fulfilled Neil's somewhat macabre vision, used his friendship with the Hawker test pilot Philip Lucas to have a manually operated rudder bias fitted to his own Hurricane.

The Hurricane Mark I had an absolute service ceiling of 33,000 feet but its effectiveness diminished at high altitude, while the temperature drop within the cockpit also became increasingly uncomfortable for the pilot. 'The Hurricane was a terribly cold aircraft in which to fly at altitude, with holes and draughts everywhere around the cockpit. And no heating either,' recalled Tom Neil, who said that, above 20,000 feet, 'even with three pairs of gloves – cape leather, silk inners and gauntlets – my hands invariably turned to stone, as did my feet'.[44] The plane was at its best at 15,000 feet, though this was still a height at which pilots had to use their oxygen since no RAF fighters had pressurized cockpits until much later in the war. Irving Smith, a New Zealander with 151 Squadron, felt that oxygen equipment on the Hurricane was awkward to operate and poorly designed: 'The oxygen systems were manually controlled and you had to keep your eye on your oxygen settings as well as your altitude to make sure that you turned on the tap enough to give you enough oxygen for your altitude. It was very difficult to pay attention to things of this nature when you were dashing around or being shot at. Our oxygen masks were so bad that the moment you put any G on, they dragged right round off your face and under your chin. So at altitude, when you started hauling your plane round, you ended up with no oxygen. All this affected your vision, your performance. Nonetheless, one survived.'[45]

Establishing twelve kills as a pilot with 249 Squadron in 1940, Neil was able to give a compelling insight into what happened during a typical moment of combat in the Battle of Britain. Having been at readiness since dawn on 27 September, he was scrambled at 8 a.m. from his base at North Weald in Essex to intercept a German formation over Dover. On his approach towards the enemy at 18,000 feet:

> I checked my cockpit for the umpteenth time; oil pressure 70 pounds; radiator temperature 85 degrees; oxygen on and flowing; gunsight on but a little bright – I turned it down a fraction; gun-button to 'Fire'; everything else in order. With tension mounting, I wriggled in my seat. Satisfied, I heightened it up a notch to allow me just to see that little bit more, then flicked up the unlocking device on my straps in order to lean forward. Satisfied, I pushed my shoulders firmly to the rear so that lock clicked into position – didn't want the gun-sight thumping me between the eyes, did I? Rock hard that brutal device.

Soon Neil was heading towards a defensive circle of Me 110s. Instinctively, he fired into the 'tilting silhouette of one', then gave another a quick burst. 'The sky seemed full of Hurricanes, climbing and diving, wings whirling, a mass of aircraft racing in all directions.' Then he managed to get on the tail of an Me 110. He opened fire. The German rear gunner responded as the Messerschmitt levelled out. Neil pressed his gun button again. 'More fire from the rear cockpit, twisting and flicking in my direction, so close that I flinched, expecting the metallic thud of bullets.' But Neil raced even closer, 'less than 50 yards and all fear erased by a flood of surging adrenalin. The gunner ignored – forgotten. I fired again, tracer, sparks and twinkling flashes everywhere. Right up its backside with a clear sight of the twin rudders, wobbling.' The Me 110 started to fall from the sky, with Neil's Hurricane in pursuit, still firing. 'A brief bubble of red which produced a developing stream of the blackest smoke. I'd got him! He was going!' Fascinated by the sight, Neil kept chasing downwards, the smell of burning aircraft filling his cockpit. 'My altimeter unwinding like a clock gone mad. Faster. Steeper. The whole aircraft stiff and trembling. Pull out! Pull out! Down to 5,000 feet and going like hell. The 110 disappearing into a haze and still diving steeply. Streaming. A goner! It must be!'[46] At last, Neil pulled away and began to climb again.

Despite Neil's rich account of the headlong pursuit of the plummeting Me 110, there was a serious technical problem with the early Merlin engine, compared to the Daimler-Benz 601, when it came to sudden dives in combat. All the Merlins on the Battle of Britain Hurricanes and Spitfires tended to cut out temporarily as a result of an interruption to the fuel flow if the pilot rammed the stick forward to pitch the nose down and perform a negative G force manoeuvre. The German engine did not suffer this difficulty because it was fuel-injected, so Luftwaffe pilots gradually learnt that they could escape the RAF fighters simply by going into a dive. The only way that an RAF plane could overcome the temporary loss of engine power was by performing a half-roll so that the aircraft was subjected to positive G, but this had the disadvantage of losing time, when every second in combat was precious. The reason that Rolls-Royce had not considered using a fuel injection system on their own engines was because, before 1940, the company had not recognized that negative G forces would play such a major role in combat. It was a bigger issue for the Spitfires than the Hurricanes, whose primary responsibility was to attack the slower bombers. Nevertheless, the problem was a source of frustration throughout Fighter Command until Beatrice 'Tilly' Shilling, a young female engineer at the Royal Aircraft Establishment at Farnborough in Hampshire came up with a simple but ingenious solution. She devised a flow restrictor, shaped like a metal washer, which ensured exactly the necessary supply of fuel to the engine to maintain maximum power. By March 1941 all Merlins in Fighter Command had been fitted with this diaphragm, which, with inevitable male ribaldry, had been nicknamed 'Miss Shilling's orifice'. In the longer term, a permanent answer was found with the development of Bendix and pressure carburettors from 1943, both of which could cope with negative G.

Technical drawbacks on the Hurricane were balanced by its indomitable resilience, but even its toughness could not survive every attack. When a fighter had been hit too badly to return to base, its pilot faced the choice of either making a crash-landing or bailing out, his decision based on the extent of the damage and the location of the aircraft. Alec Ingle of 605 Squadron was once travelling back to Croydon, when cannon shells smashed into the engine, the oil tank and his starboard wing. As well as having no aileron control, he could not see out because the windscreen was covered in black oil. As his plane rapidly lost height, he slid the hood open so he could peer out. To his horror, there were trees and a railway cutting ahead. 'I thought to myself, "This is an impossible situation." I watched my knees literally knock together till they hurt.' But he pulled himself together, avoided the trees and brought the plane down 'with a rather pronounced bang' on a field just beyond the railway. 'It's funny when you arrive with a loud bang on the ground, you stop very quickly because your wheels are up. Suddenly there is an absolute silence except for the hiss of the coolant escaping. It is most incredible. From being very noisy, there is this tremendous stillness. You get out very quickly because you don't know what is going to happen next.'[47] Fortunately for Ingle, the plane did not burst into flames. Only a few days later he again came under fire flying back to Croydon, this time the shells ripping into the cockpit. He later gave this memorable description of the sound of their impact. 'Suddenly there were five loud splats on my armour plate. The noise was just like dropping boiling water onto a metal surface.'[48] On this occasion, with his plane wrecked, Ingle had to bail out.

The standard procedure for bailing out was for the pilot to open the hood, undo the straps, turn the Hurricane on its back and then be sucked out by the air pressure. If the situation was desperate or the pilot was unable to manoeuvre the plane, he simply slid back the canopy, stood up in the open cockpit and dived out, hoping that he did not hit the airframe or get his parachute entangled in it. Bailing out over the sea was potentially more dangerous than over land, since the RAF, unlike the Luftwaffe, had no air-sea rescue organization. The best an airman could hope for was to be picked up by a passing boat. Only on 22 August, after vociferous complaints from Fighter Command about the mounting death toll, did the Air Ministry supply a force of 12 Lysanders to look for downed pilots at sea. It was not until 1941 that a proper rescue service was formed. Moreover, during the Battle of Britain, Hurricanes carried neither dinghies nor fluorescent liquid with which they could mark their position in the water. Even at the height of summer the temperature in the English Channel never rose above 14 degrees centigrade, with the result that a pilot, floating in his Mae West lifejacket, had a maximum of four hours before he would die of hypothermia. The plane itself was poor at ditching because its big underside radiator would scoop up water and send the aircraft under the waves in a few seconds.

One of the most agonizing experiences of being shot down over the sea was endured by Geoffrey Page of 56 Squadron, whose Hurricane was hit during a clash with a German bomber formation on 12 August over the Thames estuary. As Page went on the attack, 'I could see all this tracer coming from the whole formation. They had singled me out as the target. All these things, which looked just like lethal electric light bulbs, kept flashing past until there was an enormous bang and the whole aircraft just exploded.' It had been worked out by scientific experts at the Royal Aircraft Establishment, Farnborough, that inside a burning Hurricane cockpit the heat at

15,000 feet went from cool room temperature to 3,000 degrees centigrade in about 10 seconds. Page instinctively carried out the RAF drill: 'I released the harness that strapped me to my seat. I slid the hood back, rolled the Hurricane onto its back and kicked the control column so that the aircraft pointed its nose upwards. As I was upside down, that popped me out of the aircraft like a cork out of a toy gun.' But Page, who had not been wearing gloves, had been horribly burnt on his hands and face. Through the scorching pain he pulled the ripcord, the feeling of the cold metal ring on his burnt flesh 'like an electric shock'. After floating down into the water, he had a desperate struggle to release himself from his parachute and blow up his Mae West. To his anguish he quickly found that the lifejacket had been burnt through. 'My face was beginning to swell up from the burns at this point. I could not get my helmet off because the leather strap under my chin had been badly seared.'

Page began to swim for the Kent coast, which he could glimpse in the distance, but this was another ordeal because his 'swollen eyelids began to close'. Exhausted but still making his way to the shore, he was picked up by a small lifeboat put out by a Trinity Lighthouse vessel that had seen him come down. He was taken into Margate harbour where he was greeted on the quayside, rather incongruously, by the town mayor clad in full municipal regalia and a top hat. 'Welcome to Margate,' said the alderman. There followed a long period of hospitalization and plastic surgery at East Grinstead under the care of Dr Archie McIndoe. Remarkably, Page had recovered sufficiently from his burns to be flying again in 1943.[49]

For a Hurricane pilot who was able to make it back to his station, there was a strong sense of relief on landing. After all that the plane had been through, bringing it onto the grass of the airfield was probably the most straightforward task of the entire sortie, made all the easier by the Hurricane's forgiving undercarriage. Paul Richey of 1 Squadron wrote this deliberately staccato description of the usual method for landing the fighter: 'Throttle right back now. Slow down to 160 mph. Wheels down. Now flaps. Turn in now. Open the hood. Hold speed at 90. Tailwheel right back. Over the boundary. Hold off a fraction. Sink, sink – right back now with the stick. Bump, rumble, rumble, rumble – fine. No brakes – plenty of room. Tiny bit heavy that one. Not quite right. Oh well. Taxi – run the petrol out of the carburettor, switch off ignition, brakes off, undo safety and parachute harness and jump out.[50]

Once the Hurricane had come to a halt, the ground crew went into action: refuelling and rearming the plane, checking for damage, and carrying out repairs. For the pilots, the phalanx of riggers, fitters, electricians, radio mechanics and armourers were the unsung heroes of the Battle of Britain. The intensity of work at the height of the conflict was recalled by former armourer Robert Spalding:

> When one of our Hurricanes landed, a sharp lookout was kept to see if the patches on the gun ports were still intact. If not, it meant the plane had been in action and that a quick refuel and rearm was necessary to get back into the air. On such occasions speed was essential and many a time the armourer would be removing the gun panels before the propeller had stopped revolving. Meantime his assistants had arrived with the belts of ammo which were deftly fed into the boxes – each gun was provided with an ammunition box containing 350 rounds – using a side-to-side motion so as to eliminate any chance of entanglement when the guns were used.[51]

The pressures on the ground crews were alleviated by a powerful camaraderie, said Arthur Hudson of 605 Squadron: 'Relations with the pilots were very good. There was a wonderful spirit in 605. I had never experienced anything like it, this feeling of everyone pulling together.' Hudson was also proud of his job. 'Being an armourer was the best trade in the air force. We always regarded the pilots as chauffeurs for our guns.' But it was a role that could have its dangerous moments, as he found once when a Hurricane had been taken to the hangar to have its guns cleaned and harmonized. While two of the armourers where working on the muzzles, a young, inexperienced aircraft hand climbed into the cockpit and somehow let off the guns. By a miracle, at the very moment he pressed the button, the two armourers had bent down to pick up some fresh cleaning cloths. 'The whole lot went off. You're talking 350 rounds each out of eight guns. He was literally paralysed with his hand on the firing button. He couldn't loosen it. As you can imagine, with the doors shut, there was a terrific row in the hangar. We were full of smoke. Everyone was dashing round to see who was dead. Amazingly no one had been hurt. The hangar door had been virtually blasted away.' According to Hudson, it was later discovered that some of the rounds had gone through the top of the hangar door and actually hit the weathercock on Chichester Cathedral two miles away.[52] Like the fighter pilots, most ground crewmen were filled with admiration for the Hurricane, a feeling that was well put by Frank Hartley, based at Manston airfield in Kent: 'I have a vivid recollection of one Hurricane landing with tail planes, elevators and rudder reduced to a mere framework, with pieces of fabric hanging loose. As we surveyed the damage I remember thinking that this kite had defied all the known laws of aerodynamics as the pilot had coaxed it home.'[53]

Every iota of the Hurricane's celebrated resilience was needed in the weeks from mid August, as the RAF fought for survival and the Luftwaffe stepped up its attacks on southern England. On 18 August, after a lull the day before, Göring launched another major offensive in what became known to Fighter Command as 'the Hardest Day'. In a series of massed raids that lasted from noon until the evening, the Germans flew 970 sorties, mostly against 11 Group airfields. Biggin Hill in Kent and Kenley in Surrey were particularly badly hit, the Kenley Sector Operations Room having to move to a local shop. On patrol at 17,000 feet, Ken Lee of 501 Squadron was one of the casualties of the clash over Kent. 'A bullet hit me in the back of the leg. Immediately there was smoke and flames coming out from underneath the main tank.' He rolled the Hurricane onto its back and pushed himself out, coming down in a cornfield, where he was met by the Home Guard and taken to a local golf club, some of whose members had a rather odd set of priorities. 'We went in and I was given a brandy. There were all these people. "You know, old chap, I was on the fourth tee and this aircraft came so low it made me miss my stroke!"'[54]

Only too aware of the deadly earnestness of the struggle, Keith Park, commander of 11 Fighter Group, had every squadron in action that day, and he also had to call on the assistance of the Hurricane and Spitfire squadrons from Leigh-Mallory's 12 Group to protect his airfields north of the Thames estuary. Further west, the largest formation of Stuka dive-bombers ever dispatched against Britain was targeted at naval airfields around Southampton in Hampshire and the radar station at Poling near Littlehampton in West Sussex, though the choice of bases belonging to the Fleet Air Arm rather than Fighter Command may have represented another error by German Intelligence, which generally performed badly throughout the Battle of Britain, from underestimating the RAF's strength to providing poor reconnaissance. The Stuka assault as it crossed the English coast was an intimidating sight, 109 dive-bombers escorted by 157 Messerschmitt 109s and 110s along a 25-mile-long front. Again, Park had to call on outside help to cope, with 68 fighters from Quintin Brand's 10 Group scrambled to lend support. Against the faster RAF planes, there was to be no safety in numbers for the vulnerable Ju 87s, which were badly mauled. Indeed, despite the damage to some of the 11 Group airfields, this turned out to be another disappointing day for the Luftwaffe, of which 60 aircraft were destroyed in comparison to the RAF's 35 losses. In addition, 94 German aircrew had been killed and 40 captured.

Fighter Command was meant to have been crumbling by now, according to Göring's *Adlerangriff*, but in the previous week the Luftwaffe had lost over 300 aircraft. Park was understandably gratified by the performance of his Group, and sent a memo to his sector stations, congratulating them on their success on 18 August. In his communications with his commanders he also gave some tactical advice, stressing that the primary duty of the fighters was to bring down the German bombers, which ideally should be attacked before they reached their targets. 'Against mass attacks dispatch a minimum number of squadrons to engage enemy fighters. Our main object is to engage enemy bombers, particularly those approaching under the lowest cloud cover,' he wrote.[55] Furthermore, he urged that interceptions should take place over land to avoid losing pilots in the Channel, while he recommended the use of direct head-on attacks when the bombers had a large escort. In addition, he emphasized the need for 10 and 12 Groups to provide cover over the airfields of 11 Group when his own fighters were engaged in tackling the enemy intruders, an instruction that was soon to cause friction with Leigh-Mallory who felt his squadrons should be given a bigger role in the Battle of Britain than merely mounting defensive patrols.

Göring, too, was in talks with his senior officers, but he was in a far less equable frame of mind. At a conference on 19 August, held in his majestic hunting lodge of Karinhall north-west of Berlin, he raged at the heavy losses his force had suffered, then ordered three major changes of strategy. First, the hopeless Ju 87s were to be withdrawn from action. 'Until the enemy fighter force has been broken, Stuka units are only to be used when circumstances are particularly favourable,' he said.[56] Secondly, the bomber formations had to be given better protection, with the Me 109s taking the primary role as escorts, though he also urged the continuation of freelance fighter sweeps to draw up the RAF. Most importantly, the Luftwaffe was to concentrate all its efforts on the Fighter Command in the south-east, having at last realized that his airforce had been dissipating its resources by spreading them across a wide range of targets. 'We have reached the decisive period of the air war against England. The vital task is to turn all means at our disposal to the defeat of the enemy air force. Our first aim is the destruction of the enemy fighters. If they no longer take to the air, we shall attack them on the ground,' Göring declared.[57] This was precisely the approach that Dowding and Park had feared: the full might of the Luftwaffe focused exclusively on the destruction of 11 Group. So far, a steady flow of fighters from the factories and pilots from the operational training units had made up for losses, but a prolonged increase in the rate of attrition would be unsustainable. Already, over the previous nine days before 19 August, Dowding had lost eighty-eight pilots, many of them irreplaceable in terms of experience.

During the next three days from 20 August, there were only minor skirmishes, as both sides regrouped. Then, on 24 August, the Battle of Britain entered its most lethal phase for Fighter Command. Huge raids pounded the airfields, the planes on the ground and the control organization. Hornchurch and North Weald airbases in Essex, and Manston in Kent, were all badly damaged on 24 August. The following day saw an attack by 300 German planes targeted at Warmwell in Dorset and Middle Wallop in Devon. 'My mouth feels hellishly dry,' wrote Ian Gleed of 87 Squadron, based at Exeter, recalling how he was sent up to counter the vast German formation. 'There is a strong sinking feeling in my breast. Thank God a doctor isn't listening to my heart. It's absolutely banging away.'[58] An account of another ferocious clash, this one over the Thames estuary on 26 August, was provided by Kenneth Grundy of 257 Squadron, based at Debden in Essex, in a letter to his girlfriend. Having told her that he was instructed to intercept a large formation of Me 110s and Me 109s, acting as escorts for Dornier bombers, he explained that his section got split up:

> by a few stray Jerries buzzing around, and the next thing I knew was a ruddy great earthquake in my aircraft and my control column was almost solid. On my left another Hurricane was floating about over a complete network of smoke trails left by cannon shells and incendiary. We had been attacked by another unseen bunch of Me 110s. After shaking the bleeder off my tail I managed to get some fairly close but ineffective deflection shots into him but he used his extra speed and dived away clean out of range, leaving me with plenty of others to contend with. I joined up with another Hurricane and Jerry just seemed to dissolve. We couldn't find any at all. When I landed afterwards I found that my tail was all shot to hell and that my flap spar was bust in two up near the wing root and my starboard aileron was split in two halves and jammed against the wing. In my excitement of getting away I had wrenched the broken part free. I haven't yet had a real chance of getting my own back.[59]

As the raids continued towards the end of August, the RAF's losses began to approach those of the Luftwaffe for the first time in the Battle of Britain. On 26 August, 27 RAF planes were destroyed, compared to the Luftwaffe's 34. On 30 August, flying an unprecedented 1,054 sorties, Fighter Command sustained 20 losses, just four less than the Germans. Parts of the control organization were stretched almost to breaking point. When Biggin Hill was hit again, with thirty-nine of its personnel killed and power supplies cut, its Operations Room had to be transferred to Hornchurch.

Worse followed on the last day of August as the Luftwaffe again used massed attacks on the approaches to London. Biggin Hill, Croydon, Debden, Hornchurch and North Weald all suffered. Compared to the German losses of 39 aircraft, Fighter Command had

37 aircraft destroyed, 9 pilots killed and 18 others badly wounded, the worst single day of the battle so far. Peter Townsend, leader of 85 Squadron, having fought so indefatigably for months, was one of the Hurricane pilots shot down after being scrambled to intercept a large enemy formation heading for Croydon and Biggin Hill. As he prepared to take off on that fateful sortie, 'I glanced at my squadron which had formed up behind me. They looked superb, all those Hurricanes – straining against the brakes with their long eager noses tilted skywards and the sun glinting on their whirling propellers.' The order came from the controller to take off and 'we were racing forward with a bellow of twelve thousand horsepower'. Straining their airframes, the Hurricanes climbed to reach the target, a formation of Me 110s and Me 109s. Soon Townsend was on the tail of one German, but did not realize another was just behind him. 'My thumb was on the firing button, but I never fired. A blast of shot splattered my Hurricane, my left foot kicked off the rudder bar, petrol gushed into the cockpit. The shock was so terrific that I went into a steep dive.' Townsend managed to straighten up the Hurricane, then bailed out. As he came down, 'I watched my poor Hurricane dive into the trees and blow up.' Seriously injured, Townsend would miss the rest of the Battle of Britain.[60]

Even more traumatic was the experience of Squadron Leader Tom Gleave of 253 Squadron, another superb Hurricane ace who only the day before had shot down an incredible four Me 109s south of Maidstone in Kent, one of them with a brilliant piece of deflection shooting. 'Top speed is not everything when you come to a melee. Manoeuvrability was the answer and the Hurricane's manoeuvrability was clearly superior to the 109s,' he said, explaining his success. As he flew on the afternoon of 31 August at 12,000 feet, he admitted that he 'looked forward to another chance to put my firing skill into action'. Just over Biggin Hill he saw a large formation of Ju 88s, 1,000 feet above him and moving in parallel lines. He decided to lead the squadron on the attack using the unorthodox method of firing from underneath. 'So I rocked my wings, telling the others to follow. I raked number five in the line of Ju 88s on the outside. I turned at the top of my climb, dived and repeated the process on number three.' But just as he was about to go for another bomber, 'I received an incendiary shell in my starboard tank and my own aircraft burst into flames.' As he prepared to bail out, he was engulfed in fire. 'I tried to get out but couldn't because of my burns. Then the aircraft blew up and I was thrown clear.' Somehow, even with his ravaged hands, Gleave managed to pull the ripcord and float down in a field. He was now in agony. 'All the skin on my right leg and most of my left leg were like balloons. And my hands and face.'

An open Austin 12 tourer arrived on the scene to take Gleave to hospital. 'The wind was playing on my injuries. I kept saying, "For Christ's sake do something. How much longer?"' Having reached Orpington hospital in south London, he was immediately pumped full of morphia. 'The first few weeks, I don't remember, I was barmy.'[61] When he had recovered sufficiently, Gleave was allowed to receive a visit from his wife, though he was understandably worried about her reaction, given that a mask covered his grotesquely swollen face. 'Peering through the slits in my mask, I heard the footsteps approaching the bed. My wife stood gazing at me. She flushed a little, then asked: "What on earth have you been doing, darling?" I found it hard to speak. "Had a row with a German," I managed to say eventually.'[62]

The tide was now running in favour of the Luftwaffe. Göring's strategy of attacking the English airfields and giving his bombers heavier fighter escorts had brought results. By the first week of September, Fighter Command was gripped by crisis. Thirty-nine of Dowding's ninety-seven flight commanders had been killed or wounded since 1 July, and in August the total number of pilots lost had been just over 300, for whom there had been only 260 replacements. Furthermore, the new pilots emerging from the Operational Training Units had nothing like the necessary experience on fighters. Typical was Bill Green, who was sent to 501 Squadron at Gravesend in Kent having had just seven hours and forty-five minutes flying on a Hurricane. 'I really didn't know what it was all about. I was Green by name and green by nature,' he recalled. 'But I don't think they had any option but to make me operational.'[63] Gus Holden of 501 Squadron thought that some of the new recruits 'should never have been there. I remember one young chap, very nice but he was not strong enough or good enough. I could see him being shot down in no time at all.' Holden was right. The novice was killed on his very first sortie.[64]

Because of the shortage of manpower, experienced pilots had to remain on duty even when they were exhausted. 'I had just taken about as much as I could bear,' said the ace Ginger Lacey, one of the toughest of all pilots. 'My nerves were in ribbons and I was scared stiff that one day I would pull out and avoid combat. That frightened me more than the Germans and I pleaded with my CO for a rest. He was sympathetic but quite adamant that until he got replacements I would have to carry on.'[65] More fortunate was Teddy Donaldson, whose 151 Squadron was moved from North Weald to Digby to re-group after enduring heavy losses. 'I was fantastically tired and utterly depressed. My squadron had been in heavy fighting since May without a break.' One of the reasons for his exhaustion, he said, was the Hurricane. 'Flying a Hurricane, which was 50 mph slower than my adversary, I had to be brave, simply because I could not run away. Perhaps more important I could not attack, simply because I could not catch my foe. We envied Spitfire pilots. At least they could catch their foe, whereas the Hurricane pilot had to wait to be attacked and then fight like hell.'[66]

Other pilots were sickened at the increasing dominance that the Germans were establishing over the southern skies, as Donald 'Dimsie' Stones of 32 Squadron eloquently put it: 'We were seeing the enemy in large numbers streaming above the glorious countryside of Kent. I felt a sense of outrage. It was like the rape of a sleeping beauty. Their black Prussian crosses looked malevolent enough, but the crooked cross of the Swastika on their tails now seemed idolatrous and obscene.'[67] On 1 September the RAF lost three times as many planes as the Luftwaffe, 15 to 5, while Biggin Hill airbase took another hammering and was put out of action completely. So lethal was the German offensive against the 11 Group sector airfields that Keith Park felt compelled to maintain standing patrols over them, a move that not only ran counter to the responsive flexibility of the Dowding system but also reduced the number of fighters available for interception. The balance of losses was once more against the RAF on 3 September, with 25 British planes destroyed to the Luftwaffe's

22. The next three days saw the major airfields in 11 Group so heavily bombed that they could barely function. The mood of anxiety on 6 September could be glimpsed in the dry prose of an account written by Park himself:

> The damage to sector stations and our ground organization was having a serious effect on the fighting efficiency of the squadrons, who could not be given the same good technical and administrative service as previously. The absence of many essential telephone lines, the use of scratch equipment in the emergency operations rooms and the general dislocation of ground organization was seriously felt.[68]

The crisis exacerbated the simmering tension between Park and the 12 Group commander Leigh-Mallory, who felt that Fighter Command's whole strategy, based on caution and preservation of numbers, was fundamentally wrong. What Leigh-Mallory advocated was the use of large fighter formations, comprising at least three squadrons and known as 'Big Wings' to bring down as many of the German raiders as possible. He felt that his 12 Group planes were not being employed properly, because they waited to be called upon to protect the airfields rather than going directly into action. A key ally of Leigh-Mallory's was Douglas Bader, leader of 242 Squadron, who was frustrated by the long hours of idleness at Duxford while he knew that the real action was happening over 11 Group. From the end of August he began to experiment with Big Wings, claiming great successes that were not always justified by the evidence.

But all this was an anathema to Park, who believed that sending up massed formations of fighters was exactly what the Luftwaffe wanted the RAF to do. Since Fighter Command was heavily outnumbered, he argued, such an approach was the surest way to the destruction of its forces at the hands of the German fighters. In addition, a Big Wing was in his view simply impracticable because it would take so long to assemble that it would usually arrive at the point of interception too late to prevent the Germans bombing their target. Most of the pilots outside the Duxford squadrons shared Park's analysis. 'The Big Wings were far too unwieldy, took far too long to climb to height and were difficult to control,' said Fred Rosier of 229 Squadron. Within the Fighter Command, there was also a deeper feeling of respect towards

Park than Leigh-Mallory. Flying round the airfields in his own Hurricane, Park was regarded as a real 'fighter boy'. In the words of Jeffrey Quill, the Supermarine test pilot who flew with 65 Squadron during the peak of the battle, 'it did everyone good when he visited. We all thought highly of him.'[69] In contrast, Tom Neil of 249 Squadron wrote that Leigh-Mallory 'had not impressed me as a leader' when they met. 'Stiff-looking, immaculate and with a very un-airmanlike appearance, he conveyed to us all an aura of pomposity.'[70] The friction over tactics was worsened by the personal animosity between the two men. Leigh-Mallory regarded Park as too proprietorial over the conduct of the Battle of Britain; Park thought the 12 Group commander scheming, ambitious and disloyal. It is one of Dowding's few glaring failures during 1940 that he took no action to resolve a potentially disastrous quarrel between two of his leading commanders, an oversight that was to cost him dearly in the months to come.

By 7 September Dowding's chief concern was not tactics but how long Fighter Command could survive. In the previous week, 161 of his fighters had been destroyed in air battles alone. At a meeting that day with his senior officers he spoke of his force 'going down hill' and stressed the need to increase the number of trained pilots reaching the squadrons.[71] Despite the battering that 11 Group had taken, Park warned against pessimism. 'I've been looking at these casualty figures,' he told one of his controllers, 'and I've come to the conclusion that at our present rate of losses we can just afford it. And I'm damned certain that the Boche can't. If we can hang on as we're doing, I'm sure we will win in the end.'[72] As it turned out, Park's confidence was to be justified far more quickly than he could have imagined. For that very day the Germans were to commit a calamitous strategic error, one that was to cost them the Battle of Britain.

The origins of this spectacular mistake lay in a raid carried out by the Luftwaffe on the night of 24–5 August, when a fleet of more than 100 bombers was sent to attack the Shorts aircraft factory at Rochester and the oil depot at Thameshaven. Due to poor navigation, however, they dropped their loads right over London, hitting the East End, the City and Oxford Street. At this stage of the battle, such wholesale bombardment of the capital was strictly against Luftwaffe policy, the Führer reserving for himself the right to take such a far-reaching political decision. In retaliation for the attack, Churchill personally ordered a series of raids by Bomber Command against Berlin itself over five nights up to 31 August. The damage was minor, the consequences enormous. Hitler was furious and now abandoned all restraint. On 2 September he gave Göring the order 'for the start of the reprisal raids against London'.[73] This was to be total war in all its gruesome horror. Any ambivalence about pulverizing Britain had evaporated. To a cheering audience in Berlin the Führer fulminated: 'We will eradicate their cities. The hour will come when one of us will go under, and it will not be National Socialist Germany.'[74]

Contrary to his claims at the post-war Nuremberg trials that he 'told the Führer again and again' that he could never force the English people 'to their knees by attacking London', Göring was in fact only too delighted to carry out this instruction.[75] Like several others in the Luftwaffe High Command, most notably Albert Kesselring, he thought a massed assault on London would force Fighter Command to throw all its force in defence of the capital. Victory, he felt, was in his grasp. In the afternoon of 7 September he turned up at Cap Gris Nez, near Calais, so he could watch his vast aerial armada sweeping across the Channel to obliterate London and what he believed were the last remnants of the RAF. Clad in a powder-blue uniform, complete with gold braid, he watched with a beaming smile as 348 bombers, stacked in layers from 14,000 to 20,000 feet, roared through the clear sky above, accompanied by 617 fighters.

Across the water in England the Air Ministry, having been warned by Intelligence about the build-up of an unusually large force on the northern French airfields, had issued an Invasion Alert to its commands. At readiness in his Hurricane in 'the eerie light' of the early morning, Bob Foster of 605 Squadron was one of the many pilots who believed that the moment of truth had arrived:

Dawn came and there wasn't a sound to be heard. It was a strange morning and an equally strange feeling as I looked along the line of silent aircraft, each with a familiar face peering over the rim of the cockpit looking distinctly apprehensive. Sitting about were our ground crews ready to start up the machines, as each fighter had its trolley accumulator plugged in ready for contact. The only sound in my ears was some soft music from Henry Hall's music show made possible because we could tune the aircraft's radio into the BBC with our early sets. It was all very surreal.[76]

It turned out to be an anxious but wasted morning. The action did not take place until 4 p.m., when the enemy planes first appeared on the radar screens. At first, 11 Group thought another onslaught on its airfields was underway, but it soon became obvious that London was the target for the giant formation, which covered an astonishing 800 square miles. By 4.30 every 11 Group squadron was in the air, and assistance had been called from 10 and 12 Groups. For the first time Douglas Bader could put his Big Wing properly into action, but the results were disappointing. Bader claimed that he had been scrambled too late and therefore had a disadvantage because, when attacking the bombers, the fighters were coming down on them from the sun, according to a report from Leigh-Mallory.[77] The late call was to be a perennial complaint of Bader's, which the Big Wing's critics said only highlighted the ineffectiveness of the tactic.

There was other fierce fighting over the capital that day. Having executed a daring frontal attack on a Dornier bomber, Donald Stones was turning to take on an Me 110 when suddenly he was hit by fire from a 109. Immediately his Hurricane went into an uncontrollable spin. In desperation he prepared to bail out but found 'the canopy jammed through damage. I remember I prayed for a miracle and it was answered as I felt the spin slowing down and gradually we straightened out.' Stones was now at 2,000 feet and somehow was able to coax his damaged plane down to a nearby airfield. 'Someone climbed on the wing to wrench open my bent canopy and help me out. The rear fuselage and tail of my sturdy Hurricane was tattered and torn. Once more, I was grateful for the ruggedness of that machine.'[78] John Carpenter of 222 Squadron was a victim of shell fire, not from the enemy but from London's own anti-aircraft batteries. As he explained in a letter from his hospital bed to his parents: 'I am not shooting you a line when I say that the machine just disappeared from under me in one big BANG!' Fortunately, the impact propelled him from the Hurricane cockpit and he came down in a nearby wood. 'I was carted off to hospital with many scratches and cuts, where they chloroformed me and did a lot of needlework.'[79] In the true spirit of the Battle of Britain, Carpenter was back in a Hurricane within weeks.

Fighter Command took heavy blows from the Luftwaffe during the daylight action on 7 September, losing 31 aircraft, including 6 Hurricanes from 249 Squadron. Nor were the attacks over when the darkness descended. The German bombers carried on their assault until 5 a.m. the following morning, inflicting terrible devastation on the capital. Housing estates, warehouses, factories and high streets were all hit. The munitions depot at Woolwich went up with a huge explosion whose flames reached hundreds of feet into the air. More than one million tons of timber at the Surrey docks were set alight. Across the capital 448 people were killed. 'It must be terrible down there,' recorded the Ju 88 pilot Peter Stahl in his diary. 'One could not imagine that people could endure this continuous crushing burden for long.'[80]

Yet out of the nightmare of the inferno came hope. For the first time since 24 August, the airfields and 11 Group's control organization had been spared. At last, the attritional slide towards doom had been halted. With harsh realism, Park instantly recognized this as he flew over London in his Hurricane that night. 'I looked down and said, "Thank God for that," because I knew the Nazis had switched their attack from the fighter stations, thinking they were knocked out. They weren't, but they were pretty groggy.'[81] It was the turning point in the Battle of Britain. Fighter Command had been given the chance to re-group. The men of the Hurricane squadrons shared Park's assessment: 'When the airfields were being bombed, we were at rock bottom. But the change to bombing the cities gave us breathing space. Once we started to build up again, it was a matter of time until the German defeat,' said Richard Mitchell of 229 Squadron.[82] Norman Hancock's stark view was that 'if the Germans had carried on bombing the sector stations, the outcome of the battle could have been very different within ten days'.[83]

Further heavy raids on London followed on 9 and 11 September, but, once more, the airfields and control network avoided damage.

The task of rebuilding was helped by banks of drizzle and thick cloud which moved across southern England in the week after 7 September, further hampering the German attacks. On the three days from 12 September there were no more than a few reconnaissance operations and minor raids from the Luftwaffe during daylight hours. Experienced pilots were able to have some rest, new pilots more training. Hurricanes and Spitfires arrived from the factories in such numbers that by the second week in September, despite the intensity of the battle in the skies overhead, the RAF had more fighters than at the end of July. For the first time since mid August, every squadron in 11 Group had its full complement of men and machines.

Yet the German High Command continued to live with the delusion that Britain was on the verge of defeat. At a conference with his military chiefs on 14 September, Hitler declared that 'the operations of the Luftwaffe are beyond all praise' and said that preparations must continue with the highest priority for Operation Sealion, which would be launched on 17 September.[84] An imminent spell of good weather, he proclaimed, would give the German air force the opportunity to inflict the last mortal blows against the RAF.

The climax of the Battle of Britain came on 15 September, the day that was meant to herald the completion of air superiority for the Luftwaffe. It was a bright, sunlit morning as another huge Luftwaffe formation, comprising a hundred Dornier bombers escorted by over 200 Me 109s, gathered over the Channel at 11 o'clock. Taking their cue from their deluded commanders, the German pilots felt assured of victory against a hopelessly weakened RAF. To their shock, they were met on their way to London by no fewer than 250 fighters. Hans Zonderlind, a front gunner in a Dornier 17 bomber, confessed that he 'thought this bombing run would be easy' as he reached Kent, but then:

> We saw the Hurricanes coming towards us and it seemed that the whole of the RAF was here. We had never seen so many British fighters coming at us at once. I saw a couple of comrades go down and we got hit at once, but it did no great damage. All around us were dogfights as the fighters went after each other, then as we were getting ready for our approach to the target, we saw what must have been a hundred RAF fighters coming at us. Where were they coming from?[85]

These reinforcements, exaggerated in number by Zonderlind, were the five squadrons of Douglas Bader's Duxford Wing, made up of three Hurricane and two Spitfire units. In a classic division of labour, the Spitfires tore into the German fighter escorts, while the Hurricanes took on the bombers, smashing the formation apart, as Leigh-Mallory reported in glowing if embellished terms in his subsequent account to Dowding:

> The Hurricanes were able to destroy all the Dorniers which they could see and one of the squadrons saw a further small formation of Dorniers, which had no doubt broken away from the main formation in the first attack and promptly destroyed the lot. One of the Spitfire squadrons, seeing the enemy fighters were getting out of range, also came down and took part in the destruction of the enemy bombers. In this engagement, the pre-arranged idea worked perfectly, for there were sufficient numbers of Spitfires to attack the enemy fighters and prevent them from exercising their primary function of protecting their own bombers, which were destroyed by three Hurricane squadrons at their leisure. The enemy were outnumbered and appeared in the circumstances to be quite helpless.[86]

Bader himself described the action as 'the finest shambles I've ever been in'.[87]

Eager to enhance the reputation of the Big Wing, Leigh-Mallory and Bader may have overstated its effectiveness. But there was no doubt that the German air fleet was badly mauled and was unable to concentrate on its key targets, instead scattering bombs ineffectually across a wide area. A new spirit of confidence surged through the British fighter squadrons, symbolized by a remarkable incident when Ray Holmes of 504 Squadron deliberately rammed a lone Dornier that was attempting to bomb London's West End. Through previous combats that morning, his ammunition had almost been finished, but Holmes was determined to stop the German at any cost. He dived down straight at the bomber. With just seconds left before he collided, he felt for the firing button and pressed. Almost immediately the guns stuttered to a halt. He had no bullets left. Still he refused to abandon his mission and turn away. 'How flimsy the tailplane looked as it filled my windscreen, as fragile as glass. The tough little Hurricane would splinter it like balsa wood,' said Holmes in an account he gave on the fortieth anniversary of the Battle of Britain.[88] He aimed his port wing at the nearside fin of the Dornier's twin tail. 'I felt only the slightest jar as the wing of the Hurricane sliced through.' The Dornier's tail came away. Then the whole plane disintegrated, some of its bombs falling on Buckingham Palace, the rest of the wreckage coming down on the forecourt of Victoria Station and the shaken crew landing on the turf of the Oval cricket ground.

Holmes's own plane, meanwhile, went into a spiralling dive. 'I unlocked and slid back the hood. The cloud thickened around me, blindingly white, hurting my eyes and the screech of the dive was deafening.' At first, when he tried to bail out, 'the buffeting was so violent that for a moment I thought my head was caught in the propeller'.[89] Then he discovered that he had forgotten to unplug the radio lead. Having disconnected it, he just managed to get out as the Hurricane went into a vertical spin. After pulling the ripcord, he floated down on some flats near Victoria Station, ending up with his feet in an empty dustbin and his parachute entangled in a drainpipe. The Hurricane had plunged into a crossroads nearby, its impact so great that it drilled fifteen feet into the ground. A large crowd gathered to cheer Holmes, who was only bruised in his right shoulder, as he released himself from his parachute and was then taken by the Home Guard to Chelsea barracks for a medical inspection and a welcome drink.

Badly shaken by the events of the morning of 15 September, the Luftwaffe mounted another large offensive in the afternoon, made up of 150 bombers and 400 fighters staggered in three waves. But again the RAF was ready for them. The German losses were just as bad, their bombing just as ineffective. The exhilaration of the British fighter squadrons, now competing on superior terms, was captured by Eric Bann of 238 Squadron in a letter to his parents. 'My gosh, for every bomb dropped upon the King and Queen, old 238 gave them hell. We got 12 Huns in one scrap. We just went in as one man and held our fire until very close range and then blew them right out of their cockpits.'[90] This sense of jubilation was shared by Tom Neil of 249 Squadron, who called 15 September 'a momentous day'. He experienced at first hand the RAF's command of the sky when he shot down a Dornier in the early afternoon. 'The whole of the port side of the German aircraft was engulfed by my tracer. The effect was instantaneous; there was a splash of something, like water being struck with the back of a spoon. Beside myself with excitement, I fired again, a longish burst.' Moments later, the German crew had to bail out. Soon afterwards Neil joined a Spitfire in taking down another bomber over Gravesend in Kent. 'It was easy. Without interference, we took turns in carrying out astern attacks and were gratified to see a translucent stain of dark smoke emerge from one, then both of the engines.' Back at dispersal, 'I found a queue of pilots leading to the Intelligence officer, everyone in a high state of excitement. It had been a fantastic fight, no one missing and a mounting tally of Huns – seven – eight – nine "destroyed" and a similar number "probable" or "damaged". What a to-do! Crashed Huns burning on the ground everywhere.'[91]

The action on 15 September was an overwhelming triumph for the RAF. Fighter Command's dominance had been the finest vindication of the Dowding system and Park's brilliant management of his resources. The press were exultant, claiming 183 German aircraft had been shot down. Typically overblown was the coverage of the *News Chronicle* next day: 'It is the RAF that strikes like lightning and it is the Luftwaffe that is stricken. Our planes race out above the Channel – whose waters are as much ours as they have ever been – and rip Göring's bombers out of the skies so that they fall like flies before the onslaught of an antiseptic syringe.'[92] The *Daily Express* gloated: 'Göring may reflect that this is no way to run an invasion.'[93] As so often in the Battle of Britain, the initial claims of kills had been greatly exaggerated. In fact, the real figure of German losses was 56. But this still represented one of the the worst days of the battle for them, especially because Fighter Command had lost less than half that total. Even the German High Command, normally so full of bombast about imminent victory, admitted there had been 'great losses', which meant that 'the day's operations had been unusually disadvantageous'.[94] One German pilot, Horst Schulz, put it even more starkly: 'We came to realize that if there were many more missions like that, our chances of survival would be nil.'[95]

On the day when the RAF had so successfully beaten back the invaders, Churchill's private secretary Jock Colville wrote in his diary: 'It looks as if Hitler cannot keep up this pressure for long.'[96] He was right. Two days later, on 17 September, the Führer announced the indefinite postponement of Operation Sealion.

8

'The world's greatest fighter revitalized'

⟶ ⟵

THE BATTLE OF BRITAIN was won on 15 September 1940. The Germans were never to return in such numbers. For several more weeks the Luftwaffe limped on, mounting the occasional heavy raid, but all hope of victory had vanished. In any case, the postponement of Operation Sealion, allied to the onset of autumn, made the declining struggle for air superiority over England less strategically vital. Two further attempts to batter the RAF's fighter defences, on 27 and 30 September, both ended in disaster, the Germans losing a combined total of more than 90 planes. 'The Luftwaffe was bled to death,' wrote Göring's Chief of Operations Werner Kreipe, 'and suffered losses which would never be made good again throughout the course of the war.'[1] A few intermittent daylight raids over Britain were held in October to little effect. Gunther Busgen, an Me 109 pilot who was shot down over Kent in the first week of October by a Hurricane, lost all faith in Germany's military leadership after 15 September. 'The flights to London we regarded as completely unnecessary. They brought no results for us. In October, the Battle of Britain was all over – the first part of a lost war.'[2] In contrast, the pilots of Fighter Command revelled in their new supremacy. Tony Pickering of 501 Squadron recalled the successful challenge to the German raid of 30 September: 'You could see for miles and there wasn't a Hun that came anywhere near us. All you could see was a squadron of Hurricanes here and a squadron of Spitfires. The morale of the pilots . . . leapt up when we realized we were still in command of the sky. It absolutely amazed me and my morale went up 100 per cent.'[3]

The Hawker Hurricane carried a large share of responsibility for this achievement. The victory was the plane's Finest Hour as well as

Britain's. Since May 1940 the aircraft's record in combat had made a mockery of the early German belief in its chronic inferiority. Indeed, it was a sign of the fighter's impact on Nazi sensibilities that Lord Haw-Haw, the alias of the notorious British traitor William Joyce who broadcast for the Reich, claimed in one of his fraudulent radio transmissions towards the end of the Battle of Britain that RAF pilots were refusing to fly the Hurricane because it was such a vicious air-craft, an announcement of patent absurdity that only revealed the desperation of Hitler's regime. Accurate statistics about losses in the battle have been notoriously difficult to compile because of over-claiming by pilots, the political impulse to distort figures for propaganda purposes and differing methodologies for assessing whether a plane was destroyed or only badly damaged. Historical analyses vary. In the groundbreaking, authoritative work *The Narrow Margin* by Derek Wood and Derek Dempster, written in 1961, the total aircraft losses were put at 1,733 for the Luftwaffe and 915 for Fighter Command.[4] Winston G. Ramsay, in his 1980 book *The Battle of Britain Then and Now*, estimated the losses to be higher, at 1,882 for the Luftwaffe and 1,017 for Fighter Command, though even his assessment of German losses was still significantly lower than the total of 2,741 claims made by RAF pilots between 1 July and 31 August.[5] RAF fighter casualties were inevitably far fewer than the Luftwaffe's, not just because of the margin of victory, but also because the force was over its own territory and its single-seater planes had smaller crews than the German bombers. Most studies have put Fighter Command's death toll at 544 pilots, almost one in five who flew, compared to 2,698 for the Luftwaffe. Turning to specific types, Patrick Bishop wrote in his chronicle *The Battle of Britain*, published in 2009, that 603 Hurricanes and 359 Spitfires were destroyed beyond repair between July and October 1940.[6] Some of these losses, however, were due to accidents rather than combat.

For all the disagreements about the detailed numbers, two trends are nevertheless obvious from the statistics. The first is Fighter Command's clear ascendancy over the Luftwaffe. From the opening weeks of the convoy patrols in early July, the ratio of German to British losses was generally two to one. Tellingly, that was true both of 18 August, 'The Hardest Day', and 15 September, which later was officially recognized as 'Battle of Britain Day'. Even for the most optimistic Germans, such a rate of attrition could not be sustained. Generalfeldmarschall Albert Kesselring later admitted that the day-light raids had to be called off 'because our losses were too high; because we didn't have enough fighters to escort the bombers'.[7] The second trend is the vital importance of the Hurricane in the battle. Of Fighter Command's 2,741 claims of German losses, 55 per cent were made by pilots from Hurricane squadrons, compared to 43 per cent from Spitfire squadrons. That same proportion of around 55 per cent can be found throughout all the estimates of the actual losses. Even the research by John Alcorn, which put the total of Luftwaffe planes destroyed by fighter action at just 1,218, still held that the Hurricanes were responsible for 54 per cent of the kills.[8] Nor did the Hurricane prove anything like the easy target for the Messerschmitt 109s that the Germans had expected. The historian Stephen Bungay, who reckoned that 770 Hurricanes and Spitfires were shot down by German fighters, wrote that 'the 109s's margin of superiority over the Hurricane was too small to allow the sort of aerial massacres needed'.[9]

Within aviation circles there was recognition of the Hurricane's central part in the Battle of Britain. 'The success of the Hurricane in a year of War has placed it among the great aeroplanes of all time,' proclaimed the *Aeroplane* magazine in an article of September 1940, extolling its 'fine qualities', 'aerodynamic excellence' and a structure that 'is designed for simplicity and efficiency both in production and service'.[10] With a more romantic flourish, another article in *Aeroplane* compared the Hawker plane to 'the famous blades' of history, such as 'Brainbiter', the sword of Hereward the Wake. 'Few names could be more appropriate to the weapon with which our young men are scourging the Hun than the one it was given in an inspired moment: the Hurricane.' The magazine went on to glory in 'the inestimable role which the Hurricane has played and is playing in the history of mankind – no less'.[11]

Yet by the autumn of 1940 this admiration among experts had not been translated into similar enthusiasm among the general public. It was the Spitfire that prevailed in the sentiments of the nation. The glamour of the Supermarine plane gave it a greater appeal. 'Spitfire funds' were organized to raise money for the fighter campaign. Spitfire imagery predominated on official posters. The crucial months of 1940 became known as 'Spitfire summer'. At the end of the Battle of Britain, a reporter from *Flight* magazine reflected on this apparent injustice. The rush 'to subscribe to Spitfire funds here, there and everywhere' prompted the question: 'Why not Hurricane funds?' The reason, he said, was 'simple'. People 'are taken in by the name and the appearance and the performance' of the Spitfire, he wrote. 'Knowing nothing of the performance figures they have instinctively chosen this particular type as the paragon of protective types, though any pilot will tell them that the Hurricane is equally remarkable in its own particular way. Slower but more robust, easier to handle on and near the ground, and consequently ideal for work from less well-prepared airfields near the front-line of any war. A machine, in fact, which has had far less than its due attention from a somewhat fickle public.'[12] Some Hurricane pilots bristled at this neglect after the battle. 'We seem to be forgotten, sir. It seems nobody loves us,' Peter Wykeham of 43 Squadron said to one of his commanders.[13]

Another factor behind the general public's relative indifference to the Hurricane was that the Spitfire, in its sleek modernity and scope for development, was seen as representing the future, whereas the Hurricane, with its fabric-covered fuselage, increasingly evoked the past. It was undoubtedly true that, given the rapid changes in aviation technology, the Hurricane was at risk of becoming outmoded as the daylight air battle drew to a close. Its greatest victory was also its last truly effective performance purely as a combat interceptor. This glorious peak was soon followed by a rapid descent in the capability of the plane as a fighter until other roles were found for it, particularly through the use of new weaponry and bomb-carrying. This anticlimactic sense of decline was revealed almost immediately after the Battle of Britain when the Hurricane had to take on night-patrol duties against the German bombers, a job for which it was ill-suited.

The Luftwaffe's defeat in the daylight campaign meant that it had to switch its efforts to the night bombing of British cities, using darkness rather than Messerschmitts as cover. With Operation Sealion abandoned, the two aims of this new offensive were to crack the morale of the civilian population and smash Britain's industries. Beginning in earnest in September 1940, the Blitz reflected Hitler's apocalyptic vision at its most savage. 'Have you ever looked at a map of London? It is so closely built up that one source of fire alone would suffice to destroy the whole city,' he told his henchman and chief architect Albert Speer in the summer of 1940.[14] Though the night raids could not directly menace Britain's air force, the threat to the public was severe. Almost 7,000 Britons were killed in September, another 6,300 in October, while 18,000 tons of bombs fell on London in the last four months of the year. The problem for the government was that the RAF initially had no means of effectively tackling this offensive. It had just a handful of night-fighter units equipped with the dangerously vulnerable two-seater Boulton Paul Defiants, which just had a rear turret and no forward-firing armament. Once the Battle of Britain had ended, however, five full squadrons of Hurricanes were painted black and transferred to night operations. Though the plane had not been designed as a night-fighter, it should in theory have been a success in the dark, with its good forward view, steadiness and wide undercarriage. Before the war John Gillan of 111 Squadron, who made the famous record-breaking flight from Turnhouse near Edinburgh to Northolt in February 1938, carried out some night trials on the Hurricane, and in his subsequent report he was full of praise for its handling: 'The Hurricane is a simple aeroplane to fly by night. There is no glare in the cockpit, either open or closed, from the cockpit lamp or luminous instruments. The steady, steep glide at slow speed which is characteristic of this type makes landing extremely simple.'[15]

But in practice the plane proved woefully ineffective against the German night intruders during the long winter of 1940–1. Hurricane squadrons rarely even saw a bomber, never mind intercepted one. By far the biggest difficulty was the lack of any method of guiding the fighters onto their targets, for Airborne Interception (AI) radar had only just been developed and was being tested on the new Bristol Beaufighter, a long-range twin-engined aircraft. Without any navigational aids, the Hurricane pilots could do nothing more than grope in the dark, as Graham Leggett, now with 96 Squadron, a newly formed night-fighter unit based at Cranage, Cheshire, recalled: 'We had VHF radio. That's all. With the radio we could communicate with the ground controllers whose job it was to put us in a position to make an attack on an enemy bomber. But all hinged on one's ability to see an aircraft in a dark sky. On a pitch black night, when there was no moon, it was virtually impossible to expect any form of contact at all. One night, when there was a huge fire in Liverpool and the glow lit up everything around, you would have thought that it would have been quite easy to spot aircraft but I didn't.'[16] Dennis David of 87 Squadron felt that 'the idea of the Hurricane fighting at night in 1940 was an absolute waste of time because the approaching speeds were phenomenal. To see anything at night, with approaching speeds of six miles a minute, just doesn't work. You've got to have AI.'[17]

Roland Beamont, also of 87 Squadron, was one of the few Hurricane pilots who actually had a sight of the enemy at night during 1940. On a patrol over Exeter he managed to make out a Ju 88, the German plane having been briefly illuminated by the searchlights from one of the anti-aircraft batteries on the ground. He opened the throttle, moved closer and then opened fire. As he later wrote, the images of that moment always remained with him:

> The dark outline of the hood frame, the glimmer of the instruments and glowing red bead of the gunsight in the centre of the windscreen and outside nothing but a confused jumble of brilliant beams of light. In the centre an aeroplane, light grey in the glare with little white flashes appearing all over it and apparently connected to my aircraft by slightly curving lines of red and white tracer bullets looking like tramlines on a wet night. The whole, seen through the glare of flame from the gun muzzles in the wings at each burst, gave the mounting impression that there was no earth and sky.[18]

In the darkness, however, Beamont could not confirm whether he had shot down the bomber. His action was a rare case. The German raiders, pouring their lethal incendiaries on urban Britain, were largely unchallenged by the Hurricanes. Even on the night of 14 November, when the Luftwaffe's bombers turned the centre of Coventry into a vast inferno, the Hurricanes sent to defend the city could do nothing. Douglas Bader, the leader of 242 Squadron, was in a section patrolling the target area. 'None of us saw a thing except fires and gun flashes below,' he recorded.[19]

With the civilian death toll rapidly mounting, the failure of the night operations in late 1940 created a political crisis that brought about wholesale changes at the top of the RAF. The government was so concerned about the weakness of the night defences that a committee of enquiry was established under Sir John Salmond, a former Chief of the Air Staff. Salmond, never an admirer of Sir Hugh Dowding, came to the conclusion that the RAF had shown insufficient dynamism in setting up an efficient night-fighter force. Through a series of vituperative letters to Churchill and other influential figures, he urged that both Dowding and the current Air Chief, Sir Cyril Newall, be sacked. Dowding, he argued, 'has not got the qualifications of a commander in the field, as he lacks humanity', while Newall's 'strategic judgement is completely at fault'.[20] Such opinions were held by other senior air leaders and the Secretary of State for Air, Sir Archie Sinclair, though not by Churchill himself, who described Dowding as 'one of the very best men' in the RAF.[21]

The accusation that Dowding had been too passive about night-fighting took no account of the technical difficulties that his command faced. Indeed, throughout the early autumn Dowding organized a series of experiments in night interception at Kenley airfield, south London, using various innovative techniques such as predicated searchlight beams which could automatically track a bomber. But none of them inspired much confidence. The only real hope, Dowding knew, lay in Airborne Interception (AI) radar. 'It is imperatively necessary that blind flying apparatus be fitted in all aircraft,' he wrote:

> Our task will not, therefore, be finished until we can locate, pursue and shoot down the enemy in cloud by day and night and the AI must become a gun sight. We have a long way to go before we can even approach this ideal, but nothing less will suffice for the defence of this country. Every night that I spend watching attempts at interception confirms me in the conviction that haphazard methods will never succeed in producing more than an occasional fortunate encounter.[22]

After the victory in the Battle of Britain, Dowding was understandably bitter at the intrigue against him, and since 1940 many
historians have shared his anger, claiming that the opposition to his
continued leadership was a monstrous injustice, akin to sacking the
Duke of Wellington after Waterloo. But, apart from night-fighting,
there were other factors working against him. One was his age. He
was older and had held his command for longer than anyone else at
the top of the RAF. Since mid 1938, his retirement had been regularly discussed, only to be postponed because of the deepening fighter
crisis. Furthermore, the Big Wing controversy, in which he had
failed to settle the combustible quarrel between his two senior group
commanders, Park and Leigh-Mallory, had done little for his reputation towards the end of the battle. By September he had become a
curiously detached figure, having delegated most of the running of
the battle to Park. His closest aides admitted that he was exhausted
and 'almost blind with fatigue', in the words of Chic Willet, one of
his staff at Bentley Priory.[23] Even Churchill had accepted the widespread pressure for change, some of which had been orchestrated
within the Tory party by the MP Peter MacDonald, who also happened to be Douglas Bader's adjutant at 242 Squadron and was a
strong supporter of the Big Wing concept.

The government tried to lessen the pain of Dowding's retirement
by putting him in charge of the British Air Mission to the USA,
which was to investigate the purchase of American aircraft types for
the RAF. In an interview with Dowding on 13 September, Sinclair
stressed the job was of the utmost importance and required a man
'of strong personality' who could 'command' the Americans'
respect.[24] Filled with resentment at the way he had been treated,
Dowding at first tried to resist the appointment, then said that he
would only accept if it were a temporary posting, enabling him to
return as head of Fighter Command in 1941. Asserting more authority than usual, Sinclair said that such a return would be impossible.
Still indignant, Dowding talked of visiting Churchill to press his
case. But he soon saw there was no chance of any shift in the
government's stance and therefore accepted the new role. On 24
November, he left Bentley Priory for the last time as Fighter
Command's chief. Before he did so, he sent a poignant message to

his 'dear Fighter Boys', quoting the words of Winston Churchill about 'the few' and adding: 'The debt remains and will increase. In saying goodbye to you, I want you to know how continually you have been in my thoughts and that, though our direct connection may be severed, I may yet be able to help you in your gallant fight.'[25] He was succeeded by Sholto Douglas, who had been Deputy Chief of the Air Staff since April 1940 and was more aggressive in his thinking than Dowding, though less trusted by his pilots. The government also decided that Keith Park should be rested, so he was moved to a senior post at RAF Training Command, with the leadership of 11 Group handed to his bitter rival, Trafford Leigh-Mallory. Further up the hierarchy that autumn, Sir Cyril Newall was replaced as Chief of the Air Staff by Sir Charles Portal, previously the head of Bomber Command, a cool, politically astute operator.

The changes in personnel had no impact on the Hurricane night-fighter operations for the rest of 1940. The position improved a little, however, in early 1941, as the pilots gained more experience in both handling and tactics. One method frequently used by the squadrons was known as 'Jacob's Ladder', whereby the Hurricanes flew in a layered formation, as Kenneth McGlashan of 245 Squadron described: 'We would fly at levels above Angels 12 hopefully to remain out of the range of our own anti-aircraft batteries. Separated by a mere 500 feet, up to ten fighters would fly along pre-designated routes and look earthward for enemy fighters silhouetted against the glow of the overcast or the inferno of devastation below. Additionally a pair of Hurricanes might be freed up to patrol at will, clear of the ladder. Where we should fly and at what levels was all predetermined at one of the radar installations.'[26]

Landing was assisted by the introduction of the Drem lighting system, which had been developed in 1940 by Richard Atcherley, the dynamic, unorthodox commander of the Drem fighter base near Edinburgh. Gerald Edge of 605 Squadron was one of the first pilots to use it: 'Basically, we had a red light on a prominent position, like a hill nearby. From there you flew on a compass course, losing height to a given level where you would find another red light. If you followed that, you would get to the aerodrome and there you would find some heavily shaded lights, with amber above, green in the middle and red at the bottom. If you saw red, you were too low; amber you were too high and green you were all right.' The Hurricane pilot then descended over the edge of the aerodrome and, after lowering the flaps, was guided onto the airstrip by a set of blue, hooded marker lights. 'They were like little torches. If you flew down and got them in line, you just pulled the stick back and you were rolling along. You could do better landings by night than you did by day with the system. And it was totally invisible to anyone high up,' said Edge.[27] The Air Ministry was so impressed by Atcherley's innovation that the system was adopted throughout the RAF.

A further technical improvement on the Hurricane night-fighter was the installation of metallic shrouds to obscure the flames from the exhaust stubs when the fighter was at full throttle. In addition, pilots adopted a range of unconventional measures to improve their eye-sight at night. They ate carrots, sat in darkened rooms and wore sunglasses in the mess or at dispersal, though, as Kenneth McGlashan remembered, these efforts to boost night vision could quickly be undone. 'When called to scramble we would no sooner have clam-bered into the cockpit than a flurry of torch beams would flash in your face as the airmen set about strapping you in.'[28]

All these innovations, combined with the arrival of the AI radar-equipped Beaufighters, led to a significantly better record for the night-fighter squadrons in the spring of 1941. By March the monthly toll of German bombers brought down had risen to 22, up from just 3 in January. In May 138 Luftwaffe planes were destroyed, 96 by night-fighters. In one spectacular evening on 10–11 May the Hurricanes of 1 Squadron shot down 7 Heinkel 111s and 1 Junkers 88. The most deadly of the night-fighter aces was Richard Stevens, whose almost pathological hatred for the Germans led him to fly without any regard for his own safety in his determination to get close to the enemy. Before 1939 he had been a commercial pilot on the Croydon–Paris route, gaining over 400 hours' experience of flying in all conditions. When the war started, he was already thirty-two, much older than most Fighter Command airmen. What transformed him into a devastating killer was the beginning of the

Blitz, as his wife and children were killed in one of the early Luftwaffe raids on Manchester. A grief-stricken, solitary widower, he was now filled with a seething passion for revenge. The black Hurricane was his chosen instrument for lethal retribution.

Serving with 151 Squadron based at RAF Wittering near Peterborough, Stevens had his first kill on 15–16 January, when he embarked on a long, twisting pursuit of a Dornier. At 30,000 feet he finally caught it at the top of its climb and opened fire from just 25 yards, sending the plane plunging to earth in a ball of flame. Stevens's manoeuvres in this chase had been so violent that the underside of his Hurricane's fuselage was cracked. It was the start of a savage mission of vengeance, in which his fury was combined with uncanny vision and superb marksmanship. 'He was quite remarkable. He could identify planes when no one else could see a thing,' thought Irving Smith of 151 Squadron.[29] By June 1941, when the Blitz came to an end, Stevens had shot down ten German planes. Another of his fellow pilots in 151 Squadron, John Wray, said of him:

> He was a loner. He associated with virtually nobody. I'm one of the few people who knew him at all. Steve's tactics were in accord with his character. He would take off from Wittering, and having got airborne, he would turn off his r/t and disappear into the night. Nobody knew where he had gone. He would then go into an area where he felt that there might be Germans approaching. Steve always said that while the British anti-aircraft guns could never hit anything, they were very good at tracking the enemy. So if he saw some British anti-aircraft guns firing, then in front was a Hun. Many of the Germans he attacked, he picked up in this way.

But Wray always 'felt that one day he would stick out his neck too far'.[30] On 12 December 1941, having shot down four more enemy aircraft in the autumn, Stevens went on a sortie over Holland, never to return. 'His end was inevitable,' said the legendary Johnnie Johnson, officially the highest scoring RAF ace of the war.[31]

The success of the Hurricane night-fighters in 1941 was only relative to their dismal performance in 1940. Without proper blind-flying equipment, they were still not up to the job. Of his own night sorties in Wales, Donald Stones wrote that 'we stooged blindly around the Welsh mountains and valley trying to intercept the Germans on courses given to us on the r/t by equally blind ground controllers and searchlight batteries. Usually the first sign of the enemy's presence would be flashes of their bombs and incendiaries as they hit targets below us. We had no success whatsoever at this new game.'[32] Battle of Britain hero Ray Holmes of 504 Squadron found that the intensity of searchlights could be just as uncomfortable as the darkness. On a patrol with his squadron during a heavy raid on Plymouth in Devon, he glimpsed the outline of a Heinkel 111, then suddenly was caught in a searchlight's beam. 'The effect on my flying was shattering. My carefully positioned quarter attack became a drunken lurch. I was blinded by the diamond dazzle boring through my skull,' wrote Holmes. 'I was endeavouring to fly the Hurricane by feel rather than vision and failing miserably. Vertigo took over. I felt sick and lopsided.'[33] He landed soon after losing the Heinkel.

It was precisely the disconcerting power of the searchlight that the RAF later sought to exploit in a daring experiment that aimed to enhance dramatically the vision of their pilots. The scheme was based on the concept of a Hurricane night-fighter working alongside a Douglas Havoc light bomber equipped with both AI radar and a powerful Turbinlite searchlight in its nose. Guns could not be carried in the Havoc because of the combined weight of the radar set and the Turbinlite, which was built by GEC and had 2,700 million candlepower. The Hurricane, therefore, was to take on the role of providing the firepower. The theory was that the Havoc would use its radar to find the enemy intruder, illuminate the target with its Turbinlite, and then the Hurricane would go on the attack. Early trials seemed promising, and the pairing of the Havoc and Hurricane first went operational in May 1941. Eventually, there were no fewer than ten Turbinlite squadrons in Fighter Command by the end of 1942. Yet in practice the results never lived up to expectations, partly because it was difficult for the two very different types of aircraft to operate in unison. The pair would become split up, or the Hurricane would be out of position when the target was illuminated. 'The Havoc itself at certain heights was faster than the Hurricane, so the theory that the Hurricane would roar ahead and shoot down the target was a bit academic if the Havoc was going flat out,' said Cyril Brown of 253 Squadron, his words being another reflection of how swiftly the Hurricane declined as a fighter after 1940.[34] Furthermore, the Havoc's very act of switching on the Turbinlite served as a warning to the enemy of an imminent attack, destroying the element of surprise, while the brilliantly illuminated target also cast shadows, making it difficult for the Hurricane pilot to aim accurately.

But there were occasional successes. In July 1942 John Ellacombe, who had transferred to 253 Squadron the previous year, executed a textbook charge on a Dornier which had been lit up by the Havoc. As his combat report stated: 'I did a beam port attack closing to 40 yards firing a long burst. There were strikes on the port inner plane and fuselage. I had to pull up sharply to avoid ramming, climbed up and half rolled to observe enemy aircraft. The enemy aircraft rolled on his back and fell vertically to the ground.'[35] The issue of night-fighting increasingly became an irrelevance during 1942 as the Germans ceased their intruder raids and were forced to concentrate on their own defences in response to the start of RAF Bomber Command's mighty strategic offensive that was to devastate the Reich. In early 1943 the last of the Turbinlite squadrons were disbanded. Kenneth McGlashan was not sorry at their demise. 'The relatively cumbersome pairing of bomber and fighter had proved ineffective and the ever-present danger stemmed from the potential collision and not from our foe.'[36]

While the RAF struggled to find the ideal night-fighter, a much more fundamental drive was underway to improve the overall performance of the Hurricane. As far back as the outbreak of the war, the Air Ministry and Sydney Camm himself had recognized that the plane would soon head for obsolescence unless changes were made. Indeed, in early 1940 the government briefly discussed the idea of phasing out the Hurricane altogether in 1941, forestalling the need for any design improvements. 'As the policy was to concentrate on the Spitfire and the Hurricane production programme was to be completed by July 1941, it was not necessary to increase the performance of the Hurricane as had been done with the Spitfire,' concluded a research meeting of the Air Ministry in February 1940.[37] But this negative outlook never gained any real traction, particularly as the Hurricane was proving itself in combat and the Spitfire production was so badly behind schedule. The more realistic alternative to phasing out the Hawker plane was to enhance its capability through the introduction of a more powerful engine and higher-calibre weaponry.

By early 1940 Rolls-Royce had developed a more advanced version of the Merlin, featuring a two-speed supercharger. Called the Merlin XX, it delivered 1,300 horsepower, compared to 1,030 hp from the original. It also gave a stronger performance at altitude and raised the efficiency of the engine because it used a mix of 30 per cent glycol and 70 per cent water, rather than pure glycol. Well aware of the qualities of the Merlin XX through his closeness to Rolls-Royce's managing director Sir Ernest Hives, Camm sent the Air Ministry in March 1940 a proposal to install the engine on the Hurricane. He emphasized that no design changes were needed in the plane to accommodate the new power-plant, apart from a slightly longer front fuselage and a larger coolant radiator. The Air Ministry approved the proposal and told Hawker to produce the prototype of what soon was officially entitled the Hurricane Mark II Series A.

In May the arrival of Lord Beaverbrook at the Ministry of Aircraft Production (MAP), combined with the growing intensity in fighter combat, gave new impetus to the Mark II project. On 24 May 1940, MAP agreed that the Hurricane IIA 'must have first claim' over the Spitfire and the Beaufighter on Rolls-Royce's production of the Merlin XX because of the vital need to improve the Hawker fighter's performance. The need to clear the prototype design for production was 'a matter of the highest urgency', stressed MAP.[38] The question of armament also arose at this time, with Hawker and the government agreeing that the 12 Browning guns should be fitted to the new version. As it turned out, fears about a shortage of Brownings during the Battle of Britain meant that the early Mark IIs retained the eight-gun configuration.

The prototype first flew at Hawker's Langley plant near Slough on 11 June 1940 and its qualities were obvious. Flown by Philip Lucas, it achieved 348 mph, the highest speed ever attained by a fully armed Hurricane in level flight. The government at once ordered the aircraft into production, the cost of each plane to be £4,000. The importance of the new plane was reiterated by Sir Archibald Sinclair, Secretary of State for Air, in a letter to Beaverbrook on 29 August: 'The Hurricane needs the Merlin XX if it is to keep its place in the forefront of the battle . . . I am convinced that we must have Merlin XXs for all our Hurricanes.'[39] The first models emerged from the Langley works in September 1940, going into service initially with 111 'Treble One' Squadron and then replacing Mark Is in other Fighter Command units over the coming months. Bob Foster of 605 Squadron recalled his satisfaction at the new machines: 'It is no exaggeration to say that everyone was pleased with them. They had a Merlin XX engine which gave us higher speeds and a much better rate of climb.'[40] It was a sentiment shared at first by Tom Neil of 249 Squadron. The arrival of the new Hurricane at North Weald in Essex left him 'excitedly impressed. Like my first Hurricane nine months earlier, it was tight and bouncy, the engine silk smooth and there was heady, intoxicating aroma of new paint.' In the air the superiority of the Mark II was evident: 'The manually controlled two-speed supercharger, when engaged, came in with a disconcerting thud but increased the performance above 20,000 feet very substantially.' In the Mark I, Neil had never been optimistic going into combat above 25,000 feet whereas the Mark IIA 'was still pretty active at something over 30,000 feet'. Hawker had further improved the plane by fitting a rudder bias for the climb and blanking plates at the wing roots to reduce the risk of fire. One defect the company had not addressed, always a bugbear of Neil's, was the absence of cockpit heating. 'We were going to operate at temperatures around minus 60 degrees centigrade, without a vestige of heat. I was in despair.'[41]

The end of the Battle of Britain meant an end to any concerns about the supplies of Brownings, so from November 1940 Hawker began production of the 12-gun Hurricane, now designated the Mark IIB. Nearly 3,000 of this version were built, compared to 3,857 of the Mark I and just 415 of the Mark IIA, but the gun arrangement was never satisfactory, as Philip Lucas, the Hawker test pilot, explained: 'Although the effect of increasing the fire power by 50 per cent was quite devastating on the receiving end, this version was not popular for aerial combat because the extra weight of the guns and the ammunition had a significant effect on the rate of climb. Worse still, the inertia effect of the extra weight far outboard seriously affected lateral manoeuvrability and rate of roll.'[42] Both Hawker and the government recognized that, to achieve a real advance in lethality, the answer was not an increase in the number of Brownings but exchanging them for cannons. The installation of 20-mm cannon had been considered on the original Hurricane prototype back in 1935, but the idea was dropped because the French Hispano guns were then unreliable and it was feared that the fabric-covered wings would not stand their recoil. Four years later a single Hurricane armed with two cannons did actually take to the air, as part of the testing programme for new Hispano and Swiss Oerlikon cannons, which were both currently being manufactured under licence in Britain. As requested by the Air Ministry, Hawker conducted trials of a Hurricane equipped with two Oerlikons, one under each wing, though the experiment was not deemed a success as the weapons were judged to be too heavy for the single-engined fighter.

Despite such a verdict, this one-off cannon Hurricane went on to fight with some success in 151 Squadron during the Battle of Britain, taking down at least one enemy aircraft on Eagle Day. The power of its weapons was described by its pilot Roderick Smith in his account of the action. 'I opened fire at about 300 yards with my cannon, firing into the general mass as the enemy were in exceptionally close formation. One immediately burst into flames and another started smoking when my windscreen front panel was completely shattered by enemy fire and I broke downwards and returned to North Weald.'[43] The greater power of the Merlin XX led Sydney Camm in May 1940 to put forward a new proposal for a four 20-mm cannon Hurricane. The government was unsupportive, describing his scheme as 'problematical' and urging that cannon development be concentrated on the Spitfire and Beaufighter.[44]

But with typical resolution, Camm refused to be dissuaded. During the summer of 1940 he arranged for a Hurricane, which had been taken out of action because of wing damage, to be repaired and fitted with four Oerlikons. Using hand-tooled gun mountings, the plane proved sufficiently successful for trials to be conducted in the autumn using 30 more wing-damaged Hurricanes. A few problems emerged with the reliability of the wing-mounted drum-feed ammunition gear, so Hawker decided to switch to a belt feed. Otherwise the results were satisfactory enough for the Air Ministry finally to order the plane, designated the Mark IIC and armed with the lighter Hispano 20-mm gun rather than the Oerlikon. But even with all its experience, Hawker found mass production of the Mark IICs' wing mountings difficult, prompting complaints from MAP and pleas for understanding from Camm, who pointed out that the delays were partly caused by the government's own initial coolness towards the project. 'I do not want to make any excuses but I am sure you will agree that the atmosphere surrounding this particular conversion has not been a happy one, because we could not get approval for further action apart from the 30 experimental sets which I put through myself,' he wrote on 12 February to MAP.[45] Fighter Command, which feared that the Germans would soon start another major air campaign against Britain in the spring, was also exasperated. 'I am anxious about the slow progress made to date in arming our fighters with the 20mm Hispano gun . . . The Hurricane II situation is one which calls for the most urgent action,' wrote Sholto Douglas to Beaverbrook on 30 January 1941. 'Pilots ask me, during my visits to squadrons, when the cannons are coming and tell me that it is imperative to have them before the offensive starts, if we are to repeat last year's successes. If they do not get them, their morale is likely to be damped and they may feel that we are drifting into a policy of quantity rather than quality.'[46] Next day Beaverbrook assured Douglas that he shared 'to the full your anxious desire that the fighter squadrons should be assured of the most powerful armament' and promised that the programme would be accelerated.[47]

As so often before, the Minister made his influence felt. By the end of February, the first Mark IIC had been delivered to the Aeroplane and Armament Experimental Establishment (A&AEE) at Boscombe Down in Wiltshire, and production was soon up to eight sets of wings a month. Weighing 8,100 pounds, the standard Hurricane IIC was significantly heavier than previous versions, though it still had a maximum speed of 336 mph. Moreover, its wing had a remarkable versatility, capable of carrying bombs or long-range petrol tanks in addition to the cannons. The Mark IIC had the highest production run of any Hurricane, reaching 4,711 by 1944, and was used in a wide variety of roles, proving particularly deadly against ground targets, its four cannon pouring out 600 pounds of explosive shell per minute.

The new Hurricane type sparked another of *Aeroplane* magazine's patriotic effusions. 'The world's greatest fighter revitalized,' said an article on 3 October 1941. 'As our chief defender in the Battle of Britain the Hurricane earned a place in history such as few of man's mechanical achievements can claim.' But with 'a new version of the Rolls-Royce Merlin' and 'phenomenal armament', the improved Hurricane 'gives more promise of years of historic achievement'.[48]

The brief setback in Mark IIC production was a rarity at Hawker Siddeley, which operated at a high level of efficiency throughout the war. Unlike Supermarine, the company never had to disperse its manufacturing as a result of air attacks, despite the proximity of the Langley and Kingston plants to the capital. During the later part of the Battle of Britain, the Luftwaffe launched four raids against the Brooklands plant in Surrey. The first three missed the target completely but on the fourth raid, though the Germans were again largely inaccurate, some bombs hit the toilet block and dope shop, while one 250-pound delayed-action high explosive landed in the main Hurricane assembly works. A brave, quick-thinking soldier, Lieutenant John Patton of the Royal Canadian Engineers, calmly loaded the unexploded bomb onto a makeshift sled and dragged it outside where it blew up harmlessly. The Langley plant received just one hit during the Blitz, but the damage was superficial. A more serious raid on 3 October hit the Kingston plant, where bombs destroyed much of the Design Office and killed a workman on fire-watch duty. Fortunately, most of the workforce had gone to the night shelters when the alarm sounded. According to Beaverbook's report on 27 October to the War Cabinet, 50 Hurricanes were destroyed.[49] The production lines soon recovered, but the damage to the offices necessitated a move for Hawker's design, experimental and administrative teams.

The company's new headquarters at Esher in Surrey could hardly have been a greater contrast to the dingy, cramped premises where the Hurricane had first been envisioned. With the backing of MAP, Hawker took over the magnificent eighteenth-century Palladian mansion of Claremont, which had been built by Lancelot 'Capability' Brown for Baron Clive of India. Later the house had been bought by Queen Victoria for one of her children, and it subsequently passed through several hands before ending up as a girls' school in 1930. Evacuation of the pupils at the start of the war meant that Camm and his staff could quickly move into the empty building, where they remained for the duration of the war. 'It was quite a place, a marvellous old house with a marble staircase, tennis courts and an outdoor swimming pool,' recalled Jack Cousins, who was a weight-control expert at Hawker.[50]

The only other major structural change to Hawker's operations was the end of Hurricane production at Brooklands and the transfer of the site to Vickers. This was made possible not only by the expansion of the Langley and Gloster factories, but also by output from the Canadian Car company of Montreal and Austin Motors Longbridge, which was subcontracted to build 300 Hurricanes. At its peak, in the second quarter of 1942, Hurricane production reached 725 aircraft and this level was largely sustained until late 1943 when other, more powerful Hawker fighters like the Typhoon and the Tempest began to predominate. The total manual workforce engaged on the Hurricane at this time was 13,200, in addition to 2,700 white-collar staff. The Hawker employees, around a third of whom were female, had to work long hours. At the Kingston assembly line, for example, the day shift ran from 7 a.m. until 6.30 p.m., with an hour's lunch break, and the night shift also lasted eleven and a half hours.

Despite the long working days and nights, there was little evidence of widespread absenteeism or industrial unrest from the trade unions. According to Jack Cousins, the well-oiled organization was part of the reason for this. 'The Hawker factories ran remarkably well. The managers, led by Frank Spriggs, a very forthright man, were great at getting the job done and telling people where they had gone wrong. You were never short of engines, with plenty of Merlins waiting to be fitted. There were no industrial troubles so people were less Bolshie.'[51] Doris Webb, who worked in the wages office at Langley, also remembered a happy place. 'We weren't badly paid, the canteen was good and we had some entertainment. Max Miller, the comedian, came to Langley. So did the singer Petula Clark. She was only ten years old then.' The workforce's motivation was also assisted by a sense of purpose. 'The Hurricane was the best plane there was. We were very proud of working there because we knew what a great little fighter it was.'[52] That was not, however, a universal attitude. An inquiry by the Ministry of Labour in February 1942 found that there were a few 'persistent absentees who know they "can get away with it"'. The solution, said the report, was for 'proved malingerers to be sent to the fighting services. A few examples would have a most salutary effect.'[53] But with output remaining high such a tough step was never taken by the government, especially as there were far more serious labour problems in other factories and industries.

A picture of life on the Hurricane production line was left by John Corbett, who worked at Gloster's Hucclecote plant in Gloucestershire: 'I have a vivid memory, on entering the production hangar in the morning, of seeing the beginning of the line with the familiar centre-sections and the wooden aft-sections almost buried beneath fitters assembling the machines. The aircraft at the head of the line would probably be ready for flight by lunchtime.'[54] One of the few women in a senior engineering position in the aircraft industry was Beryl Platt, a Cambridge graduate who became a technician at Hawker. 'It was very hard work, often 70 hours a week. The atmosphere was intense and it was a very crowded production line. I always remember Hawker tea, which didn't taste of tea at all but it was hot and wet. Someone once told me that they put bicarbonate of soda in it. But there was great camaraderie. People did pull together and that's why I speak with such affection of the people I worked with on the shop floor. We knew we could rely on each other.'[55]

Once an aircraft had been finished, it had to be checked by Hawker's pilots before being sent to the squadrons. Bill Humble, a former mining engineer and air racer, production tested over 450 Hurricanes during his time at Langley. 'All we were doing was seeing if the plane worked as it should, that there was no vibration from the propeller and that the thing flew level. Most of them behaved themselves fairly well. I had a couple of forced landings through engine failure.' On one occasion, flying at 20,000 feet, Humble noticed that his oxygen gauge was showing zero. 'Sheer terror gripped me. I shoved the nose down and the engine over-ran. The constant speed unit didn't seem to work. There was a hell of a bang from the front end and the cockpit filled up with smoke, the bang being the fact some of the connecting rods had gone through the bottom of the crankcase. There was oil all over the place.' Humble thought the plane was on fire and prepared to bail out, but then he realized that there was only smoke, no flames. 'I decided to hang on. Sure enough, the smoke died off. I could see Langley, large as life. I put the wheels down and force-landed.'[56] Humble's experience was a further demonstration of the Hurricane's resilience in a crisis.

The job of delivering the Hurricanes to the fighter stations belonged to the Air Transport Auxiliary, the organization set up by the government in 1939 to provide logistical support to the RAF. At first it was intended that the ATA would carry only mail and medical supplies, but the wartime demands on the RAF meant that ferrying aircraft became the ATA's primary role. By 1944 it was a key part of the war effort. With its unofficial slogan 'Any aircraft, anywhere', the service had more than 1,300 pilots at 14 ferry pools across the country, supported by nearly 3,000 ground staff. Peter Garrod, a British civilian pilot who served with the ATA from 1941 to 1945, was amazed at the speed of the Hurricane on his first flight: 'That was a wonderful experience. When you first flew it, it left you behind. I mean I was six or eight miles clear of the airfield before I caught up with where I was. But later you would find that the Hurricane was slow. It is amazing how your reactions build up. When you had flown Typhoons and Tempests, and you went back to the Hurricane, you'd think, "What a slow old barge this is."'[57]

The ATA was the only wartime air service that allowed female recruitment and altogether 166 women served, among them the celebrated aviator Amy Johnson, who was killed on an ATA trip over the Thames. Another ATA heroine was Margaret Gore, who recalled her first thrill at flying the Hurricane in 1941: 'I hadn't flown anything comparable to it. We really felt we were getting somewhere when it arrived, a real fighter, particularly because we had seen the Battle of Britain going on overhead the autumn before. It really was extremely exciting.'[58] All too predictably, the female pilots of the ATA were nicknamed 'Spitfire Girls', another indicator of the disregard for the Hawker fighter.

The developments in the Hurricane's weaponry from 1941 were testament to the advantages of the thick wing and strength of the plane. The same robustness and versatility also made the Hurricane ideal for wide-ranging experimentation throughout the war, most of the trials being aimed at increasing the fighter's range or enabling it to cope with special circumstances. One early scheme, prompted by the Norway campaign, was for a Hurricane on floats that could operate as a seaplane. The idea was abandoned when it was found that the drag was excessive. Two radical proposals were put forward to give the Hurricane a long-range capability, something that Fighter Command felt it needed as the air war moved from defence to offence. The first was for a Hurricane to be towed along, like a glider, by a Vickers Wellington medium bomber fitted with a winch and cable. According to the theory, the Hurricane would take off normally but then in mid-air would link up with the Wellington using a winch and steel cable, enabling the fighter to save fuel. At the moment of attack, the Hurricane pilot would switch on his engine again and release the cable. But the practical difficulties of making the connection and preventing the Hurricane's engine from freezing proved insuperable. In January 1943 the trials were abandoned.

A second plan, which never left the drawing board but appealed to the Royal Navy, desperate for protection against Luftwaffe bombers attacking convoys, was for a Hurricane to be carried on the back of an American-built B24 Liberator. Sydney Camm told the Air Ministry in February 1941 that the idea seemed feasible and Hawker was 'prepared to do the complete conversion work on the Hurricane'.[59] But Lord Beaverbrook, normally so attracted by the unconventional, was lukewarm, saying the risks of an accident at separation were too great. Another key opponent was Sir Charles Portal, Chief of the Air Staff, who told Churchill that the effort to construct these special planes 'would be out of all proportion to any results which might be achieved, even if they could be given a sufficiently long range'.[60] The composite was never built. Even more bizarre was a project code-named Sunflower Seed, which involved a Hurricane firing a rocket vertically into the belly of an enemy bomber. The equipment for this upward-firing weapon consisted of little more than a metal tube six inches in diameter, mounted behind the cockpit. Maurice

Allward, who worked in the Hurricane design office under Camm, recalled that in the first test, the pilot wore an army-style helmet and flew with the sliding hood removed. 'The first test rocket fired severely damaged the fairing around the tube. The damage, however, was soon repaired and the area locally protected by duraluminum sheeting, after which further firings were made satisfactorily if rather frighteningly.'[61] The scheme was never adopted. Another intriguing but fruitless experiment was the Hillson Hurricane biplane, developed by the light aircraft manufacturer F. W. Hill and Son of Manchester. With the aim of providing more lift from short airstrips, a Mark I Hurricane was fitted with an extra top wing that could be jettisoned in flight. But the arrangement, which served as a reminder of the Hurricane's origins in the Hawker Fury, proved too clumsy and heavy during its trials.

One unusual Hurricane innovation proved extremely cheap. Most Hurricanes built during the war cost between £4,000 and £5,000 but there was one large batch of them that had a price tag of just £50 each. These were dummy aircraft, made of wood and cardboard, which were placed on decoy airfields to mislead enemy bombers. Identical in size and shape to the real Hurricanes, these dummies were extremely realistic and over 500 of them were built by the firm of Green Brothers of Hailsham, Sussex, specialists in the production of high-quality folding furniture. To heighten the deception, the mock airfields were installed with landing lights and flare paths. Altogether, there were nine of these false Hurricane stations operating between 1940 and 1941, part of a larger RAF network of decoy bases. A few of them attracted German raids, proving that they could be effective. Some the dummy Hurricanes were also sent overseas to be used on bases in the Mediterranean and North Africa.

Yet probably the most outlandish proposal proved both workable and successful. This was the 'Catafighter', or 'Hurricat', a seaborne fighter rocket-catapulted from a ship to provide convoy protection against air attack. Since the fall of France in June 1940, the Battle of the Atlantic had raged with a new intensity. Britain's shipping supplies were being put under severe threat not only by the German U-boats, which now had access to the Atlantic ports in France, but also by the deadly Focke-Wulf (Fw) 200 Condor bomber. Converted from a pre-war four-engined airliner, the Condor had a range of over 2,000 miles and could carry naval mines or a 2,000-bomb load. As well as powerful cannon, it was equipped with sophisticated radar equipment that enabled it to conduct reconnaissance for the 'wolf packs' of the U-boat fleet. Between June 1940 and February 1941, it was estimated that the Fw 200s sank 365,000 tons of Allied shipping, prompting Churchill to call the plane 'the scourge of the Atlantic'.[62] To counter the Condor's threat, the obvious answer would have been the use of aircraft carriers, but the Royal Navy simply did not have enough of them after losing both the *Courageous* and the *Glorious*. The alternative, therefore, was to equip a number of merchant ships with catapult-assisted fighters.

There was nothing new about the use of catapults for launching aircraft at sea. Indeed, as early as 1904 the Wright brothers had experimented with such equipment, and the Royal Navy extensively operated catapults on its vessels during the inter-war years. The problem in 1940 was that the traditional naval apparatus was too heavy and awkward to install on the convoy merchantmen, so lighter structures with rocket motors had to be adopted. The next task was to find a plane with the strength, firepower and handling characteristics to cope with this unique job. 'Of the various aircraft, the Hurricane appears most suitable on account of its performance and its smaller weight and size than the Fleet Air Arm fighters,' reported the Air Ministry on 31 December 1940.[63] Sydney Camm was so confident that he urged the catapulting equipment for the Hurricane be ordered immediately, since the conversion would require only minor alterations. 'I think the suggestion is a sound one. There is no reason to doubt the structural security of the Hurricane so modified,' said MAP at the end of the month.[64] Progress in the new year was rapid, with Churchill ruling 'that extreme priority is to be given to the fitting of the merchant ships'.[65] Rocket tests were successfully carried out Farnborough in Hampshire.

The conversion of 200 Hurricanes then began, a programme that required the installation of catapult spools and attachments, as well as a heavily padded headrest so the pilot could absorb the shock of the launch. Thirty-five merchantmen were fitted out with the equipment and pilots were recruited for the newly established Merchant

Ship Fighter Unit, which came under the control of the Admiralty as part of the Fleet Air Arm. It might have been imagined that there would be few volunteers for this role, since the pilots had no chance of landing their Hurricanes back on the ships and would have to bail out into the freezing waters of the Atlantic or the North Sea when they ran out of petrol. The fact that there was no shortage of recruits is another tribute to the remarkable fighting spirit of the RAF.

The training for the new unit was held at Speke airport near Liverpool, where a rocket catapult was erected similar to the structure used on the merchant ships. This consisted of a metal track 70 feet long and a trolley, which was loaded with a Hurricane and then propelled down the rails by 13 rockets, sending the plane into the air at the end of the line. The instructor for the Hurricat pilots at Speke was Louis Strange, a First World War veteran, who, at the age of forty-nine, began by giving an assured demonstration of how the system worked. 'If an old boy like me can do it, it won't mean a thing to lads like you,' he said, trying to persuade them not to be intimidated by the huge sheet of flame and loud explosions given off by 150 pounds of cordite.[66] Later in the war, after the project was no longer secret, a lively account of a Hurricat training flight was provided by the *Evening Standard* newspaper, in which the structure was described as looking 'rather like a straight track of scenic railway'. When the pilot gave the signal, continued the *Standard*'s account, 'the explosive charge is ignited and with a roar the cradle carrying the Hurricane hurtles along the "scenic railway track". Belching flame from behind, it gathers speed until at 70 mph or more it dashes into the buffers at the end of the railed track and shoots the Catafighter into the air. The Hurricane takes to the air with only a few feet to play with and usually dips a little as it leaves the catapult. Then quickly it gains height, does a few circles round the airfield and comes down, the practice flight over.'[67]

The first of the 35 CAM (Catapult Assisted Merchantmen) ships, the SS *Michael E*, set sail in a convoy from Belfast to Halifax, Nova Scotia on 18 May 1941. It was not an auspicious start. The vessel was sunk by a torpedo in the mid-Atlantic, though the Hurricane pilot, Sub-Lieutenant M. Birrell, survived and, with the Hurricane breed's characteristic defiance, soon returned to Catafighter duties. Early

CAM launches were undermined by problems with non-firing rock-ets. But over the summer of 1941, with further experience and improvements to the equipment, the Hurricats began to prove more effective. The first victory was achieved on 3 August, when a Condor was shot down by Lieutenant Robert Everett, sailing with the CAM *Maplin*. Everett was one of the most colourful figures in the Fleet Air Arm. Born in Australia, he had been an amateur pilot and a brilliant jockey, winning the Grand National in 1929 on Gregalach. All his gallant spirit went into this fight against the Fw 200 as he was launched from the *Maplin*, then chased the bomber for over thirty-five miles despite heavy return fire. Finally, after blazing away until his guns ran out of ammunition and his own engine had been hit, he saw the Condor burst into flames and plunge into the sea. After struggling back to the *Maplin*, Everett had to ditch his own Hurricane, a near-fatal task as the plane turned over and sank the moment it touched the water, dragging him down thirty feet. Somehow he managed to struggle free and reach the surface, where he was picked up by another destroyer in his convoy. His heroic action earned him the DSO.

Other successes followed, and by the end of 1941 six Condors had been destroyed by the Hurricats. A further technical advance in the autumn was the introduction of 44-gallon jettisonable long-range fuel tanks, which reduced the fighters' manoeuvrability but improved their chances of reaching land. The pilots still needed to show incred-ible bravery, however, as the CAM ships continued their convoy operations during 1942. Neil Hulse, a naval officer serving on the merchantman *Empire Lawrence*, was full of admiration for his vessel's Hurricane pilot, Alastair Hay, who brought down two Heinkel bombers during an arctic convoy trip to Russia. 'Here was one brave Hurricane, like a sparrowhawk, going into these formations of German bombers.' Hulse had been smoking on the bridge with Hay when the message came through that the enemy had been sighted. 'He butted out his cigarette and put it in his flying jacket. He had no hope of landing on friendly territory. We watched as he took off and remained in communication with him. On the speaker, we could hear him going in and hear his cannon fire in the cockpit of the plane. He got one and there was smoke trailing from the other. Then we heard his cry that he'd been hit.' But he managed to return to the convoy and bail out near HMS *Volunteer*, which picked him up from the water after only ten minutes. 'We got a message from the *Volunteer*. Your pilot is safe. He is having a bullet removed from his thigh.'[68]

Less fortunate but equally brave was Flying Officer John B. Kendall, who also served as a Hurricat pilot on the *Empire Morn* in one of the Arctic convoys. Early on 25 May 1942 he and his plane were catapulted off their merchantman when enemy aircraft were sighted in the area. First he chased a Blohm and Voss 138 Flying Boat, which fled at his attack; then he dived on a Ju 88, shooting it down. Two other German planes withdrew after this kill, but tragedy quickly followed, as Captain W. L Cruickshank of the *Empire Morn* recorded in his diary:

> As Kendall had exhausted his ammunition he circled a destroyer on our starboard quarter with the object of bailing out. With a very low ceiling I think he must have misjudged his height when he bailed out. The machine crashed into the sea and he close behind it but unfortunately the parachute did not open until he was close to the water and he hit the water with a terrific force, seriously injuring himself, from which he died shortly afterwards. He was buried at 2 p.m. the same day from the destroyer. The attack was magnificently carried out with skill and daring, against superior numbers. He showed British mettle against the Hun.[69]

Ironically, for all the extreme dangers of the Hurricats, Kendall was the only pilot to lose his life on one of their sorties.

The CAM fighters were estimated to have shot down at least nine German planes, most of them Fw 200s. The CAMs were gradually phased out from mid 1942 because of the increasing availability of a new generation of small escort carriers, known as MACs (Merchantman Aircraft Carriers). These could carry Hurricanes that had undergone minor conversions to operate at sea through the installation of arrester hooks for deck-landings, the work carried out by General Aircraft Ltd. The first Sea Hurricanes, designated Mark IBs, had gone into service in July 1941 aboard the elderly Royal Navy carrier HMS *Furious*. Further naval versions followed in 1942, including the Mark IC with four cannon and the Mark IIC, which was equipped with naval radio gear. The Sea Hurricane saw action in a wide range of theatres, including the Mediterranean and Russia, but, apart from its strength, it was not particularly suitable for maritime work because of its large size, slow climb and poor ditching qualities in the water. Sammy Mearns, an 804 Squadron pilot with the Fleet Air Arm, who flew a Sea Hurricane until 1943, recalled some of the disadvantages:

> The Hurricanes did not have folding wings which was a most inhibiting factor, in that you had to put the aircraft onto lifts to take them down into the hangar underneath the flight deck. To do this you had to put them on a trolley to sidetrack them. Once you got them into the hangar you had to push them off the trolley. You can imagine that doing this at sea, with the ship rolling and pitching, with several tons of aeroplane bumping off a little trolley which rolled along the deck, could cause all sorts of problems, particularly in the close confines of a hangar.

Mearns further remembered that the pitching and rolling 'could be very hard on undercarriages. There were a number of accidents. People used to go over the side.' The carrier decks had a strong wire net which was meant to stop any aircraft that missed the arrester hooks, but 'if you went straight into the barrier that would mean a prop wrecked. On other occasions, aircraft could bounce over the barrier and hit the flight deck park fore of the bridge.' But Mearns's squadron did have some successes, especially against the slow four-engined reconnaissance plane the Ju 290:

> We had all our Hurricanes painted white as we found that white was a very useful camouflage. We were the only squadron to do that. Certainly the Ju 290s did not see us much. We shot down three of these shadowers. They were quite heavily armed but they were a big target and in that respect they were easier to hit. We had a good 150 mph of extra speed over them. We were armed with 20 mm cannon, a highly effective weapon with semi-armour piercing rounds and high explosive incendiaries. It only needed one or two of these rounds to do vast damage to an aircraft. In fact you could see them striking targets. They exploded on impact, very lethal.[70]

During the war, 537 Sea Hurricanes served with the Fleet Air Arm, and in total around 1,200 Hurricanes were converted for maritime use. But they came to be heavily outclassed by the enemy from 1943 and were replaced by other, more modern aircraft, particularly the American Grumman Widcast. In April 1944 the last Sea Hurricane was withdrawn from carrier service. On land, however, the Hawker fighter was still on operations, having emerged triumphantly from a series of brutal ordeals.

9

'In every corner of the globe'

❦

JUST AS THE summer of 1940 had been the Finest Hour of the war for both the Hurricane and Britain, so the period from early 1941 until mid 1942 was disastrous for both the plane and the British cause. In almost every theatre from the Mediterranean to the Far East, the Hurricane, like the wider British military, proved ineffectual against German and Japanese power. There was an air of continual retreat and defeat. Neither the armed forces nor the Hawker fighter seemed up to the task. After the catastrophes in the Far East in early 1942, when Singapore and Burma fell to the Japanese, the commander of forces there, General Henry Pownall, wrote: 'We need a tougher Army, based on a tougher nation . . . We must cultivate mobility of mind as well as of body, ie imagination; and cut out the great hampering "tail" which holds back rather than aids the "teeth".'[1] At about the same time, on 21 March, Arthur Tedder, the RAF Commander in the Middle East, wrote despairingly to Sir Charles Portal, Chief of the Air Staff, that: 'the days of the Hurricane I for offensive work are over and even for Army Co-Operation work it is now far too slow. I see, however, no prospect of being able to equip the Army Co-Operation squadrons with anything better for months.'[2] Looking back on the string of setbacks, Harold Nicolson, the National Labour politician, wrote privately: 'There is something deeply wrong with the whole morale of our army.'[3] When the RAF Commander Basil Embry made a tour of inspection of Malta's fighter defences in early 1942, he kept hearing vociferous complaints about the Hurricane. 'I am informed that the German fighter pilots often fly in front of our Hurricanes in order to show off the superiority of the 109s. This is bound to have an increasingly adverse effect on morale,' he wrote.[4] The plane certainly had an adverse effect on the morale of 249 Squadron's Tom Neil, who said that he was 'struck dumb' when told by the RAF in April 1941 that during operations in Malta he would be fighting in a Hurricane Mark I: 'Oh no, not again! We are back again on the old out-distanced, out-performed, out-everythinged Mark I.'[5] The Hurricane, like the British military, participated in a few impressive victories over the forces of the Italian empire and the French Vichy regime, but such triumphs alone were never going to decide the outcome of the war.

The main deployment of the Hurricane since its creation had been in the defence of Britain and western Europe. But the government always considered that it might be required for operations much further afield, particularly North Africa and the Middle East, vital regions for the protection of Britain's imperial trade routes and oil supplies. As early as February 1939 the Air Ministry had asked Hawker to study the feasibility of converting a Hurricane for tropical use, a step that would require the installation of cockpit ventilation and a filter in front of the carburettor air intake to prevent abrasive sand wrecking the engine.[6] The heavy demands on production for the home front meant that little urgency was attached to the project until December 1939, when the Air Ministry stressed that the scheme had to be 'given priority' because of the need for the RAF 'to be in a position to replace the Gladiators by Hurricanes in the Middle East by the early spring should this be necessary'.[7] The conversion now proceeded rapidly, and in early 1940 one experimental Hurricane, serial number L1669, was fitted with the tropicalized filter, built by the Surrey company of Vokes Limited. The plane was then flown out to Egypt for trials. In March a report from the headquarters of RAF Middle East Command in Cairo stated that the tests had been 'very satisfactory'. From a technical aspect, 'the performance, fuel consumption, oil and water temperatures are almost identical to Hurricane aircraft operating under temperate conditions'. There had been 'no trouble as regards the maintenance of the airframe and engine', while 'the guns have proved to be suitable for conditions in this country'.[8] Moreover, it was claimed that the Vokes filter led to a drop in the maximum speed of only 5 mph, though in combat later this turned out to be over-optimistic.

Once the trials were completed, L1669 was handed over to Air Vice Marshal Raymond Collishaw, a Canadian veteran of the First

Hurricane of 85 Squadron preparing for night patrol. Without airborne radar, the Hawker fighter was ill-equipped for this role

A maritime version of the Hurricane on the flight deck of HMS *Indomitable*, August 1942, part of a convoy bringing essential supplies to the island of Malta

A specially adapted Hurricane being lowered on to the catapult structure of a merchant ship. Known as 'Hurricats', these fighters did valiant work in protecting the Atlantic convoys

The fuselage of a Hurricane is pulled from its packing crate at the RAF base of Takoradi on the Gold Coast. Once assembled with their wings and tailplanes, the Hurricanes were then ferried to the north African theatre

A damaged Hurricane is lifted on to a Queen Mary trailer in the western desert, early 1942. The plane's resilience and ease of repair were two of the ingredients of its success

A Hurricane pilot shows the remarkable manoeuvrability of the plane, early 1942. 'She handled so beautifully,' recalled one airman

Hurricanes of 1 Squadron, South African Air Force, in action over Libya, January 1942

Below: A Hurricane IID, justifiably known as the 'Tankbuster', gives a demonstration of the lethal firepower from its 40mm cannons

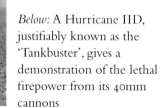

A Hurricane Mark IIC under construction. The thickness of the plane's wings, which enabled it to carry a wide variety of armaments, is clearly evident

Wooden fuselages lined up at the huge Hawker factory in Langley, Slough. More than 7,000 Hurricanes were built at this vast plant

The instrument panel inside the cockpit of a Hurricane

Fitters and armourers of the Women's Auxiliary Air Force servicing a Hurricane at RAF Sealand, Wales

Below: A pilot of 121 Squadron tests the engines and guns of his Hurricane in March 1941, while four of the ground crew sit on the tail to hold the plane down

A crated Hurricane is unloaded at the Vaenga airfield, north Russia, September 1941. Two RAF Hurricane squadrons, making up No. 151 Wing, were sent to Russia that autumn in response to the German invasion

Hurricanes of the Soviet Air Force, flown by Russian pilots, go on the attack. Altogether 2,952 Hurricanes were supplied to Russia during the war

A British anti-aircraft gun crew at an airfield in Bengal wave to a Hurricane on its return from a sortie over Arakan, Burma, December 1944

A Hurricane Mark IIC of 42 Squadron attacking a bridge near a Burmese settlement on the Tiddim Road. 'It was very gratifying to see the explosions,' said one pilot

The old and the new. An ox cart passes a Hurricane Mark IIC of 34 Squadron at Palel, Burma, November 1944

The last Hurricane type to go into service, the Mark IV, pictured during a test flight over Langley in August 1943

The end of an era. The very last Hurricane to be built by Hawker, designated serial number PZ865 and known as 'The Last of the Many'. The plane was later handed over to the Battle of Britain Memorial Flight and still flies to this day, a tribute to the durability of Sir Sydney Camm's design

World War who was now Commander of 202 Group, the RAF's Western Desert Force. When Italy formally declared war against the Allies on 10 June 1940, precipitating the state of hostilities in the Middle East that Portal had feared, Collishaw flew this single Hurricane from one airfield to another near the frontier of Libya, Mussolini's North African colony, in an attempt to persuade the enemy that modern RAF fighters were arriving in Egypt. As it turned out, the Italians were reluctant to go on the offensive, despite all Il Duce's bombast. But the RAF in the Middle East, led by Sir Arthur Longmore, knew that Collishaw's daring pantomime was no substitute for genuine fighter reinforcements against the Italian threat and urged that more Hurricanes be sent. Even in the face of the pressures from the impending Battle of Britain, the government accepted Longmore's case. A small number of tropicalized Hurricanes were dispatched to Alexandria in early June 1940, making a gruelling journey via war-torn France, Tunisia and Malta before reaching Egypt, where they joined 80 Squadron whose chief task was guarding the Royal Navy's eastern Mediterranean fleet.

Almost as soon as they arrived, however, four of the Hurricanes had to be sent back to Malta, the strategically vital island that was coming under attack from Italian aircraft based in nearby Sicily. At the time the Maltese garrison comprised just a handful of Gladiator biplanes, nicknamed *Faith*, *Hope* and *Charity* for their stoicism in the face of a numerically superior enemy. The seven-strong combination of Gladiators and Hurricanes performed beyond expectations and by the end of July had accounted for twelve Italian aircraft. Inevitably, just as in the Battle of Britain, the phenomenon of 'Spitfire snobbery' reared its head. When a pair of Hurricanes shot down a Regia Aeronautica bomber along with one of its Fiat CR42 biplane escorts, the returning Italians claimed to have been attacked by 'two Spitfires'.[9]

The RAF had their own losses, however, including the death of Flight Lieutenant Peter Keeble, the first Hurricane pilot to die in the long struggle to defend Malta. Carter Jonas, the commander of the airfield at Luqa, described the incident: 'The sound of firing and diving had almost ceased when Peter Keeble was killed, his Hurricane rocketing down out of a patch of blue sky, flattening out for a moment as if to attempt some form of landing and then diving into the ground.'[10] The Hurricane pilots also found the Fiat CR42 biplanes surprisingly manoeuvrable, as Dick Sugden described in his account when he went into combat with them:

> The whole aircraft shakes as the eight guns rattle. I see the nose drop, the engine cuts and picks up again and I am just going to fire again when – what is this? Red sparks shooting past me, over each wing, coming from the sea. I hear a hiss and a crack and do a steep turn to the left. Oh my God! There are six little CR42s dancing up and down behind me. They follow me easily on the turn, much more manoeuvrable than the Hurricane. There's only one thing to do and I half-roll onto my back and go down vertically, leaving them standing.[11]

By August 1940 there were just three planes left in the Malta Fighter Flight, the RAF unit responsible for the island's aerial defences. Fortunately, more Hurricanes were on their way from Britain. The inspirational example of 46 Squadron, led by Kenneth Cross, in the Norway campaign showed that it was feasible for Hurricanes to take off from an aircraft carrier. The process was now repeated in the Mediterranean in Operation Hurry, as the venerable 14,550-ton aircraft carrier HMS *Argus*, with 12 Hurricanes on board, headed for Malta. As the ship passed south of Sardinia on 2 August 1940, the planes prepared for take-off, their journey to be guided to the island by two Blackburn Skua maritime fighters. Hurricane pilot Jim Pickering of 501 Squadron recalled the anxious moments before the flight on the crowded deck. 'The leading Skua had the shortest take-off run. The ramp on the *Argus* bumped it into the air at too low an airspeed for comfort and at obviously too steep an angle for attack. It sank slowly below the level of the *Argus*'s bows. I was next off and scores of permutations of circumstances cascaded through my mind . . . but all was well. The Hurricane leapt from the deck without even full throttle.'[12] Flying eastwards in vic formation at 6,000 feet over the sea, they all landed on the island, where they were amalgamated with the Malta Fighter Flight to form 261 Squadron.

Because of the Battle of Britain, no more Hurricanes were delivered to the island until later in the autumn. The next attempt to strengthen the fighter defences, code-named Operation White, took place in November, with the *Argus* carrying another cargo of 12 Hurricanes. But this time the execution was disastrous. A heavy Italian naval presence in the western Mediterranean meant that the ship was more 400 miles west of Malta when the Hurricanes took off early in the morning of 17 November. Not only was this distance stretching the limit of the planes' fuel endurance, but the pilots had also been badly briefed for the journey. They were told to fly at 2,000 feet, when in reality the most economical altitude was 10,000 feet where the air was lighter. Furthermore, unlike the Operation Hurry aircraft, which had two-speed, variable-pitch airscrews, the Hurricanes of Operation White had constant-speed propellers, with which the pilots were unfamiliar. They therefore did not know how to adjust the engine speed to optimize their range. Tragically, only four of the Hurricanes made it to the island, the rest running out of fuel and dropping into the sea. Just one of the pilots was rescued by an RAF flying boat sent out in support of the operation. A subsequent investigation into the tragedy put most of the blame on inadequate briefing for pilots in the use of the constant-speed units, stating the result of the decision to fly the Hurricanes at 'the "best" engine speed of 2,200 revolutions per minute', as opposed to 'the most economical' speed of 1,800 rpm, was 'to decrease their range by 15 per cent, that is to 415 miles'.[13] Lessons were learnt for future deliveries, but until the New Year of 1941 Malta was protected by only the most meagre fighter force.

Supplies of Hurricanes were also urgently needed in North Africa, where in September 1940 Mussolini finally persuaded his large army to go on the offensive into Egypt. But the RAF faced enormous logistical difficulties in meeting this requirement. The fall of France meant that fighter planes could no longer be flown through western Europe and on to Tunisia. Sending them through the Mediterranean was fraught with danger, as the Operation White fiasco demonstrated, while the southern journey around the Cape to Egypt could take seventy days. The solution was found in the far-flung nature of Britain's African empire. A new RAF terminus was opened at the port of Takoradi on the Ghanaian coast, where the fighters could either be flown off aircraft carriers or unloaded from ships in crates and reassembled. Having been tested, the planes then embarked on a journey of over 4,000 miles across central and northern Africa to Cairo. Masterminded by Group Captain Henry Thorold, the former head of RAF maintenance during the Battle of France, the Takoradi base was an impressive operation, complete with airstrips, hangars, workshops, living quarters, heavy plant, gantries and communications. 'The whole show is a first-class piece of improvisation, from the devices for unloading the extremely awkward cases to the excellent accommodation fixed up for the troops,' Tedder told Portal on 19 December after making a tour of inspection.[14] The creation of the Takoradi route provided a vital lifeline for the RAF in the Middle East from the moment it was established, as Sir Arthur Longmore, head of RAF Middle East Command, recalled in an early wartime analysis of the RAF's desert operations. 'By October 1940, our aircraft supply situation was much improved. Hurricanes had begun to replace Gladiator fighters. It seemed likely that at last we could adequately support our rapidly growing British army.'[15] The flow rapidly increased in the New Year. Between January 1941 and the Battle of El Alamein in October–early November 1942, over 1,500 Hurricanes were dispatched along the route.

For the pilots, the trip could be an arduous experience, involving stops in Nigeria at Lagos and Kano, followed by a long stretch over hostile Vichy French territory, then further refuelling halts in the Sudan at El Fasher, Khartoum and Wadi Halfa before flying on to the final destination, the RAF base at Abu Sueir, seventy miles northeast of Cairo. Maurice Leng was one of the first Hurricane pilots to complete the route, when his 73 Squadron was sent out to Africa in November 1940 aboard the carrier HMS *Furious*. 'We had never been on an aircraft carrier before and never flown off one before. Unfortunately one pilot took off in coarse pitch and fell off the bow. He was swept along the keel and had to be rescued by a destroyer that had come with us. He lost his aircraft but all he had was a cut chin. I got off uneventfully.' After taking off again from Takoradi for Egypt, Leng was all too aware of the dangers. 'The worst part was flying over the jungle. If your engine packed up over the jungle you were never found again because there was nowhere to land. And if you parachuted out you would never be found. That jungle was impenetrable for 250 miles from Lagos to Kano.' Other aspects of the journey were more tolerable. 'At these staging posts, we would usually stay in the District Commissioner's house. We were well fed, well treated. The black population was very friendly, pleasant. I don't think they knew there was a war.'[16] The ferocity of the heat in Africa was what Sam Fletcher, another pilot with 21 Squadron, remembered most. 'I found Khartoum a bit like an oven. When the aircraft were left, say if we went for a meal, when we came back they would be red hot. You could burn yourself on the surface.'[17] The stresses of the crossing meant that the Merlin engines were often damaged when they reached Abu Sueir and had to undergo extensive repairs or even replacement.

But the Takoradi route could also reveal the robustness of the Hurricane, that never-ending theme of the air war, as demonstrated by an experience of Ken Lee's. Posted to the Middle East with 112 Squadron in December 1941, Lee landed at El Fasher, where his Hurricane had to undergo minor repairs to a wing tip. While he was waiting, he was asked whether he could fetch another Hurricane which had been forced to crash-land in the desert nearby. So, with the propeller from his own Hurricane on the back of a truck, he set off with some mechanics:

> We eventually found this place where the aircraft had crashed. All the bush was being cleared away by local natives, who were being bribed. They dug a hole under the aircraft, then let the wheels down and pulled it slowly back up a ramp. It was pretty tattered and torn with the crash landing. The wings were fabric so they got some natives with bone needles and sinews to stitch up the slits on the Hurricane. They put my airscrew on, we revved it up, they stood back and off we went and flew it back to the base. The airscrew was then put back on my aircraft and I joined the next convoy.[18]

The stream of Hurricanes was a crucial addition to the British forces in the Middle East as their commander, General Archibald Wavell, prepared to fight back against the Italians. On 9 December 1940 he launched Operation Compass, an audacious counter-offensive led by the commander of the Western Desert Force Richard O'Connor. At first, Compass aimed only to drive the Italians out of

Egypt, but it soon proved such a dazzling success that Wavell and O'Connor were able to seize the eastern Libyan province of Cyrenaica. In just two months the British forces, despite being heavily outnumbered, had destroyed ten Italian divisions, taken the vital ports of Tobruk, Benghazi and El Agheila, and captured 130,000 prisoners-of-war, 1,200 guns and 400 tanks. Based in 33, 73, 208 and 274 Squadrons, the Hurricanes played a valuable role in this sweeping victory, establishing air superiority over the slower Italian biplanes and bombers, providing reconnaissance for the army and strafing ground targets. The Australian journalist Alan Moorehead, who was an eloquent witness to the Desert War, wrote in his contemporary account of the British fighters that they were 'like a line of black geese in the red sky', swooping down on the Italian bombers and putting 'them to flight'. In another passage Moorehead described how the 'Hurricanes, flying only 30 or 40 feet above the ground, were ranging back and forth over the whole of eastern Cyrenaica, blowing up staff cars and transports, machine-gunning troops and gathering information of the movements of the enemy. By the time Tobruk fell in January 1941, the Italian air force was utterly defeated, and it was never to be restored to superiority.'[19] O'Connor personally wrote to Collishaw to pay tribute to 'the wonderful work of the RAF units under your command, whose determination and fine fighting qualities have made this campaign possible. Since the war began you have consistently attacked the enemy air force, dealing blow after blow until finally he was driven out of the sky and out of Cyrenaica.'[20]

Wavell's triumphant counter-offensive against Italy was not confined to North Africa. In the east of the continent British forces under Major-General William Platt drove the Italians out of Somaliland, Eritrea and Abyssinia after a series of tough battles, the Hurricanes of 3 Squadron in the South African Air Force proving invaluable by providing air superiority against the outdated CR42 biplanes. Following the action from Addis Ababa, Hiram Blauvelt, the well-known correspondent of the *New York Herald Tribune*, claimed that 'One squadron of only nine Hurricanes destroyed over 100 enemy planes, countless trucks, automobiles, transports and trains while operating from makeshift desert airfields.'[21] In one astonishing incident on 15 March 1941 that reflected the selfless bravery of the South Africans, the Hurricane of Jack Frost was badly hit by ground fire as he carried out a low-level ground attack on an airfield in the Ethiopian city of Dire Dawa. With glycol streaming from his engine, Frost had to make an emergency landing at a satellite airstrip. He then immediately jumped out of the plane, set it on fire to prevent its capture and ran for cover as he came under attack from Italian artillery and troops. Almost surrounded, his fate appeared to be sealed. But then his SAAF comrade Bob Kershaw, who had seen Frost make his emergency landing, swept down on the same airfield and yelled to Frost to leap on board. Moments later, Kershaw was airborne again, Frost on his lap and bullets racing past the Hurricane. Squeezed in the cockpit together, they were somehow able to make it back to their base, Kershaw operating the rudder's pedals and Frost the control column. This was the spirit of determination against which the Italians could not prevail. By 10 April the Italian air force had been almost wiped out. At the end of the month Jack Frost, back in his own Hurricane cockpit, shot down the last airworthy Savio-Marchetti 79 bomber. Shortly afterwards, the Italians in East Africa surrendered.

But this victory took place against a backdrop of deepening crisis for the British, fuelled by renewed German aggression on several fronts. Wavell and O'Connor, after their overwhelming triumph in February, had wanted to press on with their attack to Tripoli and throw the Italians out of Libya altogether. The War Cabinet, however, put a brake on the continued assault because military reinforcements were desperately needed as the flames of conflict swept through the Balkans and threatened Britain's position right across the eastern Mediterranean. Mussolini had invaded Greece in October 1940, but the assault had failed as dismally as other Italian offensives at this time. The Greeks resisted heroically, then counterattacked, seizing southern towns in Italy's colony of Albania. The fight continued into the winter, Britain lending support to its ally by taking over the defence of the island of Crete and providing fighters for the Greek cause. 'Keeping the Greek front in being must weigh hourly with us,' wrote Churchill on 6 January 1941.[22]

Three squadrons of Gladiators were sent to Greece, their pilots including a twenty-six-year-old South African called Marmaduke Pattle, better known within the RAF by his nickname 'Pat'. Pattle's exploits never became as famous as those of Douglas Bader, 'Cobber' Kain or 'Ginger' Lacey, yet there is some justification for describing him as the greatest Hurricane ace of the war. A quiet, serious man with a natural authority, crack marksmanship and excellent eyesight, Pattle was born in Cape Province, the son of English parents who had emigrated to South Africa. Consumed with a youthful passion for flight, he joined the SAAF as a cadet on leaving school. But amazingly, in view of his subsequent record, he was not accepted for aircrew training. In bitter disappointment, he returned to civilian life, starting work for a mining company. Yet the ambition to be a pilot remained too strong, so in 1936 he travelled to England where he joined the RAF. On receiving his commission as a pilot officer, he was posted to the Suez canal zone. When war broke out against Italy, he was immediately in action on army co-operation duties, shooting down two enemy fighters. It was in the Greek campaign that he enjoyed his greatest success. Despite flying the obsolete Gladiator in the first months of fighting, he gained a reputation as a bold tactician with a gift for timing his attacks to perfection. On 2 December 1940 he shot down two observation planes, and on the 4th three CR42s were added to his tally. His deadliness reached new heights in February 1941, when the RAF began to replace the Gladiators with Hurricanes. At this stage the Greeks were stepping up their campaign to drive the Italians out of Albania, and Pattle was the ideal figure to shatter the enemy's morale. During the Greek attack on Tepelini, he led the three fighter squadrons in a concentrated support operation that destroyed no fewer than 27 Italian aircraft, Pattle himself claiming three kills in his Hurricane. By the middle of March, when he was awarded the DSO, he had 23 victories. But the war was about to become much tougher.

Exasperated by the failures of the Italian campaign and determined to crush an anti-Axis revolt in Belgrade, Hitler launched a massive invasion of Greece and Yugoslavia on 6 April 1941, using 45 divisions, 1,200 aircraft and the same Blitzkrieg methods that had been so successful in western Europe. Desperately outnumbered, the three Hurricane squadrons were withdrawn to Athens. For the RAF it was like the Battle of France again, heroics against overwhelming odds in a doomed cause. But Pattle, now in command of 33 Squadron, showed no sign of flagging. On 8 April he shot down two Me 109s, and the following day his first German bomber. One of his squadron, Bill Winsland, was awestruck by the sight of Pattle in action against the Messerschmitts. 'I shall never forget it. What shooting too. A two-second burst from his eight guns at the first enemy machine caused a large piece to break off in mid-air, while the machine turned over vertically onto one wingtip as the pilot bailed out. A similar fate awaited the second enemy which went spirally down in flames.'[23] The destruction could not be sustained. As the Germans pulverized the Greek defences, the Hurricane losses mounted. After mid April, Pattle himself grew exhausted and sick with fever, though he still insisted on fighting. 'He was a very small man and very soft-spoken. He possessed the deeply wrinkled doleful face of a cat that knew all nine of its lives had already been used up,' wrote another of his comrades, the author Roald Dahl, whose dramatic wartime career encompassed spells as a Hurricane ace, a Washington air attaché and a spy.[24] With characteristic disregard for his own safety, Pattle led the fighters on more gruelling missions throughout 20 April, a day of almost continuous combat. 'Pattle, who was leading our formation of 12 Hurricanes over Athens, was evidently assuming that we could all fly as brilliantly as he could and he led us one hell of a dance above the city,' wrote Dahl:

> Suddenly the whole sky around us seemed to explode with German fighters. They came down on us from high above, not only 109s, but twin-engined 110s. Watchers on the ground say there cannot have been fewer than 200 of them around us that morning. I can remember seeing our tight little formation all peeling away and disappearing among the swarms of enemy aircraft . . . I threw my Hurricane around as best I could and whenever a Hun came in my sights, I pressed the button. It was truly the most breathless and in a way the most exhilarating time I have ever had in my life.

When he landed, Dahl began to walk to the Operations Room. 'As I walked across the grass I suddenly realized that the whole of my body and clothes were dripping with sweat. Then I found my hand was shaking so much I couldn't put the flame to the end of the cigarette. The doctor, who was standing nearby, came up and lit it for me.'[25] Five of the twelve Hurricanes were destroyed that day, among them Pattle's. As with so many heroes, his was a tragically early end, just nine months into his war. Yet in that brief period he had shot down at least 34 aircraft and possibly as many as 50. If the latter figure were true, it would make him the greatest RAF ace of the war, beating the 38 confirmed kills of Spitfire ace Johnnie Johnson. But differences between the source materials mean that the exact number of victories can never be definitely known.

Pattle's death was symbolic of the failing Allied campaign. A day later, 21 April, Wavell ordered the evacuation of British and Commonwealth troops from Greece to Crete. Supposedly to provide air cover for the withdrawal, the last remnants of the three Hurricane squadrons, amounting to only 20 planes, remained at the Argos airfield on the Peloponnese peninsula. But the small force was soon mutilated in a raid by 40 Me 110s, which destroyed 13 of the Hurricanes on the ground. The last seven of them joined the retreat to Crete, where a trickle of fighter reinforcements had arrived from Egypt. With Greece having fallen, the eastern Mediterranean island was the next target for the Axis. Air supremacy would be vital in this looming conflict, for without command of the sea against the Royal Navy, the Germans would have to mount an airborne invasion using paratroopers. Yet little attempt was made by the RAF to strengthen Crete's fighter defences. Alongside a scattering of Gladiators, Bristol Blenheims and Fleet Air Arm Fulmars, the number of Hurricanes on the island never rose above 16, compared to a German fleet of 700 transport machines, 430 bombers, 180 fighters and 80 gliders preparing for the airborne invasion. The outcome was all too predictable. In a series of pre-invasion raids, the Luftwaffe continued to wear down the RAF.

One indicator of the fierce pressures on the small band of fighter pilots on Crete was the experience of Edward Howell, who had taken over from the late 'Pat' Pattle as commander of 33 Squadron, despite having no experience of flying the Hurricane. When a marauding party of Me 109s strafed his unit at the Maleme airfield on 14 May, Howell had to jump into a Hurricane cockpit for the first time, glance around the instrument panel and try to take off, as he later recounted: 'I opened the throttle and saw a string of five Messerschmitts coming over the hill firing at me. It seemed an age before my wheels came off the strip. I went straight into a turn towards the approaching 109s, my wing tip within inches of the ground. The faithful old "Hurribus" took it without a murmur, the enemy flashed past and I went over instinctively into a steep turn the other way.'[26] To his credit and that of his plane, he actually managed to shoot down one Me 109. But such victories were all too rare. By 19 May there were only four Hurricanes left on Crete and they were ordered to fly back to Egypt. Once the invasion of the island started the next day, the lack of aerial opposition to the Luftwaffe was crucial, bravely though the army and navy resisted. During the height of the battle, the RAF made an attempt to send 12 Hurricanes of 73 Squadron back to the island, but it was a hopeless task. Some were fired on by the Royal Navy. Others became lost and returned to Egypt. The few that reached their destination were quickly obliterated. A batch of Hurricanes with 44-gallon fuel tanks flew from Egypt, but even with their extra range they could spare only a few minutes flying over the island.

Even then, they achieved some surprising successes. Dudley Honor, commander of 274 Squadron, destroyed or damaged six enemy aircraft before he was shot down himself on 26 May over the sea. As his plane plunged into the water, he was pulled 40 feet below the surface before he managed to escape from the cockpit. After swimming to the shore and sheltering in the coastal hillside for six days, he was picked up by a Sunderland flying boat. Yet such intermittent victories as Honor's only emphasized what might have been achieved by a far bigger fighter force. Even though they ultimately prevailed on Crete, the Germans suffered such heavy losses that Hitler ruled out any further airborne invasions after the fall of the island to the Germans on 1 June. As the British Air Ministry later put it in its official analysis, 'the history of the RAF in the Cretan campaign was primarily negative, the story of the disaster in its absence'.[27]

The reason that the RAF Middle East Command could not lend more support to Greece and Crete was the severe pressure exerted on its resources as a result of German action in the desert and Malta. In

February 1941, following Italy's defeat in the eastern Libyan province of Cyrenaica, Hitler had sent General Erwin Rommel to recover the position of the Axis in North Africa. Backed up by the Afrika Korps and the Luftwaffe, he soon went on the offensive in his masterly style, driving Wavell's forces back towards Egypt. Yet again, the Hurricanes found themselves outnumbered and in retreat. What made the situation even worse was the arrival of the Me 109, which had been further improved since the Battle of Britain by better armament and wing design. Considered the finest Messerschmitt fighter of them all, the Me 109f went into desert action in April and immediately proved its marked superiority over the Hurricane Mark I, which was still being operated by Middle East Command. Dickie Martin of 73 Squadron was one of the pilots on the receiving end of the 109's new punch when he went on patrol over the port of Tobruk on 23 April. 'I can well remember being heavily engaged by all these planes, then seeing this chap on the right. I thought to myself: "I won't worry about you. No one can hit me with a full deflection shot." I thought the guy in the 109 was a beginner because it was so difficult to hit anybody across your bows. But after I had turned my attention to the front again, the chap put a whole lot of cannon shot into the plane and it caught fire. I had to jump out. I was only at about 1,000 feet so the parachute was swinging pretty wildly when I reached the ground.'[28] Martin broke his shoulder on impact, but was picked up by some Australian troops and flown to an emergency hospital.

The Germans' toughness on the ground was what impressed Richard Mitchell of 229 Squadron. 'The German blighters were good at firing back. I remember once we were doing a sweep. We came over some sand dunes and there right in front of us was a complete German convoy. Unfortunately it was stationary. We had ten Hurricanes, some with ten guns, some with eight. So you could say we had over 100 guns firing, which must have been terrifying on the ground, but they fired back. They hit me in the oil sump. When we got back to base, about half a gallon of oil fell out of it.'[29] Another Hurricane pilot, Maurice Leng of 73 Squadron, was fed up with the conditions in North Africa. 'Nobody wants to fight in the desert. We had very few facilities and very little water. Food was very scarce. All we had was corned beef and biscuits. It was the most unpleasant part of the war. Funnily enough, we were all very fit. Few of us got ill. One fellow died of dysentery, the doctors reckoned from wiping his bottom with a newspaper.'[30]

As the RAF's losses mounted in the face of Rommel's advance, Sir Arthur Longmore complained bitterly about his lack of men and machines despite the Takoradi route and the arrival in May at Alexandria in Egypt of a Royal Navy convoy, code-named Tiger, carrying 220 tanks and 43 Hurricanes. Back in England, Churchill believed that Longmore was grossly mismanaging his stocks and was even fiddling his figures to exaggerate shortages. Such conduct, the Prime Minister believed, was all too indicative of Longmore's faint-heartedness. 'I have long been more than doubtful whether he is making efficient and effective use of the enormous air personnel at his disposal. He has been most pessimistic and cautious at every turn,' Churchill told Portal on 22 February.[31] Having learnt of Longmore's claim that he had only received one Hurricane from Takoradi in March, a charge unsupported by the Air Staff's own statistics, Churchill fired off an angry telegram directly to him. 'We are as fully informed as you of what you are getting,' wrote Churchill on 23 March with a hint of menace, adding that the complaint about the delivery of a single Hurricane in March was 'absurd'.[32] Churchill's belief that there 'must be frightful mismanagement and futility'[33] led to his complete loss of faith in Longmore and at the end of May he had him sacked. Churchill's action is often seen by his critics as another example of his high-handed unreasonableness, yet his anger at Longmore's disorganization was borne out by this memory from Dickie Martin of 73 Squadron about the RAF base at Heliopolis near Cairo. 'The eerie thing was the number of spare aircraft lying around. You could normally lay your hands on anything you wanted, either for a weekend jolly or to pick up booze. I remember at one stage there were so many planes parked around the perimeter at Heliopolis that they closed the place. I think there were 156 aircraft unaccounted for, everything: Hurricanes, Beaufighters, Bostons.'[34]

Longmore's position as head of Middle East Command was taken by Arthur Tedder, one of the great wartime commanders, a pioneer of army co-operation in the desert and a future Chief of the Air Staff. But neither he, nor increased supplies of Hurricanes, could halt the

British reverses. Another failure was the attempted counter-offensive against Rommel in June, code-named Battleaxe and aimed primarily at relieving the port of Tobruk, which had become besieged by the German advance through Libya. The air fighting around Tobruk was often intense, the Hurricanes again inflicting severe damage on the lumbering Ju 87s, as one British soldier within the garrison, Frank Harrison, wrote: 'The RAF pilots took off from the airfield under constant attack, tore into an enemy far more numerous than themselves and made dive-bombing as dangerous for the Stuka crews as it was for the men on the ground.'[35] But such bravery was not enough to break the German forces. After this setback, another major change was made in the British High Command, with Claude Auchinleck taking over from Wavell, who was shifted to the command of military forces in India. A sense of stalemate now descended on the Desert War, the British seeking to re-group, the Germans turning their attention to Russia.

Vital to Rommel's Afrika Korps were the supply routes through the Mediterranean. That is why the Germans were determined to destroy the resistance of Malta, which remained a strategic threat as long as it was in British hands. Shortly before Rommel was sent to Africa, Fliegerkorps X, the air corps that had proved so effective in the Norway campaign, was sent to Sicily in January 1941 to assist the Italian Regia Aeronautica in seizing control of the island. In the months that followed, Malta came under sustained bombardment from the 350 planes of the Fliegerkorps. The increase in concentration was signalled in mid January as an allied convoy, led by HMS *Illustrious*, was constantly attacked from the air as it struggled to make its way into Valetta harbour. That the *Illustrious*, though badly damaged, was able to dock, unload and then set sail again for Alexandria was partly a tribute to the fight that Hurricanes put up against the German raiders, as well as the massive anti-aircraft barrage that the Maltese ground defences fired over the harbour. As so often before, the Ju 87s were fatally vulnerable, as shown by this account from Jim Pickering of 501 Squadron as he described one successful combat. 'The gunner started firing long before I was in range but after I fired one well-aimed burst, he packed up and I could see his gun pointing harmlessly in the air. The rest was fairly plain sailing. I closed in to about 100 yards and gave him five or six squirts. Clouds of smoke came from his engine and as he rolled into his last dive, I could see vivid tongues of flame streaking back from his wing root. I watched him go in and turned for home.'[36]

But the successful combat over the harbour, in which the RAF had brought down at least 40 German aircraft to protect the convoy, left Malta desperately short of fighters, especially as the Me 109s had started to make aggressive sweeps from Sicily. At the end of January six more Hurricanes arrived from the Middle East, but the fight in the air remained hopelessly imbalanced, with Germany establishing air superiority over the island by March. Despite all the pressures from other theatres, the government recognized that urgent measures were needed. At the beginning of April, therefore, 12 Hurricanes were flown off the aircraft carrier HMS *Ark Royal,* the ship having taken the precaution of sailing closer to the island than the *Argus* had done the previous November, while the planes were also fitted with 44-gallon long-range fuel tanks. Later in the month the *Ark Royal* sent another 20 Hurricanes to the island. The nerve-racking moment of take-off was described by one of the pilots, Doug Robertson of 261 Squadron:

> When it was my turn to take off, I held back the control column, kept my feet pressed on the brakes, then opened up the throttle until the aircraft came off the deck. I then eased the brakes and gave the engine full throttle. My forward acceleration seemed to be slower than I would have liked. Would I become airborne on reaching the end of the deck? The Hurricanes ahead of me were in the air, so I figured I could do it. The raised ramp at the end of the deck lifted my plane, only to sink towards the sea. The downward motion gave me the lift needed and I climbed away from the carrier. Oh boy, I made it.[37]

A further 48 Hurricanes were delivered to Malta by carrier in May 1941, none of them having a more awkward or exhausting trip than the flight led by Tom Neil of 249 Squadron. Never an admirer of the Hurricane Mark I, Neil had felt tense at dawn on 21 May as he climbed into his plane. The journey, for which a Fairey Fulmar would act as guide, was due to take two and a half hours and cover a distance of 450 miles, comfortably within the range of a Hurricane equipped with drop tanks. The planes carried no ammunition, the boxes being used instead to store the pilots' gear because the Hurricane had no extra space in its cockpit for any baggage. 'If the enemy were sighted en route,' wrote Neil, 'we would be able to give them a quick squirt of Macleans toothpaste from all eight guns.' For all his apprehension, the take-off was straightforward but, just as he began to climb away from the carrier, 'there was a loud bang, as though a paper bag had been exploded in my left ear. The aircraft dropped a wing and began to fly sideways in an alarming manner.' It turned out that a gun panel had become loose and was sticking up at an angle of 45 degrees. For a terrible moment the Hurricane seemed to be heading towards the sea but with a hard right rudder Neil was able to bring it back under control. He considered for a moment trying to land back on the *Ark Royal* but deemed it too dangerous, given the damage to the plane and its lack of any arrester hook. There was no alternative but to fly on, even though his leg was already starting to ache badly.

After about an hour's flying in 'acute discomfort', Neil faced a new problem: the guiding Fulmar suddenly disappeared from the sky in front of him. It later turned out that an engine pipe on the Fulmar had burst, leaving the windscreen covered in black oil, so the pilot had dived away to return to the carrier. Neil was bewildered. Without any maps he was now completely lost, yet the other Hurricanes were dependent on him. Against all rules, he broke radio silence and spoke to his comrades. No one else had any idea how to reach Malta. Neil decided he had to lead the squadron westwards and take the risk of landing on the *Ark Royal*. But just he approached the ship, another Fulmar appeared to put them back on course, the navy having worked out what happened. Neil's men now embarked on their second attempt to reach the island. In agony from his leg, he was then gripped by a new fear. Having already been in the air for more than two hours, his Hurricane would be at the absolute limit of its endurance by the time it reached Malta. The journey dragged on. The needle on his petrol gauge sank lower. The horizon continued to stretch ahead. Then, when he had just ten gallons left, Malta appeared below him 'with magical suddenness'. Overwhelmed with relief, he came down and landed in a cloud of dust at Luqa in the middle of an air raid. His leg, released from his numbing incarceration against the rudder, immediately went into spasm. But Neil had survived. 'We had been airborne for five hours and 25 minutes, probably the longest operational trip ever made by the Hurricane.'[38]

The Hurricane reinforcements, augmented by a further dispatch from the *Ark Royal* in late June, had enabled Malta to weather the storm of the German onslaught. During the summer and the second half of 1941, the raids greatly diminished as the Luftwaffe units were moved up to Russia. The RAF was sufficiently confident even to use the Hurricanes to carry out occasional night intruder attacks on the Italian airfields in Sicily. Graham Leggett, who arrived in June to join Neil's 249 Squadron, nostalgically described the latter part of 1941 as:

> a delightful period of my life. Here I was on a nice warm Mediterranean island, surrounded by friends and decent aeroplanes to fly. There did not appear to be too much enemy activity at the time. What we had was a private war between three squadrons of Hurricanes and the Italian air force in Sicily, which was very much a comic opera affair. The Luftwaffe had been in Sicily in considerable strength, had done a lot of damage but had then been sent to the Russian front. The Italians were not really interested in this war. They did not bother us much.[39]

Yet even in the uneasy peace that descended on Malta, there was still deep concern among military leaders about the strength of the fighter forces and the performance of the Hurricane as an interceptor. Typical was the complaint from Sir Wilbraham Ford, the Vice Admiral of Malta, who wrote to Sir Arthur Longmore on 15 May that heavy RAF losses to the Luftwaffe in the first half of 1941 were 'the result of inferior aircraft to those of the enemy'. Sir Wilbraham asserted that 'unless modern fighters are exchanged for the Hurricane Mark I and sent immediately we are riding for bad falls and will be unable to protect harbour shipping or population'.[40] His martial spirit bristling, Churchill thought that this was just another example of his senior officers' pusillanimity. 'It is well known,' he told Portal on 16 May, 'that in air warfare when morale declines from any cause the first symptom is dissatisfaction of the pilots with their machines. The Hurricane I, though outclassed at extreme heights, can cope with the Me 109 at 16,000 feet and it is at these lower heights that most of the combats over Malta have been fought.'[41]

But Churchill's accusation was ill-judged. According to Tom Neil's account, it was the poor quality of the Hurricanes that reduced morale, not the other way round. In the space of his first eight weeks, Neil suffered no fewer than five engine failures. 'Scarcely a day passed when I did not sit there during take-off, stiff with apprehension, waiting for the loss of power or stoppage that would pitch me into the hill ahead,' he wrote. At one stage he was so furious with the Hurricane that 'I determined never to fly the damned thing again.' Even the arrival of the Mark II did not assuage his despair, because the versions his squadron received were not tropicalized so they 'managed to suck in every particle of dust and filth whipped up by our whirling airscrews'. When Tedder visited Malta in the autumn Neil told him that 'we really ought to have some Spitfires in Malta if we are to do anything worthwhile'. Neil's negative view has been backed up by historical analysis. As James Holland has pointed out, during the two months that the Me 109 fighters of the elite Fliegerkorps X unit led by Joachim Muncheberg were in Malta, 'they had claimed at least 42 Hurricanes in the air'. Even more 'had been destroyed on the ground. There can hardly be a better illustration of German fighter supremacy and the woeful inadequacy of the battered Hurricane.'[42]

One of the worst aspects of the strain put on the overseas squadrons during 1941 was that Fighter Command in Britain had never been so well endowed. As Neil pointed out to Tedder, while the Hurricane pilots toiled in the Mediterranean and African campaigns, there were vast numbers of Supermarine and Hawker machines at home with no real threat to face. Ironically, the domestic fighter force was far larger in September 1941 than at the peak of the Battle of Britain. It had no fewer than 75 squadrons, made up of 31 Hurricane units, 43 Spitfire units and one using the American P-39 Airacobra. The rationale for such strength was that the Germans might renew their daylight offensive, but by the autumn it was obvious, with the Russian front having opened up, that this argument no longer was applicable. Even so, the Fighter Command chief Sholto Douglas and his commanders still regarded any instruction to send fighters to other theatres as a drain on their own establishment. This attitude was clearly demonstrated by Douglas's opposition in October to supplying any Spitfires to the Middle East. A few Hurricane Mark IIs would be adequate, he argued to Portal on 1 October, adding several spurious technical reasons for keeping the Spitfires in Britain. 'It is scarcely necessary for me to point out the disadvantage of adding yet another type of fighter to the many different types at present in the Middle East. A further and more serious point is that I very much doubt that the Spitfire will stand up to the rougher conditions and wear and tear in the Middle East. It is a far less robust aircraft than the Hurricane. It is in fact rather fragile. And I am afraid that the crash rate on the rough desert aerodromes will be high.'[43] Portal had little time for this pleading, whose speciousness was proved by the Spitfire's magnificent performance during subsequent campaigns in Malta and Italy. The balance between home and the Middle East 'is not in accordance with strategic needs', he told Douglas on 5 October, adding that the morale of the overseas command 'would be raised by the presence of our best fighters'.[44]

Throughout 1941 and early 1942, Fighter Command tried to justify the existence of its vast fleet not merely by talking up a future German threat but also by operating offensive raids against Nazi-occupied northern France. There were two main types of operation: first, 'circuses', where Hurricane or Spitfire formations accompanied packs of RAF bombers attacking military or industrial targets; second, 'rhubarbs', in which pairs or small groups of fighters carried out low-level raids against gun installations, railways, transport depots, road convoys or wireless installations. But the results of these offensive sweeps were heavily outweighed by the loss of men and machines over France. The Battle of Britain had proved how hard it was to crack an enemy's defences even with mass, daily, concentrated raids. Fighter Command's sporadic ventures were of little strategic value, neither causing any real damage to the Reich's war machine nor raising the morale of the French. On the other hand, Fighter Command paid a high price. Douglas Bader, now flying Spitfires, was one of the many pilots downed during these pointless exercises. His collision with a Messerschmitt 109 over France in August 1941 meant that he was a prisoner in Germany for the rest of the war. Bader had switched aircraft because, by July 1941, the RAF recognized that the Hurricanes were no longer a match for the Me 109s on these offensive combat duties over France and had to be gradually replaced by Spitfires. Tellingly, when the biggest fighter sweep of 1941 was carried out on 6 August, out of the 18 fighter squadrons that took part only 2 were Hurricane units, 71 and 275 Squadrons.

The one type of raid that the Hurricanes successfully carried out from home stations during 1941 was known as the 'Channel Stop', where groups of eight fighters would organize low-level attacks on German shipping and coastal convoys. The master at this art was Denys Gillam, commander of 615 Squadron. On a typical 'Channel Stop' operation, he explained, the Hurricane formation approached the convoy in two sections of four in line abreast formation. 'At the right distance from the target, the two leaders throttled back, thus allowing the outside men to get ahead. Then all eight Hurricanes pulled up and dived on the target, with cannons and machine guns blazing. As soon as we passed over it, we were down on the water and jinking away. Out of range, we would re-form and have a second go in a different direction.'[45] The attacks could be devastating to smaller vessels, said Gillam: 'E-boats, if you hit them, burned up very nicely. A good burst at a small coaster generally disabled it enough to finish it off. About 3,000 tons was the maximum we could deal with.'[46] But the German convoys were also heavily defended and could send up a murderous barrage against the Hurricanes. 'The trouble is that they formed a cone of fire over the central ship which you had to fly through. Quite a few didn't get through.'[47] At one stage in 1941 Fighter Command was losing five Hurricanes a week on these raids. Gillam himself once had to bail out over the Channel when he got an anti-aircraft shell in his engine, stopping it immediately. But such an incident could not diminish his admiration for the Hurricane. 'It was the finest gun platform of them all. It also took a staggering amount of punishment.'[48]

The instinct of Fighter Command to hoard its planes had to be overridden by Portal and Churchill in other theatres apart from Malta and the West African desert. A batch of nine Hurricanes were sent up to Iceland in the summer of 1941 to cover the withdrawal of the British garrison, which had first been established there in 1940 to act as a deterrent to a potential German invasion. This threat had evaporated with the German assault on Russia, though the Icelandic Hurricanes, formed into 1423 Flight, remained on the island until December to give some protection to north Atlantic and Arctic convoys. Another Hurricane squadron, 94 Squadron, was sent in May 1941 to Iraq, where the large RAF base at Habbaniya, 50 miles west of Baghdad, had come under attack from pro-Axis rebels, backed up by the Luftwaffe, following an anti-British coup led by the nationalist politician Rashid Ali. The Hurricanes, some of them equipped with long-range tanks, were in action immediately, carrying out strafing attacks on the Iraqi troops and transport, as well destroying a number of Heinkel 111s and Me 110s. Alongside British and Arab ground forces, the RAF helped to lift the siege of Habbaniya, quell the rebellion and drive Rashid Ali from power.

There was a poignant legacy to the Iraqi conflict. One of the Hurricane pilots killed on a raid in May 1941 against the Luftwaffe was Sir Roderic MacRobert, son of Lady Rachel MacRobert, the American-born widow of a self-made millionaire from Aberdeen. Sir Roderic was one of three brothers who were all killed serving with the RAF. Devastated by her loss, Lady Rachel donated £25,000 to purchase a Stirling bomber and £20,000 to buy four Hurricanes, three of which were named after each of her beloved sons and adorned with the family crest, the other one called *Salute to Russia* as a tribute to Soviet resistance. All four of these fighters, collectively known as 'the MacRoberts Hurricanes', flew with 94 Squadron in the desert. The family motto was 'Not for Self, but for Country', a maxim that perfectly embodied the spirit of the RAF.[49]

Further north, Hurricanes were also part of the Commonwealth force that defeated the Vichy regime in Syria during the summer of 1941, Churchill's War Cabinet fearing that a pro-German stronghold there could threaten Britain's entire position across the Middle East. Driven by Gallic pride and contempt for the British, the Axis French fought with surprising toughness. They also had a bigger air fleet than the RAF, though their Dewoitine and Morane fighters were not of the same class as the Hurricanes. In co-operation with Bristol Blenheims and American Curtiss Tomahawks, the Hurricanes of 80 and 260 Squadrons carried out strafing operations on French troops, low-level attacks on airfields and cover patrols for the army and navy. It was in this conflict that Roald Dahl achieved his status as an ace, but his record was far surpassed by that of Bill 'Cherry' Vale of 80 Squadron, whose three kills in Syria brought his total to at least 30.

The slim, moustachioed son of a Royal Marines captain, Vale had joined the RAF in 1931 as a fitter before training as a pilot five years later. He spent the first two years of the war entirely in the Middle East, shooting down 10 enemy planes in his Gloster Gladiator and probably another 20 in his Hurricanes. The Syrian campaign marked the end of his operational career, as he then took up a series of administrative and training posts in Egypt and England. Another member of 80 Squadron, Ben Bowring, recalled the sense of exhilaration at the successes of the campaign, some of it bred from co-operation with the British troops. 'We had good liaison with the army. We learnt the times that the Warwickshire regiment was likely to be attacked.' On one pair of operations over two successive days, his squadron shot down 18 French aircraft. 'It was very emotional afterwards because we flew low over the British troops and we could see them throwing their helmets in the air and waving to us as we returned home.' Some of the strafing was done against trains. 'We would go for the engine, try to get the firebox. We did not wait to see the results.' But the favourite target was the French air force on the ground. 'We destroyed quite a lot of aircraft. The squadron flew at least eight hours a day, but the best time to attack was lunchtime because the French being French always had their break then.' It was not always the best time, however, for the Hurricanes, some of which did not have the Vokes tropical filters and could therefore be prone to over-heating. 'With these old Hurricanes, even at the higher altitudes, the glycol temperatures would be in the red. Most people would not have flown in those conditions.'[50] According to Bowring, it was 'an extremely bloody' campaign, but it was ultimately a triumphant one. On 18 July the Vichy commanders accepted an armistice, the first surrender by French military to Britain since Waterloo.

The actions in Syria and Iraq were important for the survival of Britain as a force in the Middle East, but they paled beside the titanic struggle between the Third Reich and the Soviet Union, which began when Hitler ordered the invasion of Russia on 22 June,

Operation Barbarossa. Immediately after it started Churchill broadcast to the world: 'Any man or state who fights against Nazidom will have our aid . . . It follows, therefore, that we give whatever help we can to Russia and the Russian people. The Russian danger is our danger and the danger of the United States, just as the cause of any Russian fighting for his heart and home is the cause of free men and free peoples in every corner of the globe.'[51] The question was the form that British aid should take. With a wild lurch into fantasy, Joseph Stalin initially asked for 30 divisions, a request that took no account of the disastrously weakened state of the British army after all the setbacks since 1940. Churchill had a more realistic solution. The Hawker Hurricane would be the instrument of British military support for Russia, along with supplies of war materiel. After negotiations with Ivan Maisky, the Soviet ambassador in London, the War Cabinet initially agreed to supply 200 Hurricanes. 'These would be eight and 12-gun Hurricanes which we have found very deadly in action,' Churchill told Stalin.[52]

The Prime Minister recognized that the Russians would have to receive instruction in how to assemble, operate and maintain the Hurricane, so he quickly arranged for an advance party to be dispatched to the Soviet Union. This expeditionary force, designated 151 Wing and commanded by the rugged New Zealander Gynes Ramsbottom-Isherwood, was made up two squadrons, 81 Squadron under Tony Rook and 134 Squadron under Tony Miller, with a total of 40 Hurricanes and 550 airmen, including pilots and ground crews. The wing was to be based at the airfield of Vaenga, about six miles north-east of Murmansk, a strategically important port in the north-western extreme and the world's largest city north of the Arctic Circle. As well as providing instruction, the 151 Wing Hurricane pilots would be required to assist in the defence of Murmansk against German bombers attacking the naval base and the railway that supplied the Russian front.

Preparations were made with remarkable speed. By early August both squadrons were ready to depart. Because of the size of the expedition, the journey to Russia had to be made in two separate waves. The first, leaving on 16 August, was led by the SS *Llanstephan Castle*, a former luxury liner, which carried most of 151 Wing's personnel, while 16 of the Hurricanes went in heavy wooden crates in the convoy's other seven merchant ships. Accompanied by a powerful Royal Navy escort, they travelled up to Iceland, where they picked up more fuel and cargo, before embarking on the long voyage eastwards. 'For days on end we saw nothing from the *Llanstephan Castle* but grey rolling water and other ships in our convoy,' recalled the Battle of Britain hero Ray Holmes, now with 81 Squadron.[53] The second, smaller wave left three days later, on 19 August. At the heart of this convoy was the warhorse of earlier Hurricane deliveries in the Mediterranean, the aircraft carrier HMS *Argus*, this time with 24 Hurricanes on board. It had originally been planned that, on arrival in Russian waters, the *Llanstephan Castle* convoy would dock at Murmansk to unload its crated Hurricanes, but the threat of German aerial activity meant that the merchant ships had to travel further south to the city of Archangel for disembarkation. The assembly of the 16 Hurricanes there was initially beset with problems. Facilities were primitive. Equipment was missing. Spanners could not be found. One plane had been damaged beyond repair in transit. But with a mixture of ingenuity, determination and improvised tooling, the job of putting together the remaining 15 Hurricanes was completed in just nine days.

Ray Holmes, who had been depressed by the poverty and political oppression he saw around him in Archangel, cheered up on 9 September when he participated in the air tests for the first batch of reassembled Hurricanes, certain that the fighter would impress the Russians. 'There was tremendous excitement both among our boys and their Russian counterparts. Russian admirals, generals, colonels, their Air Ministry representatives, technical experts, engineers – all were there to get their first glimpse of a Hurricane going through its paces.' Holmes and his two comrades were briefed to show just what the plane could do. 'If we'd flown like this at a British airfield we'd have been court-martialled. The cloud was below a thousand feet, so the three of us were able to circle the aerodrome in cloud, then spiral out at full throttle, sweeping at ground level across the grass straight at the delegation, and climbing up over their heads a hundred yards short of them.' At one moment, the dignitaries flung themselves to the ground as the Hurricanes roared over. 'We tore out from behind hangars at them vertically banked over their heads, until red Very lights from the control tower indicated that they had seen enough. We did a couple of rolls and went into tight formation to land in a vic of three.'[54]

While the 15 Hurricanes from the *Llanstephan Castle* were assembled and tested at Archangel, the other 24 were flown directly to the Vaenga airfield from the deck of the *Argus*, which had arrived near Murmansk on the morning of 7 September. The launch did not go entirely smoothly, for two of the Hurricanes smashed their undercarriages on take-off, again highlighting the reality that the fighter was not designed for maritime work. Charlton Haw of 81 Squadron had the misfortune to be behind one of the errant pair. 'The *Argus* had this ramp at the end, which the Grumman Martlets – there were two of them on board for the defence of the carrier – were stressed to hit and be thrown in the air. Of course the Hurricanes weren't stressed. The first to go hit this ramp with an almighty clank and knocked his wheels back. So the first RAF aircraft to land in Russia landed with his wheels up. I don't know what the Russians thought of that. I had watched this and by my turn I had got the form. I opened it up and at the last minute dragged it back and got off.'[55] The Hurricanes, including the two damaged ones, managed to reach Vaenga without further incident, though the airstrip itself made landings awkward. 'It was just one big sandy strip. They had huge rollers on it, like the rollers used at cricket grounds,' recalled Haw, who said it was even worse when the snow fell. 'They just rolled the snow flat. You had no control over the aeroplane. You just put it down and it slid all over the place. It was pretty dodgy.'[56]

By the second week in September, 151 Wing was ready for its first operations. Ground crews and other pilots had been brought from Archangel by Russian air transport and by train, and the first of the reassembled Hurricanes had made the awkward journey, guided by a Pe-2 light bomber. Four planes from 134 Squadron made the wing's debut patrol on 11 September, but it was not an auspicious beginning as two of them had their engines cut out in mid-flight, the Merlins only coming back to life through vigorous use of the priming pump. The engine problems were due to the 95-octane fuel used by the Soviets, whereas the Merlin needed 100-octane petrol for its best performance. The next day saw the Hurricanes' first combat in Russia, as they attacked a group of Me 109s and a Henschel 126 observation aircraft at 3,500 feet west of Murmansk. 'I don't think they knew we were there because they turned away from us, allowing us to fly behind them and shoot them down,' recalled Haw, who shot down one Me 109.[57] Altogether four German aircraft were destroyed. One Hurricane pilot, Norman Smith, was killed while trying to make a force-landing after being hit by a 109. One of his comrades, Basil Rigby, wrote philosophically in his private diary that evening: 'This was my first fight and I did not feel any fear – much – but given a bit more time on the way home I was quite glad it was over! Pity Smith was killed but I suppose it's all in the foul cause of war.'[58] This combat gave another early boost to 151 Wing's reputation among the Russians. 'The RAF's first action gave us confidence that the hands we were about to shake were those of good comrades-in-arms,' said the Soviet officer Captain Zakhar Sorokin.[59]

Further victories followed in the next few weeks as more of the reassembled Hurricanes arrived from Archangel. During an interception on 17 September, Charlton Haw took down an Me 109, a kill that he attributed, with typical modesty, to a large degree of luck: 'I suddenly saw white tracers just missing my wing tip. I had seen nothing before that. Then this 109 presented itself right in front of me. I couldn't believe it. I shot him down, but had he not used tracer bullets I would not have seen him.' Two days later Haw was involved in a ferocious dogfight, in which he ran out of ammunition and ended up with an Me 109 on his tail:

> I knew that the German was not out of ammo. I was climbing like mad and I did the only thing I could. I sort of threw my aeroplane at him and he sheared away. We were at 5,000 feet. Then I put my Hurricane upside down, and went straight down to the ground and I flew back kissing the ground. I don't think I have ever been so shaken in all my life. I could see this yellow nosed thing behind me. If you fly low there is no way they can shoot you down because they cannot possibly look at you without hitting the ground. Though I say it myself, that was sheer flying skill that got out of that one. I was shaken, very shaken. I was so relieved when he pulled up. I almost felt like saluting him. We had a terrific fight that morning, but my God, I thought to myself, 'I'm only 21 but I'm getting old.'[60]

The main operational duties of 151 Wing were to provide defensive patrols over Murmansk and escorts for the Russian bombers attacking German targets. The latter was not always an easy task, recalled Haw, because of the speed of the Russian aircraft. 'They were terrific. They were faster than the Hurricanes. We had an awful job to keep up with them.'[61] But the Hurricanes proved effective enough. During almost forty escort patrols they carried out, not a single Russian bomber was shot down. Yet that statistic also reflects the fact that the air battle over Murmansk never reached anything like the intensity that 151 Wing expected, largely because the overwhelming concentration of German forces in Operation Barbarossa was much further south on the vast front from Leningrad to the Crimea. Furthermore, the bitter Russian winter was approaching and by October most of the daytime was shrouded in darkness. The number of patrols were reduced. Combats became rare. The last encounter with the Luftwaffe on this mission occurred on 6 October, when the Germans carried out a light raid on Vaenga airfield but little damage was done.

Remarkably, the only RAF pilot to die in action over Murmansk was Norman Smith, though there were two other fatalities in a tragic accident on 26 September. Because of heavy snow in the region, it had become the practice for a pair of crewmen to lie on the tail of each Hurricane to prevent the plane tipping forward on its nose while it taxied over the bumpy ground before take-off. On this fateful occasion, pilot Vic Berg, having spotted a reconnaissance Ju 88 heading towards the airfield, was so desperate to get into the air that he opened up the engine and roared over the snow without realizing that the two men had not yet jumped off the tail. As the plane hurtled forward, they were now pinned down by the force of slipstream. Fellow pilot Ray Holmes recorded: 'When the Hurricane reached flying speed and became airborne, the weight of the two men dragged the tail down, the nose climbed vertically and the aircraft spun in and cartwheeled as the propeller hit the ground. The unfortunate fitter and rigger were hurled high into the air to land 150 yards from the wrecked plane. Both were killed instantly.'[62] Despite severe injuries to his head and legs, Berg managed to survive, his cockpit being the only part of the Hurricane that did not disintegrate during the crash.

The pilots of 151 Wing achieved 16 victories in all, Charlton Haw being the leading scorer with three kills. As important as combat was the training they provided to the Russians in flying and maintaining the Hurricanes. 'We assured them that the Hurricanes had no vices and that any fool could fly them,' said Holmes. The plane again proved its worth, not only in its ease of handling for novices but also in how it coped with the Arctic conditions. As the Russians gained experience, the Hurricanes were transferred to their squadrons, the supply of fighters soon to be supplemented by the arrival of the first 100 of the additional planes that Churchill had promised Stalin. By 22 October all the aircraft of 151 Wing had been formally handed over to the Russians. There followed a tiresome period of enforced idleness for the pilots. To their outrage, having expected to be brought back to England on the completion of their mission, they were told that they might be sent to the Middle East or even the Russian front further south. Boredom was now mixed with fear. 'How we are all longing to get home. Tempers are very near the surface these days,' read one diary entry by Basil Rigby.[63] 'Nothing to do is fine for a day or so, but a month of it is too much even for me. I honestly think that most of us are borderline and much longer of this will take us the whole way,' read another some three weeks later.[64] Eventually, the plan to send the pilots south was abandoned, the Russians telling London that the pressures on their own supply lines meant that they could not provide the British with the rations and support needed for the 3,000-mile journey. At the end of November, to their enormous relief, the personnel of 151 Wing embarked for England, leaving behind a small staff of technicians.

In public at least, the British government treated the Murmansk exercise as a great success, a stance that was helped by Soviet propaganda. Portal told the Russian High Command that the Hurricane operations were the 'beginning of ever wider and closer collaboration between our two air forces, each of which is already straining to the utmost to hasten the final defeat and collapse of the Nazi aggressors!'[65] The Russians responded warmly, lavishing praise on the RAF and awarding the Order of Lenin to four of the pilots: the 151 leader Gynes Ramsbottom-Isherwood, the two squadron commanders Tony Miller and Tony Rook, and the top ace Charlton Haw. It was the only time during the war that this medal was presented to any Allied airmen.

But this celebratory tone, which has generally been adopted by aviation histories, was hardly the whole picture, as the official archives demonstrate. In reality, Churchill was angrily disappointed at the limited scope of the expedition and the refusal to extend RAF Hurricane operations to the main Russian front. 'The most serious mistake we have made about the Russians was not in sending eight fighter squadrons, which would have gained great fame, destroyed many German aircraft and given immense encouragement all along the front,' the Prime Minister told Portal on 24 October.[66] In his reply Portal admitted that 'the story of the Murmansk operations is not a very satisfactory one'. He told Churchill that the Air Staff had at one time proposed that the two Hurricane squadrons 'should be transferred complete from Murmansk to the Russian left flank'. But this, he explained, would have involved 'going back on our offer to give the Russians 40 Hurricanes or what was left of them', so when the weather closed down, 'it was considered politically expedient' to drop the idea. The next plan was for the personnel to be sent to the Middle East once the Hurricanes had been transferred to the Soviet air force, but the 'congestion and confusion' of the Russian railway system made that logistically impossible. A return to England was therefore the only option. Then, in a fascinating passage, Portal revealed one of the real explanations for the restricted scale of the operation: 'In dealing with the criticism of the smallness of the force sent to Russia, I suggest we should bear in mind that at the time it was decided to send them, we had no idea how successful the Russian resistance to the German invasion would prove.'[67] Churchill was still dissatisfied, calling the episode 'most painful'.[68] He even went so far as to draft a telegram to Stalin that concluded: 'I am sorry we have not done more.'[69] Portal dissuaded him from sending it.

In the longer term Churchill's disappointment at Britain's contribution to the Russian air war turned out to be misplaced. The first 39 Hurricanes of 151 Wing were just the precursor of a huge influx of Hurricanes that reached the Soviet Union during the war. So great were the numbers that the RAF opened a major base at Basra, Iraq, in 1943 to provide an overland supply route in addition to the arctic convoys. Altogether 2,952 Hurricanes were supplied to Russia from 1941, more than a fifth of the entire production, the majority of them either Mark IIBs, with 12 guns, or Mark IICs, with 4 cannon. It has often been claimed that the Russians were delighted with the machines, their only complaint being that not enough were handed over. An example of this attitude was said to be contained in a 1942 edition of the propaganda sheet *Soviet Air News* in which the Hurricane was praised for its 'speed' and 'excellent lateral manoeuvrability', which had resulted in a series of 'splendid victories'.[70]

But again, this is not the whole story. As archival records show, there were also elements of friction and dissatisfaction in the relationship between Britain and Russia over Hurricane supplies. Indeed, strife began soon after the big convoys, with their cargoes of crated Hurricanes, began to arrive in Archangel at the end of 1941. The Air Ministry had sent a large party of mechanics, engineers and supervisors, under Wing Commander H. H. Hilliar, to oversee the assembly of the Hurricanes, but the men were ostracized by the Russians, who claimed that, after their experience with 151 Wing, they needed no help. 'All equipment personnel who came to Russia with great enthusiasm to render the Russians every possible assistance are much disheartened by their reception and the Russian attitude,' Hilliar told the Ministry on 6 January 1942. 'Unless they return to England with all possible speed there is a grave danger of their becoming demoralized because the conditions are bad and there is literally nothing else to do but eat and drink. Exercise is impossible because of the extreme cold.'[71] Hilliar became so exasperated with Soviet obstinacy that he urged a halt in supplies of Hurricane equipment. 'The Russians look. upon our aid as a mere drop in the ocean and consider we owe it to them. Now that they have the ball at their feet they are becoming contemptuous and high-handed,' he complained in another missive a week later.[72] The dispute was eventually resolved through the creation of better liaison arrangements and Soviet co-operation, though a later source of conflict arose over the supply of Hurricane spares, the Russians arguing that the quantities sent by Britain were inadequate because they took no account of the vastly different conditions in the Soviet Union, especially the intense cold and the poor quality of the airstrip surfaces.[73]

Nor was the Soviet government as pleased with the Hurricane as is sometimes claimed. Through Ivan Maisky, the Soviet ambassador to London, Stalin asked in January 1943 whether Britain 'could not let him have a small number of Spitfires in the fighter quota from time to time and not only supply him with Hurricanes'.[74] The request was accepted and in May 1943 the first of 1,331 Spitfires arrived to operate in the Red Air Force. The real attitude of Soviet pilots to the Hurricane, beyond the propaganda, is revealed in an unpublished wartime memoir by Colonel Igor Kaberov, who flew Hurricanes from May 1942, having previously used the Yak fighter. After the arrival of the new aircraft at his base, he wrote: 'First of all the size of the Hurricane struck us. Both in length and wing span, it was almost half as big again as our Yak. Humpbacked, on long legs, it seemed rather strange.' Like many other Soviet Hurricane units, Kaberov and his comrades were unhappy with the rifle calibre guns of the Mark IIB and its armour plating, so they had both changed, installing 0.5-inch cannon and a thicker plate behind the pilot's seat. Overall, this was his summary of the Hurricane:

> I thought that the name Hurricane hardly matched the technical qualities of the machine. The armament on it was now good. The armour plating was fine. Such protection was like a stone wall. The horizon indicator was a wonderful indicator. It was easy to fly in the clouds with it. The radio worked magnificently, like a domestic telephone; neither noise nor crackle. But the speed, the speed . . . No, this aircraft was far from being a hurricane. It was slow to gain height and was not good in the dive. As for vertical manoeuvrability – not good at all! Yefimov, our commissar, got it right. 'The aircraft is fine. It's metal, so it won't catch fire. You can shoot from it. But instead of manoeuvrability and speed – you'll have to use your Russian wits.'[75]

But the greatest weapon for the Soviet air force, concluded Kaberov, was the hatred of the enemy. 'We did have the strength to kill the Fascist scum. We swore to destroy them like mad dogs.'[76]

The problem for the RAF at the beginning of 1942 was that the enemy showed no signs of breaking. On the contrary, the British remained under severe pressure. Exhausting stalemate continued in the North African desert after months of bitter fighting. Launched on 17 November 1941, Operation Crusader, General Auchinleck's masterplan for driving Rommel out of the eastern Libyan province of Cyrenaica, had only partially succeeded. The siege of Tobruk had been lifted and the Germans had retreated to El Agheila, a coastal city in the far west of the province. But in January 1942, having reinforced his troops, Rommel struck back, recapturing the port of Benghazi and making the British take up defensive positions just west of Tobruk. The Hurricanes, which now made up 25 of the 40 fighter squadrons in the Middle East, had played a valuable role in supporting the initial advance of Crusader, lessons having been learnt about the importance of army co-operation. But, as in so many other theatres, the plane was showing its age badly. Ron Cundy, an Australian with 260 Squadron, who first went into action with the plane in November 1941, having previously flown the Curtiss Kittyhawk, later recalled:

> Frankly the Hurricane was out of date when the war began. It was too slow and it didn't have the ceiling. Certainly it was manoeuvrable. That was its only saving grace. But it was an incompetent aircraft. Its armament did not impress me, eight .303s. I was much more impressed with the six .5s on the Kittyhawk, much better hitting power. From the point of view of ground-strafing, when you were in a Hurricane and you hit a truck or something, I never had the impression that I was doing any fantastic damage to the truck.[77]

With the Hurricane once more outmatched by the Me 109, the losses for the RAF had been severe. When Crusader was broken in January, 440 RAF planes had been destroyed, compared to 260 of the Luftwaffe's. It was the same story in Malta, against which the Luftwaffe, equipped with latest Me 109g, had resumed its attacks in December 1941. 'It shows that the Huns have returned from Russia and mean to spend a happy winter in the Mediterranean. Not good for the Hurricane boys here, the 109s having a much superior performance,' wrote Sonny Ormrod of 605 Squadron in his diary.[78] As the raids intensified in the new year, the siege of the island became desperate, the Hurricane unable to provide effective protection against the storm. On 25 January 1942, a dozen Me 109s swooped on a formation of Hurricanes trying to guard a supply convoy at Valetta harbour. Seven of the British fighters were shot down, and another three were forced to return to their base with engine failure. During the month, no fewer than 50 Hurricanes were destroyed on the ground or in the air. Out of the 340 Hawker planes that had been dispatched to the island since the autumn of 1940, just 28 remained serviceable. 'The defence was a cruel task, quite beyond our capacity,' wrote Sir Hugh Lloyd, the Air Officer Commanding Malta in the spring of 1942. 'One raid would follow another so quickly that it was impossible to land the Hurricanes and rearm and refuel them for the next contest. It was a non-stop performance. The Hurricane was a wonder in manoeuvre and would out-turn a 109 but it lacked the speed and firepower. It was clean out of its class. We wanted more speed, more aeroplanes and heavier armament as the task was to kill.'[79]

Exactly the same words could be used about an even worse military crisis that engulfed Britain at the turn of the year, as Japan launched its dramatic strike against Britain and America in the Pacific, following its attack on Pearl Harbour on 7 December 1941. At the start of the war in the Far East, the RAF in Malaya and Singapore was pitifully ill-equipped, with a small force of Lockheed Hudsons, Bristol Blenheims, Brewster Buffalos and Vickers Vildebeests, obsolete biplane light bombers that had first gone into RAF service in 1928. To strengthen the air defences, the government sent 51 crated Hurricane Mark Is by sea around the Cape of Good Hope but they did not arrive until 3 January 1942, by which time British morale had been dealt a shattering blow through the destruction by the Japanese air force on 10 December of two mighty Royal Navy vessels, the 35,000-ton battleship HMS *Prince of Wales* and the 26,500-ton battlecruiser HMS *Repulse*. The disaster not only left Britain 'weak and naked' over 'all this vast expanse of waters', to quote Churchill's words,[80] but also exposed the empire's lamentable lack of air power in the region. Yet there remained the wildly optimistic belief that the Hurricanes, with their reputation still glowing from the Battle of Britain, would prove to be the saviours once again. 'It was confidently expected that the Hurricanes would sweep the Japanese from the sky,' wrote Sir Paul Maltby, the commander of Singapore's air defences.[81] Churchill himself saw the planes as crucial to the defence of Singapore. 'The whole battle turns on the arrival of the Hurricanes,' he told Portal.[82]

This sense of faith led to further dispatches of reinforcements to the region, as 48 Hurricanes were flown off the carrier HMS *Indomitable* to the island of Sumatra, and another 39 were delivered in crates to the southerly neighbouring island of Java. But the hope invested in these aircraft was mistaken. The Hurricanes that arrived in Singapore were not even assembled until 19 January, at which stage the Japanese army was already making a swift advance through the Malayan peninsula. Even worse, having originally been intended for the combat in the desert, they were the tropicalized version fitted with Vokes filters. Nor did the pilots have sufficient experience of combat, as Portal admitted later to Churchill on 23 February. 'We have had a good deal of evidence during the war of the indifferent performance of hurried collections of pilots and aircraft without unit Esprit de Corps and a period of collective training. But in the Far East emergency, there was nothing to be done except try to get what pilots and aircraft we could to Singapore in time.'[83]

The first day of action, 20 January, seemed to bode well for the Hurricanes, as they shot down eight Japanese bombers that had embarked on a raid of Singapore. It was a moment of false promise. The reality dawned the next day as an escort of Mitsubushi Zero fighters destroyed five Hurricanes without loss. That was to be the pattern for the rest of the campaign as the British fighters were overwhelmed and outclassed by the Japanese. By 28 January there were just 20 left of the original 51 Hurricanes first dispatched. Arthur Hudson, an armourer who served in the East Indies with 605 Squadron, was frank about the weakness of the Hurricanes: 'The Zeros were fantastic. They were running rings round the Hurricanes, which could not turn as fast. The Zero was basically a flying engine attached to the lightest possible frame. It could go at a hell of a speed. The Hurricane never beat the Zero.'[84] In desperation, some ground crews removed the two outer Browning guns and one petrol tank to improve the performance of the plane, but to no avail. 'The Hurricanes never really got going and they were shot down very quickly. Certainly the Mitsubishi Zero was far, far superior,' recalled Richard Pool, one of the naval commanders in the Far East.[85]

The end came swiftly and with appalling inevitability. On 10 February the last seven Hurricanes were removed from Singapore and sent to Sumatra, which had been under continual bombardment since mid January. Five days later, in a humiliating scene, the commander of the British forces at Singapore, General Arthur Percival, raised the white flag and surrendered to the Japanese, the shame all the greater because the British had outnumbered the enemy by four to one. Soon afterwards the Hurricanes were again in retreat, this time from Sumatra to Java. They briefly hampered the Japanese ground invasion, but their numbers were too small to have any impact. 'It was a shambles. There was nothing we could do,' said Arthur Hudson.[86] By 7 March there were just two Hurricanes left on the island. In accordance with their orders, the remaining airmen set fire to the pair of planes. Soon afterwards the men were captured by the Japanese, beginning a long, often savage period of incarceration as prisoners of war. The following day the Japanese seized control of Java. All British resistance in the East Indies was over.

Winston Churchill described the fall of Singapore as 'the worst disaster and largest capitulation in British history'.[87] After its part in that ignominious episode, the Hawker Hurricane appeared to be doomed. But true to its robust nature, the old fighter was not finished yet. Refashioned from the wreckage of defeat, it was about to experience a rich new lease of life.

10

'A magnificent striking force'

～～

'You smell that?'
'What?'
'Napalm, son. Nothing else in the world smells like that. I love the smell of napalm in the morning.'[1]

This exchange in the 1979 film *Apocalypse Now* between the flamboyant, deranged Lieutenant Colonel Bill Kilgore, memorably played by Robert Duvall, and a young American soldier has become one of the most famous pieces of dialogue in cinema history. The lines have such power because they are held to typify the nihilistic excesses of America's campaign in Vietnam. Kilgore is seen as the classic bloodthirsty lunatic who revelled in the savagery of the war. Napalm is regarded as the quintessentially American weapon of the 1960s, a terrifying petroleum gel that brought death to soldiers and civilians alike by burning through their flesh. The very word is now redolent of technological barbarity. Yet it is an incongruous fact that, almost twenty years before the first American air operations in Vietnam, the Hawker Hurricane was dropping napalm in the jungles of Far East Asia. Long after the disasters of 1941, when the plane looked to be finished, it was still in action on Britain's last front of the Second World War, deploying this highly experimental type of bomb. 'Maybe I should not say this but for the last couple of months of the war we were filling our long-range tanks with napalm. The Japs did not like that at all,' recalled George Butler, who served in Burma with 60 Squadron.[2] The use of napalm by the RAF was not only a reflection of how brutal the war had become since the early, more restrained days of the Phoney War, but also a tribute to the surprising longevity of Sydney Camm's fighter. 'The Hurricane

282

has certainly outlived what everybody thought would be its useful life because of its value for aggressive action against land targets,' said the government's chief scientific adviser Sir Henry Tizard on 7 September 1942, during an Air Ministry discussion about future fighter production.[3]

The key to that length of service was the creation of a new role for the Hurricane as a bomber and ground attack aircraft. The battles over Greece, Malta and Singapore had proved that the plane was no longer viable as an interceptor against the Japanese or the Germans, especially as the Luftwaffe had introduced in early 1942 the Fw 190, a raging bull of a fighter that, for a time, outclassed even the Spitfire. But through the development of new weaponry, the Hurricane was able to prolong its operational life right until the end of the war. Bombs, rocket projectiles and large-calibre cannon were the ingredients of this renaissance. The Hurricane's thick wing, which even Camm had regarded as a cause for regret, became one of its assets since it enabled the plane to carry easily a variety of armaments. So tough and versatile was the plane that the increase in weight had little effect on its handling. Without much difficulty, the Hurricane could easily carry two 500-pound bombs, exactly the same load as was carried by the Vickers Vildebeest, a plane that had been specifically designed as a bomber and had fought alongside the Hurricane in Singapore.

The development of the Hurricane as a bomber began in makeshift fashion. As Deputy Commander of the RAF in the Middle East from November 1940, Arthur Tedder, never a conventional thinker, had experimented with the use of four 40-pound bombs slung under the wings of his own personal Hurricane in the desert. Though he did little damage with such a minimal load, he showed that the idea was feasible. Similarly, during 1941, 249 Squadron based in Malta tried a few raids against the Italian airfield of Gela on Sicily using Hurricanes equipped with even smaller 20-pound bombs. Graham Leggett was one of the pilots. 'We were armed up with bomb racks and they put these little 20-pound bombs – eight of them – under the wings. We set off at first light, arrived at Gela and did our bombing bit. We pressed the button and let these little bombs go off. They made a lot of noise and probably frightened the Italians, but I don't think they did much good.'[4] Further raids on Sicily at night proved ineffectual, but again the practicability of the Hurricane as a bomber had been demonstrated. The experiments captured the interest of the Ministry of Aircraft Production and in March 1941 tests were carried by the A&AEE at Boscombe Down in Wiltshire on a Hurricane Mark I loaded with two 250-pound bombs. The trials were a success. 'There are no difficulties in loading the two 250-pound bombs,' noted a report from Boscombe Down. 'The handling of the aircraft with the bombs on is normal under all conditions, as also is the handling with one bomb on and one bomb off. Dropping of the bombs in no way affects the stability.'[5] The only change in performance was a fall in the top speed by about 15 mph to 285 mph at 16,000 feet. After this favourable outcome, Hawker was authorized to start producing the fighter-bomber version, which quickly acquired the nickname the 'Hurribomber'. Some of the new planes were sent out to the Middle East, where the RAF faced its toughest operations, though many were retained by Fighter Command for use as intruders against occupied France and as attackers against Channel shipping.

Along with the new equipment, pilots were issued with instructions on both the technical and tactical aspects of the Hurribomber: 'The electrical release gear of the Hurricane bomber consists of four switches: one fusing switch, two selector switches and one firing switch,' explained the notes. 'The fusing switch and the two selector switches are grouped together on the starboard side of the cockpit, near the parachute flare release, and the firing switch consists of a push button on the top of the throttle lever. The selector switches enable the pilot to select his bombs so that when he presses the firing switch he can release at will either of the two bombs or both bombs together.'[6] To protect themselves from the blast, pilots were told to attack from a minimum of 650 feet if their bombs were fused to go off immediately, and 400 feet if they were using delayed-action bombs. 'The lower you make your approach, the less likely you are to be seen by the enemy,' urged another set of instructions.[7] Other advice included: 'Don't jink on your bombing run. It will put you off your aim. Make up your mind you are going to hand out much more than you are getting and concentrate on hitting and planting your bombs slap on the target.' Immediately after the release of bombs 'is the time to start jinking, and then do it violently.'[8]

The Hurribomber went into action from the autumn of 1941. Most of the planes converted to the bomber role at this time were either Mark IIBs or Mark IICs, rather than the old Mark Is or Mark IIAs, which were being phased out of operations. In the desert the RAF found that the bombing capability, when combined with the Vokes filter, lowered the maximum speeds considerably more than the tests at Boscombe Down had suggested, falling as much as 25 mph on the Mark IIC to 275 mph. Yet given that the Hurribomber was not intended for direct combat against the enemy, this was less important than the damage the plane could inflict, especially because a new tactic was devised whereby Spitfires would sometimes act as escorts on ground-attack missions.

A compelling description of the experience of flying the new Hurribomber was given to the BBC on 18 November 1941 by the Canadian officer Vaughan Corbett of 402 Squadron, after he had returned from a sortie to France:

In our Hurricane bombers, we don't have to dive onto our targets. We come down almost to ground level before we reach them and drop our bombs in level flight with a greater degree of accuracy than can be achieved in dive-bombing. The whole thrill of the Hurribomber is in this ground-level flying over the target. There we are, like a close formation of cars sweeping along the straight of a race track, only, instead of fast car speeds, we are going along at between 200 and 250 miles per hour. Even though we are travelling so fast, there would be a risk of being hurt by the blast from our own bombs if they were of the ordinary type which burst on contact. But our bombs are fitted with delayed action fuses so that they do not explode until we have got well outside their blast range. It might seem that flying onto the target at only a few feet altitude, we would be easy meat for Bofors [anti-aircraft guns] or machine-gun posts. We would be – if the gunners could see us coming. But they seldom see the low flying fighter until it is almost overhead, then they have to be remarkably quick to get the gun trained on the aircraft. What is more, they have little time to calculate what deflections to allow in their aim. I have seen flak and machine-gun fire pelting at my aircraft from all angles, but none of it has hit me.[9]

Paying tribute to the Hurribomber, *Flight* magazine reported in November 1941 that its pilots 'are quite confident that they could fit two 500-pounders without sacrificing much in the way of performance'.[10] This is precisely what Sydney Camm told the Ministry of Aircraft Production should be done, and on 22 February 1942 successful tests were carried out on a Hurricane IIB with two 500-pounders. Such a version soon went into service, though the 250-pounders remained the standard load. By mid 1942 the Hurricane was the RAF's premier fighter-bomber for army co-operation duties, superseding the Bristol Blenheim, as Portal explained during an Air Ministry meeting on 16 June to discuss the future bomber programme. 'The Chief of the Air Staff said that the army's needs would best be fulfilled by aircraft of the Hurribomber type. The day of the Bristol Blenheim was over. Nothing less handy than a fighter could deliver attacks from very low heights in the way needed for close support of the army.'[11]

The arrival of the Hurribomber was soon followed by another advance: the introduction of 40-mm anti-tank cannon. The move had been suggested to Camm by the Vickers company which had been working on this high-calibre gun, known as the 'S' type, since 1939 but had only come up with a reliable model in 1941. The Air Ministry gave its approval to the project and, after the conversion work had been completed at Langley, a Hurricane fitted with the two guns was delivered to Boscombe Down on 19 September. Leslie Appleton, a senior Hawker engineer, was present at the trials:

> The target was a Vickers Valentine tank, which looked rather forlorn in the middle of the range. I asked an officer of the Armoured Corps in attendance how they would remove the damaged tank. He said they would drive it away – which was not very encouraging! The trial pilot was Wing Commander Dixie Dean of the A&AEE Flight. He made several attacks, firing pairs of single shots from each gun until finally, in a fit of exuberance on his final pass, he fired a burst of four or five rounds per gun. When we examined the target, we saw that out of 28 rounds fired, Dixie had scored about 20 hits. More important, any single one of some 10 rounds had disabled the tank – either by track or engine damage, or by penetrating the turret, which was not a pleasant sight. I did not see my army friend again.[12]

The impressive results led immediately to a production order for the new 40-mm cannon Hurricane. It was given the official designation of the Mark IID, though within the RAF it was more commonly known as 'the tankbuster', or 'the flying can opener' because of how it could rip open enemy armour. John Wray of 137 Squadron experienced the formidable striking power of the Mark IID on operations over western Europe. 'Each 40-mm cannon had 16 shells. Once the guns were harmonized, someone who was a good shot could hit something like a telegraph post. It was a very, very accurate weapon. It had a firing rate of about one round every two seconds. Every time it fired, the pilot rose in his seat about three inches. It revolutionized things. When we hit a train, the boiler just blew off. When we hit solid targets, we really damaged them.'[13] According to Denys Gillam, the expert on Channel shipping attacks, the 'recoil from these large-calibre cannons was tremendous and reduced the speed by 40 to 50 mph'.[14] Altogether 800 Mark IIDs were built, the majority of them serving in the tank battles of the Middle East or on the Russian front. Even Joseph Stalin, eagerly seeking Spitfires in early 1942, welcomed the tankbuster a year later. 'I am very grateful for your offer to send us 60 Hurricanes IID armed with 40 mm cannon. Such planes are very needed especially against heavy tanks,' he told Churchill on 12 April 1943.[15]

A further expansion of the Hurricane's armoury occurred when a version was developed to carry rocket projectiles, an even more lethal weapon than the 40-mm cannon. Impressed with reports of the use of air-to-ground rockets on the Russian front, the Air Ministry asked Hawker in November 1941 to prepare three Hurricanes for tests in this role. This involved the installation of wing attachment points for the rockets' launching rails, firing selector switches in the cockpit and additional wiring. The rockets themselves were astonishingly crude. They comprised nothing more than a 40-pound cast-iron shot screwed into a three-inch iron pipe that contained the propellant. A cruciform of rectangular fins was bolted on to the rear end of the pipe. The three Hurricanes, each with six rocket projectiles under their wings, were sent to Boscombe Down in the spring of 1942. The trials proved largely successful, though the weapons were less accurate than had been hoped. Once the plane went into production, the number of rockets was raised from six to eight, while the weight of the high-explosive warhead was increased from 40 to 60 pounds. The warheads and the rocket equipment made this the heaviest Hurricane of them all, putting up its overall take-off weight to 8,450 pounds. The stronger punch came at the price of further reduced performance, recalled John Wray of 137 Squadron: 'With the mounting, the rails and the rockets, the whole installation was very heavy, which meant that the Hurricane – which had never been the best of climbers – had its rate of climb reduced to almost nil; not that we needed much rate of climb at this stage.'[16]

The rocket-armed Hurricanes first operated in June 1943, eventually serving with 137, 164 and 184 Squadrons in western Europe until they were replaced by Hawker's own much bigger Typhoon fighter-bomber, though they carried on fighting in the Far East until the end of the war. For John Wray the destructive power of the rockets was awesome: 'The 40-mm gun just wasn't in the same league. We really discovered this the first time we had a go at an "M" class mine-sweeper. In the past we'd found that we could hit one with half a dozen bombs and smoke would come out as it went limping along. But when we hit one with eight rockets the thing just turned over and disappeared in a flash.'[17]

The advent of bombs and rockets on the Hurricane played their part in the creation of a new variant, the Mark IV, the last type to go into production. The logical successor to the Hurricane Mark II should, of course, have been the Mark III, and indeed Hawker's designers were working on a prototype of just that designation in late 1941. This was a version fitted with an American-built Packard Merlin 28 engine, its creation reflecting the deep concern of the Ministry of Aircraft Production that the supply of Rolls-Royce Merlin engines might be insufficient for the output of Hurricanes. But thanks to Sir Ernest Hives's managerial brilliance and the dedication of his Rolls-Royce workforce, this problem never arose and no Hurricane Mark III was ever built. However, the Packard-Merlin was installed on most of the Hurricanes manufactured in Canada, where the planes, despite having the same airframes as the English types, had their own designations ranging from the Mark X to the Mark XII. Back in Britain, the development of the Hurricane

IV resulted from the Air Ministry's determination to introduce an all-purpose 'universal wing', which could carry several different external loads, including rockets, bombs or long-range fuel tanks, depending on the type of operation. The Mark IV was also fitted with two Vickers 40-mm and two .303 Brownings, while the power-plant was the Merlin 27 engine, which incorporated a redesigned oil system and also offered a better performance at low altitude where the Hurricane now tended to operate in its ground-attack role. Other changes on the Mark IV were a deeper radiator and additional armour around the front fuselage. A total of 524 Mark IVs were built and they operated in all theatres.

Hawker and the Air Ministry planned one further Hurricane type, the Mark V, which featured a Merlin 32 boosted engine giving 1,700 horsepower at low level. With tropical filters, anti-tank guns and a four-bladed Rotol propeller, it was primarily intended for action in Burma, but tests at Boscombe Down revealed a susceptibility to over-heating and the Mark V never went into production.

Apart from bludgeoning the enemy with its variety of weapons, the Hurricane performed another role over occupied territories, one for which it was ill-suited because of its structure and handling. It was in North Africa in 1941 that the RAF first set up a tactical reconnaissance (Tac R) unit equipped with a number of Hurricanes. In addition to its armament, each of these planes was fitted with three cameras behind the cockpit. Geoffrey Morley-Mower, who flew the Hurricane on reconnaissance in the desert with 451 Squadron, described how primitive the conversion was: 'The Hurricane was not designed to take such heavy, awkwardly shaped objects as cameras and it was a sight to see the modifications that the riggers had performed in the narrow space between the rear of the cockpit and the tail. It was a crude carpentry job, a "lash-up", and the spars looked too frail to support the dense, spiky mechanisms, facing downwards at differing angles from the large hole cut in the underside of the fuselage.'[18] Morley-Mower also explained the method for taking the photographs: 'The middle camera faced directly down and the other two were angled to cover the areas on either side of the air-craft's path. A timing device opened and shut the lenses at the correct intervals for the speed flown. The pilot simply had to press a button to start the whole thing off.' Tight precision was required, with little margin for error. 'If the wings tilted at all, an incorrect tract of country would be photographed.' The ideal speed was 180 mph but it could be an exhausting job. 'The massive old fashioned cameras weighed the tail down so badly that the nose would rise in flight even with the elevator trim fully forward. On these aircraft, thick elastic chords fastened the stick to the dashboard, relieving the pilot of the physical effort to move the stick from its position of maximum dive. Half a notch on the elevator trim and the aircraft would lurch forward as if released by a giant hand. This effectively turned a racehorse into a carthorse.'

The common tactic on these sorties was to fly in pairs, one making the reconnaissance, the other keeping a lookout for enemy fighters. But Morley-Mower confessed that on one of his first trips, flying behind the highly experienced Lewis 'Molly' Malone, he was gripped with such fear when they had to fly through a savage anti-aircraft barrage, that he briefly deserted his leader: 'I could hear the crack of near misses above the engine noise and felt the thumps against the fuselage as they discharged . . . The sheer terror of immediate extinction overwhelmed me. I turned my Hurricane on my back and barrelled down through the dense explosions and out into the clear. Intoxicated with relief, I held my dive towards the earth, levelling out at 100 feet.' Soon afterwards he caught up again with Malone, who had barely even noticed his disappearance.

On another occasion Morley-Mower was sent on a solo two-hour flight to photograph German army positions: 'The whole situation, 6,000 feet above the German army, taking photographs in a clapped out Hurricane, burdened with long-range tanks and three heavy cameras, was out of some old pilot's nightmares.' When he had completed his mission, 'the accumulated tension led me to perform a wild descent at maximum power.' As he roared downwards, he saw a line of German trucks and immediately opened fire. 'It was glorious to strike back,' he wrote. To his surprise, the convoy erupted with a string of explosions, revealing that the lorries had been carrying munitions. I was so close to the ground that I had the impression that the world was blowing up in my face.'[19] He escaped and flew back to base without any further incident.

Despite the tough experiences of Morley-Mower's unit, other types of Hurricane reconnaissance planes were deployed in the desert and Burma. One tactical version had a forward-facing F24 camera or a cine camera in the starboard wing root. Another had its guns replaced by extra fuel tanks in the wings to give it greater range, and, with four F24s in the fuselage, flew at over 30,000 feet. But neither of these alternatives did anything to contradict the evidence that the Hurricane was not up to this job. Arthur Tedder himself, the RAF Commander in the Middle East, admitted on 22 October 1942 to Sir Charles Portal, Chief of the Air Staff, that the reconnaissance pilots 'have a pretty grim task' because 'the poor old Hurricane is becoming more and more out of date', but he could not 'possibly afford to give them Spitfires'.[20] As the war entered 1943, however, more reconnaissance Spitfires became available and took over from the Hurricanes. Harry Hawker, who carried out photographic duties with 208 Squadron, was only too glad to make the exchange. 'My problems were over. The Hurricane was like a beautiful old beast. The Spitfire was a completely different animal, a different sensation flying. I very much preferred the Spitfire. The Hurricane was an old aeroplane, even in the Middle East.'[21]

Yet this creaking venerability did not stop the Hurricane giving admirable support as a ground-attack aircraft during the later part of the Allied campaign in the desert. After they had arrived in North Africa for the start of Operation Crusader, General Auchinleck's attempt to push Rommel out of Cyrenaica and lift the siege of Tobruk in eastern Libya, the Hurribombers went into battle for the first time on 20 November 1941 when six of them from 80 Squadron attacked a batch of German motor vehicles. The same squadron's Hurribombers saw heavier action the next month. On 8 December they caused severe damage to another motorized convoy, leaving a trail of burning transports that stretched almost a mile along the main coast road. But flying at low level, the Hurribombers were themselves vulnerable. In a single action on 12 December four of the squadron's aircraft were shot down by ground fire. All the pilots survived but were taken prisoners of war. The tactical reconnaissance Hurricanes were also deeply involved in Crusader, providing crucial information for the army on German movements. Murray Gardner of 451 Squadron in the Royal Australian Air Force recalled of one his first recces: 'The view from 18,000 feet over the edge of the Mediterranean was fabulous, though I could not spare too much attention on that. This was particularly true during the actual photographic runs, when it was necessary to stop looking round for enemy fighters for a while and concentrate entirely in the cockpit, keeping a steady height, speed and setting. Coming down was exhilarating and a great relief.' Gardner also tried to fly above the anti-aircraft fire. 'I found in the desert it was just as easy to spot a tank at 10,000 feet as it was at 4,000 feet, and much safer, even allowing for some extra exposure to enemy fighters.'[22]

In the heat of the battle Gardner's activities were not confined to photographic runs. On the morning of 12 December, while on a recce over Timimi, 60 miles west of Tobruk on the Libyan coast, he noticed dust rising from an aerodrome, and then glimpsed an Me 109 heading for the coast:

> I watched him closely and, as he levelled off, I got carefully into position and gave him a three-second beam shot with the aid of the Hurricane's excellent reflector gun sight. I did this deliberately as many German aircraft had armour plating front and rear but nothing on the sides. My eight Browning machine guns did their work and raked the enemy aircraft from nose to tail. I saw it slow down and it looked as if it intended to land among the bushes on the right-hand side of the road. There was no time for half-measures, as we had been subjected to considerable shelling and bombing in Tobruk and I had seen what damage the Me 109s, with their nose-mounted cannons, could do.[23]

Actions like those of Gardner's helped Crusader achieved some of its goals, especially in relieving Tobruk. But, much to Churchill's anger, the operation then petered out in the sands like previous initiatives, allowing Rommel to replenish his supplies and strike back. As the Germans advanced in the new year of 1942, the Hurribombers, now arriving in greater numbers, again achieved some successes, most notably on 26 January when 120 enemy lorries were destroyed, though the standard fighter Hurricanes again were generally outclassed by the Me 109. One humiliating incident on 14 January saw two 109s shoot down four Hurricanes. Fred Rosier, who won the

OBE for his heroism during Crusader, admitted that the squadrons 'fought with great courage' but their Hurricanes 'were no match for the 109s. They needed time to build up their strength and they needed better fighters, Spitfires and Kittyhawks.'[24]

A lull descended after Rommel's counter-attack ended at the beginning of February 1942, once he had recaptured the western port of Cyrenaica which meant that he could reinforce his Afrika Korps with supplies from Tripoli and the Mediterranean. The RAF also welcomed the chance to reorganize their forces. Crucial in the preparations for the next phase of the campaign was the leadership of Sir Arthur 'Mary' Coningham, a tough, dry Antipodean who had been appointed Commander of the Western Desert Air Force in October 1941. Born in Australia, Coningham was the son of a Test cricketer and fraudster whose scandalous conduct resulted in the family's departure from Sydney to New Zealand, a move that led to Sir Arthur's RAF nickname: 'Mary' had nothing to do with effeminacy but was just a distortion of the word 'Maori'. Despite his instinctive reserve, which was a reaction against his father's behaviour, Coningham was a daring innovator. Working closely with Tedder, he pioneered a new concept of army co-operation, whereby the whole of his force was used tactically in support of the ground forces. It was an approach that ran counter to the RAF's traditional ethos of independence, in which co-operation was regarded as nothing more than a minor adjunct to the two main tasks of fighter defence and strategic bombing. Central to Coningham's vision of the RAF as a form of flying artillery was the role of ground-attack aircraft, and the development of the Hurricane as a bomber and anti-tank weapon gave him the flexibility he needed.

The introduction of the Hurribomber into the desert force was followed in May 1942 by the arrival of the Hurricane IID, which first went into service with 6 Squadron, led by Roger Porteous. The men of this squadron underwent some urgent training with their new armament. At first they used a piece of canvas, mounted between two vertical rails and painted with a lifesize picture of a tank. Then they wangled a captured German tank from the army and put a can of petrol inside it. As Canadian Al Simpson of 6 Squadron recalled: 'We attacked it and the results were quite dramatic. Later we inspected the damage and agreed that we had an effective weapon. Our skill level was also high; we had an average of more than 70 per cent hits, firing six to ten shots per attack.'[25]

The entry of the 'Tankbuster', with its heavyweight Vickers guns able to penetrate 20 mm of armour plating, coincided with the resumption of Rommel's offensive. With his characteristic boldness, the Desert Fox soon had the Allies falling backwards in another retreat, even though their ground forces actually outnumbered the Germans. In May at Gazala in Libya the Afrika Korps smashed through the British lines, while further to the south-east, at Bir Hakeim, the Free French garrison was isolated and crushed after ten days of gallant resistance. It was during this battle that the Hurricane IID went into action. Donald Weston-Burt of 6 Squadron described how the assault on German tanks was made after 'a run-in at about 20–40 feet above the ground. Opening with the first pair at about 1,000 yards, two more pairs could be got away accurately before breaking off the attack. It is no exaggeration to say that any good pilot would guarantee to hit his target with one or more pairs on each attack.'[26] But for all the firepower of the Hurricane IIDs, they were vulnerable to ground fire from the Panzers and anti-artillery guns, something Al Simpson found when he opened up his cannon against a German convoy during the fierce fighting around Bir Hakeim: 'As we neared the target, we dove to pick up speed and attacked from about 1,000 yards at ten feet off the deck. When a bullet is coming towards you, you can see it even though it is not tracer or incendiary. I remember the one that hit me. I saw it coming, the way you see a snowflake coming at your windshield. Flak normally breaks away from an aircraft like snowflakes, too, as I had seen it in France and Belgium. But this one kept coming. An explosive bullet, it detonated when it entered the hull of my aircraft by my left hand. It burst a few inches in front of my chest.' Covered in blood, Simpson thought he was mortally wounded. 'My initial reaction was to cost the enemy as much as possible, and so I continued my attack on the German III tank, then lined up another at which I got a good run, and then a truck.'[27] But then hot glycol started to pour from the engine, which had also been hit. Simpson had no alternative but to bail out. He managed to drag the plane up to a sufficient altitude and jumped out, pulling the rip cord as soon as he passed the tail. When he landed, badly injured, in terrible pain and short of breath, he was fortunate to be rescued by the Royal Signals Corps and taken to hospital at Tobruk.

By the end of June the Hurricane IIDs had destroyed 26 tanks, 31 armoured troop carriers and many other trucks and guns. But the tide of the desert war was running against the Allies. Sadly, neither Auchinleck nor the commander of the 8th Army, Neil Ritchie, had the vision or the coolness of Tedder and Coningham. The break-throughs at Gazala and Bir Hakeim were quickly followed by the fall of Tobruk to the Germans on 20 June 1942. Churchill called the capture of the port 'one of the heaviest blows of the war'.[28] The Allies retreated deep into Egypt, taking up a defensive position on a line running south from the coastal town of El Alamein. The Suez Canal and Britain's very existence in the Middle East now seemed under threat. As a sense of crisis swept through the British High Command, Auchinleck and Ritchie were forced out. In August Harold Alexander became Commander-in-Chief of the Middle East, and Bernard Montgomery head of the 8th Army. The effect of these changes was electric. Montgomery brought an energetic new sense of purpose to the desert campaign, building a strong relationship with Tedder and Coningham based on an instinctive understanding of air co-operation. Communications and planning were radically improved, morale boosted. 'No longer was the ground situation allowed to become so confused that air support became limited. We knew where the enemy were and we were able to attack them in relays with light bombers and fighter bombers,' remembered Hurricane pilot Fred Rosier of 229 Squadron.[29] The journalist Alan Moorehead, who had been fol-lowing the campaign from its inception, was similarly impressed by Montgomery's influence. 'The RAF was working at a rhythm and speed that eclipsed all previous efforts,' he wrote.[30]

Yet even in the Allies' darkest hour Rommel was weaker than his victories might suggest, since his supply routes through the Mediterranean were constantly under threat from the Royal Navy. This difficulty emphasized the vital strategic importance of Malta, whose defences had been under constant bombardment from the Luftwaffe since December, with the RAF no longer able to offer much resistance. By March 1942, with the Germans flying 600 sorties a week, the Hurricanes on the island had been all but obliterated. So severe were the shortages of aircraft that some of the pilots of 249 Squadron were reduced to the job of standing on the rooftops of Valetta to act as plane spotters. 'In the early months of 1942, it was to be a grossly unequal contest. The Hurricanes, totally outperformed, were soon reduced to impotence,' wrote the squadron's Tom Neil.[31] But salvation was at hand for the island. During March the first Spitfires had been ordered to Malta, taking off from the aircraft carrier HMS *Eagle*. Graham Leggett, a Hurricane pilot with 249 Squadron, saw the relief that surged through the Maltese public at the arrival of the new fighters. 'The Spitfires came in from the southwest corner and flew right across the island at low level in formation and out across Valetta harbour. The Maltese practically went mad. They knew the score. They knew the Hurricanes were having a tough time against the 109s. We were losing a lot of planes and a lot of people. The Maltese rushed through the streets shouting "Spitfire, Spitfire".'[32] Throughout the spring more reinforcements arrived, enabling the RAF to challenge the Luftwaffe's air supremacy. A further boost to the fighter defences came when Sir Keith Park, the mastermind of the Battle of Britain, was appointed Air Officer Commanding Malta, by which time the last remaining Hurricanes had been pulled out of the front line, some sent to the desert, some retained for night-fighting and Hurribomber duties against the Sicilian airfields.

Though the final months of the Malta campaign represented a heroic failure for the Hurricane as an interceptor, they witnessed the Sea Hurricane's greatest triumph of the war. During the summer of 1942, with the fight for North Africa still in the balance, two major Allied supply convoys were sent to Malta, both of them coming under ferocious assault from the Luftwaffe and the German U-boats. The first convoy, code-named Operation Harpoon, passed through the Straits of Gibraltar on 12 June, its six merchantmen protected by Sea Hurricanes on HMS *Eagle* and Fairey Fulmars on HMS *Argus*. Two days later the Axis attacks started, led by 150 dive-bombers escorted by over 100 fighters. In the furious battle that followed, the Germans succeeded in sinking four of the merchant ships, but the sea fighters put up enough resistance to allow two of them to make it to Valetta harbour, bringing 15,000 tons of food and ammunition to the island.

There was an even bigger clash in August when Operation Pedestal was launched, featuring a huge convoy of 13 freighters, an American oil tanker, 7 Royal Navy cruisers, 26 destroyers and 3 aircraft carriers, with 39 Sea Hurricanes of the Fleet Air Arm among the fighters on board. This time over 500 German and Italian aircraft went on the attack. The fighting, lasting four days, was intense, as Hugh Popham of 880 Squadron described: the ships 'were enclosed in a sparkling net of tracer and bursting shells, a mesh of fire. Every gun in the fleet and convoy was firing, and the darkling air was laced with threads and beads of fire.' Popham's section took down one Ju 88 that had become separated from its formation. 'He turned away and we stuffed the nose down, full bore, willing our aircraft to make up on him. At extreme range, we gave him a long burst; bits came off and smoke poured out of one engine, and then he vanished into the thickening twilight.'[33] The Sea Hurricanes were estimated to have shot down between 30 and 40 enemy aircraft while losing 4 of their own number. The most remarkable of the pilots was the Fleet Air Arm ace Dickie Cork, who destroyed one German and three Italian aircraft during the battle, winning the DSO in the process. The cost to the convoy was severe: nine merchantmen, an aircraft carrier, two cruisers and a destroyer were all sunk. Yet enough ships made it to Malta for the island's desperately low stocks to be replenished. Most crucially of all, the American oil tanker reached Valetta, despite such severe damage that she had to be towed into the harbour. The siege of the island was over. Malta had been saved as a base from which to menace Rommel's lifeline.

The momentum of the desert war had continually shifted since the summer of 1940. But now, with Malta secure, the British forces confident under new leadership, the RAF well organized and Rommel overstretched, it moved decisively in favour of the Allies. By October, having beaten back further thrusts by the Afrika Korps, Montgomery and Tedder were ready to break out from behind the line at El Alamein. The Hurricanes, in their different guises, remained an integral part of the Desert Air Force, making up 22 of its 48 fighter and fighter-bomber squadrons. On the eve of the offensive, spirits were high. 'Monty was not the usual "Old Boy" type,' said Hurricane pilot Murray Gardner. 'He was more of a roundhead than a cavalier. He believed in personal contact, in seeing things for himself. Perhaps his greatest merit was his insistence on everybody knowing what the plan was and what his own part was in it. He didn't claim to be the Messiah but he came very close to that.'[34] A thunderous barrage from the British artillery on the night of 23–4 October signalled the start of the Battle of El Alamein, the turning point of the war in the West. Standing by his tent on the British lines, Graham Leggett who had been transferred to 73 Squadron shortly before the battle, watched the guns opening up. 'It was quite spectacular. The whole sky was lit up. You could feel the ground trembling. Coffee mugs on the table would start shaking. It was quite extraordinary.'[35] Later that same night Hurribombers and Mark IIDs with their 40-mm cannons roared over Italian and German positions, destroying vehicles, tanks, supply dumps and troop carriers. Donald Burton-West of 6 Squadron was in action from the morning after the barrage and continued to mount sorties throughout the battle:

> I was set off with six Hurricane IIDs on a target of 15 tanks and two half-tracks. We found them, attacked and did considerable damage. I personally claimed three tanks definitely hit . . . On November 3rd we were let loose along with all the other squadrons to play as much havoc as possible with the now retreating German and Italian forces. My logbook states that I claimed four mechanical transports hit and two tanks. I also recall one bus which spewed forth several dozen Italians which we gleefully and callously mowed down as they ran for their lives.[36]

Flying over the enemy lines at night gave Graham Leggett a sense of exhilaration: 'El Alamein was a good place from where to watch the war. It was an incredible sight: flashes, flares and clouds of dust all going up, tracer going off in all directions, bombs bursting everywhere. It really was fantastic.'[37] From 4 November the withdrawal of the Axis forces began to turn into a headlong, disorganized retreat across the desert, harried all the way by the RAF. The battle was the Germans' first land defeat by Britain. Tobruk was taken on 12

November, and three days later Churchill ordered the church bells to be rung across all of Great Britain. More than two years earlier such a sound would have meant a German invasion was underway. Now it heralded victory. The Hurricanes, like the rest of the Desert Air Force, had played a significant part. As the historian Frank Mason pointed out, between 23 October and 8 November 6 Hurricane squadrons alone had claimed a total of 39 tanks, 212 lorries and armoured troop carriers, 26 bowsers (fuelling tankers), 42 guns and over 200 other vehicles.[38]

This time there was no halt in the Allies' offensive. With the Axis forces in retreat, their convoys were easy prey for the ground-attack aircraft now that the RAF had full air superiority. The threat to the Germans and Italians was compounded in early November by the Allied landings on the coasts of Vichy French-occupied Algeria and Morocco in Operation Torch, led by Dwight D. Eisenhower. As the 8th Army and Desert Air Force headed westwards, and Torch quickly crushed pro-Axis resistance, Rommel's forces were trapped in a pincer movement. Once more, Hurricanes were in the front line of the Allies' advance. Within an hour of the Americans seizing the Maison Blanche airfield at Algiers, Hurricane IICs of 43 Squadron had landed to fight off any German attempts to recapture the base, a job that they did successfully, quickly shooting down three Ju 88 raiders. By the end of 1942 five Hurricane squadrons were operating from airfields in former Vichy-held Africa. When Allied troops took Tripoli on 23 January 1943, Sir Arthur Coningham ordered two Hurricane squadrons up to the airfields far ahead of the 8th Army, so they could attack the retreating German and Italians from the rear. Soon after Rommel had been driven out of Libya, Montgomery paid this tribute to the RAF: 'On your behalf I have sent a special message to the Allied Air Forces that have co-operated with us. I don't suppose that any army as ever been supported by such a magnificent striking force. I have always maintained that the Eighth Army and the RAF in the Western Desert together constitute one fighting machine and therein lies our strength.'[39] Trapped in Tunisia, the position of the Axis quickly became hopeless, the Americans and British advancing overland, the RAF and USAAF controlling the air. According to a report from Harry Broadhurst, who in late January took over from

Coningham, 6 Squadron alone inflicted serious damage on the enemy during just one month of the Tunisian campaign, destroying 46 tanks, 13 armoured cars and 17 lorries between 10 March and 8 April. These were all 'ideal targets for the Hurricane IIDs and the knowledge that we have a force of tank busters' compelled the enemy 'to exercise considerable caution in the employment of his armour,' wrote Broadhurst in a report on 12 May, while he also added his praise for the robustness of the Hawker fighter: 'Hurricane aircraft have always proved to be able to stand severe structural damage in fuselage and mainplanes. This has been upheld in operations undertaken by the Hurricane IID.'[40] Attempts to airlift the German and Italian troops from Tunis in a convoy of Ju 52 transports failed disastrously when the Luftwaffe aircraft were attacked by Allied fighters including Hurricanes. On 13 May the Axis forces surrendered in North Africa: 230,000 German and Italian troops were taken prisoner.

The North African campaign was the last great offensive against Germany in which the Hurricanes participated in any significant numbers. After operations in Tunisia, they were shifted to secondary duties in the Mediterranean and played little part in the invasion of Italy from July 1943. Only 73 Squadron, now based in Malta, was given a front-line role at all, that of shooting up enemy searchlights on the invasion coast, but even that job was soon handed over to Spitfires. Graham Leggett had mixed feelings when he was told in Tunisia that his squadron would be changing to Spitfires: 'There was jubilation from many pilots, though personally I was perfectly happy with the Hurricane. It was a plane I knew and could rely on. You could plop it down almost anywhere. Its rigidity had saved my neck more than once. So although I was quite excited about the transfer, I was not glad to see the back of the Hurricane.' But, like others, he soon grew to like the Spitfire. 'Visibility on the whole was that much better. Handling, the Spitfire responded very well. Aileron control was probably better. Response to the throttle was very good and there was a good rate of climb.' Moreover, he found that he could fly the whole time with the canopy shut, whereas on the Hurricane, because its windscreen was often 'scratched and marked', he had generally kept the hood open up to 12,000 feet. But the change of planes ended a remarkable relationship that stretched back to 1937 when

Leggett had first joined Hawker as an apprentice, the Hurricane becoming 'so much part of my life'.[41]

The last Hurricanes to fly in combat in the Mediterranean theatre were those of 6 Squadron. Based at Grottaglie in southern Italy, the 6 Hurricane Mark IVs successfully carried out operations against German shipping in the Adriatic in early 1944, before being transferred to the anti-Axis Balkan Air Force, in which role they were regularly called upon by the Greek and Yugoslav partisans to attack German positions, troop movements and naval convoys. Just a week before VE Day on 8 May 1945, rocket-carrying Mark IVs of 6 Squadron forced the surrender of a flotilla of 25 enemy ships in the Gulf of Trieste.

In northern Europe the Hurricane was also phased out from 1942 as the Typhoon, Tempest and Mosquito became available, in addition to the latest versions of the Spitfire. The Hurricane took part in the notorious fiasco of the 'Channel Dash' in February 1942, when three German warships, the *Scharnhorst*, the *Gneisenau* and the *Prinz Eugen*, sailed from Brest on the north-western tip of France, right through the naval blockade in the Channel and into their home bases on the North Sea coast. RAF efforts to halt their journey were frenetic but unavailing, due to poor visibility, powerful flak and dire communications. Four Hurribombers from 601 Squadron were vectored too far south, while three other squadrons claimed to have found the ships but caused little damage in the face of enemy fire, which brought down two of their number.

Later that year, on 19 August, Hurricanes participated in another failed operation, the raid on Dieppe on the northern French coast. This ill-conceived venture had the twin aims of testing the German coastal defences in occupied France and trying to draw the Luftwaffe into the air. But in truth its main achievement was to cause the deaths of about 1,000 men and the capture of some 2,400 more, in addition to the loss of 119 aircraft. Eight Hurricane squadrons, include two of Hurribombers, were instructed to carry out attacks in three waves on gun positions around Dieppe and the two headlands east and west of the harbour. But throughout the day planes encountered intense flak from the Germans as they approached the port, as Kenneth McGlashan of 245 Squadron recalled: 'The sky was absolutely thick with the black smoke of exploding shells. I couldn't believe that I had made the coast without being hit by some form of flying metal.' McGlashan's task had been to take out some German gun emplacements, but, in a reflection of the poor planning of the operation, he was almost blown up by the RAF's own Hurribombers as he made a low-level attack at exactly the moment that they dropped their loads on the same target. 'I was down in the dirt, the wall of the gun's parapet lay ahead at eye height and I readied for one last pass when all hell broke loose. A deafening explosion erupted directly below me and threw my Hurricane hundreds of feet into the air. The percussion and "G" force starved my Merlin carburettor of fuel causing all to go quiet up front. I was seemingly hanging in mid-air with a choking engine, for a few seconds that seemed to take forever.' Fortunately, his Merlin quickly started up again and he was somehow able to nurse the crippled Hurricane back across the Channel. When he landed at Tangmere in Sussex he found 'the bottom of my aircraft was pulp. In the sagging canvas hung wires, pipes, and numerous other pieces of the Hurricane's anatomy, literally hanging by a thread.'[42] Altogether 20 Hurricanes were shot down on the Dieppe raid, 12 were damaged and 15 Hurricane pilots were either killed or captured. John Ellacombe of 253 Squadron, who was hit over the Channel by a Fw 190, had to bail out into the sea and was picked up by a landing craft, gave this verdict: 'It was not a good day for Hurricanes.'[43]

There were to be no further large-scale operations by the Hurricane in this theatre, not least because Dieppe proved that the 250-pound and 500-pound bombs were inadequate for heavily fortified positions. The Mark IID 'Tankbuster' went into service with only one home squadron, 184 Squadron, from December 1942, but was confined purely to training exercises with the army. In mid 1943, 164 and 137 Squadrons were equipped with the Mark IVs carrying rocket projectiles and carried out several missions over occupied Holland and Belgium, attacking goods trains, barges and transport. One of the more daring of these attacks was Operation Twitch, held on 2 September, which aimed to destroy lock gates on the Hansweert canal in Holland. Because of the limited range of the Hurricane, the 12 planes were instructed to head towards Holland at just 120 mph to conserve fuel, then fly at full throttle over the target area as they released their rockets. John Wray of 137 Squadron remembered how difficult the operation was. Cruising over the water at such a 'pitifully slow' speed, 'it was as if we were in a balloon standing still. Directly we hit the coast the guns opened up. We were flying at less than 50 feet. I am not exaggerating in saying that one could actually hear the fast-firing, multiple machine guns that were being used.' One Hurricane was hit but the other eleven continued on the painful journey, the stress made all the worse by the poor visibility. 'When we arrived at the target, the whole thing became a bit of a mish-mash.' Flying alongside J. L. De Houx, his commanding officer, Wray headed for the target. But just as De Houx 'was about to open fire, he was hit by anti-aircraft fire, and flew straight into a house on the side of the lock gate, instantly blowing up in a ball of flames and smoke. I fired my rockets but was unable to see the result because I was over the lockgates and dodging down to zero feet again.' Wray throttled back to 120 mph and, feeling 'utterly vulnerable', headed out towards the North Sea. 'It seemed improbable that we could undertake such an attack and not attract German fighters', but Wray made it back to Manston airfield in Kent without incident. Sadly, after all that trauma and the loss of two men, reconnaissance revealed the next day that little damage had been caused because of a fault in the arming device of the rocket's warheads.

A week later Wray took part in an even more ineffectual operation. It was code-named Starkey and was meant to be a mock invasion of France at the northern port of Boulogne, featuring 250 naval craft and over 1,000 Allied planes. The three aims of this little-known sham attack were to entice the Luftwaffe into the air, to divert German troops from the Italian front and to convince Hitler that the real invasion would be mounted across the straits of Dover. But the Germans did not fall for the hoax. The vast force had to return to England, having achieved nothing except the deaths of 500 innocent French civilians in the accidental bombing of a coastal village. 'It really was a complete and utter failure,' said Wray.[44] 137 Squadron converted to Typhoons soon after this, but a few squadrons kept their Hurricanes until March 1944, mainly using them on raids against the heavily defended VI rocket sites. They were not particularly effective in this role, since their speed made them vulnerable to flak and German fighters, though they did put some of the sites out of action. The last RAF fighter squadron to fly Hurricanes on duty from Britain was 309 Squadron, a Polish unit that mounted patrols throughout most of 1944 to guard the east coast of Scotland against raids. Not a single German bomber was sighted during these operations and in October the squadron converted to US-built Mustangs. The Hurricane remained in RAF service within Britain in a few other roles until the end of the war: producing weather reports; testing equipment and weapons; and training pilots.

More importantly, Hurricane IICs and IVs in 63 Squadron carried out some reconnaissance operations around Dieppe during the weeks leading up to the D-Day landings of 6 June. During the great invasion Hurricanes were also used on the Air Despatch Letter Service run by 1697 Flight, carrying urgent messages and documents between Normandy and London. One of the pilots on this service was Arthur Lowndes: 'We had Hurricanes specially adapted to carry mail. They had a special space behind the pilot and it was also possible to use one of the wing tanks. We used to fly Hurricanes to the airstrips in Normandy and dispatch riders would come from the front bringing dispatches for London. It took about an hour to fly the distance back to Northolt where another dispatch rider or driver would take it straight to London, so an action which might have taken place at 7 a.m. would be reported in London by about 10 a.m.'[45]

As the Allies advanced through Normandy, the last Hurricane came off the production line. On 12 August 1944, a decade after Sydney Camm had come up with his proposal for the Hawker monoplane, a Hurricane IIC with the serial number PZ865 emerged from the vast Langley factory in Berkshire. It did not go into service. Instead, it was bought from the Air Ministry by the Hawker company and formally named 'The Last of the Many'. With this slogan painted on either side of its fuselage, PZ865 took part in a formal ceremony and flypast at Langley to mark the end of an era, Camm himself rightly having the place of honour on a dais in front of the large crowd. Equally appropriately, the man in the cockpit during this exhibition was none other than George Bulman, the test pilot who had so presciently declared the plane to be a winner after taking the prototype up for the first time almost nine years earlier. The end of Hurricane production was recognized in the press with a mixture of admiration and poignancy. 'Last of the Hawker Hurricanes: 10 years of varied service', declared the headlines in *The Times*. 'One of the most famous and versatile fighter aircraft in the world, the Hawker Hurricane, is nearing the end of its fighting career. The last of the Hurricanes has just been delivered to the RAF from the factory,' continued the article, not with complete accuracy.[46] 'At long last this old warrior, which first flew in November 1935, must give way to faster and more powerful single-seater fighters,' said *Flight* magazine. 'Its versatility, combined with its high performance and fine qualities, together with the unyielding courage and tenacity of the fighter pilots, has made the Hurricane one of the most outstanding machines in the history of aviation.'[47]

But this was not the end of the story. On the other side of the world, the Hurricane was still battling doughtily in Burma, a campaign that not only assisted in the defeat of Japan but also provided the final confirmation of the excellence of the plane. Following the classic pattern of Britain's war, the fighting in Burma started disastrously at the end of 1941, partly because of a sneering complacency towards the enemy, as John Randle, an officer in the Baluch regiment, admitted: 'We were arrogant about the Japs. We regarded them as coolies. We thought of them as third rate. My goodness me, we soon changed our tune.'[48] When Japanese bombers first attacked the capital of Rangoon in December 1941, British aerial defences were hopelessly inadequate, consisting of nothing more than 16 Brewster Buffalo fighters. To bolster the air force, 30 Hurricane Mark Is were dispatched in crates from the Middle East, arriving in January 1942. Once assembled they were flown by pilots of 17 and 67 Squadron, some of them bravely launching strikes against enemy bases in Thailand, but they could do little to halt the Japanese advance towards Rangoon. On 5 February the Air Officer Commanding Burma, Donald Stevenson, ordered the surviving Hurricanes and Buffaloes to retreat to makeshift airfields on the route between Rangoon and Mandalay, the aim being to protect the northwards evacuation of troops once the capital fell. Operating from poor surfaces hacked out of the jungle, several of the Hurricanes were fitted with bamboo skids in place of tailwheels. They had some success in deterring enemy attacks against the retreating troops, but their numbers were too small to prevent the fall of Rangoon. Given the context of continual retreat, claims by the RAF that their fighters destroyed or damaged 483 enemy aircraft in return for just 38 losses, 22 of them Hurricanes, were hardly credible. Soon the last remnants of the Burmese defences had crumbled in the face of the continued Japanese onslaught.

The remaining RAF planes were sent either to Calcutta or Ceylon in India at the beginning of March. Just as the Axis advance in North Africa appeared to threaten Britain's position in the Middle East, so the Japanese capture of Burma seemed to menace India, for so long the jewel in the crown of the British empire. One of the prime fears of British imperial government was that the narrative of Japanese conquest would fan the flames of Indian nationalism, already burning strongly. Only days after the fall of Singapore on 15 February 1942, anti-British rebels, led by the radicalized former army officer Mohan Singh, had formed the Indian National Army with the specific aim of using Japanese power to overthrow the Raj. The sense of crisis was reinforced at the start of April, when the increasingly emboldened part of the Japanese fleet, including three aircraft carriers, headed towards Ceylon.

Yet the prospects for the British were not quite as grim as they first appeared. The Japanese had neither the men nor the equipment to launch a full-scale invasion of India in 1942, for the campaign against the Americans in the Pacific was the main focus of their war, just as Hitler was far more concerned about the Russian front than North Africa. One important consequence of this lack of priority for Burma was a Japanese air force below full strength in the region. In contrast to the disasters of Singapore or Crete, the RAF was to enjoy increasing air superiority during the years of fighting that lay ahead, a vital factor not only in hitting Japanese ground forces but also in maintaining supplies to army units that were under siege in the jungle. The absence of heavy enemy combat forces was particularly beneficial to the Hurricane, since the plane could be used to its fullest extent for strafing and bombing. 'We had very little opposition from fighters,' recalled Owen Parry, who served as a Hurricane pilot in 11 Squadron in Burma during the last two years of the war. 'The RAF was very much in control. The Japanese fighter attacks were sneak raids, really of nuisance value only.'[49] Another pilot who served in the campaign was George Butler of 60 Squadron. 'We never got into dogfights with the Japanese Zeros. We went in with our bombs first, then carried out the rest of the mission and then got back to base as quickly as we could.' Having first flown Bristol Blenheims in 1942, Butler appreciated the move to Hurricanes: 'The Hurricane was able to discharge the same bomb-load as the Blenheim. We had two 250-pound bombs. The Hurricane was marvellous to fly, a lovely aeroplane. I preferred it to the Blenheim. It was more manoeuvrable and could get in and out of problems. You were in total command.'[50]

Fortunately for the RAF, the logistical problems that initially plagued the North African campaign did not arise in the Indian empire, with the result that there was a reliable supply of Hurricanes from the spring of 1942. During that summer they were arriving in India at the rate of 50 a week and by September 1943, Sir Richard Peirse, the Commander of the RAF in south-east Asia, had no fewer than 1,088 Hurricanes, a far greater force than Sir Hugh Dowding had at the start of the Battle of Britain. It would be wrong, however, to overplay the influence of the Hurricane on the Burma campaign, for other aircraft played just as decisive a role, particularly the Spitfire as a fighter and the Dakota as a transport. Indeed, Peirse complained in late 1943 to the Air Ministry that his Hurricanes were outdated and should be replaced by Spitfires. The arrival of the first Supermarine planes 'has had a most decisive effect on our operations', he wrote in a dispatch in November. 'Prior to this the enemy had been able to carry out reconnaissance flights with impunity by flying at great heights and easily outdistancing the Hurricanes which tried to intercept.' Even so, Peirse accepted that Hurricanes were doing 'particularly satisfactory' work in support of the army and had inflicted 'extensive damage' on enemy barges and trains.[51]

The evidence of Peirse's call for Spitfires contradicts the charge made by Paul Richey of 1 Squadron, one of the heroes of the Battle of France, that the RAF in the Far East had rejected the Spitfire on the grounds that the Hurricane was a superior plane for the jungle because of its sturdier undercarriage. Now an operational commander in Burma, Richey had dramatically changed his view of the Hurricane since that first conflict more than three years earlier. 'There is no doubt that the Hurricane is not up to the job and we must have Spitfires,' he wrote in one report. 'The Air Command in India has forfeited the confidence of pilots because it has deliberately shut its eyes to the inferiority of the Hurricane as an interceptor fighter.' He added that the refusal of Peirse to admit this, because of fears about lowering morale, was 'criminally irresponsible'. Richey, although he was wrong about Peirse's attitude, was right in arguing that the Hurricane was outmoded as an interceptor. But such a stance ignored the role that the plane had developed as a ground attacker, which was to be vital in the campaign.[52]

The Hurricanes were present at the start of the fightback against Japan, which began in April 1942 against the enemy aircraft marauding over the Ceylon coast. There were around 50 serviceable Hurricanes on the island, flown by 30 and 261 Squadrons, and though they suffered heavy losses, they mounted an effective challenge to the raiders from the aircraft carriers. On 5 April seven Japanese escorts were shot down and four days later, when 129 aircraft attacked airfields in Ceylon, 15 planes were lost to the British fighters. The Japanese naval commanders saw little benefit in continuing with these raids, and so withdrew to the Pacific where their carriers were needed for the battle against America. Having seen off this threat, the RAF on Ceylon was then restocked with more men and machines. The journalist Alan Moorehead was impressed by the purposeful activity. 'This was no second Singapore. The island was defended far more strongly than I could have believed. There were the increasing Hurricanes of the RAF as well as the Fleet Air Arm,' he wrote. On a visit to the capital Colombo, he watched as 'Hurricane after Hurricane went by until there were thirty or more overhead, and from the sea, two cruisers were entering the harbour. It all looked very healthy.'[53]

The British expected the next Japanese attack to be made against Calcutta in north-eastern India, near the Burmese border where the enemy forces had halted. On Peirse's orders four Hurricane squadrons, including Mark IIBs, were sent to airfields in the area. But the incursion never materialized in the spring, largely because the floods of the monsoon season severely restricted air operations. It was only when drier weather arrived in December 1942 that a few sporadic Japanese bomber raids were mounted, but they were soon abandoned because of the strong fighter opposition they met. It was, in fact, the British who tried to seize the initiative at this time, through two very different thrusts into Burma. The first, overseen by Field Marshal Archibald Wavell, the Commander-in-Chief of the Indian Army, was an orthodox offensive beginning in December 1942 through the Arakan region on the western coast of Burma, with the aim of reoccupying the Mayu peninsula and Akyab island, where there was a large airfield. Six squadrons of Hurricanes, as well as one reconnaissance unit, supported the advance and again demonstrated their effectiveness against land targets by hitting troop columns, bridges, railways and river transport. So deadly were their attacks that, on some parts of the coast road, the Japanese only dared to move under the cover of darkness. The Hurricanes also had their successes against enemy fighters. The Australian Jack Storey of 136 Squadron destroyed three single-engined Oscar fighters over Akyab. Gordon Conway, another 136 Squadron pilot, flying a Mark IIC, accounted for another Oscar while intercepting a Japanese raid against one of the captured airfields. The enemy fighter 'turned on to his tail in front of my flight. I gave this Oscar a long burst of cannon, closing from astern, as he literally fell apart. He seemed to stop in mid-air, his port wheel came down followed by his flaps and with pieces flying off all around, he flicked and spun vertically into the sea, just by the airfield.'[54] But there were casualties too, one of the most horrific of them reported to Alfred Cameron of 28 Squadron at the start of the Arakan offensive. 'We were all keyed up and things were moving at last. Forty-eight hours later the news came through that one of our flight sergeants had been shot down on the very first day. On a dawn patrol, a Japanese Zero had fired a full deflection shot at him and taken his head off. But he had his plane trimmed so that the Hurricane carried on flying and eventually flew into the beach and landed, the pilot in his seat without his head. That shook things up when the news came back. We knew the war was for real.'[55] But like Wavell's advance in the African desert in early 1942, his Arakan offensive failed because of lack of reinforcements on the ground. In May 1943 his army retreated from Burma.

The second British offensive was much more unconventional. This was the 'Chindit' expedition, named after a mythical Burmese beast, in which 3,000 specially trained troops, led by the volatile, charismatic brigadier Orde Wingate, moved deep into Burma in February 1943 to carry out guerrilla-style attacks on Japanese communications. Crucially, they were supplied from the air by Dakotas escorted by Hurricanes, a new development in the British war. Despite the heroics, Wingate's first expedition had achieved few tangible results when it ended in April 1943. Almost a third of his men were lost, while the railway system was out of commission for less than a week. But Wingate's adventure had consequences far beyond its limited physical impact on the enemy. Not only did it raise the morale of the British, as government propaganda sedulously exploited the imagery of Wingate's daredevil heroes, but it also showed that a force could be supplied directly from the air, thereby emphasizing the importance of command of the skies.

For most of the remainder of 1943 the monsoon season prevented further operations. But the British were not inactive. During this time the military command of Asia underwent a radical reorganization. Wavell was elevated to the peerage and made Viceroy of India, his place as British Indian army commander taken by Auchinleck. Earl Mountbatten was appointed to the new position of Supreme Allied Commander South East Asia and the 14th Army was formed under Bill Slim. Once the dry season arrived at the end of the year, the revamped Allies launched another offensive into the Arakan, again with close support from the Hurricanes. But in early 1944 the Japanese counter-attacked with remarkable ferocity, forcing Slim's forces right back inside India to the Imphal valley and Kohima ridge further north. Alan Sammons of 20 Squadron was one of the Hurricane pilots shot down by ground fire during this counter-offensive. 'Our trips usually consisted of searching for camouflaged vehicles and blowing them to pieces,' he recorded in a post-war memoir. On this occasion he was flying near the end of a sortie 'at about 1,000 feet when – Bang – I copped it. A lucky shot from a rifle or machine gun hit the engine coolant pipe-line and I became extremely annoyed as the steam flooded the cockpit and I became very warm indeed, a hot seat in fact. After about five minutes, the poor old engine was just about on its last legs and thumping something horrid. There was so much steam in the cockpit that I couldn't see the instrument panel. I was down to about 400 ft and crossing the Mayu River.' Through his canopy Sammons saw a large mangrove swamp island, 'so I decided to crash-land before the engine caught fire. Making a gliding turn to enable me to see where I was going I crash-landed through the undergrowth, clearing a path as I went. The aircraft slithered along slightly sideways, so that I did not get thrown forward into the reflector sight and injure my face as is usually the case. I wasn't injured but the poor old kite was a wreck; the engine was broken away and was steaming in the swampy water; the wings were torn off and the fuselage was smashed-in except for the cockpit.' Sammons jumped out and waded through the swamp to a clearing. Over the next two days, with nothing to eat but a few glucose sweets and some Horlicks tablets from his emergency pack, he tried to hide from the Japanese but, after coming across a village, was picked up and became a prisoner of war.[56]

With the Allies isolated in their defensive positions at Imphal and Kohima, it looked as though the Japanese might achieve their breakthrough and march on Calcutta. But this time there was to be no retreat. The RAF's air superiority meant the two forces under siege could hold out, while ten Hurricane squadrons based in the Imphal plain constantly harried the Japanese troops. In one action typical of this resistance, Hurricane pilot Arjan Singh, leader of 1 Squadron, was on an early evening reconnaissance patrol when he spotted a Japanese battalion moving towards Imphal. Once he made his report, 33 Hurricanes took off in the dusk and, using their landing lights, picked out the enemy columns. Immediately, they tore down, opening up with their cannons and dropping their bombs on the startled Japanese. It was later found that more than 200 men had been killed in that single attack. Such victories were vital in keeping up the morale of the squadrons, for both the geography and the living conditions made life exceptionally tough during this part of the campaign. Alfred Cameron of 28 Squadron recalled the difficulties of flying out of one of the Imphal strips. 'It was the worst-situated aerodrome I have ever seen in my life. It was a death trap. There were a lot of accidents there. You had to land facing the mountains.' If a pilot overshot on other airfields, the standard procedure on the Hurricane was to open up the throttle and go round again. But there, 'the hills were so close that if you opened up at 100 feet, you had to climb like the blazes to get round. So I never liked Imphal.' The stresses of flying were not helped by the quarters. 'The facilities were rough, very rough. We lived in native huts, on Indian beds. You put the four bed posts in syrup tins cut in half. Into that you pour some kind of oil that stops the bugs getting to you. Then you had mosquito nets. The food was grim. It was bully beef, three times a day, six days a week. That cook should have got a medal for the way he doctored the bully beef to camouflage it. On Sunday we had a "treat" of soyalink sausages.'[57] George Butler of 60 Squadron said that 'the conditions made you feel different to the enemy, living under canvas for almost two years, suffering malaria and dysentery. It was bloody awful.'[58]

But for all the misery they endured, the Hurricane pilots' operations were essential to breaking the Japanese at Kohima and Imphal. During the peak four months of the battle in early 1944, 221 RAF Group, of which the Hurricanes were part, flew 6,000 sorties a month, even when the monsoon was at its peak. The official report into the Allied air operations at Imphal showered praise on the Hawker fighter: 'The tactical reconnaissance Hurricanes searched day by day for enemy movements and positions, delivering attacks as opportunities offered.' The report continued: 'No less valuable was the work of the ground attack Hurricanes, most versatile of aircraft. They performed an indispensable service in the early period of the Japanese offensive by their persistent attacks upon the forward Japanese lines of communication at a time when the enemy was making every effort to bring up his stores and armaments westwards.'[59] The importance of the RAF was acknowledged by Colonel Ichii Sugita of the Japanese army in Burma. 'In the later operations they used vertical tactics and surprise and they had a lot of time to prepare for the attack. The British army had air superiority so it was far easier for them to use air power and change the tactics.'[60] Owen Parry of 11 Squadron said that he always felt confident of victory at Imphal. 'The possibility of defeat never occurred to us. We were being supplied from the air by Dakotas with everything from bombs to food. It seemed that the Japs were not making much progress out of the jungle. We had control of the air. We felt we were really on top of things.'[61]

Kohima and Imphal, from which the Japanese withdrew in May and July 1944 respectively, were the Burmese equivalent of El Alamein. The twin defeats marked the beginning of Japan's collapse across Burma. Racked by disease, short of supplies, her army had lost 55,000 men, compared to 17,000 Allied casualties. Her exhausted troops now stumbled into headlong retreat southwards on the road towards Mandalay and Rangoon. With total air supremacy, the Hurricanes were in their element as ground attackers. 'We were, in effect, the army's short-range artillery, performing two main duties. We had to support the army when they requested strikes and we also had to harass the Jap lines of communication by doing low-level rhubarbs along the roads from the south along which the Japs brought their supplies. We did this at both day and night,' recalled Parry, who flew Hurribombers throughout 1944. Many of the Japanese, he said, were carrying fuel or ammunition. 'It was very gratifying to see the explosions. This was our greatest pleasure, to meet a convoy and really set about it and leave it in ruins at the end of the operation.' Official policy was to leave attacks on tanks to the Hurricane IIDs, specially designed for that job, but Parry discovered that even his Brownings or 20-mm cannon could do real damage:

> We found that we could make fair progress against tanks, not obviously against the cupola or the front armour. But we aimed at the tracks or between the tracks to try and hit the fuel tank and to disable the tracks. We used to use ammo like mixing a cocktail, according to the sort of job we were doing. We could mix up the ordinary ball ammunition, incendiary, high explosive, semi-armour piercing, armour piercing. The Warrant Officer Armourer would attend to our needs very well. We found that if we had a fair amount of armour-piercing and incendiary devices amongst the mixture we could disable the tanks.

Another of Parry's methods, on discovering a convoy, was to drop one bomb at the front to form a crater and prevent the vehicles moving forward. He would drop another bomb at the rear, to create another hole that would block the retreat. Throughout these operations, there was 'a very close relationship' with the army. 'They trusted us with bomb lines which were very, very close to our troops, the bomb line being the point beyond which we were not to strafe or bomb because our troops were likely to be there.' The army, he said, developed the practice of sending the Hurricane squadrons 'strawberries': messages of thanks being the opposite of raspberries. 'It was most heartening to receive a signal after a strike where we had thought that we had done little or no good at all from the army to say that it had been eminently successful. The signal would describe in glowing terms how we had destroyed certain vehicles or killed 200 Japs. This of course was a great booster for morale.'[62]

A graphic description of the carnage caused by the Hurricanes was left by Donald Stones, whose 32 Squadron was instructed to hit an airfield and railway junction south of Mandalay. 'I could sense the rising excitement,' he wrote of the approach to the target. Flying over the aerodrome at just 50 feet, the Hurricanes caught the Japanese by surprise, setting fire to two Oscars in their pens. 'Panic reigned below us as smoke and flames from the burning Oscars added to the enemy's confusion.' Stones as squadron leader ordered a second run, in which the Hurricane formation split and went for individual targets. 'A locomotive was going up in steam and smoke, trucks were knocked over, motor transport and troops were being chased and shot up.' Making a third pass, Stones went for another Oscar in its pen. 'Turning round, I got a good burst of cannon into it and saw it collapse in bits on its belly. It did not burn which made me think it was not fuelled up. I pulled up over the wreck at about 20 feet. My over-exuberance was promptly rewarded by a loud explosion on the port side of my cockpit as the Japanese gunners finally got into the act.' But, as so often before in the war, the Hurricane 'flew perfectly' and Stones made it back to his base.[63]

It is little wonder that Bill Slim called the Hurricane 'our most successful anti-tank weapon'.[64] Hurribombers were equally lethal. During the course of the Burma campaign they dropped five and half million pounds of bombs. But the plane was not just useful in destroying the enemy. The 14th Army, in its move south from Imphal, had to march through the Kabaw Valley, reputedly the most malarial place on earth. The versatile Hurricane had the solution, spraying the whole road through the valley with DDT. As a result casualties from malaria were largely eliminated. The Hurricane also carried a far more deadly cargo in the last months of the war, when it was used to drop napalm on the Japanese lines. The chemical, a form of jellied petrol, had been used by the Americans as early as July 1944 in a raid on a fuel depot on northern France, but the Hurricane was the first RAF plane to carry it. A report from the War Office explained: 'The purpose of napalm is to slow down the vaporization of the gasoline and thereby lengthen the burning time of the fuel. Without a thickener, the gasoline vaporizes so quickly that upon ignition a flash fire occurs that has very little incendiary value. Gasoline thickened with napalm to the proper gel consistency will burn comparatively slowly, generating a great amount of heat and as such becomes an excellent incendiary fuel.' The War Office suggested that targets for napalm could include 'the built-up and congested areas of cities' where the chemical 'will cause extremely large fires to gut most buildings'.[65]

On 21 January 1945 three Hurricanes, flying in line abreast, carried out the first British experiment using napalm, as they dropped the chemical from their long-range tanks on an area of jungle at Kirvatti near Hubli in western India, this area being chosen because it was thought to resemble the Burmese jungle. But the napalm appeared to have little incendiary effect, for the fires 'burned out after a few minutes in the normal fashion'. The experts felt the problem was in the composition of the gel itself. 'It is thought that if the petrol gel mixture had been less viscous and more easily sprayed, there might have been a better chance of success.'[66] The mixture was therefore refined and proved more successful in further trials, leading to its deployment with the Hurricanes in Burma from February 1945. 'The technique used for dropping napalm was no different to that used in dropping bombs. We dropped from about 8,000 feet, sometimes less depending on the weather and the cloud,' recalled George Butler of 60 Squadron.[67] Napalm was not widely used, since in its early form was not as dangerous as other more traditional weapons.

But its combustible shock value could undermine enemy morale, and even the Allied forces were stunned by the sight of its explosions. Army reports noted a tendency 'on the part of troops to watch the exhibition rather than get on with the attack'.[68]

During the last months of the conflict in Burma many of the Hurricanes were replaced by Spitfires or the massive American Thunderbolts. But there were still significant numbers in action. On 19 February Mark IVs from 20 Squadron, armed with 40-mm cannon, tore into a large convoy of Japanese armoured vehicles and tanks west of Myinmu, north west of Mandalay, destroying eleven of them. The local British army commander sent a grateful punning message to the Hurricanes. 'Nippon Hardware Corporation gone bust. Nice work, 20 squadron. Tanks, repeat, tanks.'[69] Flying along-side US Thunderbolts and Mitchell bombers, Hurricanes also played their part in the recapture of Fort Dufferin, a key supply depot and garrison at Mandalay. Operating from nearby airstrips cut in the jungle by the Royal Engineers, Hurribombers blasted holes in the fort's huge earthworks, allowing Allied troops to pour into the compound. Their defences shattered, Japanese troops had to make a desperate escape from the fort through sewers and drains. Retreating southwards, the Japanese continued to fight, but their cause was now doomed. In another spectacular attack on the Pegu Road, north of Rangoon, the Hurricanes of 20 Squadron destroyed 46 vehicles in a single day at the end of April. On 3 May British troops entered Rangoon after a seaborne assault. The war ended in Europe five days later as the Nazi regime surrendered after the collapse of Berlin. Even after the defeat of Germany and the fall of Rangoon, the remnants of the Japanese army continued to put up stiff resistance. Part of its force battled in the low-lying central hills between the Irrawaddy and Sittang rivers until they were overwhelmed by the Allies in late July when they tried to break out from their positions. Another element remained in control of the long, narrow Kra isthmus in the southern-most part of the country, forcing the Allies to contemplate further airborne landings. But the dropping of the atomic bombs on Hiroshima and Nagasaki brought a dramatic halt to the struggle. Isolated and broken, the Japanese accepted the Allies' demand for unconditional surrender on 14 August. Fittingly Sir Keith Park, titan of the Battle of Britain, was the Air Officer Commanding South East Asia at the moment of Japan's final capitulation. And within the huge Allied air fleet he commanded in those last days of the war in Burma were three squadrons of fabric-covered, thick-winged, unconquerable and undaunted Hawker Hurricanes. Sydney Camm's fighter had made it through to the end.

Epilogue

THE HAWKER HURRICANE was the only fighter to serve in every British theatre during the Second World War. But it did not remain long with the RAF once the conflict was over. The arrival of the first combat jet planes, beginning with the Gloster Meteor and the De Havilland Vampire, heralded a new age in military aviation. By the beginning of 1946 there was just one Hurricane squadron still in service. This was 6 Squadron, which had flown with Marshal Tito's partisans in the Balkans in the last months of the war and now carried out army co-operation duties from its base in Palestine. After moving to Cyprus in September 1946, the squadron was re-equipped with Hawker Tempests on 15 January 1947. It was almost twelve years since the Hurricanes had first been delivered to 'Treble One' Squadron at RAF Northolt.

In the immediate post-war years a few Hurricanes continued to fly with air forces abroad. Two squadrons operated on the north-west frontier with the Indian air force until 1947, remaining with training units once they had been withdrawn from the front line. The last such Hurricane, a Canadian-built Mark XII, retired in 1953. Thirteen Hurricane Mark Is and Mark IIs served with the Irish Free State's air force until 1947, while some also flew with the Turkish and Egyptian air forces. Hawker sold 50 Hurricanes, some of them with long-range tanks, to Portugal, which used them in the Defence of Lisbon Fighter Squadron until 1951. A year later a number of these Portuguese Hurricanes returned to England for filming in the movie *Angels One Five*, a British classic starring Jack Hawkins and John Gregson about life on an RAF base during the summer of 1940. Hawker sold another batch to Persia, including a specially converted two-seater Hurricane trainer. Both cockpits on this trainer version, which had been on the

Hawker drawing board since 1940, were left uncovered, with the front position protected just by a windscreen and the rear by a simple transparent fairing. But trials showed that, even at low altitudes, this arrangement was too cold and draughty for the pilots, so a sliding hood, adapted from the Tempest, was installed. With modifications complete, the two-seater, with a top speed of 320 mph, was delivered to Persia in 1947.

The final plane to be built by Hawker, PZ865, was placed on the civil register once it had completed the farewell ceremonies for the Hurricane in its exhibition role as 'The Last of the Many'. With its guns removed, painted dark blue and gold, and given the new civilian serial number of G-AMAU, it flew as a racing aircraft throughout the 1950s before it was restored to military colours in 1960 and returned to Hawker. Based at the company's testing site of Dunsfold in Surrey, PZ865 was regularly used in target-tug trials and even acted as a chase plane for the P1127 Hawker Siddeley jump-jet prototype, the aircraft that was to win worldwide fame as the Harrier. The historian Jarrod Cotter explained why the Hurricane was so well suited to this role: 'The Hurricane's low-speed envelope was found to be ideal for monitoring the P1127 during the transition between conventional flight and jetborne lift.'[1] In a happy link with the Hurricane's past, the veteran fighter also participated in several movies, most notably the 1969 *Battle of Britain* epic, in which it portrayed the aircraft personally flown by Sir Keith Park. Three years later, after a brief spell as a static exhibit in Hawker's unofficial museum at Dunsfold in Surrey, it was presented to the Battle of Britain Memorial Flight. As a much-cherished member of the Flight, PZ865 has remained airworthy ever since, the hum of its Merlin and its sturdy lines delighting crowds wherever it travels.

One other Hurricane joined the Memorial Flight, LF363, which was built in 1944 and served with the last Hurricane unit to operate within Britain, the Polish 309 Squadron based in Scotland. Following a period of neglect immediately after the war, LF363 was restored by the RAF and took part in several high-profile events, including Battle of Britain flypasts, the state funeral of Sir Winston Churchill in 1965 and the ceremony in 1967 for the closure of Fighter Command at Bentley Priory. Like PZ865, the aircraft was also enrolled in the *Battle of Britain* movie, taking the high-profile part of Douglas Bader's Hurricane in 242 Squadron. The plane went on to serve for many years in the Memorial Flight until September 1991, when disaster struck during rehearsals for another Battle of Britain flypast. Squadron Leader Allan Martin described what happened as he flew over RAF Wittering near Peterborough, at 2,500 feet, in formation alongside a Lancaster and Spitfire: 'There was an almighty bang and the engine started running roughly. I tried changes of boost and fuel mixture on the engine to try to restore smooth running and got the best I could, but I was clear I was not going to be able to maintain height.' Martin headed for RAF Wittering to try to put the plane down. Just as he lined up the runway, the engine gave a final cough and the Hurricane stalled. 'The aircraft hit the runway and slid backward down it. I can remember looking down through the Perspex panel in the floor and seeing showers of sparks going down the fuselage. We came to a halt and the cockpit immediately erupted in flames. Fortunately the escape hatch on the starboard side of the Hurricane had fallen off with the initial impact and I just unstrapped and legged it over the side.'[2] Beyond some minor burns and a broken ankle, Martin had suffered no serious injuries. But LF363 was a wreck, the fire having destroyed much of its structure. A subsequent inquiry blamed the incident on engine failure caused by a broken camshaft. But in another, final indicator of the Hurricane's astonishing strength, the aircraft was rebuilt over a period of three years by the Essex company Historic Flying Ltd. Seven years later LF363 was back in the air and remains part of the Battle of Britain Memorial Flight to this day.

Like his famous fighter, Sydney Camm enjoyed an impressive longevity. His energy, fertile mind and driving leadership enabled him to carry on working at Hawker in the decades after the war. During these years he designed not only the Hunter, for a time the fastest jet fighter in the world, but also the Harrier, the pioneering vertical take-off aircraft. Given that Camm had started work as an apprentice at Martin and Handasyde on fabric-covered biplanes during the First World War, it was a record of remarkable ingenuity and vision. During the post-war years he became one of the most distinguished figures in British aviation, was showered with honours, awarded a knighthood in 1953 and made President of the Royal Aeronautical

Society. Amidst all this distinction, there was little sign of his temper mellowing. 'With regard to his own staff, it must be said that he did not suffer fools gladly, and at times most of us appeared to be fools,' said Dr John Fozard, who became Hawker's Chief Designer in 1965.[3] Diligent as ever, Camm was still on the board of Hawker Siddeley when he died suddenly on 12 March 1966 while playing a round of golf near his home at Thames Ditton. He was seventy-two. According to *The Times*, he had been:

> one of the most consistently successful designers the aircraft industry has ever had . . . He had ample reason to be satisfied with the success a lifetime of devotion brought him and it made him forceful and somewhat intolerant of his own conclusions. Over the years these proved so often to be right that Camm came to be accepted in the industry with slightly amused affection as one who was entitled to be eccentric and aggressive, particularly as those characteristics were based on solid convictions, the product of careful thinking and shrewd appraisal.[4]

An eloquent later summary of Camm's work and character was provided by one of his successors as President of the Royal Aeronautical Society, Sir Peter Masefield, who wrote in 1981: 'His sensitive nature, carefully concealed, led him to display a kaleidoscope of attitudes – alike to those who knew him well as to mere acquaintances. He was, successively, modest and arrogant, exasperating and appreciative, deprecating and supercilious, caustic and congratulatory, humorous and severe, enthusiastic and offhand – but always shyly glad of friendship.' Camm, he concluded, was 'a man in whom, as a master of engineering and design, there glowed an "eye for an elegant line" and for sound, simple structures; rarely qualified and never surpassed. From the Hart and Fury to Hurricane, Hunter and Harrier, under the paternal guidance of Sir Thomas Sopwith, Camm saw more of his aircraft in service with the Royal Air Force than most other designers put together.'[5]

Among all Camm's rich achievements, the Hurricane was the most significant. If he had not persisted with his design, the future history of Britain and even of mankind might have been very different. As *Flight* magazine put it in a tribute to the Hurricane towards the end of the war: 'Without detracting in any way from the magnificent courage, skill and endurance of the fighter pilots, the British victory was in some measure due to Hawkers, who produced the aircraft in time and sufficient numbers to enable the pilots to turn the day.'[6] The Hurricane lifted the nation in its hour of peril, a mood captured in this evocative prose from the British propaganda magazine *The War in Pictures*, written at the height of the Battle of Britain: 'Hurtling to meet the enemy at 500 feet a second, power-diving to the attack, at half as fast again, the world-renowned Hurricane fighters spell annihilation to the raider who is unable to flee from them in time. This is the quality of the British machines which have asserted as clear a superiority over German aircraft as British pilots have shown in handling them.'[7] The summer of 1940 was the moment when German invincibility was shattered for the first time, and it was the Hurricane that turned the once distant hope of victory into a triumphant reality.

Notes

INTRODUCTION: 'SHE WAS A DREAM TO FLY

1. Paul Gallico, *The Hurricane Story*.
2. Patrick Bishop, *The Battle of Britain*.
3. Stephen Bungay, *The Most Dangerous Enemy*.
4. Interview with Arthur Hudson, IWM sound archive tape 13923.
5. Mass Observation archive, 3 September 1940.
6. Paul Gallico, *The Hurricane Story*.
7. Wing Commander Tom Neil, *Gun Button to Fire*.
8. Matthew Parker, *The Battle of Britain*.
9. Alexander McKee, *Strike from the Sky*.
10. Peter Townsend, *Duel of Eagles*.
11. Interview with Eustace ('Gus') Holden, IWM sound archive tape 11198.
12. Interview with Graham Leggett, IWM sound archive tape 27075.
13. Interview with Ben Bowring, IWM sound archive tape 12173.
14. Interview with Roland Beamont, IWM sound archive tape 10128.
15. Donald Stones, *Dimsie*.
16. *Picture Post,* 10 August 1940.
17. Wing Commander Tom Neil, *Gun Button to Fire*.
18. Wing Commander Geoffrey Morley-Mower, *Messerschmitt Roulette*.
19. Douglas Bader, *Fight for the Sky*.
20. Dr John W. Fozard, *Sydney Camm and the Hurricane*.
21. Interview with Charlton Haw, IWM sound archive tape 12028.
22. Interview with Eric Brown, IWM sound archive tape 12279.
23. Interview with Dennis David, IWM sound archive tape 10092.
24. Chaz Bowyer, *Hurricane at War*.
25. Dr John W. Fozard, *Sydney Camm and the Hurricane*.
26. 'The Sayings of Sir Sydney Camm', undated memorandum by Harold Tuffen, Hawker archive, Brooklands Museum.

27. Dr John W. Fozard, *Sydney Camm and the Hurricane*.
28. Stephen Darlow, *Five of the Few*.
29. Interview with Beryl Platt, IWM sound archive tape 10698.

CHAPTER 1: 'I'M ONLY INTERESTED IN DESIGNING FIGHTERS'

1. Camm to Deputy Director of Technical Development, 6 January 1934, National Archives AIR 2/605.
2. Director of Contracts to Camm, 9 March 1934, National Archives AIR 2/605.
3. Memo by J. S. Buchanan, Deputy Director of Technical Development, 19 February 1934, National Archives AIR 2/605.
4. Undated Air Ministry memorandum, 1931, National Archives AIR 20/167.
5. Ellington to the Deputy Chief of the Air Staff, 13 July 1933, National Archives AIR 2/2741.
6. John Terraine, *The Right of the Line*.
7. *The Times*, 10 November 1932.
8. Broadcast on the BBC Forces programme, 13 April 1942, quoted in Dr John W. Fozard, *Sydney Camm and the Hurricane*.
9. *Flight* magazine, 20 April 1912.
10. *Flight* magazine, 22 February 1913.
11. *Flight* magazine, 5 April 1913.
12. Broadcast on the BBC Forces programme, 13 April 1942, quoted in Dr John W. Fozard, *Sydney Camm and the Hurricane*.
13. Edward Bishop, *Hurricane*.
14. Interview with Beryl Platt, IWM sound archive tape 10698.
15. Dr John W. Fozard, *Sydney Camm and the Hurricane*.
16. Dr John W. Fozard, *Sydney Camm and the Hurricane*.
17. Interview with Robin Balmer, IWM sound archive tape 17828.
18. *Air International*, May 1979.
19. All quotations from an article entitled 'The Wit and Wisdom of Sydney Camm', newsletter of the Hawker Association, autumn 2005.
20. Newsletter of the Hawker Association, autumn 2006.
21. Memorandum by Salmond, 13 July 1931, National Archives AIR 20/167.
22. Historical note by the Ministry of Aircraft Production on the development of the Hurricane, National Archives AVIA 46/114.

23. Note on F7/30 Design Conference, 27 May 1932, National Archives AVIA 46/114.
24. Broadcast on the BBC Forces programme, 13 April 1942, quoted in Dr John W. Fozard, *Sydney Camm and the Hurricane*.
25. Dr John W. Fozard, *Sydney Camm and the Hurricane*.
26. Dr John W. Fozard, *Sydney Camm and the Hurricane*.
27. Paul Gallico, *The Hurricane Story*.
28. Handwritten note by Dowding, 25 February 1934, National Archives AIR 2/605.
29. Dr John W. Fozard, *Sydney Camm and the Hurricane*.
30. Handwritten note by Captain Liptrot, 27 July 1934.
31. 'The Wit and Wisdom of Sydney Camm', newsletter of the Hawker Association, autumn 2005.
32. Proposal for Interceptor Monoplane, 4 September 1934, National Archives AIR 2/605.
33. Buchanan to Cave-Brown-Cave, 10 September 1934, National Archives AIR 2/605.
34. Cave-Brown-Cave to Buchanan, 13 September 1934, National Archives AIR 2/605.
35. Cave-Brown-Cave to Buchanan, 13 September 1934, National Archives AIR 2/605.
36. 'Factors involved in the conception of the eight-gun fighter', memorandum 6 May 1945, Sorley papers AC/17/19/16/2.
37. Robert Jackson, *Hawker Hurricane*.
38. Paul Gallico, *The Hurricane Story*.
39. Sorley to Ludlow-Hewitt, 5 July 1934, National Archives AIR 2/2471.
40. Brooke-Popham to Ludlow-Hewitt, 1 August 1934, National Archives AIR 2/2471.
41. Note by Pierse, 28 July 1933, National Archives AVIA 8/167.
42. Minutes of Air Staff Conference, 9 August 1934, National Archives AIR 2/2471.
43. Minutes of Mock-up Conference, 10 January 1935, National Archives AIR 8/166.
44. Hawker to F.W.Cowlin, 30 April 1935, National Archives AVIA 8/166.
45. Sorley to Ludlow-Hewitt, 1 May 1935, National Archives AIR 2/2471.
46. Note by Verney, 4 May 1935, National Archives AIR 2/2824.

47. Dr John W. Fozard, *Sydney Camm and the Hurricane*.
48. Joshua Levine, *Forgotten Voices of the Blitz and the Battle for Britain*.
49. Ian Kershaw, *Making Friends with Hitler*.
50. Minutes of the Ministerial Committee on Air Parity, 13 May 1935, National Archives CAB 27/518.
51. Minutes of Cabinet, 17 May 1935, National Archives CAB 27/518.
52. Dr John W. Fozard, *Sydney Camm and the Hurricane*.
53. Minutes of 6th Progress Meeting, 17 September 1935, Swinton papers.
54. Minutes of 11th Progress Meeting 22 October 1935, Swinton papers.
55. Paul Gallico, *The Hurricane Story*.

CHAPTER 2: 'THE FASTEST FIGHTER IN THE WORLD'

1. *Flight* magazine, 4 April 1946.
2. Dr John W. Fozard, *Sydney Camm and the Hurricane*.
3. Edward Bishop, *Hurricane*.
4. Paul Gallico, *The Hurricane Story*.
5. Bernard Clark, Directorate of Technical Development, to Air Ministry, 6 December 1935, National Archives AVIA 8/166.
6. Report by A&AEE on Hawker monoplane, April 1936, National Archives AVIA 18/635.
7. Minutes of the 20th Progress Meeting, 17 December 1935, Swinton papers.
8. *Daily Express*, 6 December 1935.
9. *Flight* magazine, 14 November 1935.
10. *Flight* magazine, 5 December 1935.
11. *Flight* magazine, 12 December 1935.
12. Courtney to R. H. Verney, 31 December 1935, National Archives AIR 2/2822.
13. Verney to Courtney, 2 January 1936, National Archives AIR 2/2822.
14. Dr John W. Fozard, *Sydney Camm and the Hurricane*.
15. Minutes of the 27th Progress Meeting, 6 February 1936, Swinton papers.
16. Minutes of the 27th Progress Meeting, 6 February 1936, Swinton papers.
17. Report by Newall to 28th Progress Meeting, 26 February 1936, Swinton papers.

18. Minutes of the 28th Progress Meeting, 26 February 1936, Swinton papers.

19. Minutes of the 29th Progress Meeting, 28 February 1936, Swinton papers.

20. Minutes of the 29th Progress Meeting, 28 February 1936, Swinton papers.

21. Report by A&AEE on Hawker monoplane, April 1936, National Archives AVIA 18/635.

22. *Flight* magazine, 16 July 1936.

23. Graham Stewart, *Burying Caesar.*

24. Edward Bishop, *Hurricane.*

25. Robert Wright, *Dowding and Fighter Command.*

26. Verney to Dowding, 14 April 1936, National Archives AVIA 10/9.

27. Minutes of the 42nd Progress Meeting, 16 June 1936, Swinton papers.

28. Minutes of the 59th Progress Meeting, 10 November 1936, Swinton papers.

29. Minutes of the 68th Progress Meeting, 2 February 1937, Swinton papers.

30. Newsletter of the Hawker Association, autumn 2005.

31. Minutes of the 72nd Progress Meeting, 2 March 1937, Swinton papers.

32. Interview with Graham Leggett, IWM sound archive tape 27075.

33. Dr John W. Fozard, *Sydney Camm and the Hurricane.*

34. Newsletter of the Hawker Association, summer 2009.

35. Edward Smithies, *Aces, Erks and Backroom Boys.*

36. Interview with Graham Leggett, IWM sound archive tape 27075.

37. *Daily Express*, 23 December 1938.

38. Interview with Graham Leggett, IWM sound archive tape 27075.

39. Minutes of the 42nd Progress Meeting, 16 June 1936, Swinton papers.

40. Memorandum by Frank Cowlin, DTD, 22 June 1936, National Archives AVIA 10/9.

41. Minutes of the 43rd Progress Meeting, 22 June 1936, Swinton papers.

42. Sir Ian Lloyd and Peter Pugh, *Hives and the Merlin.*

43. Dr John W. Fozard, *Sydney Camm and the Hurricane.*

44. Dr John W. Fozard, *Sydney Camm and the Hurricane.*

45. Dr John W. Fozard, *Sydney Camm and the Hurricane.*

46. Minutes of the 100th Progress Meeting, 19 November 1936, Swinton papers.

47. Minutes of the 100th Progress Meeting, 19 November 1936, Swinton papers.
48. Dr John W. Fozard, *Sydney Camm and the Hurricane*.
49. Chaz Bowyer, *Hurricane at War*.
50. Interview with Ronald Brown, IWM sound archive tape 12404.
51. *The Times*, 11 January 1938.
52. Interview with Ronald Brown, IWM sound archive tape 12404.

CHAPTER 3: 'THIS THUNDERING GREAT MONSTER'

1. *Flight* magazine, 9 September 1938.
2. *Daily Mail,* 11 February 1938.
3. Interview with J. W. Gillan, *Daily Mirror*, 6 October 1938.
4. *Daily Mirror*, 11 February 1938.
5. *Daily Mail*, 11 February 1938.
6. *The Times*, 4 May 1938.
7. *Flight* magazine, 10 March 1938.
8. Report by J. W. Gillan, 14 January 1938, National Archives AVIA 10/19.
9. Report by J. W. Gillan, 21 February 1938, National Archives AVIA 10/19.
10. Verney to Directorate of Research and Development, 26 March 1938, AVIA 10/19.
11. John Dibbs and Tony Holmes, *Hurricane: A Fighter Legend*.
12. Interview with Douglas Grice, IWM sound archive tape 10897.
13. Larry Forrester, *Fly For Your Life*.
14. Interview with Dickie Martin, IWM sound archive tape 11906.
15. Peter Townsend, *Duel of Eagles*.
16. Robert Jackson, *Hawker Hurricane*.
17. Interview with Peter Down, IWM sound archive tape 11449.
18. Interview with Roland Beamont, IWM sound archive tape 10128.
19. Minutes of the Cabinet, 7 November 1938, National Archives AIR 8/250.
20. Entry on 1st Baron Newall, *Oxford Dictionary of National Biography*, by Vincent Orange.
21. Memorandum by Inskip, 9 December 1937, National Archives AIR 8/226.
22. Newall to Inskip, 11 December 1937, National Archives AIR 8/226.

23. Leo McKinstry, *Spitfire*.
24. Air Ministry note, 26 April 1938, National Archives AVIA 46/114.
25. Hansard, 10 May 1938.
26. *Daily Express*, 13 May 1938.
27. Air Ministry memorandum, September 1938, National Archives AIR 75/2.
28. Bruce-Gardener to Mrs Anne Chamberlain, 1954, Chamberlain papers NC11/12/1.
29. Spriggs to Freeman, 26 September 1938, National Archives AVIA 10/19.
30. Freeman to Spriggs, 29 September 1938, National Archives AVIA 10/19.
31. Spriggs to Freeman, 30 September 1938, National Archives AVIA 10/19.
32. Freeman to Fisher, 30 September 1938, National Archives AVIA 10/19.
33. Vincent Orange, *Dowding of Fighter Command*.
34. Peter Townsend, *Duel of Eagles*.
35. Peter Townsend, *Duel of Eagles*.
36. Clark to Air Ministry, 29 January 1936, National Archives AVIA 8/166.
37. Minutes of meeting at Directorate of Technical Development, 21 February 1936, National Archives AVIA 8/166.
38. Minutes of 38th Progress Meeting, 5 May 1936, Swinton papers.
39. Note by Frank Cowlin, 19 March 1936, National Archives AVIA 8/166.
40. Progress minute by Air Ministry, 12 October 1936, National Archives AVIA 46/114.
41. Minute by Sir Ernest Lemon, 5 September 1938, National Archives AVIA 46/114.
42. Tedder to Frank Spriggs, 1 November 1938, National Archives AVIA 10/19.
43. Directorate of Technical Development note, 5 July 1938, National Archives AIR 2/2822.
44. Douglas to Robert Saundby, Deputy Director of Operational Requirements, 20 July 1938, National Archives AIR 2/2822.
45. 'Pitch Panic', *Flight* magazine, 9 December 1943.
46. L. F. E. Coombes, *The Lion Has Wings*.
47. Report by Mechanical Test Department, 23 November 1938, National Archives AIR 2/3353.

48. Francis K. Mason, *The Hawker Hurricane*.
49. *Daily Mirror*, 6 May 1939.
50. *The Times*, 2 February 1939.
51. Interview with Charlton Haw, IWM sound archive tape 12028.
52. Interview with Harold Bird-Wilson, IWM sound archive tape 10093.

CHAPTER 4: 'REAL WAR AT LAST'

1. Quote from Eric Clayton, from *Fighter Boys* by Patrick Bishop.
2. Bob Cossey, *A Tiger's Tale*.
3. Bob Cossey, *A Tiger's Tale*.
4. Andrew Roberts, *The Holy Fox*.
5. Interview with Douglas Grice, IWM sound archive tape 10897.
6. Interview with Harold Bird-Wilson, IWM sound archive tape 10093.
7. Interview with Eustace ('Gus') Holden, IWM sound archive tape 11198.
8. Peter Townsend, *Duel of Eagles*.
9. Peter Townsend, *Duel of Eagles*.
10. Interview with Charlton Haw, IWM sound archive tape 12028.
11. Interview with Hugh Ironside, IWM sound archive tape 13101.
12. Paul Richey, *Fighter Pilot*.
13. Interview with Dickie Martin, IWM sound archive tape 13114.
14. Interview with Dickie Martin, IWM sound archive tape 11906.
15. Roland Beamont, *My Part of the Sky*.
16. Paul Richey, *Fighter Pilot*.
17. Interview with Dickie Martin, IWM sound archive tape 11906.
18. Adrian Stewart, *They Flew Hurricanes*.
19. Interview with Peter Matthews, IWM sound archive tape 10451.
20. Interview with Maurice Leng, IWM sound archive tape 12217.
21. Paul Richey, *Fighter Pilot*.
22. Roland Beamont, *My Part of the Sky*.
23. Donald Stones, *Dimsie*.
24. Interview with Kenneth Cross, IWM sound archive tape 10481.
25. Interview with Kenneth Cross, IWM sound archive tape 10481.
26. Interview with Richard Earp, IWM sound archive 11772.
27. Interview with Richard Earp, IWM sound archive 11772.
28. Adrian Stewart, *Hurricane*.
29. Interview with Kenneth Cross, IWM sound archive tape 10481.

30. Roland Beamont, *My Part of the Sky.*
31. Donald Stones, *Dimsie.*
32. Patrick Bishop, *Fighter Boys.*
33. Stephen Darlow, *Five of the Few.*
34. Stephen Darlow, *Five of the Few.*
35. Letter by Squadron Leader T. G. Pace, 2 November 1940, IWM archive 01/35/1.
36. Interview with Group Captain Dennis David, IWM sound archive tape 10092.
37. Interview with Peter Down, IWM sound archive tape 11449.
38. Brian Cull, Bruce Lander and Heinrich Weiss, *Twelve Days in May.*
39. Interview with Norman Hancock, IWM sound archive tape 10119.
40. Adolf Galland, *The First and the Last.*
41. Brian Cull, Bruce Lander and Heinrich Weiss, *Twelve Days in May.*
42. Letter by Squadron Leader T. G. Pace, 2 November 1940, IWM archive 01/35/1.
43. Peter Townsend, *Duel of Eagles.*
44. Roy Jenkins, *Churchill.*
45. Peter Townsend, *Duel of Eagles.*
46. Minutes of War Cabinet, 16 May 1940, National Archives CAB 65/7/21.
47. Minutes of War Cabinet, 16 May 1940, National Archives CAB 65/7/21.
48. Brian Cull, Bruce Lander and Heinrich Weiss, *Twelve Days in May.*
49. Vincent Orange, *Dowding.*
50. Minutes of War Cabinet, 17 May 1940, National Archives CAB 65/7/21.
51. Minutes of War Cabinet, 17 May 1940, National Archives CAB 65/7/21.
52. Minutes of War Cabinet, 17 May 1940, National Archives CAB 65/7/21.
53. Interview with Gerald Edge, IWM sound archive tape 12674.
54. Interview with Fred Rosier, IWM sound archive tape 10157.
55. Interview with Pete Brothers, IWM sound archive tape 10218.
56. Interview with Pete Brothers, IWM sound archive tape 10218.
57. Interview with Harold Bird-Wilson, IWM sound archive tape 10093.
58. Interview with Fred Rosier, IWM sound archive tape 10157.
59. Interview with Brian Young, IWM sound archive tape 6803.
60. Robert Jackson, *Hurricane.*

61. Brian Cull, Bruce Lander and Heinrich Weiss, *Twelve Days in May*.
62. Brian Cull, Bruce Lander and Heinrich Weiss, *Twelve Days in May*.
63. Paul Richey, *Fighter Pilot*.

CHAPTER 5: 'A MAD STRUGGLE FOR SURVIVAL'

1. Interview with Fred Rosier, IWM sound archive tape 10157.
2. Robert Wright, *Dowding and Fighter Command*.
3. Vincent Orange, *Dowding*.
4. Interview with Hugh Ironside, IWM sound archive tape 13101.
5. Vincent Orange, *Dowding*.
6. Interview with Christopher Foxley-Norris, IWM sound archive tape 10136.
7. Ray Holmes, *Sky Spy*.
8. Matthew Parker, *The Battle of Britain*.
9. Interview with George Johns, IWM sound archive tape 11616.
10. Paul Richey, *Fighter Pilot*.
11. Paul Richey, *Fighter Pilot*.
12. Minutes of meeting at Hawker, 21 July 1938, National Archives AIR 2/3353.
13. Note by Operational Requirements Directorate, 2 June 1939, National Archives AIR 2/3353.
14. Report by H. V. Rowley, Operational Requirements Directorate, 29 August 1939, National Archives AIR 2/3353.
15. W. S. Douglas to Operational Requirements Directorate, 25 September 1939, National Archives AIR 2/3353.
16. Note by Directorate of Technical Development to Hawker, 20 October 1939, National Archives AIR 2/3353.
17. Stephen Bungay, *The Most Dangerous Enemy*.
18. Tom Neil, *Gun Button to Fire*.
19. Alex Kershaw, *The Few*.
20. Tom Neil, *Gun Button to Fire*.
21. Wing Commander Geoffrey Morley-Mower, *Messerschmitt Roulette*.
22. Paul Richey, *Fighter Pilot*.
23. Steve Darlow, *Five of the Few*.
24. Donald Stones, *Dimsie*.
25. Steve Darlow, *Five of the Few*.
26. Steve Darlow, *Five of the Few*.

27. Ray Holmes, *Sky Spy*.
28. Patrick Bishop, *Fighter Boys*.
29. Steve Darlow, *Five of the Few*.
30. Kenneth McGlashlan, *Down to Earth*.
31. Douglas Bader, *Fight for the Sky*.
32. Patrick Bishop, *The Battle of Britain*.
33. Adrian Stewart, *Hurricane*.
34. Interview with Wing Commander Richard Mitchell, IWM sound archive tape 11364.
35. Interview with George Johns, IWM sound archive tape 11616.
36. Norman Franks, *The Air Battle for Dunkirk*.
37. Interview with Geoffrey Page, IWM sound archive tape 11103.
38. Interview with Harold Bird-Wilson, IWM sound archive tape 10093.
39. Alex Kershaw, *The Few*.
40. Peter Townsend, *Duel of Eagles*.
41. Statistics from Norman Franks, *The Air Battle for Dunkirk*.
42. Ulrich Steinhilper, *Spitfire on My Tail*.
43. Norman Franks, *The Air Battle for Dunkirk*.
44. Interview with Geoffrey Page, IWM sound archive tape 11103.
45. Adolf Galland, *The First and the Last*.
46. The words of Ian Nethercott, quoted in Phil Craig and Tim Clayton, *Finest Hour*.
47. Joshua Levine, *Forgotten Voices of the Blitz and the Battle of Britain*.
48. Interview with Harold Bird-Wilson, IWM sound archive tape 10093.
49. Interview with Douglas Grice, IWM sound archive tape 10897.
50. Tom Neil, *Gun Button to Fire*.
51. Winston Churchill to the House of Commons, 4 June 1940.
52. Winston Churchill to the House of Commons, 4 June 1940.
53. Tim Clayton and Phil Craig, *Finest Hour*.
54. Interview with Eustace ('Gus') Holden, IWM sound archive tape 11198.
55. Interview with Norman Hancock, IWM sound archive tape 10119.
56. Interview with Eustace ('Gus') Holden, IWM sound archive tape 11198.
57. Interview with Dennis David, IWM sound archive tape 10092.
58. Basil Collier, *Leader of the Few*.
59. Jonathan Fenby, *The Sinking of the Lancastria*.
60. Interview with Norman Hancock, IWM sound archive tape 10119.
61. Winston Churchill to the House of Commons, 18 June 1940.

CHAPTER 6: 'OUR AIR FORCE IS SUBLIME'

1. Derek Robinson, *Invasion 1940*.
2. Martin Davidson and James Taylor, *Spitfire Ace*.
3. Stephen Bungay, *The Most Dangerous Enemy*.
4. Peter Townsend, *Duel of Eagles*.
5. Peter Townsend, *Duel of Eagles*.
6. Report of the Luftwaffe High Command, Section 1c, 16 July 1940, Militärarchiv–Bundesarchiv Freiburg RL2II/935.
7. Alex Kershaw, *The Few*.
8. Alexander McKee, *Strike from the Sky*.
9. Peter Townsend, *Duel of Eagles*.
10. Paul Gallico, *The Hurricane Story*.
11. The full story of this extraordinary scandal is told in Leo McKinstry, *Spitfire*.
12. L. F. E. Coombes, *The Lion has Wings*.
13. Douglas Bader, *Fight for the Sky*.
14. Interview with Eric Davis, IWM sound archive tape 13928.
15. Interview with Roger Wilkinson, IWM sound archive tape 10216.
16. Joshua Levine, *Forgotten Voices of the Battle of Britain and the Blitz*.
17. Edward Smithies, *Aircrafts, Erks and Backroom Boys*.
18. Interview with James Goodson, IWM sound archive tape 11623.
29. Stephen Darlow, *Five of the Few*.
20. Donald Stones, *Dimsie*.
21. Interview with Christopher Foxley-Norris, IWM sound archive tape 10136.
22. Ray Holmes, *Sky Spy*.
23. Interview with Ben Bowring, IWM sound archive tape 12173.
24. Paul Gallico, *The Hurricane Story*.
25. Paul Gallico, *The Hurricane Story*.
26. Matthew Parker, *The Battle of Britain*.
27. Tom Neil, *Gun Button to Fire*.
28. Interview with Dennis David, IWM sound archive tape 10092.
29. Interview with Jeffrey Quill, IWM sound archive tape 106874.
30. Matthew Parker, *The Battle of Britain*.
31. Interview with Eric Brown, IWM sound archive tape 12279.
32. Report to AASF Headquarters, 2 May 1940, Mike Williams archives.
33. Patrick Bishop, *Fighter Boys*.
34. Patrick Bishop, *The Battle of Britain*.

35. Patrick Bishop, *Fighter Boys*.
36. Interview with Ronald Brown, IWM sound archive tape 12404.
37. Alexander McKee, *Strike from the Sky*.
38. Interview with Geoffrey Page, IWM sound archive tape 11103.
39. Patrick Bishop, *The Battle of Britain*.
40. Interview with Douglas Grice, IWM sound archive tape 10897.
41. Peter Townsend, *Duel of Eagles*.
42. Dilip Sarkar, *The Few*.
43. John Ray, *The Battle of Britain*.
44. Tim Clayton and Phil Craig, *Finest Hour*.
45. Peter Townsend, *Duel of Eagles*.
46. Patrick Bishop, *The Battle of Britain*.
47. Derek Robinson, *Invasion 1940*.
48. Richard Overy, *The Battle of Britain*.
49. Battle of Britain Historical Society, *Chronology of the Battle*.
50. Battle of Britain Historical Society, *Chronology of the Battle*.
51. Battle of Britain Historical Society, *Chronology of the Battle*.
52. Peter Townsend, *Duel of Eagles*.
53. Malcolm Brown, *Spitfire Summer*.
54. Matthew Parker, *The Battle of Britain*.
55. Robert Rhodes James, *Chips: The Diaries of Sir Henry Channon*.
56. Patrick Bishop, *The Battle of Britain*.
57. John Colville, *Fringes of Power*.
58. Diary entry 14 August 1940, 5039.3, Mass Observation archives.
59. Patrick Bishop, *The Battle of Britain*.
60. Interview with Roland Beamont, IWM sound archive tape 10128.
61. Interview with Douglas Grice, IWM sound archive tape 10897.
62. Alexander McKee, *Strike from the Sky*
63. Stephen Bungay, *The Most Dangerous Enemy*.
64. *The Times*, 16 August 1940.
65. Francis Mason, *The Hawker Hurricane*.

CHAPTER 7: 'THE SKY SEEMED FULL OF HURRICANES'

1. Malcolm Brown, *Spitfire Summer*.
2. Interview with Harold Bird-Wilson, IWM sound archive tape 10093.
3. Interview with Dennis David, IWM sound archive tape 10092.
4. Interview with Gerald Edge, IWM sound archive tape 12674.

5. Interview with Teddy Donaldson, IWM sound archive tape 12172.
6. Interview with Pete Brothers, IWM sound archive tape 10218.
7. Interview with James Goodson, IWM sound archive tape 11623.
8. Interview with Roland Beamont, IWM sound archive tape 10128.
9. Stephen Bungay, *The Most Dangerous Enemy*.
10. Entry in *Oxford Dictionary of National Biography*.
11. Robert Ebert, *Chicago Sun-Times*, 30 June 1968.
12. Entry in *Oxford Dictionary of National Biography*.
13. Michael Burns, *Bader: The Man and His Men*.
14. John Frayn Turner, *The Bader Wing*.
15. Douglas Bader, *Fight for the Sky*.
16. Interview with Ben Bowring, IWM sound archive tape 12173.
17. Martin Davidson and James Taylor, *Spitfire Ace*.
18. Chaz Bowyer, *Hurricane at War*.
19. *London Gazette*, 15 November 1940.
20. Dilip Sarkar, *The Few*.
21. Stephen Bungay, *The Most Dangerous Enemy*.
22. Stephen Bungay, *The Most Dangerous Enemy*.
23. Alex Kershaw, *The Few*.
24. Interview with Pete Brothers, IWM sound archive tape 10218.
25. Interview with Peter Matthews, IWM sound archive tape 10451.
26. Interview with Brian Considine, IWM sound archive tape 10961.
27. Ray Holmes, *Sky Spy*.
28. Interview with Harold Bird-Wilson, IWM sound archive tape 10093.
29. Ray Holmes, *Sky Spy*.
30. John Dibbs and Tony Holmes, *Hurricane: A Fighter Legend*.
31. Interview with Graham Leggett, IWM sound archive tape 27075.
32. Interview with Francis Twitchett, IWM sound archive tape 12047.
33. Kenneth McGlashan, *Down to Earth*.
34. Ray Holmes, *Sky Spy*.
35. John Dibbs and Tony Holmes, *Hurricane: A Fighter Legend*.
36. John Dibbs and Tony Holmes, *Hurricane: A Fighter Legend*.
37. Dowding to Group commanders, 1 August 1940, Dowding papers AC71/17.
38. Nick Thomas, *RAF Top Gun*.
39. Interview with Ray Holmes, IWM sound archive tape 2807.
40. Interview with Peter Down, IWM sound archive tape 11449.
41. Stephen Darlow, *Five of the Few*.

42. Dowding to Group commanders, 1 August 1940, Dowding papers AC71/17.
43. Tom Neil, *Gun Button to Fire*.
44. Tom Neil, *Gun Button to Fire*.
45. Interview with Irving Smith, IWM sound archive tape 11754.
46. Tom Neil, *Gun Button to Fire*.
47. Interview with Alec Ingle, IWM sound archive tape 11338.
48. Interview with Alec Ingle, IWM sound archive tape 11338.
49. Interview with Geoffrey Page, IWM sound archive tape 11103.
50. Paul Richey, *Fighter Pilot*.
51. Robert Jackson, *Hawker Hurricane*.
52. Interview with Arthur Hudson, IWM sound archive tape 13923.
53. Chaz Bowyer, *Hurricane at War*.
54. Steve Darlow, *Five of the Few*.
55. Derek Wood and Derek Dempster, *The Narrow Margin*.
56. Stephen Bungay, *The Battle of Britain*.
57. Dilip Sarker, *The Few*.
58. Patrick Bishop, *The Battle of Britain*.
59. Letter by K. C. Grundy to 'Lovebugs', 27 August 1940, IWM archive 97/12/1.
60. Peter Townsend, *Duel of Eagles*.
61. Interview with Tom Gleave, IWM sound archive tape 10084.
62. *Daily Mail*, 6 April 2009.
63. Matthew Parker, *The Battle of Britain*.
64. Interview with Gus Holden, IWM sound archive tape 11198.
65. Patrick Bishop, *The Battle of Britain*.
66. *Daily Telegraph*, 15 September 1965.
67. Donald Stones, *Dimsie*.
68. Patrick Bishop, *The Battle of Britain*.
69. Interview with Jeffrey Quill, IWM sound archive tape 10687.
70. Tom Neil, *Gun Button to Fire*.
71. Stephen Bungay, *The Most Dangerous Enemy*.
72. Stephen Bungay, *The Most Dangerous Enemy*.
73. Derek Wood and Derek Dempster, *The Narrow Margin*.
74. Peter Townsend, *Duel of Eagles*.
75. Dilip Sarker, *The Few*.
76. Bob Foster, *Tally Ho*.
77. Report on Wing Patrol, 7 September, Leigh-Mallory papers, AC 7124/4/4.

78. Donald Stones, *Dimsie.*
79. Malcolm Brown, *Spitfire Summer.*
80. Peter Stahl, *The Diving Eagle.*
81. Len Deighton, *The Battle of Britain.*
82. Interview with Richard Mitchell, IWM sound archive tape 11364.
83. Interview with Norman Hancock, IWM sound archive tape 10119.
84. Derek Wood and Derek Dempster, *The Narrow Margin.*
85. Patrick Bishop, *The Battle of Britain.*
86. Report on Wing Patrol, 15 September, Leigh-Mallory papers, AC 7124/4/4.
87. Peter Townsend, *Duel of Eagles.*
88. *Sunday Express,* 7 September 1980.
89. *Sunday Express,* 7 September 1980.
90. Patrick Bishop, *The Battle of Britain.*
91. Tom Neil, *Gun Button to Fire.*
92. *News Chronicle,* 16 September 1940.
93. *Daily Express,* 16 September 1940.
94. Peter Townsend, *Duel of Eagles.*
95. Stephen Bungay, *The Most Dangerous Enemy.*
96. John Colville, *The Fringes of Power.*

CHAPTER 8: 'THE WORLD'S GREATEST FIGHTER REVITALIZED'

1. John Terraine, *The Right of the Line.*
2. Matthew Parker, *The Battle of Britain.*
3. Stephen Darlow, *Five of the Few.*
4. Derek Wood and Derek Dempster, *The Narrow Margin.*
5. Winston G. Ramsay, *The Battle of Britain Then and Now.*
6. Patrick Bishop, *The Battle of Britain.*
7. Peter Townsend, *Duel of Eagles.*
8. John Alcorn, 'Battle of Britain Top Guns', *Aeroplane Monthly,* September 1996.
9. Stephen Bungay, *The Most Dangerous Enemy.*
10. 'The Hawker Hurricane', *Aeroplane,* 6 September 1940.
11. 'A Hurricane in the Hand', *Aeroplane,* 6 September 1940.
12. 'This is the Spitfire', *Flight,* 26 September 1940.
13. Edward Bishop, *Hurricane.*

14. Andrew Roberts, *The Storm of War*.
15. Report by J. W. Gillan, 14 January 1938, National Archives AVIA 10/19.
16. Interview with Graham Leggett, IWM sound archive tape 27075.
17. Interview with Dennis David, IWM sound archive tape 10092.
18. Roland Beamont, *My Part in the Sky*.
19. Douglas Bader, *Fight for the Sky*.
20. Vincent Orange, *Dowding*.
21. Peter Flint, *Dowding and the Headquarters of Fighter Command*.
22. Report by Dowding, 20 October 1940, Dowding papers AC71/17/26.
23. Peter Flint, *Dowding and the Headquarters of Fighter Command*.
24. Note by Sinclair of meeting with Dowding, 13 November 1940, Beaverbrook papers BBK/D/21.
25. Vincent Orange, *Dowding*.
26. Kenneth McGlashan, *Down to Earth*.
27. Interview with Gerald Edge, IWM sound archive tape 12674.
28. Kenneth McGlashan, *Down to Earth*.
29. Interview with Irving Smith, IWM sound archive tape 11754.
30. Interview with John Wray, IWM sound archive tape 12371.
31. Johnnie Johnson, *Wing Leader*.
32. Donald Stones, *Dimsie*.
33. Ray Holmes, *Sky Spy*.
34. Interview with Cyril Brown, IWM sound archive tape 12524.
35. Stephen Darlow, *Five of the Few*.
36. Kenneth McGlashan, *Down to Earth*.
37. Minutes of Air Ministry meeting, 7 February 1940, National Archives AVIA 46/114.
38. Letter by N. E. Rowe to the Director General of Production, 24 May 1940, National Archives AIR 2/2822.
39. Sinclair to Beaverbrook, 29 August 1940, National Archives AVIA 10/233.
40. Bob Foster, *Tally Ho*.
41. Tom Neil, *Onward to Malta*.
42. Dr John Fozard, *Sydney Camm and the Hurricane*.
43. Patrick Bishop, *The Battle of Britain*.
44. Minutes of Air Ministry meeting, 29 May 1940, National Archives AVIA 46/114.
45. Camm to Patrick Hennessy, MAP, 12 February 1941, National Archives AVIA 10/234.

46. Sholto Douglas to Beaverbrook, 30 January 1941, Beaverbrook papers D/29.
47. Beaverbrook to Douglas, 31 January 1941, Beaverbrook papers D/29.
48. 'The Hawker Hurricane II', *Aeroplane*, 3 October 1941.
49. Beaverbrook to War Cabinet, 27 October 1940, Beaverbrook papers D/34.
50. Interview with the author.
51. Interview with the author.
52. Interview with the author.
53. Inquiry into Hawker Working Hours, February 1942, National Archives LAB 14/301.
54. Robert Jackson, *Hawker Hurricane*.
55. Interview with Beryl Platt, IWM sound archive tape 10698.
56. Interview with Bill Humble, IWM sound archive tape 12876.
57. Interview with Peter Garrod, IWM sound archive tape 9944.
58. Interview with Margaret Gore, IWM sound archive tape 9285.
59. Minutes of meeting at Hawker, 3 February 1941, National Archives AVIA 15/881.
60. Portal to Churchill, 2 May 1941, Portal papers, Folder 3/2/24a.
61. Maurice Allward, *Hurricane Special*.
62. Dr John Pimlott, *Luftwaffe*.
63. Report by H. Grinsted, 24 December 1940, National Archives AIR 2/2823.
64. N. E. Rowe to Directorate of Operational Requirements, 31 December 1940, National Archives AIR 2/2823.
65. Note by DOR, 10 March 1941, National Archives 10/234.
66. Adrian Stewart, *Hurricane*.
67. 'Catafighters of the Merchant Navy', *Evening Standard*, 26 November 1942.
68. Interview with Neil Hulse, IWM sound archive tape 15332.
69. Diary of Captain W. L. Cruickshank, 25 May 1942, IWM archive 5145 96/21/1.
70. Interview with Sammy Mearns, IWM sound archive tape 11088.

CHAPTER 9: 'IN EVERY CORNER OF THE GLOBE'

1. Max Hastings, *Finest Hour*.
2. Tedder to Portal, 21 March 1942, Portal papers, Folder 3/1/35.

3. Norman Rose, *Churchill: An Unruly Life*.

4. James Holland, *Fortress Malta*.

5. Tom Neil, *Onward to Malta*.

6. Report by N. E. Rowe, Air Ministry, 8 February 1939, National Archives AVIA 10/19.

7. Note of Air Ministry meeting, 6 December 1939, National Archives AVIA 46/114.

8. Report from Middle East Command, 29 March 1940, National Archives AIR 2/2822.

9. James Holland, *Fortress Malta*.

10. Adrian Stewart, *They Flew Hurricanes*.

11. Brian Cull and Frederick Galea, *Hurricanes over Malta*.

12. Brian Cull and Frederick Galea, *Hurricanes over Malta*.

13. Report of Board of Enquiry, Naval Staff Division, 14 December 1940, National Archives AIR 2/2822.

14. Tedder to Portal, 19 December 1940, Portal papers 1/1/38b.

15. 'With the RAF in the Middle East' by Sir Arthur Longmore, *Flight*, 21 May 1942.

16. Interview with Maurice Leng, IWM sound archive tape 12217.

17. Interview with Sam Fletcher, IWM sound archive tape 12557.

18. Steve Darlow, *Five of the Few*.

19. Alan Moorehead, *The Desert War*.

20. Richard Townshend Bickers, *The Desert Air War 1939–1945*.

21. James Ambrose Brown, *The War of a Hundred Days*.

22. Minute by Churchill, 6 January 1941, Portal papers, Folder 2/1/9a.

23. Adrian Stewart, *They Flew Hurricanes*.

24. Roald Dahl, *Going Solo*.

25. Roald Dahl, *Going Solo*.

26. Adrian Stewart, *Hurricane*.

27. 'The Campaign in Crete', National Archives Air 41/29.

28. Interview with Dickie Martin, IWM sound archive tape 11906.

29. Interview with Richard Mitchell, IWM sound archive tape 11364.

30. Interview with Maurice Leng, IWM sound archive tape 12217.

31. Churchill to Portal, 22 February 1941, Portal papers, Folder 2/1/31.

32. Churchill to Longmore, 23 March 1941, Portal papers, Folder 2/1/46.

33. Churchill to Portal, 5 April 1941, Portal papers, Folder 2/2/4a.

34. Interview with Dickie Martin, IWM sound archive tape 11906.

35. Frank Harrison, *Tobruk*.

36. Brian Cull and Frederick Galea, *Hurricanes over Malta*.

37. Brian Cull and Frederick Galea, *Hurricanes over Malta*.

38. Tom Neil, *Onward to Malta*.

39. Interview with Graham Leggett, IWM sound archive tape 27075.

40. Ford to Longmore, 15 May 1941, Portal papers, Folder 2/2/30.

41. Churchill to Portal, 16 May 1941, Portal papers, Folder 2/2/30a.

42. James Holland, *Fortress Malta*.

43. Douglas to Portal, 1 October 1941, Portal papers, Folder 7/2/29.

44. Portal to Douglas, 5 October 1941, Portal papers, Folder 7/2/29a.

45. Douglas Bader, *Fight For the Sky*.

46. Interview with Denys Gillam, IWM sound archive tape 10049.

47. Interview with Denys Gillam, IWM sound archive tape 10049.

48. Douglas Bader, *Fight For the Sky*.

49. 'Call to Salute the Height of Courage', *Scotsman*, 5 May 2009.

50. Interview with Ben Bowring, IWM sound archive tape 12173.

51. 'Hurricanes in Russia' by L. A. Jacketts, *Royal Air Force Quarterly*, Autumn 1971.

52. Churchill to Stalin, 25 August 1941, Churchill papers CHAR 20/42A.

53. Ray Holmes, *Sky Spy*.

54. Ray Holmes, *Sky Spy*.

55. Interview with Charlton Haw, IWM sound archive tape 12028.

56. Interview with Charlton Haw, IWM sound archive tape 12028.

57. Interview with Charlton Haw, IWM sound archive tape 12028.

58. Diary of Basil Rigby, 12 September 1941, IWM archive 92/29/1.

59. Robert Jackson, *Hawker Hurricane*.

60. Interview with Charlton Haw, IWM sound archive tape 12028.

61. Interview with Charlton Haw, IWM sound archive tape 12028.

62. Ray Holmes, *Sky Spy*.

63. Diary of Basil Rigby, 20 October, IWM archive 92/29/1.

64. Diary of Basil Rigby, 13 November, IWM archive 92/29/1.

65. Ray Holmes, *Sky Spy*.

66. Churchill to Portal, 24 October 1941, Portal papers, Folder 2/4/12.

67. Portal to Churchill, 24 October 1941, Portal papers, Folder 2/4/12a.

68. Churchill to Portal, 26 October 1941, Portal papers, Folder 2/4/12c.

69. Churchill to Portal, 1 November 1941, Portal papers, Folder 2/4/12d.

70. Maurice Allward, *Hurricane Special*.

71. Hilliar to the Air Ministry, 6 January 1942, RAF Museum B1147.

72. Hilliar to the Air Ministry, 13 January 1942, RAF Museum B1147.

73. Minutes of British-Soviet Liaison Committee, 10 February 1942, RAF Museum B1147.

74. Minute by Sir Anthony Eden, 5 January 1943, National Archives FO 954/3B.
75. Memoir of Colonel Kaberov, IWM archive 96/58/1.
76. Memoir of Colonel Kaberov, IWM archive 96/58/1.
77. Interview with Ron Cundy, IWM sound archive tape 9651.
78. Brian Cull and Frederick Galea, *Hurricanes over Malta*.
79. Brian Cull and Frederick Galea, *Hurricanes over Malta*.
80. Andrew Roberts, *The Storm of War*.
81. Francis Mason, *The Hawker Hurricane*.
82. Churchill to Portal, 27 January 1942, Portal papers, Folder 3/1/8.
83. Portal to Churchill, 23 February 1942, Portal papers, Folder 3/1/23b.
84. Interview with Arthur Hudson, IWM sound archive tape 13923.
85. Interview with Richard Pool, IWM sound archive tape 9248.
86. Interview with Arthur Hudson, IWM sound archive tape 13923.
87. Winston Churchill, *The Second World War: Volume IV*.

CHAPTER 10: 'A MAGNIFICENT STRIKING FORCE'

1. Francis Ford Coppola and John Milius, *Apocalypse Now: A Screenplay*.
2. Interview with George Butler, IWM sound archive tape 12341.
3. Memo by Sir Henry Tizard, 7 September 1942, National Archives AVIA 46/114.
4. Interview with Graham Leggett, IWM sound archive tape 27075.
5. Report of A&AEE, 28 March 1941, National Archives AIR16/695.
6. Notes for pilots, 3 October 1941, National Archives AIR 16/695.
7. Tactical memorandum, 14 December 1941, National Archives AIR 16/695.
8. Tactical memorandum, 14 December 1941, National Archives AIR 16/695.
9. Interview with Vaughan Corbett, BBC, 18 November 1941.
10. 'Fighter Bomber squadron', *Flight*, 27 November 1941.
11. Minutes of Chief of the Air Staff's meeting, 16 June 1942, National Archives AVIA 46/114.
12. Dr John Fozard, *Sydney Camm and the Hurricane*.
13. Interview with John Wray, IWM sound archive tape 12371.
14. Douglas Bader, *Fight for the Sky*.
15. Stalin to Churchill, 12 April 1943, Churchill papers, Char 20/110.
16. Interview with John Wray, IWM sound archive tape 12371.

17. Norman Franks, *Hurricane at War*.
18. Geoffrey Morley-Mower, *Messerschmitt Roulette*.
19. Geoffrey Morley-Mower, *Messerschmitt Roulette*.
20. Tedder to Portal, 22 October 1942, Portal papers, Folder 12/1/11.
21. Interview with Harry Hawker, IWM sound archive tape 10886.
22. Memoir of the Desert War by Wing Commander Murray Gardner, IWM archive 99/23/1.
23. Memoir of the Desert War by Wing Commander Murray Gardner, IWM archive 99/23/1.
24. Max Arthur, *Lost Voices of the RAF*.
25. Bruce Barrymore Halpenny, *Fight for the Sky*.
26. Chaz Bowyer, *Hurricane*.
27. Michael Lavigne and James F. Edwards, *Hurricanes over the Sands*.
28. Andrew Roberts, *Masters and Commanders*.
29. Max Arthur, *Lost Voices of the RAF*.
30. Alan Moorehead, *The Desert War*.
31. Tom Neil, *Onward to Malta*.
32. Interview with Graham Leggett, IWM sound archive tape 27075.
33. Adrian Stewart, *They Flew Hurricanes*.
34. Memoir of the Desert War by Wing Commander Murray Gardner, IWM archive 99/23/1.
35. Interview with Graham Leggett, IWM sound archive tape 27075.
36. Chaz Bowyer, *Hurricane*.
37. Interview with Graham Leggett, IWM sound archive tape 27075.
38. Frank Mason, *The Hawker Hurricane*.
39. Adrian Stewart, *They Flew Hurricanes*.
40. Report on the Employment of Hurricane IID aircraft, 12 May 1943, National Archives AIR 2/3353.
41. Interview with Graham Leggett, IWM sound archive tape 27075.
42. Kenneth McGlashan, *Down to Earth*.
43. Stephen Darlow, *Five of the Few*.
44. Interview with John Wray, IWM sound archive tape 12371.
45. Interview with Arthur Lowndes, 24 August 2004, BBC People's War Archive.
46. *The Times*, 14 August 1944.
47. 'The Last of the Many', *Flight*, August 24 1944.
48. Julian Thompson, *Forgotten Voices of Burma*
49. Interview with Owen Parry, IWM sound archive tape 11366.
50. Interview with George Butler, IWM sound archive tape 12341.

51. Dispatch on Air Operations, 21 June–15 November 1943, Liddell Hart Archives TULL 1/6.
52. Norman Franks, *Fighter Pilot's Summer*.
53. Alan Moorehead, *The Desert War*.
54. Robert Jackson, *Hawker Hurricane*.
55. Interview with Alfred Cameron, IWM sound archive tape 12215.
56. Memoir of Alan B. Sammons, IWM archive 89/12/1.
57. Interview with Alfred Cameron, IWM sound archive tape 12215.
58. Interview with George Butler, IWM sound archive tape 12341.
59. Francis Mason, *Hawker Hurricane*.
60. Richard Holmes, *The World at War*.
61. Interview with Owen Parry, IWM sound archive tape 11366.
62. Interview with Owen Parry, IWM sound archive tape 11366.
63. Donald Stones, *Dimsie*.
64. Adrian Stewart, *Hurricane*.
65. War Office report, 2 January 1945, National Archives WO 205/501.
66. Report on Jungle Burning Trials, 26 January 1944, National Archives AIR 23/2832.
67. Interview with George Butler, IWM sound archive tape 12341.
68. H. L. Thompson, *New Zealanders with the RAF*.
69. Adrian Stewart, *Hurricane*.

EPILOGUE

1. Jarrod Cotter, *Battle of Britain Memorial Flight*.
2. Jarrod Cotter, *Battle of Britain Memorial Flight*.
3. Dr John Fozard, *Camm and the Hurricane*.
4. *The Times*, 14 March 1966.
5. Dr John Fozard, *Camm and the Hurricane*.
6. 'The Last of the Many', *Flight*, 24 August 1940.
7. *The War in Pictures*, August 1940.

Bibliography

Unpublished Sources

Air Ministry papers (National Archives, Kew)
Bader, Sir Douglas (RAF Museum, Hendon)
Balfour, Harold (House of Lords Record Office)
Barrett, Frank (private)
Beaverbrook, 1st Baron (House of Lords Record Office)
Brabner, Rupert (Imperial War Museum)
Cabinet papers (National Archives, Kew)
Campbell, D. J. (RAF Museum, Hendon)
Campbell, Squadron Leader C.N.S. (Imperial War Museum)
Carey, Squadron Leader G. V. (Imperial War Museum)
Churchill, Sir Winston (Churchill Archive Centre, Cambridge)
Cruickshank, Captain W. L. (Imperial War Museum)
Dowding, Sir Hugh (RAF Museum, Hendon)
Foreign Office papers (National Archives, Kew)
Gardner, Wing Commander Murray (Imperial War Museum)
Gundry, Flying Officer K. C. (Imperial War Museum)
Hawker Aircraft papers (RAF Museum, Hendon)
Hawker Siddeley papers (Brooklands Museum)
Hilliar, Wing Commander H. H. (RAF Museum, Hendon)
Ismay, Sir Hastings (Liddell-Hart Archives, King's College London)
Kaberov, Colonel Igor (Imperial War Museum)
Kucera, Wing Commander Jiri (Imperial War Museum)
Lane, G. A. (RAF Museum, Hendon)
Leigh-Mallory, Trafford (RAF Museum, Hendon)
Liddell-Hart, Basil (Liddell-Hart Archives, King's College London)
Mass Observation Archive (Sussex University)
Ministry of Aircraft Production (National Archives)

Pace, Squadron Leader T. G. (Imperial War Museum)
Peirse, Sir Richard (Liddell-Hart Archives, King's College London)
Portal, 1st Viscount (Christ Church College, Oxford)
Rigby, Flight Lieutenant Basil (Imperial War Museum)
Sammons, Alan B. (Imperial War Museum)
Swinton, 1st Earl (Churchill Archive Centre, Cambridge)
Williams, Mike (www.wwiiaircraftperformance.org)

Transcripts of Audio Interviews and Speeches

Balmer, Robin (IWM tape 17828)
Beamont, Roland (IWM tape 10128)
Bird-Wilson, Air Vice Marshal Harold (IWM tape 10093)
Bowring, Ben (IWM tape 12173)
Broadfoot, Doug (IWM tape 17828)
Brothers, Peter (IWM tape 10218)
Brown, Cyril (IWM tape 12524)
Brown, Eric (IWM tape 12279)
Brown, Wing Commander Ronald (IWM tape 12404)
Burroughes, Hugh (IWM tape 7255)
Butler, George (IWM tape 12341)
Cameron, Alfred (IWM tape 12215)
Cape, Brian, *Service with 56 Hurricane Squadron* (BBC People's Archive of
    World War Two)
Considine, Brian (IWM tape 10961)
Corbett, Vaughan (BBC 18 November 1941)
Cousins, Jack (private interview)
Cross, Air Marshal Kenneth (IWM tape 10481)
Cundy, Ron (IWM tape 9651)
David, Group Captain Dennis (IWM tape 10092)
Davis, Eric (IWM tape 13928)
Devitt, Wing Commander Peter (IWM tape 10667)
Donaldson, Air Commodore Teddy (IWM tape 12172)
Down, Peter (IWM tape 11449)
Downham, Peter, *No Brakes or Hydraulics, But It'll Fly* (BBC People's
    Archive of World War Two)
Earp, Richard (IWM tape 11772)
Edge, Gerald (IWM tape 12674)

Fletcher, Sam (IWM tape 12557)

Foster, Bob (IWM tape 12738)

Foxley-Norris, Air Chief Marshal Christopher (IWM tape 10136)

Fraser, Ian (IWM tape 11928)

Gardner, Charles (IWM tape 1011)

Garrod, Peter (IWM tape 9944)

Gillam, Group Captain Denys (IWM tape 10049)

Gleave, Group Captain Tom (IWM tape 10084)

Goodson, James (IWM tape 11623)

Gore, Margaret (IWM tape 9285)

Grice, Wing Commander Douglas (IWM tape 10897)

Hancock, Wing Commander Norman (IWM tape 10119)

Haw, Charlton (IWM tape 12028)

Hawker, Harry (IWM tape 10886)

Higginson, Frederick (IWM tape 15111)

Holden, Wing Commander Eustace (IWM tape 11198)

Holmes, Ray (IWM tape 2807)

Hudson, Arthur (IWM tape 13923)

Hulse, Neil (IWM tape 15332)

Humble, Bill (IWM tape 12876)

Ingle, Wing Commander Alec (IWM tape 11338)

Ironside, Hugh (IWM tape 13101)

Johns, George (IWM tape 11616)

Kaye, John (IWM tape 11186)

Last, Geoffrey (IWM tape 9801)

Leggett, Graham (IWM tape 27075)

Leng, Maurice (IWM tape 12217)

Lowndes, Arthur, *A Flyer's Story* (BBC People's Archive of World War Two)

Lucas, Phillip (IWM tape 12878)

Maclachlan, James (IWM tape 2219)

Martin, Dickie (IWM tapes 13114 and 11906)

Matthews, Peter (IWM tape 10451)

Mearns, Sammy (IWM tape 11088)

Mitchell, Wing Commander Richard (IWM tape 11364)

Moore, Cyril, *My Time at Hawkers* (BBC People's Archive of World War Two)

Newman, Alan, *Battle of Britain – My Wartime Memories* (BBC People's Archive of World War Two)

Page, Sir Frederick (IWM tape 18035)
Page, Wing Commander Geoffrey (IWM tape 11103)
Parkin, Roy, *RAF in Lagos* (BBC People's Archive of World War Two)
Parry, Owen (IWM tape 11366)
Pennington, James (IWM tape 11064)
Platt, Beryl (IWM tape 10698)
Pool, Commander Richard (IWM tape 9248)
Quill, Jeffrey (IWM tape 10687)
Rosier, Air Chief Marshal Fred (IWM tape 10157)
Smith, Group Captain Irving (IWM tape 11754)
Turle, William (IWM tape 9803)
Twitchett, Francis (IWM tape 12047)
Webb, Doris (private interview)
Whittingham, Derek, *Malta: George Cross Island* (BBC People's Archive of World War Two)
Wilkinson, Wing Commander Roger (IWM tape 10216)
Wray, John (IWM 12371)
Young, Brian (IWM tape 6803)

Published Sources

Allward, Maurice, *Hurricane Special* (1975)
Arthur, Max, *Lost Voices of the Royal Air Force* (1993)
—— *Forgotten Voices of the Second World War* (2004)
Austin, Douglas, *Churchill and Malta* (2006)
Bader, Douglas, *Fight for the Sky* (1973)
Bailey, Jim, *The Sky Suspended* (1964)
Baker, E. C. R., *Ace of Aces* (1964)
Barr, Niall, *Pendulum of War: The Three Battles of El Alamein* (2005)
Beamont, Roland, *Fighter Test Pilot* (1986)
—— *My Part of the Sky* (1989)
—— 'Hurricane Baptism', *Aeroplane Monthly* (January 1994)
Best, Geoffrey, *Churchill and War* (2005)
Bickers, Richard Townshend, *The Desert War 1939–1945* (1991)
Bierman, John, and Smith, Colin, *Alamein: War without Hate* (2002)
Bingham, Victor, *Merlin Power* (1998)
Birtles, Philip, *Hurricane: The Illustrated History* (2001)
—— *Hurricane Squadrons* (2003)

Bishop, Edward, *Hurricane* (1986)
—— *McIndoe's Army* (2001)
Bishop, Patrick, *Fighter Boys* (2004)
—— *Battle of Britain: A Day-by-Day Chronicle* (2009)
Blackmore, L. K., *Hawker: A Biography of Harry Hawker* (1990)
Bowyer, Chaz, *Hurricane at War* (1974)
Braybrook, Roy, 'Two Men of their Time', *Air International* (May 1979)
Brew, Alec, *The Turret Fighters* (2002)
British Aerospace, *Hurricane: Clouded by Legend* (1985)
—— *75 Years of Aviation of Kingston* (1988)
Brown, Captain Eric 'Winkle', *Wings on my Sleeve* (2006)
Brown, Malcolm, *Spitfire Summer* (2000)
Brown, Squadron Leader Peter, *Honour Restored* (2005)
Budiansky, Stephen, *Air Power* (2003)
Bungay, Stephen, *The Most Dangerous Enemy* (2000)
—— *Alamein* (2002)
Burleigh, Michael, *The Third Reich: A New History* (2000)
Burns, Michael, *Bader: The Man and His Men* (1990)
Butler, Lieutenant Colonel Ewan, and Bradford, Major J. Selby, *Keep the Memory Green* (1950)
Clarke, R. M. (ed.), *Hawker Hurricane Portfolio* (1986)
Clayton, Tim, and Craig, Phil, *Finest Hour* (1999)
Clostermann, Pierre, *The Big Show* (1951)
Collier, Richard, *Eagle Day* (1966)
Coombs, L. F. E., *The Lion Has Wings* (1997)
Corbin, Jimmy, *Ten Fighter Boys* (2008)
Corrigan, Gordon, *Blood, Sweat and Arrogance* (2006)
Cosey, Bob, *A Tiger's Tale* (2002)
Cotter, Jarrod, *Battle of Britain Memorial Flight* (2007)
Crampton, John, *From Sopwith to Hawker Siddeley Aviation* (1968)
Cull, Brian, and Galea, Frederick, *Hurricanes over Malta* (2001)
—— *249 at Malta* (2004)
Cull, Brian, and Lander, Bruce and Weiss, Heinrich, *Twelve Days in May* (1995)
Cull, Brian, with Sortehaug, Paul, *Hurricanes over Singapore* (2004)
Curtis, Lettice, *Autobiography* (2004)
Dahl, Roald, *Going Solo* (1986)
Darlow, Steve, *Five of the Few* (2006)
Deighton, Len, *Fighter* (1977)

—— *Battle of Britain* (1980)

—— *Blood, Tears and Folly* (1993)

D'Este, Carlo, *Warlord: A Life of Churchill at War 1874–1945* (2008)

Dibbs, John, and Holmes, Tony, *Hurricane: A Fighter Legend* (1995)

Dixon, Jack, *Dowding and Churchill* (2008)

Edwards, James, and Lavigne, Michael, *Hurricanes over the Sands* (2003)

Evans, Richard J., *The Third Reich at War* (2008)

Fenby, Jonathan, *The Sinking of the Lancastria* (2005)

Fleischman, John, 'Best of the Battle of Britain', *Air & Space Magazine* (March 2008)

Foreman, John, *Fighter Command War Diaries* (1997)

Forrester, Larry, *Fly For Your Life* (1956)

Foster, R. W., *Tally Ho! From the Battle of Britain to the Defence of Darwin* (2008)

Fozard, Dr. John W. (ed.), *Sydney Camm and the Hurricane* (1991)

Franks, Norman, *Air Battle for Dunkirk* (1983)

—— *Hurricane at War: Volume 2* (1986)

—— *Hurricanes over the Arakan* (1989)

—— *The Greatest Air Battle* (1997)

Furse, Anthony, *Wilfred Freeman* (1999)

Galland, Adolf, *The First and the Last* (1954)

Gallico, Paul, *The Hurricane Story* (1959)

Gleed, Ian, *Arise to Conquer* (1942)

Golley, John, *Hurricanes over Murmansk* (1987)

—— 'Hurricanes to the Defence of Russia', *Rolls-Royce Magazine* (September 1988)

Goodson, James, and Franks, Norman, *Over-paid, Over-sexed and Over Here* (1991)

Gregory, Pat, et al, *Heroes of the RAF* (1960)

Grey, C. G., *A History of the Air Ministry* (1940)

Griffith, Hugh, 'With the Royal Air Force in Russia', *RAF Journal* (December 1941)

Halpenny, Bruce Barrymore, *Fight for the Sky* (1986)

Hamilton, Nigel, *The Full Monty: Montgomery of Alamein* (2001)

Hannah, Donald, *Hawker* (1982)

Hannig, Norbert, *Luftwaffe Fighter Ace* (2004)

Harrison, Frank, *Tobruk: The Birth of a Legend* (1996)

Hastings, Max, *Finest Years: Churchill's Warlord 1940–45* (2009)

Havers, Richard, *Here is the News: The BBC and the Second World War* (2007)

Hiscock, Melvyn, *Hawker Hurricane: Inside and Out* (2003)

Holland, James, *Fortress Malta* (2003)

Holmes, Ray, *Sky Spy* (1997)

Holmes, Richard, *The World at War* (2007)

Holmes, Tony, *Hurricane Aces 1939–40* (1998)

Jackets, L. A., 'Hurricanes in Russia', *The Royal Air Forces Quarterly* (Autumn 1971)

Jackson, Robert, *Fighter Pilots of World War II* (1976)

—— *Hawker Hurricane* (1986)

—— *Air War at Night* (2000)

James, Derek, *Hawker Aircraft Ltd* (1996)

Johnson, Air Vice Marshal Johnnie, *Wing Leader* (1956)

Kaplan, Philip, and Collier, Richard, *The Few* (1989)

Keegan, John, *The Second World War* (1989)

Kelly, Terence, *Hurricane in Sumatra* (1985)

—— *Hurricanes versus Zeros* (1985)

—— *Hurricane and Spitfire Pilots at War* (1986)

Kershaw, Alex, *The Few* (2006)

Korda, Michael, *With Wings Like Eagles* (2009)

Lancaster, Nicholas, *Brooklands: Cradle of British Racing and Aviation* (2009)

Levine, Joshua, *Forgotten Voices of the Blitz and the Battle of Britain* (2006)

Lewis, Peter, *The British Fighter since 1912* (1965)

Lloyd, F. H. M., *Hurricane: The Story of a Great Fighter* (1945)

Lloyd, Sir Ian, and Pugh, Peter, *Hives and the Merlin* (2004)

Lock, David, 'A Russian Experience', *Journal of the Spitfire Society* (Spring 1991)

Longmore, Arthur, 'With the RAF in the Middle East', *Flight* (May 1942)

Lucas, Laddie (ed.), *Wings of War* (1983)

Lyall, Gavin (ed.), *The War in the Air* (1968)

Lyman, Robert, *Slim, Master of War* (2004)

McGlashan, Kenneth Butterworth, *Down to Earth* (2007)

McKee, Alexander, *Strike From the Sky* (1960)

McKinstry, Leo, *Spitfire* (2007)

Mason, Francis, *Hawker Hurricane* (1962)

—— *Hawker Aircraft since 1920* (1991)

Moorehead, Alan, *The Desert War* (1944)

Morley-Mower, Wing Commander Geoffrey, *Messerschmitt Roulette* (1993)

Neil, Wing Commander T. E., *Gun Button to 'Fire'* (1987)

—— *Onward to Malta* (1992)

Nesbit, Roy Coyners, *An Illustrated History of the RAF* (1999)

Offenberg, Jean, *Lonely Warrior* (1969)

Oliver, David, *Fighter Command 1939–45* (2000)

Orange, Vincent, *Park* (2001)

—— *Dowding of Fighter Command* (2008)

Overy, Richard, *Why the Allies Won* (1995)

—— *The Battle of Britain* (2000)

Owen, James, and Walters, Guy (eds.), *The Voice of War* (2004)

Page, Geoffrey, *Shot Down in Flames* (1999)

Parker, Matthew, *The Battle of Britain* (2000)

Parker, R. A. C., *The Second World War* (1997)

Phillips, Reginald, *Bulldog to Matador* (1989)

Pitchfork, Graham, *Shot Down and on the Run* (2003)

—— *Shot Down and in the Drink* (2005)

Probert, Air Commodore H. A., 'The RAF in the Battle of France', *Hawk* (May 1990)

Ray, John, *The Battle of Britain* (1994)

Richey, Paul, *Fighter Pilot* (2001)

Richey, Paul, with Franks, Norman, *Fighter Pilot's Summer* (1993)

Roberts, Andrew, *The Storm of War* (2009)

Robinson, Anthony, *RAF Fighter Squadrons* (1987)

Robinson, Derek, *Invasion 1940* (2005)

Rys, Marek, *Hawker Hurricane* (2006)

Sarkar, Dilip, *Through Peril to the Stars* (2006)

—— *The Few* (2009)

Saunders, Andy, *Finding the Few* (2009)

Sciortino, Ian, *Malta* (2000)

Sebag-Montefiore, Hugh, *Dunkirk: Fight to the Last Man* (2006)

Shacklady, Edward, *Hawker Hurricane* (2000)

Sheppard, Mark, 'To Russia with Love', *Aeroplane Monthly* (March 1997)

Shores, Christopher, *Hawker Hurricane Mark 1/IV* (1971)

—— *Aces High* (1999)

Shores, Christopher, and Cull, Brian, with Malizia, Nicola, *Malta: The Hurricane Years 1940–41* (1987)

Sinnott, Colin, *The Royal Air Force and Aircraft Design 1923–1939* (2001)

Smith, Graham, *Taking to the Skies* (2003)

Smith, Richard, *Hornchurch Eagles* (2002)

Smithies, Edward, *Aces, Erks and Backroom Boys* (1990)

Spick, Mike, *Allied Fighter Aces* (1997)

Stahl, Peter, *The Diving Eagle: A JU88 Pilot's Diary* (1984)

Steinhilper, Ulrich, and Osborne, Peter, *Spitfire on My Tail* (1989)

Stewart, Adrian, *Hurricane: The War Exploits of the Fighter Aircraft* (1982)

—— *They Flew Hurricanes* (2005)

Stones, Donald, *Dimsie* (1990)

Terraine, John, *The Right of the Line* (1985)

Thomas, Andrew, 'One Way Fliers', *Journal of the RAF Association* (April 2004)

Thomas, Hugh, *Spirit of the Blue* (2004)

Thomas, Nick, *RAF Top Gun* (2008)

Thompson, H. L., *New Zealanders with the RAF* (1954)

Thompson, Julian, *Forgotten Voices of Burma* (2009)

Townsend, Peter, *Duel of Eagles* (1970)

Turner, John Frayn, *The Bader Wing* (1981)

—— *The Battle of Britain* (1998)

Vigors, Tim, *Life's Too Short to Cry* (2006)

Whittell, Giles, *Spitfire Women of World War II* (2007)

Wood, Derek, and Dempster, Derek, *The Narrow Margin* (1961)

Wragg, David, *RAF Handbook 1939–1945* (2007)

Wright, Robert, *Dowding and the Battle of Britain* (1969)

Acknowledgements

I am indebted to many people who helped to make this book possible. First of all I would like to express my thanks to the staff of the National Archives at Kew, the House of Lords Record Office, the Liddell Hart Centre for Military Archives, the library at Christ Church, Oxford, the Brooklands Museum at Weybridge, the Mass Observation archive at Sussex University and the Churchill Archive Centre at Cambridge. I am particularly grateful to Roderick Suddaby and his excellent team at the Imperial War Museum, who were unfailingly helpful over my numerous demands for material from the written and sound archives. As with my previous military aviation books, Peter Elliott and the rest of the Department of Research at the RAF Museum in Hendon gave me invaluable assistance. May I record here my special gratitude to: Peter Devitt, always a source of wisdom, encouragement and humour; Nina Burls, who showed great patience with my detailed queries and Gordon Leith, who was extremely co-operative over the photographs. Air Commodore Philip Wilkinson generously provided me with some fascinating material from his own research into 151 Wing in Russia. Memories of Hurricane manufacturing were provided by Jack Cousins and Doris Webb, while Doug Barrett kindly sent me an article with his grandfather's recollection of working at Kingston.

On the production side, I owe a huge debt to Roland Philipps and his superb team at John Murray, including Helen Hawksfield, Victoria Murray-Browne, Caroline Westmore, Anna Kenny-Ginard and Polly Ho-Yen. Juliet Brightmore carried out the picture research with her customary diligence and thoughtfulness, and Richard Mason did a magnificent editing job, correcting my many idiocies. Further research, especially on press articles, was done with her usual reliability by Alannah Barton.

Finally, I would like to thank my wonderful wife Elizabeth for all her devotion, insights and tolerance while the storm of the Hurricane was raging. The book could never have been written without her support.

Leo McKinstry
Westgate, February 2010

Index

Hurricane (aircraft) *(continued)*
298, 302; Mark III 288; Mark IV
288–302, 316; Mark V 289; Mark
XII 288, 318; rocket-carrying 301;
Sea Hurricane (aircraft) 243–4
Hurry, Operation 248–9

Iceland 266, 270
Identification Friend or Foe (IFF) 94
Illustrious, HMS 260
Imperial War Museum 16
Imphal: siege of 14, 310–15
India 14, 183, 186, 234, 260, 306–15;
air force 318; Indian National Army
306–9; nationalism 306;
Indomitable, HMS 280
Ingle, Alec 195–6
Inskip, Sir Thomas 55, 76–9; Inskip
doctrine 77–9
Intelligence: German 170–3, 200
Ipswich 47, 92
Iraq 267–8, 275
Irish air force 318
Ironside, Hugh 97, 124
Irrawaddy, River 316
Irvin, Leslie 188; Irvin flying jacket 188
Isle of Wight 171–2
Ismay, Sir Hastings 186
Italian air force 252, 263

Jabs, Hans Joachim 170
Jameson, Flight Commander Patrick
107–8
Japan 3, 279, 305, 308
Japanese air force 279, 306
Japanese army 280, 312, 316
Java 13, 280–1
jet aircraft 15, 318–20
Jodl, Alfred 158
Johns, George 128, 137
Johnson, Amy 236
Johnson, Johnnie 226, 256
Jonas, Carter 247
Jones, Ira 'Taffy' 178
Joyce, William (Lord Haw Haw) 217

jump-jet 319; *see also* Harrier
Junkers: Ju 87 (aircraft) 9, 139–40, 158,
164, 171, 175, 199–201, 260; Ju 88
(aircraft) 4, 138, 225
Jupiter engine 27; *see also* engines

Kabaw Valley 315
Kaberov, Colonel Igor 277
Kain, Edgar 'Cobber' 100, 143
Kano 250–1
Keeble, Flight Lieutenant Peter 247
Kendall, Flying Officer John B. 242
Kenley 73, 87, 199, 222
Kershaw, Bob 253
Kesselring, Generalfeldmarschall Albert
160, 208, 159
Kestrel (aircraft) 28, 32, 159
Khartoum 250–1
Kilmartin, Flying Officer John 'Killy' 94
Kingston plant: Canbury Park Road 57
Kirvatti 315
Kittyhawk (aircraft) 278
Kohima 310–13
Kreipe, Werner 162, 216
Kriegsmarine (German Navy) 103, 148,
158

Lacey, James 'Ginger' 116, 181–4, 205,
254
Lack of Moral Fibre (LMF) 180–1
Lagos 250–1
Lancaster (aircraft) 1, 148, 320
Lancastria: sinking 144–5
Langley: Hawker factory 3, 11, 60,
229–30, 233, 304
Larwood, Harold 69
League of Nations 29, 34
Lee, Ken 109, 131, 135, 154, 192, 199
Lee, Raymond 127
Leggett, Graham 5, 58–60, 189, 220,
263, 283, 296–301
Le Havre 98
Leigh-Mallory, Air Chief Marshal
Sir Trafford 126, 200, 207–9, 212,
223–4